CANADIAN ECONOMIC

PROBLEMS AND POLICIES

the editors

LAWRENCE H. OFFICER is currently Assistant Professor
of Economics at Harvard University. He obtained a
B.A. degree from McGill University and A.M. and Ph.D.
degrees from Harvard University. In addition to contributing many articles to scholarly journals, Professor
Officer has published two previous books: **An Econometric Model of Canada Under the Fluctuating Exchange
Rate** and **The International Monetary System: Problems
and Proposals** (co-editor).

LAWRENCE B. SMITH is presently Associate Professor
of Economics at the University of Toronto, and has
also taught at Harvard University. He obtained a
B.Com. degree from the University of Toronto and
A.M. and Ph.D. degrees from Harvard University. Professor Smith has contributed articles to scholarly
publications in the areas of housing, mortgage markets, monetary economics, and economic history, as
well as articles on current policy issues.

Canadian Economic Problems and Policies

edited by

Lawrence H. Officer

and

Lawrence B. Smith

Toronto

McGRAW-HILL COMPANY
OF CANADA LIMITED

Montreal
New York
St. Louis
San Francisco
London
Sydney
Johannesburg
Mexico
Panama
Dusseldorf

To our parents

Canadian Economic Problems and Policies

Copyright © McGraw-Hill Company of Canada Limited 1970. All rights reserved. No part of this publication may be reproduced, stored in a retrieval system, or transmitted, in any form or by any means, electronic, mechanical, photocopying, recording, or otherwise, without the prior written permission of McGraw-Hill Company of Canada Limited.

07-92669-7

Library of Congress Catalog Card Number: 73-112968

234567890   MB-70   9876543210

Printed and bound in Canada.

preface

A quarter of a century has elapsed since the end of World War II — a postwar period which has witnessed a multitude of changes in the Canadian economy. The purpose of this volume is to present a comprehensive collection of essays which (1) outline Canada's present economic problems, (2) discuss the various policy instruments available to Canadian governments in order to cope with these problems, and (3) evaluate the success of this policy-making in the immediate postwar period. Although a single volume cannot hope to consider every issue, we feel that the most important problems confronting the Canadian economy are covered.

The book consists of 20 essays divided into five groups — macroeconomic policy, international aspects, industry problems, urban problems, and social-welfare issues. Each essay is concerned with a particular economic problem, and each is written by a specialist in the subject-matter discussed. The essays have not been published elsewhere in their present form. Although the contributors furnished their studies at the invitation of the editors, the views expressed in each essay are the views of the individual authors and do not necessarily represent the views of the editors.

We should like to express our appreciation to Miss Rosemary L. Carter, whose typing services were instrumental in producing the volume.

Cambridge, Massachusetts   LAWRENCE H. OFFICER

Toronto, Ontario   LAWRENCE B. SMITH

table of contents

Introduction

Economic policy in the hands of non-totalitarian governments has come a long way since the 19th century. Indeed, there no longer seem to be limitations in the *scope* of government activity, i.e., the aspects or sectors of the economy in which it may intervene legitimately, but only in the *intensities* of its various actions. Thus, for example, it is considered appropriate for a democratic government to be concerned with the provision of medical care for the population, but not to the extent of nationalizing the medical industry!

Along with the expansion of the legitimate areas of government activity has come a renewed awareness of the extent to which the various policies can either compete or complement one another. In one fundamental respect, of course, all policies involving the expenditure of funds (or, in general, the allocation of resources) appear to be competitive with one another. In slicing up a pie (the economy's total production of goods and services—gross national production) the larger the part for one use, the smaller that for another. However, even this simple analogy can be misleading. Some government actions—say, appropriate stabilization policies—may maintain a high level of employment and output in the economy, thus increasing the total "pie" (the goods and services available for all uses).

When one considers detailed policies, problems of conflict may arise, even apart from the general problem of competing for scarce resources. For example, the goal of efficient production may be sought by breaking up a monopoly or preventing firms in a given industry from engaging in collusion, i.e., taking actions in concert; but such policies might weaken the industry's resistance to wage demands on the part of unions in the industry, thus increasing the economy's susceptibility to inflation, a result detrimental to the pursuit of stabilization policy. However, policies may just as well be complementary in nature. The same "efficient-production" or industrial-organization actions mentioned above may in themselves (and in fact, will, if successful) lower the cost of production in the industry, thus increasing the competitiveness of its products abroad and improving the country's balance of payments (another goal of policy).

Although governments must (or rather, should) study the various inter-relationships among policies in order to carry them out in a consistent fashion, policies must also be studied individually in order to determine the state of the particular situation and the options open to the government in that area. In other words, the "micro" as well as "macro" effects of policies should be assessed carefully by government policy-makers.

While the above discussions (and indeed parts of several essays in this volume) are sufficiently general in their scope to apply to *any* economy, this volume concentrates on an examination of the economic problems facing Canada, an assessment of the policies that Canadian governments have pursued to meet these problems in the past, and an evaluation of policy alternatives (or exposition of policy recommendations) for the future.

Although this volume focuses upon Canada, with a very few exceptions the issues discussed have a wider applicability. The discussion of macro-economic policy in Part I is by nature a general one, as fiscal, monetary, debt-management, and exchange-rate policies are common to all governments, at least in the non-Communist industrial world. However, within this general framework, reference is made to institutional and historical features peculiar to the Canadian economy. For example, considerable attention is given to the fact that Canada is the only country to have had the experience of a truly freely fluctuating exchange rate, without exchange controls, in the post-World-War-II period and to the unique fiscal relations between the Canadian federal and provincial governments.

One of the most significant single aspects of the Canadian economy today is its sensitivity to the international environment in general and the United States in particular. This sensitivity manifests itself in many ways, as numerous facets of the Canadian economy are influenced heavily by the United States, either directly *via* merchandise trade and integrated financial markets or indirectly *via* the communications media and a common technology. In addition, Canadian economic policies are often constrained by those of the United States. Consequently, Part II of this volume is devoted to international considerations.

In addition to its position as one of the major industrial countries of the world, Canada is an important agricultural producer. Thus, while Part III is concerned with conventional industry problems such as the collective-bargaining process and government regulation of industry, it also considers the special case of agriculture. Furthermore, because of the vast geographical expanse of Canada, transportation plays an important role in the economy, and it, too, is analyzed as a special industry.

Like most industrial countries, Canada is experiencing the special problems associated with a rapidly expanding urban population. Problems such as the lack of adequate housing and the existence of families living in abject poverty become accentuated in an urban context. The urban problem as such, and its special aspects of housing and poverty conditions, is examined in Part IV.

More specialized economic issues, namely, the provision of adequate medical care, the financing of higher education, the problem of pollution, regional economic disparities, and the development of the Northland, are the topics of Part V. These issues, with the exception of the Northland, are of growing concern to almost all countries, as governments seek to improve the quality of life for their citizens within the constraints of financial and political feasibility. While problems of the Northland are of less general interest, the Canadian Northland continues to stand out as the great under-developed area of the country, and as such deserves more attention than it customarily receives.

If the various essays in this volume show that Canada is experiencing difficulties in devising optimal social-welfare and urban programs, weaknesses in the institutional framework for stabilization policy, and uncertainties in its international economic policies, they should be balanced by the knowledge that Canada has just experienced its longest peacetime economic expansion on record, that its population, labour force, and productive capacity have been expanding rapidly, that its supplies of natural resources are the envy of much of the world, and that over time it has accumulated large stocks of social and industrial capital. Moreover, a wealth of knowledge has been gained by Canadian policy-makers from the experience of the past. In this regard it is our hope that the volume *Canadian Economic Problems and Policies* will serve not primarily as a critique of Canada's policy-making in the past but rather as a challenge to policy-making in the future.

I

Macro-
Economic
Policy

Macro-economic policy—the use of policy tools to influence important aggregates in the economy—generally has been considered the most important economic function of governments since Keynesian economics gained ascendance, and certainly since World War II. Perhaps the most important kind of macro-economic policy is stabilization policy, the primary goal of which is to "stabilize" the economy at certain (feasible) levels of output, employment, and price movement; so the first essay in the volume examines such policies. Other macro-economic issues discussed in Part I are: (1) incomes policies, especially in the form of wage-price guidelines (which might supplement Canadian stabilization policy in the future), (2) tax reform, (3) federal-provincial fiscal relationships, and (4) the special Canadian institution, the Economic Council of Canada.

Lawrence H. Officer and Lawrence B. Smith, in their essay, "Stabilization Policy in the Postwar Period," develop a theoretical framework demonstrating the need for stabilization policies, summarize the tools available to government for stabilization purposes, outline the feedbacks on the economy from these various tools, and evaluate government policies during the postwar period in this light. Their survey of the federal government's monetary, fiscal, debt-management, exchange-control, and exchange-rate policies indicates a mixed performance. While the government at times applied policies in a very enlightened manner, it occasionally adopted destabilizing or inconsistent policies. At one period or another, with hindsight, it is clear that each of the policies listed above was inappropriately applied. However, Officer and Smith note that policy instruments are currently em-

5

ployed in harmony with one another to combat inflation and there is hope that in the future proper coordination of policies will continue.

David C. Smith examines an anti-inflationary policy instrument which Canada has not used since the 1940's but which other countries have employed in recent years. His essay, "The Direct Control of Inflation," is concerned with "incomes policies"—wage and price guidelines set by the government. Smith adopts a cautious view on the efficacy of such policies. If an elaborate system of direct controls is not used, the success of incomes policy depends on the effects of moral suasion applied by the government to corporations and labour unions. These effects are not clear-cut, however, and depend on the circumstances involved. Smith notes that Canada now appears to be moving in the direction of some form of incomes policy, though whether it will aid the government in its battle against inflation is an open question.

The taxation side of fiscal policy is of interest not only because of its aggregate economic effects but also because it has direct and measurable influences on the spending-power of individuals in the country. In his essay, "The Use of a Normative Model to Analyze Tax-Reform Proposals," John Bossons discusses the effects of tax systems in general upon the economy, and then analyzes the implications of the major proposals made by the Royal Commission on Taxation (the "Carter Commission"). Bossons notes that the existing Canadian tax system is largely the result of histori-cal accidents. He argues that the tax system recommended by the Carter Commission would not only be more equitable, but would interfere less with individual decision-making than does the present system and would also enhance the country's economic growth.

Jacques Parizeau discusses the fiscal structure among the federal, provincial, and municipal governments in his essay "Federal-Provincial Economic Coordination." He notes the increased decentralization of the fiscal structure, and of policy-making in general, as an important feature in the evolution of Canada's federal system in recent years. Examples of federal-provincial cooperation and coordination in policy-making are few, and their impact has been slight. Parizeau argues against the view, held by some, that the decentralization and lack of coordination do not stand in the way of effective federal policy-making. This view is too sanguine for certain situations. For example, a reduction in federal tax rates would probably give rise to increases in provincial tax rates, even if the federal policy is in response to a recession.

Albert Breton's essay, "A Theory of the Economic Council of Canada," examines the origins of that institution, set up by federal legislation in 1963. Breton argues that the Economic Council of Canada was created in order to squelch the demand for economic planning on the part of Cana-dians, following the unsatisfactory performance of government policy and the Canadian economy in the late 1950's and early 1960's. He views the Council as a "blocking" institution—one that substituted for the formation of a genuine planning body, but that managed to appease the public clamour for economic planning. Breton's contention is founded on a model of government and voter behaviour in a democracy such as Canada, a model that he elaborates in the early sections of his essay.

stabilization policy in the postwar period

Lawrence H. Officer, Harvard University
and Lawrence B. Smith, University of Toronto

The economy of a country, just as the fortunes of man, seldom advances smoothly and steadily. Rather, it proceeds in a cyclical fashion, oscillating between periods of rapid economic growth and periods of economic stagnation or recession. This is not to say that there are regular business cycles of uniform duration and form, but that the economy moves in an irregular fashion which cannot be predicted easily.

Until the Second World War, the policies that most countries (including Canada) followed to cope with cycles in economic activity were usually destabilizing and pro-cyclical rather than stabilizing and counter-cyclical. For example, countries usually sought a balanced budget, so that declines in economic activity, which are accompanied by reduced government tax revenue, would precipitate an increase in government tax rates and/or a reduction in government expenditures, both of which actions exacerbate the decline. Today, thanks to the "Keynesian revolution," most governments realize that such behaviour is pro-cyclical and that precisely the opposite policies are warranted to achieve stabilizing results. However, despite the increased economic knowledge potentially in the hands of government,[1] fluctuations in economic activity are not always countered successfully and are far from becoming a relic of the past.

This essay focuses upon the problems of economic stabilization within the Canadian context, beginning in section I with a brief sketch of the postwar cycle in economic activity. In section II we develop a simple income-determination and inflation model and in section III discuss the

---

1. We use the term "potentially" rather than "necessarily," as the government may base its actions on grounds other than modern economic knowledge. Examples justifying the former term can be found readily in Canadian policy since the Second World War, as discussed in section V of this essay.

goals of stabilization policy and the conflicts among them. This is followed in section IV by a description of the basic stabilization tools available to the policy-maker. Finally, the highlights of Canada's postwar stabilization policy are analyzed and assessed in section V.

I. ECONOMIC ACTIVITY IN CANADA IN THE POSTWAR PERIOD

During the last twenty years, the real value of Canada's gross national product (GNP)—the value of all goods and services produced by Canadians in a year—has increased almost two and one-half times and the standard of living, as measured by the increase in *per capita* real GNP, has risen almost 50 percent. However, this growth has not been continuous and has often been accompanied by unemployment, inflation, or both.

Following the inflationary period of mid-1946 to 1948, which was produced by a large backlog of pent-up consumer and industrial demand, large public holdings of liquid assets, and the removal of price controls, Canada experienced a brief interlude of general economic stagnation. This stagnation soon gave way to a consumer-good-based expansion which, reinforced after the outbreak of the Korean War by defence and investment expenditures, continued until the middle of 1953. However, the Korean War placed excessive strain on the Canadian economy, and the early part of the expansion was accompanied by rapid inflation, the consumer price index (CPI) rising over 10½ percent and the wholesale price index 20 percent in one year. By 1952 the inflationary pressures eased, materials and labour became more available, and the economy expanded rapidly. This expansion softened in 1953, and unemployment, which ran 2½ to 3 percent previously, suddenly shot upward—reaching 5 percent in mid-1954. Consequently, although real GNP grew by 20 percent during the first half of the 1950's, the economy was buffeted both by a period of sharp inflation and by a period of substantial unemployment.

Led by an investment boom, which was triggered by world-wide fears of a raw-material shortage, the Canadian economy entered another period of expansion in the latter part of 1954 and early 1955. Capital investment took place at a tremendous pace, with expansion in industrial- and commercial-plant construction and power communications and public services contributing to a 20 percent increase in real GNP between 1954 and 1957. During this period, unemployment settled back down to approximately 3½ percent. However, by the middle of 1957 the expansion ran its course, industrial production began to decline, falling about 6 percent during 1957, and unemployment soon soared to 7½ percent. Once again, a substantial economic advance was accompanied by sectoral disallocations. Unfortunately, this retardation was neither as brief nor as shallow as the previous one and, with the exception of the short-lived advance of mid-1958 to early 1960, the economy stayed depressed until 1963. Unemployment in Canada remained over 5½ percent from the third quarter of 1957 until the middle of 1963, and averaged 7 percent, or 1 person out of every 14 seeking work, in 1958, 1960, and 1961.

This prolonged period of high unemployment and slow economic growth set the stage for a remarkable expansionary period which began in 1961 and has continued to the time of writing (1969). However, even this expansion, which saw real GNP rise 60 percent in eight years, was not

Figure 1 (a)

SELECTED CANADIAN ECONOMIC INDICATORS
Percentage Change in Real Gross National Product at Annual Rates

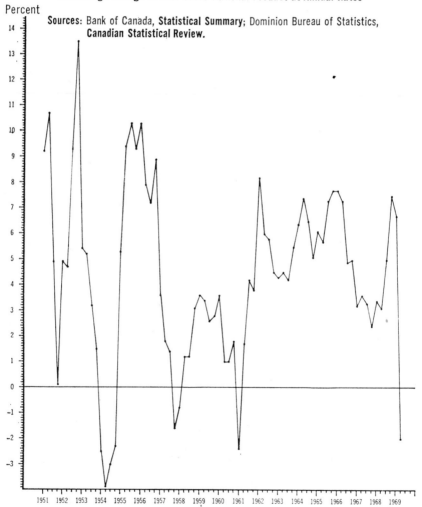

Sources: Bank of Canada, **Statistical Summary**; Dominion Bureau of Statistics, **Canadian Statistical Review.**

without its maladjustments, as 1966 saw the beginning of a persistent and severe inflation of almost 4 percent a year, which sharply eroded the purchasing power of the Canadian dollar and inflicted hardships upon those segments of the population on fixed or slowly rising incomes.

From this brief outline it is clear that the economy tended to oscillate between periods of rapid growth and expansion and periods of stagnation and retardation. Moreover, as Figure 1 indicates, fluctuations in real variables (real GNP, industrial production, unemployment, etc.) have been accompanied by fluctuations in monetary variables (money income, prices, etc.), with declining unemployment and rising prices accompanying econo-

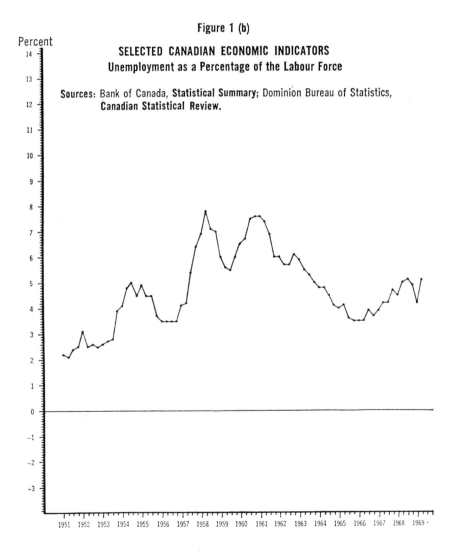

Figure 1 (b)

SELECTED CANADIAN ECONOMIC INDICATORS
Unemployment as a Percentage of the Labour Force

Sources: Bank of Canada, **Statistical Summary**; Dominion Bureau of Statistics, **Canadian Statistical Review.**

mic growth, and rising unemployment and stable or more slowly rising prices accompanying economic retardation. In consequence of the increasing downward rigidity of wages and prices, fluctuations in monetary variables now refer predominantly to movements in the *rates of change* of these variables, whereas in the pre-World-War-II period they referred to movements in the *levels* of these variables. This statement is also true for some real variables, such as aggregate output, but does not apply to others, such as unemployment and *per capita* output.

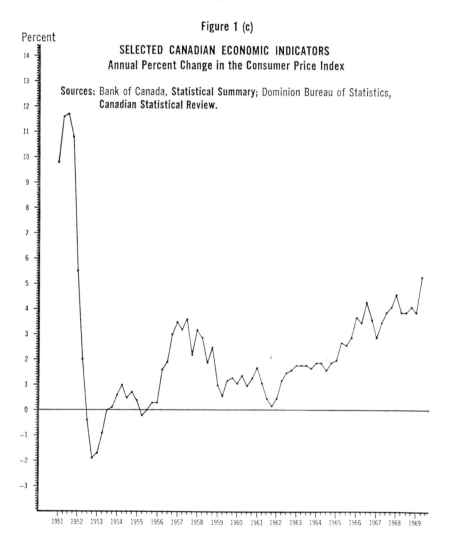

Figure 1 (c)

SELECTED CANADIAN ECONOMIC INDICATORS
Annual Percent Change in the Consumer Price Index

Sources: Bank of Canada, Statistical Summary; Dominion Bureau of Statistics,
Canadian Statistical Review.

II. A NEO-KEYNESIAN INCOME-DETERMINATION AND INFLATION MODEL

Although the reasons for cycles in economic activity are quite complex and diverse, it is often useful to consider them within the framework of a simple neo-Keynesian model. We shall examine such a model for an economy in which all factors of production are fully employed initially and which has no government sector. At any point in time, this economy would produce some volume of output which is available for consumption to the residents of the country and to the rest of the world. Simultaneously, the production of these commodities and services generates incomes, in the forms of wages, salaries, profits, rents and interest payments, which provide the various spending units in the country with a source of funds or incomes to finance their purchases. These spending units have a demand for domestic production which, together with foreign demand for domestic production, may equal, exceed, or fall short of the actual amount of domestic production. If this demand exactly equals the economy's production, the economy is said to be in full-employment equilibrium. If this demand exceeds the volume of production, the economy is in a position of excess demand, which leads to rationing and/or inflation. If this demand falls short of the volume of production, then unsold goods accumulate, production is curtailed, and unemployment develops. Therefore, from this simple model it is clear that unless aggregate demand equals full-employment output, the economy will be in a state of either unemployment or inflation.

However, even if aggregate demand and output are equated at a given point in time, there is no assurance that this will continue in the future. The problem here arises because some of the current production is devoted to investment, which increases productive capacity. Therefore in the next period potential output is increased, necessitating a corresponding increase in aggregate demand if full employment is to be attained. If aggregate demand does not grow by the exact amount that productive capacity increases, then in the next period the economy will have moved from a full-employment equilibrium position to a simple inflationary or excess-capacity position. Although there are a number of reasons why demand will increase with productive capacity, there is no particular reason why their growth should always bear a one-to-one correspondence, and hence the likelihood of either inflation or unemployment in the absence of government action is great.

The model we have been discussing so far is extremely simplified, allowing for either inflation or unemployment but not both simultaneously. If such an either-or situation existed in the real world, the guidelines for stabilization policy would be pure and simple. Unemployment, which would be accompanied by price declines or, at the limit, price stability, could be combatted by expansionary economic policies; while inflation, which would be caused by "over-full employment," could be combatted by contraction-ary economic policies, and the possibility of "full employment without inflation" would become a reality.

However, as is discussed in more detail in section eight of the chapter by John Crispo, our modern economy is so inflation-prone that price increases occur simultaneously with unemployment and excess capacity, even though the rate of inflation is lower the greater is the amount of unemployment. This relationship between the rate of inflation and the unemployment rate, which is known as the "Phillips' curve,"[2] means that the "ideal" policy target of zero inflation *and* zero unemployment is virtu-ally unattainable in a non-socialist economy.[3]

One reason why such a policy target is probably impossible to achieve is that literal full employment, in which the entire labour force is employed, is itself most unlikely because of frictional, seasonal, and structural impedi-ments. In a free and evolving society the matching of job vacancies and available workers happens neither instantaneously nor precisely, but involves numerous delays and imperfections, especially when not only local but also regional and national alternatives are considered. The unemploy-ment arising from these frictions is further aggravated seasonally in a country such as Canada by climatic influences which in the winter, for example, reduce construction activity and close the St. Lawrence River— a natural transportation route for Canada's foreign trade. Finally, in econo-mies experiencing rapid technological change, structural unemployment often develops as some people, though willing to work, lack the necessary training and ability required for modern industry. Because of the inevitabil-ity of some frictional, seasonal, and structural unemployment, economists generally define "full employment" not literally as zero unemployment but rather as unemployment of two or three percent of the labour force. Here-after we will follow this same convention.

In addition to the obstacles in obtaining literal full employment, there are several other reasons why unemployment and inflation co-exist. First, it is quite possible that while demand equals or is less than full-employment output in the aggregate, the demand for *some* commodities exceeds their supply. In such a situation we should expect prices to rise in those sectors experiencing excess demand and unemployment to arise in those sectors experiencing overproduction, thereby generating rising prices and unem-

2. The term "Phillips' curve" refers to the economist who first estimated this relation-ship. See A. W. Phillips, "The Relation Between Unemployment and the Rate of Change of Money Wage Rates in the United Kingdom, 1861-1957," *Economica,* New Series, XXV, No. 100 (November 1958), 283-99.
3. This is not to say that the use of all-pervasive controls by a socialist country would achieve "full employment without inflation" with impunity. Inefficiencies in production and distribution, poor quality of goods, and an over-emphasis on investment- relative to consumer-goods output might very well be a high price to pay for this accomplish-ment.

ployment simultaneously.[4] Moreover, if the excess demand occurs for items which are inputs in the production of other commodities, the cost of producing these other commodities will rise, and consequently prices will increase, even if we began in equilibrium in these sectors, giving us both a demand-pull and cost-push inflation. A variant of this, which is prevalent in an open economy such as Canada, occurs when the cost of imports increases. To the extent that imports are used as inputs in production, costs will rise and inflation will develop even with unemployed resources. If these imports are consumer goods, then the cost of living will rise automatically, thereby possibly fostering inflation *via* unions' demands for higher money wages to offset the increased cost of living.

Second, costs of production tend to increase as the economy moves toward full employment, generating inflationary influences while unemployment is still prevalent. These increases arise from qualitative differences in labour skills, whereby additional workers on a given salary are less productive than their previously hired counterparts, from the payment of higher wage rates for overtime, and from the bottlenecks that arise in production and distribution as full capacity is approached. All these factors increase the cost of production, and consequently prices, not only when full employment is *reached* but also while it is being *approached*.

Third, "impurities of competition" in the form of excessive market power in the hands of trade unions and firms in many industries give an inflationary bias to the economy even in the presence of unemployment. When organized labour seeks wage parity with more-productive workers in other countries or other unions in the same country, or when wages are automatically adjusted upward for cost-of-living increases without regard to productivity gains (so-called "escalator clauses" in labour contracts), inflationary pressures are built into the economy. If wage settlements are sought on a parity basis with workers whose productivity is increasing more rapidly, industries experiencing slowly rising productivity will experience wage increases in excess of their productivity increases, thus raising the per unit cost of output, and necessitating price increases if profits are not to decline. This in turn, *via* escalator clauses, leads to automatic wage increases which can trigger or maintain an inflationary spiral in the midst of unemployment.

In bargaining for wage rates beyond the competitive level, trade unions give management incentives to restrict employment, either by reducing output or by substituting real capital (machines) for men, the latter giving rise to so-called "technological unemployment." Management, also, often asserts its market power—by raising prices above the level which would

---

4. This situation would last until factors of production (especially labour and capital) could be shifted from overproducing to underproducing sectors.

occur under pure competition. Such price increases are both inflationary and restrictive, since the higher price lowers demand for the product, leading to reduced output and employment.

From this discussion a picture of the economy emerges in which unemployment is the consequence of frictional, seasonal, and structural factors as well as aggregate demand failing to keep pace with productive capacity, while inflation is the result of a multitude of demand and cost forces which make inflation likely even when the economy is operating with excess capacity.

III. THE GOALS OF STABILIZATION POLICY AND THE TRADE-OFFS AMONG POLICY OBJECTIVES

In view of the above discussion, it is useful to examine the relationship between the rate of inflation and the level of unemployment for the Canadian economy. A Phillips' curve estimated for the historical period 1953-1965 is shown in Figure 2 and confirms that although the rate of inflation declines with the level of unemployment, a zero-unemployment zero-inflation point does not exist to serve as an automatic goal of policy. Consequently, policy-makers must choose as their target that combination of unemployment and price inflation which they consider appropriate, given as a constraint the set of feasible points that lie on the Phillips' curve.

Of course, the Phillips' curve itself need not be stable. It changes autonomously over time; for example, moving outward (more inflation corresponding to a given unemployment rate) as inflationary expectations increase and labour unions become more powerful and more determined in their wage-rate demands. Also, the Phillips' curve may be amenable to policy actions, such as wage and price guidelines, adult education, and better labour-market information.

A rational choice of the appropriate point on the Phillips' curve requires the policy-makers' assessment of the relative *costs,* in terms of their own *preferences,* of marginal changes in unemployment and in inflation. The costs of unemployment are, in the first instance, a loss of output, which restrains the growth of consumption and investment production, thereby delaying improvements in the standard of living and increases in the productive power of the economy. Unemployment also carries with it the personal tragedies of the unemployed themselves, involving both economic difficulties and social stigma. These personal costs may weigh even more heavily than the opportunity loss in output, from the standpoint of the policy-makers who are also politicians and desire a satisfied electorate.

The costs of inflation, on the other hand, are not so evident but are just as important. In the case of a moderate inflation, where prices rise by a few percent a year, the costs may be primarily distributional in nature. Families

Figure 2

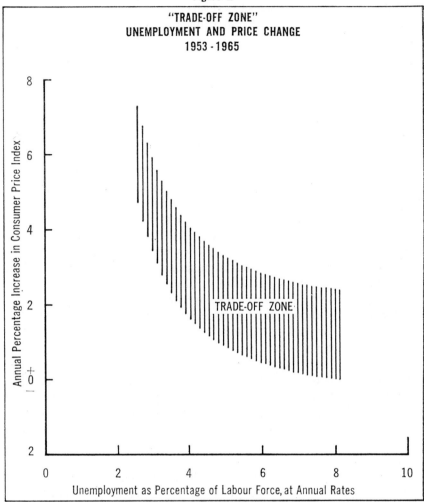

Source: Economic Council of Canada, **Third Annual Review** (Ottawa: Queen's Printer, 1964), p. 144.

on relatively fixed income—such as pensioners, salaried employees, and unorganized workers—find a steady deterioration in their standard of living as price increases outpace increases in income.[5]

A second and potentially very important disadvantage of such inflation occurs if a substantial proportion of an industry's cost increases are thought to be reversible, such as costs arising from bottlenecks in production or

_____

5. Even where income increases are proportionate to price increases, the progressive income tax leaves families with a lower after-tax purchasing power.

distribution, from the unavailability of skilled manpower, or from high interest rates which are expected to decline. In this case investment decisions may be postponed, leading to a slowing-down or reduction in economic activity, which may have a cumulative effect culminating in an economic recession. In an open economy, where exports have strong linkages to the rest of the economy, this severe downward spiral may be initiated by domestic price increases outpacing those of trading partners, thereby eroding the country's international competitive position. In addition, inflation has a symbolic effect of depreciating the purchasing power of the dollar, and politicians might be quite sensitive to charges of abetting such a result.

Runaway inflation, also called "hyperinflation," is another case entirely. In this situation the real costs are enormous, as inflationary expectations come to dominate spending and saving habits and cause major disruptions and misallocations. Everyone strives to spend money (and sell money-fixed assets in general) before prices rise all the more, and this very action fosters even greater inflation. A breakdown of the economy, as in post-World-War-I Germany, may result from such a chaotic situation.

Nevertheless, it is not hyperinflation which a country such as Canada faces but rather what is called "creeping" inflation. Prices change not in astronomical proportions but by a few percent a year, the exact amount of which can be determined by the location of the Phillips' curve and by the amount of unemployment in the economy.

A third important goal of economic policy is economic growth, which may be defined as the growth in *per capita* real output. The relationships between this goal and the goals of price stability and full employment (in terms of feasibility rather than government preferences) are complicated. Clearly, unemployment involves income foregone and causes an opportunity loss in savings and investment thereby retarding the growth in productive capacity of the economy. In this respect, low unemployment and rapid growth are complementary. As for inflation and growth, this relationship is controversial. Some distinguished economists, such as Joseph Schumpeter and Sumner Slichter, have argued that moderate inflation is conducive to growth, indeed that it is inherent in the growth process.[6] For example, innovators desiring to apply improved techniques in production must bid up the prices of labour and capital in order to attract these factors. However, most economists see inflation and growth as competitive rather than complementary, partly because of the fear that creeping inflation might develop into hyperinflation, partly because inflation leads to a misallocation of resources which may cause a postponing of investment

---

6. See Joseph A. Schumpeter, *Business Cycles* (New York: McGraw-Hill Book Company, 1939) and Sumner H. Slichter, "Thinking Ahead on the Side of Inflation," *Harvard Business Review* (September-October 1957), pp. 15-22.

projects if a large proportion of the higher costs are considered to be reversible, and partly because in an open economy such as Canada inflation greater than that abroad may destroy or seriously handicap the country's competitive position. Therefore, in view of (1) the strong likelihood that anything which promotes general economic stability will also foster economic growth, (2) the difficulty of determining the correspondence between any point on the Phillips' curve and economic growth,[7] and (3) the fact that the policies designed primarily to foster economic growth usually would be supply- rather than demand-oriented (such as developing educational and training institutions, improving transportation and communication facilities, etc.), we feel that stabilization policies need not be aimed directly at the goal of economic growth.

Another important aspect of stabilization policy, which is particularly relevant to Canada, is the sensitivity of the economy to its international environment. This appears as constraints placed upon Canadian policymakers both by Canada's physical proximity to and economic interdependence with the United States and by the need to maintain a long-run equilibrium in Canada's balance of payments.

The Canadian economy is extremely open, with imports providing 25 percent of goods and services consumed and exports accounting for 23 percent of production. This very large foreign-trade component of 24 percent of GNP (averaging imports and exports) compares with 47 percent for the Netherlands, 26 percent for Sweden, 20 percent for the United Kingdom, 19 percent for West Germany, 14 percent for France, 12 percent for Japan, and 5 percent for the United States. The vast majority of Canada's foreign trade is with the United States, which receives over 60 percent of Canadian exports (14 percent of total Canadian production) and supplies over 70 percent of Canadian imports (17 percent of all goods and services absorbed in Canada). Because of (1) the importance of this Canadian-American trade to Canada, (2) the amount of American ownership and control of Canadian industry (discussed in the essay by A. E. Safarian), (3) the close cooperation between Canadian and American labour unions, (4) the tremendous two-way tourist trade and (5) exposure to American radio, television, magazines, and newspapers, which influence Canadian consumer preferences and business expectations, United States economic conditions and environment have a pronounced impact upon the Canadian economy, usually causing it to move in harmony with the U.S. economy. When the U.S. economy is bouyant, favourable American expectations and strong American demand for Canadian goods and services stimulate Canadian production and transmit U.S. growth to the

---

7. Of course, if it were known that certain points on the Phillips' curve correspond to higher rates of growth, this would be an additional factor in favour of policy-makers aiming at these points.

Canadian economy. On the other hand, when the U.S. economy is sluggish, unfavourable U.S. expectations and slackening American demand for imports have restraining growth and employment consequences for Canada. In addition to these interrelationships, Canadian and American financial markets are well integrated with a highly developed set of institutional links, so that slight variations in relative interest rates can cause substantial capital flows. Consequently, Canadian monetary conditions are strongly influenced by American conditions, and Canadian stabilization policy is constrained significantly by corresponding U.S. policy.

A summary of a country's transactions with the outside world is provided by its balance of payments, a deficit indicating that a country spent more foreign exchange than it received during the year and a surplus indicating that the country spent less than it received. A deficit in the balance of payments involves losses in the country's holdings of international reserves (for Canada, predominantly gold and U.S. dollars), and ultimately may lead to a foreign-exchange crisis. Such a crisis, involving loss of confidence in the value of a country's currency *vis-à-vis* other currencies, is analogous to hyperinflation, the latter involving a loss of confidence in the domestic purchasing power of the currency.

A balance-of-payments deficit, to the extent that it is reflected in the current account (the value of a country's imports of goods and services exceeding that of its exports) has a direct retarding effect on the economy, compared to balanced trade in goods and services. Whether this result is desirable or not depends upon the state of the economy. It would be tolerable or desirable in an inflationary period, undesirable in a recessionary or high-unemployment period. Analogously, a balance-of-payment surplus on current account has an inflationary and stimulating effect upon the economy, which could be desirable during periods of economic stagnation but decidedly unwarranted during boom periods of high employment.

The relationship between the balance of payments and unemployment and price movements is clear. As a country moves along its Phillips' curve to points of lower unemployment and higher inflation, its balance of payments deteriorates. The greater the amount of inflation in one country relative to that in the rest of the world, the less competitive are its domestically produced goods, both at home and abroad, and hence the greater its imports and the less its exports. Furthermore, the higher income associated with lower unemployment involves an increase in the demand for imports.

As far as a balance-of-payments goal is concerned, ordinarily the policy-maker would aim at equilibrium or perhaps a small surplus (in order to achieve additions to the country's holdings of international reserves). Thus the goals of stabilization policy are price stability, full employment, and balance-of-payments equilibrium (or a small surplus). There is a "feasibility frontier" of attainable values of (1) the rate of change of prices, (2) unemployment and (3) the balance of payments, and these are called "target variables" or "policy targets." The Phillips' curve is a cross-section of this frontier.

Rational stabilization-policy-making involves the following four steps: (1) delineation of the "feasibility frontier" of the target variables; (2) selection of a point on this frontier, i.e., determination of the *values* of the target variables that stabilization policy will aim to achieve; (3) consideration of, and integration of stabilization policy with, other socio-economic policies, such as housing, education, medical care, etc. (many of which are discussed in other essays in this volume); and (4) the use of policy tools to attain the selected values of the target variables.

Of course, sensible policy-making aims also at *improving* the "feasibility frontier," for example, moving the Phillips' curve inward. However, we do not define such actions as *stabilization policy*, important though they may be, and do not discuss them further in this essay.[8] One should note at this point that if the government does not perceive the true "feasibility frontier," it might select inconsistent values of the target variables in step (2). Even if the government's goals are feasible, inappropriate use of policy tools might also prevent their realization. Before examining the record of Canadian policy-makers in this regard, we turn to a discussion of the tools available to policy-makers for stabilization purposes.

IV. THE TOOLS OF STABILIZATION POLICY

The traditional free-market tools for stabilization purposes are monetary and fiscal policies, where monetary policy refers to variations in the money supply emanating from the actions of the central bank and fiscal policy refers to variations in government spending and taxation policy.[9]

Monetary policy exerts its impact upon the economy directly by altering the availability of liquid assets in the economy, thereby affecting the ability of consumers and investors to finance their expenditures, and indirectly by altering interest rates, which influences the desirability and profitability of consumer and investor expenditures. Monetary policy has diverse sectoral impacts, affecting new-residential-construction and public-utilities expenditures most strongly, and business investment and consumer expenditure least strongly. It also has a substantial impact upon the balance of payments, affecting portfolio-capital flows by altering the interest differential between the home country and the rest of the world and influ-

---

8. For analysis of some of these policies, see the essay by David C. Smith.
9. For an elaboration of the material in this and the preceding section, see the Royal Commission on Banking and Finance, *Report* (Ottawa: Queen's Printer, 1964), chs. 19-25.

encing the current-account balance by changing domestic expenditure.

In Canada, the central bank (Bank of Canada) has several techniques for conducting its monetary policy. The most usual technique is open-market operations, in which the central bank purchases (sells) government securities from the public, including the chartered banks,[10] thus increasing (decreasing) the amount of cash in the hands of the public. If the transaction is with a chartered bank, the cash reserves of the banking system are immediately increased (decreased), providing a base for multiple credit expansion (contraction). If the transaction is with the non-bank public, the cash shortly finds its way into (out of) the banking system in the form of deposits, again altering the cash reserves of the banking system.[11]

A second technique is changing the reserve requirements of the chartered banks. The banks are required to hold cash (currency and deposits at the Bank of Canada) equal to 12 percent of their demand deposits and 4 percent of their other deposits (savings and notice deposits).[12] Decreasing (increasing) these percentages reduces (increases) the amount of reserves required to be held against existing deposits, thereby freeing additional reserves to support a further multiple credit expansion (requiring a multiple credit contraction).[13]

A third technique of monetary policy is varying the bank rate, the rate at which the central bank will lend cash to the chartered banks.[14] In addition to controlling the bank rate, the Bank of Canada sets other lending terms, such as the maximum amounts of credit it will provide. Because the chartered banks only occasionally borrow from the Bank of Canada, changes in the bank rate historically have had more of an "announcement"

---

10. Commercial banks in Canada are called "chartered," because they operate under charters from the federal government.

11. The money supply may be altered also *via* cash-management techniques, i.e., the shifting or allocating of government deposits between the Bank of Canada and the chartered banks. This is used more to smooth day-to-day fluctuations in the money supply than as a long-run technique.

12. Prior to 1967 there was a unit reserve requirement against all Canadian deposit liabilities of the chartered banks. The dual system of required reserves has the disadvantage of permitting swings between demand and other deposits to frustrate monetary policy, or at least to make the operations of monetary policy technically more difficult. Thus, although the dual system was part of a set of banking-legislation changes to remove inequities against chartered banks as distinct from other financial institutions, it was a step backward from the standpoint of providing a favourable framework for stabilization policy. However, such a dual system has been in existence in the United States for some time.

13. In addition to these "primary" (cash) reserve requirements, the chartered banks face "secondary" reserve requirements—minimum holdings of treasury bills, and day-to-day loans as a percentage of deposits. These secondary requirements, too, may be altered by the Bank of Canada.

14. The Bank of Canada also provides loans to money-market dealers, who themselves lend cash to the chartered banks as part of their operations.

than a "borrowing" effect. For example, an increase in the bank rate signals stronger anti-inflationary policies.

A fourth way of implementing monetary policy is by "moral suasion," that is, extra-legal limitations on chartered-bank actions. The small number of chartered banks in Canada fosters this kind of tactic on the part of the central bank. Indeed, prior to its enactment into legislation, the secondary-reserves requirement was based on an extra-legal agreement between the Bank of Canada and the chartered banks.

Unlike monetary policy, which operates in an indirect fashion on expenditure, fiscal policy is quite direct in both its discretionary and automatic forms. Discretionary fiscal policy refers to deliberate changes in taxation rates and government expenditure, while automatic fiscal policy refers to changes in government tax collections and spending which occur automatically (i.e., without any parliamentary action) when recession or inflation threaten. Two important forms of automatic fiscal policy are the graduated (progressive) income tax and variations in government spending and collections under transfer-payment programs (such as unemployment insurance). Under both kinds of fiscal policy, variations in tax collections alter the amount of funds that individuals and corporations have at their disposal for expenditure, thereby affecting consumption and investment expenditures, while alterations in government spending programs have direct and indirect income-generating effects.

In addition to the problem of timing, to which all government policies are subject, fiscal policy in a federal state such as Canada is hampered by the need to harmonize federal and provincial spending and taxation programs. This issue is discussed in the essay by Jacques Parizeau, and in the remainder of our essay fiscal policy refers exclusively to that conducted by the federal government.

A stabilization tool that is ancillary to both fiscal and monetary policy is debt-management policy, in which the government alters the term structure of its public debt. This is done by issuing or calling in debt that is concentrated at either the short- or long-term end of the maturity structure. *Ipso facto*, short-term debt adds more heavily to the liquidity of the private sector of the economy, and hence is expansionary compared to longer-term issues. Furthermore, since government long-term debt competes with long-term private securities issued to finance long-term investment projects, long-term financing is considered more contractionary than an equivalent amount of short-term financing. A third effect of a change in the term structure of the government debt is a shift in the yield curve for government securities: increased long-term borrowing raises long-term interest rates relative to short-term rates, compared to an equivalent amount of short-term financing.

Monetary, fiscal, and debt-management policies all influence—to a greater or lesser extent—the same monetary and real variables in the economy. Thus these policies are all intertwined. This may be seen clearly if we assume, for example, that the government wishes to reduce unemployment by increasing its spending. In this case the government has the option of increasing its deficit (or reducing its surplus) by running down cash assets, by increasing the money supply through security sales to the central bank, or by issuing securities directly to the public. If the government chooses to reduce its cash assets by spending balances held at the Bank of Canada, it increases the money supply, thus simultaneously conducting a form of monetary policy with its fiscal policy. If it runs down balances held with the chartered banks, there is no such monetary-policy effect.

If the government chooses the second alternative—selling securities to the central bank—the government's cash position is protected, but the money supply is increased as in the first case, in which deposits at the Bank of Canada were run down. Finally, if the government raises its funds by security sales to the public, the money supply is left unaltered but the term structure of the debt, and therefore debt-management policy, probably will be changed. Consequently, pursuit of any one tool of stabilization policy inevitably involves a decision as to the form of all other tools of such policy to be followed. Therefore it is often misleading to study the application of a policy tool in isolation. Rather, the whole mix of stabilization-policy instruments should be considered.

Finally, we come to the matter of exchange-rate policy, which assumes great importance in an open economy, especially when that economy is heavily influenced by one or two other countries, as is Canada. Canada was on a freely fluctuating exchange rate in the period 1950-1962. Such a system has the advantage that the balance of payments is always in equilibrium, kept there by market forces; thus no deficit can arise. However, its principal virtue for an open economy is the enhanced scope that it gives to stabilization policy compared with a fixed-rate system. Suppose that Canada pursues expansionary policies. Under a pegged exchange rate this would lead to a balance-of-payments deficit (assuming that the country starts from a position of balance-of-payments equilibrium). This development, in turn, might either act as a constraint on the application of the expansionary policies or require the use of other policies to cope with the deficit. Under a fluctuating exchange rate, no such problems exist. The incipient deficit would be corrected by an automatic depreciation of the exchange rate.

Of course, the enhanced scope that a fluctuating exchange-rate system gives to an open economy need not be advantageous. If the policies followed are inappropriate, the constraining influences of a pegged exchange rate ought to be welcomed. If the Canadian government can pursue more effective stabilization policy than can the United States, then it ought to revert to a fluctuating exchange rate. If not, then it is wise in remaining on the pegged-rate system.

The use of a pegged exchange rate under the Articles of Agreement of the International Monetary Fund provides an additional tool of policy, namely, the possibility that the value of the pegged rate itself may be changed. All countries must register a par value of their currency with the International Monetary Fund, this value defined in terms of the U.S. dollar, and must keep all transactions in their currency within one percent of parity.[15] A country may change the par value of its currency unilaterally, providing the new parity does not exceed 10 percent of the par value initially registered at the Fund. Otherwise, permission of the Fund is required for the change, although in practice exchange-rate changes often take place *before* formal permission is given (especially if the country concerned is powerful economically and politically on the world scene).

Canada has not changed the par value of its currency (at $1.00 Can. = $.925 U.S.) since it reverted to a pegged rate in 1962, although it did alter the par value twice between 1946 and the adoption of the fluctuating exchange rate in 1950. Under the present international monetary system, countries are reluctant to change the par value of their currency, say, to depreciate their currency in order to cure a balance-of-payments deficit, for the following reasons: (1) the action may provide a windfall gain to speculators who foresaw the devaluation; (2) it might set off competitive devaluations, as countries strive to lower the prices of their products in foreign markets; (3) politically, devaluation tends to be interpreted as an event which lessens the prestige of a country and its government; (4) devaluation has a deleterious effect on the standard of living in a country, by increasing the cost of imported goods.[16]

These disadvantages of currency-depreciation mean that a country tends to postpone devaluation until a time of great crisis in its foreign-exchange market, thus exacerbating some of the disadvantages, especially the gain to speculators, who sell the currency about to be devalued, thereby weakening the exchange rate of the country. In effect, then, Canada's replacement of its freely fluctuating exchange rate by a pegged exchange rate added a policy target (balance-of-payments equilibrium, fulfilled automatically in the former system) without providing a policy tool (discrete changes in the exchange rate) except under the most trying circumstances.

---

15. The United States, in turn, pegs its currency to gold at $35 an ounce.
16. In fact, unless either sufficient slack in the economy exists initially or strong deflationary measures are applied, devaluation is likely to generate inflationary forces throughout the economy, not just in the trade sector.

V. HIGHLIGHTS OF CANADIAN STABILIZATION POLICY IN THE POSTWAR PERIOD

We now turn to a discussion of how the tools of stabilization policy have been applied in practice, taking as our subject some important episodes in Canada's postwar experience. One way to proceed would be to analyze Canadian stabilization policy on a year-by-year basis, summarizing the policy changes as they occurred. Another way, which we feel is more meaningful, is to discuss the *highlights* of the stabilization policies undertaken in postwar years, by considering the following seven episodes:

1. Retention of Exchange Control
2. Adoption of a Freely Fluctuating Exchange Rate
3. Acceptance and Rejection of "Keynesian" Fiscal Policy
4. The Conversion-Loan Fiasco
5. Perverse Monetary Policy
6. Reversion to a Pegged Exchange Rate
7. The Battle Against Inflation

These seven policy developments are arranged roughly—though not precisely—in chronological order. Although we shall be discussing each of these measures in turn, they cannot properly be analyzed in isolation, and therefore attention is also given to the interrelationships among them. The interested reader can put these episodes into even stronger historical perspective by referring to official policy declarations and the relevant statistical data.[17]

1. retention of exchange control

All-out war in modern times inevitably involves foreign-exchange control instituted by the governments of the countries engaged in hostilities (and indeed by governments of many neutral countries as well). Canada declared war on Germany shortly after Britain did in September 1939, and Canada's entry into the war was followed immediately by the setting-up of exchange control. The exchange-control system, while modified over the years, remained in essentially the same form after the conclusion of hostilities and still existed even after the unpegging of the Canadian dollar in September 1950.[18]

Basically, exchange control involved restrictions on both the disposition

---

17. The basic source information on stabilization policy in Canada is the *Annual Reports* of the Bank of Canada, the *Budget Speeches* of the Minister of Finance, and the *Annual Reviews* of the Economic Council of Canada. Also relevant are speeches and press releases of the Governor of the Bank of Canada and press releases of the Minister of Finance. Macro-economic statistics are found in the Bank of Canada's *Statistical Summary* and the Dominion Bureau of Statistics' *National Accounts, Income and Expenditure* and *The Canadian Balance of International Payments*.

18. Details of the various changes in the exchange-control system over time are found in the *Annual Reports* of the Foreign Exchange Control Board (1946-1951).

and the acquisition of foreign exchange. Canadian residents were required to sell all foreign exchange that they had obtained to a dealer authorized by the government, i.e., to a chartered bank. On the other side, permits were required for the purchase and use of foreign exchange.

The purpose of exchange control is to help mobilize the resources of the country in a direction desired by the government. In wartime this means, for example, the restriction of luxury consumer-goods imports and the fostering of raw-material imports needed for the armaments industry. Also, it must be remembered that Canada entered the Second World War two years earlier than did the United States. This raised the possibility that Canadians might try to shift their Canadian-dollar assets and their acquisitions of foreign currencies into U.S. securities and deposits in U.S. banks, thereby weakening the Canadian dollar (possibly even bringing about a foreign-exchange crisis) as well as dissipating foreign exchange needed for the war effort. The operation of Canada's exchange-control system in the war years is considered generally to have been successful in the achievement of its purposes. As one observer of the experience notes:

> Exchange stability was maintained and the country's resources were conserved for essential purposes. Domestic war financing was not hampered by non-resident selling; in fact, the magnitude of the subscriptions received from some American institutional investors during the later Victory Loan campaigns was even a source of some embarrassment. Confidence was maintained in the Canadian dollar and the Canadian economy and there was little opposition to the control even from American investors; indeed, those with a large stake in Canada recognized that for the long term their investments were safeguarded rather than endangered by its existence. Without foreign exchange control it is hard to see how these results could have been achieved.[19]

The problem with foreign-exchange control, like that of economic controls in general, is the distortions and inefficiencies that result. True, the shift of resources to the military and supporting industries is a *desired* distortion in wartime. More important, the Second World War involved feelings of patriotism and self-sacrifice on the part of Canadian citizens. This made the administration and policing of exchange control easier than it would otherwise have been. Even so, the man-hours spent in administering the system (filling out permits, filing forms, deciding on the acceptance or rejection of applications for foreign exchange, etc.) were indeed substantial. The Foreign Exchange Control Board alone employed as many as 553 workers at one time,[20] quite apart from the resources expended on the system by the chartered banks, other private institutions, and by individual citizens.

---

19. Alan O. Gibbons, "Foreign Exchange Control in Canada, 1939-51," *Canadian Journal of Economics and Political Science*, XIX, No. 1 (February 1953), pp. 52-53.
20. *Ibid.*, p. 37.

The decision to continue foreign-exchange control after the war cannot be viewed as sound policy. Without the inherent patriotism associated with a war effort, the incentives for the public to evade rather than cooperate in the exchange-control system inevitably increase. The distortions in an exchange-control system imply windfall gains for those able to avoid the regulations. For example, the resale of smuggled luxury goods (otherwise restricted by controls) could be quite profitable, in view of their higher prices in Canada compared to the source of supply, say, the United States. Furthermore, without a firm national goal as to the disposition of resources (such as the fostering of military-related industries), the tremendous paperwork involved in carrying out and administering the controls becomes a deadweight loss. However, the retention of exchange control after the war was related intimately to Canada's exchange-rate policy at the time, which brings us to our next topic.

2. adoption of a freely fluctuating exchange rate

Canada had a floating exchange rate over most of the period between the two world wars, but this experience was divided by adherence to the gold standard in 1926-1929. In 1939, with the outbreak of the war, the government pegged the Canadian dollar at a discount of about 10 percent in relation to the U.S. dollar. The government sold U.S. dollars at $1.11 Can. (reduced to $1.105 in 1945) and bought U.S. dollars at $1.10 Can. The spread enabled the government to make a small profit on exchange transactions.

Canada entered the postwar period with a huge pent-up demand for consumer goods. As an anti-inflationary measure, the Canadian dollar was appreciated to parity with the U.S. dollar[21] in 1946—one of the few instances of currency *appreciation* by any country in the postwar period. While this action helped to contain inflation, experience proved it to be too drastic a change in the exchange rate, resulting in an over-valued Canadian dollar, which led to a foreign-exchange crisis in 1947. *This crisis was countered not by depreciating the exchange rate but by increasing the severity of the exchange-control system.*

In September 1949, when Britain devalued the pound sterling, Canada— along with some thirty other countries—followed suit, depreciating the Canadian dollar by about 10 percent in relation to the U.S. dollar (selling the U.S. dollar at $1.105 Can. and buying at $1.10 Can.). Within a year it became apparent that Canada had erred once more in the selection of a new par value. This time it had *depreciated* by too much.

Belief that the Canadian currency was undervalued and would soon be

---

21. Actually, the government's selling rate for the U.S. dollar was $1.005 Can. and its buying rate $1.00 Can.

appreciated led to a capital inflow which reached intolerable proportions in 1950. The government feared the inflationary implications of this flow, as well as its deleterious effect on monetary policy and the bond market. The Bank of Canada must purchase foreign exchange in the last resort; but such a purchase is equivalent to a purchase of government bonds in the same amount, as far as the credit-expansion implications for the banking system are concerned. Offsetting the foreign-exchange purchases by government-bond *sales* could be done to some extent, but was limited by the "thinness" of the bond market, which meant bond prices would fall (and, correspondingly, interest rates rise) drastically, if the operations continued.

Uncertain of what to do next, afraid of appreciating because of the windfall gains that speculators would obtain, baffled by the difficulty of selecting a true equilibrium par value of the Canadian dollar (having over-reacted twice in the past four years in this connection), the government decided upon a brilliant solution to the problem of the undervalued Canadian dollar: it would let the dollar float freely in the exchange market. As the Minister of Finance announced on September 30, 1950:

> Today, the Government, by Order in Council under the authority of the Foreign Exchange Control Act, cancelled the official rates of exchange which, since September 19 of last year, had been calculated on the basis of a 10 percent premium for the United States dollar in Canada. It has been decided not to establish any new fixed parity for the Canadian dollar at this time, nor to prescribe any new official fixed rates of exchange. Instead, rates of exchange will be determined by conditions of supply and demand for foreign currencies in Canada.[22]

The exchange-control system still existed even after the unpegging of the Canadian dollar. As the Minister of Finance noted in his announcement: "From what has been said, it will be seen that the change from a fixed rate of exchange to a market rate does not involve the abandonment of the foreign exchange control system."[23] However, the exchange-control system was loosened considerably after the adoption of the floating exchange rate, and exchange control was terminated a year later, in December 1951. Much of the credit for the elimination of the exchange-control system must go to the floating exchange rate, which automatically equilibrates demand and supply of foreign exchange, thus obviating the need to ration foreign exchange in order to finance balance-of-payments deficits.

The 1950 decision to free the exchange rate was surely one of the most remarkable economic decisions ever taken by a government. For one thing, because the Canadian dollar had been pegged at too low a rate relative to the U.S. dollar, the shift to a rate determined only by private (non-govern-

---

22. *The Unpegging of the Canadian Dollar: A statement issued by Mr. Douglas Abbott, Minister of Finance, at Ottawa on September 30, 1950, regarding the Canadian exchange rate*, Department of External Affairs (Ottawa), p. 1.
23. *Ibid.*, p. 2.

ment) supply and demand would involve an inevitable appreciation of the Canadian dollar, decreasing the prices of Canadian imports at home and increasing the prices of its exports abroad, thereby adversely affecting both exported and import-competing goods. Second, permission of the International Monetary Fund had to be obtained in order to free the dollar legally, as a pegged rate is mandatory according to the Articles of Agreement of the Fund. Furthermore, it is presumed that the United States— Canada's foremost trading partner—had to grant acquiescence to this move, which might have been done through U.S. representation in the Fund.

Canada's policy-makers showed laudable economic sophistication in opting for the floating exchange rate in 1950. And the freely fluctuating rate worked well, with changes in the rate occurring only gradually. True, the rate was usually above parity with the U.S. dollar, but there were no disruptions of trade or capital flows. In fact, the Canadian experience with the floating rate put an end (or should have put an end) to the economic myth that equates a *floating* rate with an *unstable* rate.[24] In the light of Canada's admirable decision to float the rate, the story of the demise of the floating rate is all the more saddening—a story which is outlined as episode 6 below.

3. acceptance and rejection of "Keynesian" fiscal policy

Following the Korean War, which began in 1950, Canada entered a period of rapid economic growth, with unemployment averaging less than 3 percent in the years 1951 and 1952 and just 3 percent in 1953. However, in 1954 signs of a recession appeared, and the unemployment rate increased to 4.6 percent. The fiscal-policy response to this slowdown was to revise the personal income-tax schedule so as to reduce the tax payable by 12-13 percent and to reduce the corporate tax rate (on profits above $20,000) by 2 percentage points. Moreover, the Minister of Finance followed clear Keynesian reasoning in arriving at his tax reductions. As H. Scott Gordon has noted:

> In his Budget Speech of April 1955 [the Minister of Finance] Mr. Harris made a clear statement of the economic budgeting principle and then went on to apply it to the existing economic circumstances. First he estimated what the budget balance would be at existing tax rates. This calculation resulted in a small deficit. Then he noted that the revenue side of this estimate was based on a level of economic activity which, for the fiscal year as a whole, was below full employment. He accordingly re-estimated the budget balance on the assump-

---

24. For a detailed discussion of the Canadian fluctuating exchange rate, see Paul Wonnacott, *The Canadian Dollar 1948-1962* (Toronto: University of Toronto Press, 1965).

tion of full employment. This calculation resulted in a substantial surplus. He then decided on tax reductions of a magnitude that would deepen the estimated deficit of the fiscal year, but which would represent a balanced budget at theoretical full employment level. A Keynesian could not have much quarrel with this procedure.[25]

The economy gained momentum in 1955 and 1956, with unemployment falling to 3.4 percent in 1956. Tax changes were only minor in this period, although they were on the easing side, helping the economy to expand.

The economy faltered again in 1957, with unemployment averaging 4.6 percent once more. A recovery began in 1958, but did not take hold, and the economy plummeted into a severe recession—with unemployment averaging 7.1, 6.0, 7.0, and 7.2 percent in each of the years 1958 to 1961, respectively. In 1957 and 1958, the government responded by continuing to reduce taxes, but only moderately, whereas large-scale reductions were required. In the 1959 budget, however, taxes were *increased*, the government guessing wrongly that the 1958 recovery would be sustained. As it turned out, the tax increases were the wrong policy, but only hindsight could provide this judgment. The March 1960 budget introduced no significant tax changes, and although 1961 and 1962 saw some tax reductions, they were not particularly significant in magnitude. As Gordon notes:

> There were virtually no tax changes of any importance in this period. The treasury ran substantial deficits, but these were of the passive variety and reflected the effect of the recession itself, rather than positive efforts to combat it. The deficit rose very considerably in 1961, largely as a result of increases in expenditures on defence, interest on the national debt, payments to the railways, and federal contributions to vocation training and health programs. The greater part of these expenditure increases was due to programs that were quite independent of the general state of the economy, and the resulting rise in the deficit in fiscal 1961-62 cannot be construed as due to a decision on the part of the government to combat unemployment by Keynesian policies applied on the expenditure side of the budget.[26]

This drift away from Keynesian economics was completed in 1963 by the virtual abandonment of Keynesian principles in Canadian fiscal policy. Again, as H. Scott Gordon notes:

> Mr. Walter Gordon, who succeeded to the finance portfolio when the government changed in the spring of 1963 . . . [applied] the [anti-Keynesian] principle of balanced budgeting. Despite the existence of unemployment rates almost twice the full employment level of three percent, taxes were raised in 1963. The Minister spoke in pleased terms of the recovery of government revenues in 1964 and 1965 and

---

25. H. Scott Gordon, "A Twenty Year Perspective: Some Reflections on the Keynesian Revolution in Canada," in *Canadian Economic Policy since the War*, Montreal: Canadian Trade Committee of the Private Planning Association of Canada, 1966, p. 38.
26. *Ibid.*, pp. 40-41.

was proud to announce that the budget had been "brought under control" by the elimination of deficits. . . . The tax cut of 1965 was no doubt influenced to some extent by the adoption of a tax reduction policy in the United States, but its primary bases were simply that revenues had risen to the point where the Minister felt that the treasury could afford it, and that it was politically desirable to offset by tax reductions the compulsory contributions that would have to be made by taxpayers to the projected federal pension plan.[27]

We may also speculate that the 1965 tax reduction gave an extra boost to the economy, just as it was beginning to feel inflationary pressure.

The above summary of Canadian fiscal policy for the period 1954-1965 suggests that even the *inclination* of governments to apply rational fiscal policy at all times is by no means assured. Furthermore, the Canadian government cannot claim to have compensated for its misuse of fiscal policy in the postwar period by the sound application of other tools of stabilization policy, as our discussion of further episodes shows.

4. the conversion-loan fiasco

The Conversion-Loan episode of 1958 was the most important action of debt-management undertaken by the Canadian government in the postwar period. Unfortunately, this massive operation, which extended the average maturity of public holdings of government debt from 96 months on June 30, 1958, to 178 months on September 30 in the same year, created considerable difficulties. It complicated the government's stabilization policy for some years to come, because *liquidity in the economy was substantially reduced in the midst of a recession.*

In 1958 the government became concerned about the amount of its debt issued during the Second World War that would have to be refinanced over the next few years. In particular, $947 million of Victory Bonds were to mature in January 1959, another $1,165 million in June 1960, and a further $4,304 million in 1962, 1963, and 1966. Rather than be faced with a problem of continuous large-scale financing, some of which could arise at an inopportune time, the government decided to convert its shortly-maturing Victory Bond issues into longer-term securities. During a two-month period, from mid-July to mid-September, in a campaign reminiscent of the war-bond drives, $5,806 million, representing 45 percent of the outstanding market debt, were converted to longer-term issues.[28]

This vast conversion of long- for short-term debt, which almost doubled the average term to maturity of public holdings, had numerous immediate and long-term consequences. First, by substantially reducing the liquidity of the public it contributed significantly to the upward movement in interest

27. *Ibid.,* p. 42.
28. See Royal Commission on Banking and Finance, *Report,* pp. 454-55.

rates that occurred at the time, and to the maintenance of relatively high rates thereafter. Whether such an increase in interest rates is desirable or not depends, of course, upon the state of the economy. Since unemployment during 1958 averaged 7 percent and growth in GNP and industrial production was sluggish, higher interest rates and reduced liquidity were clearly inappropriate, as they exacerbated the recession and helped to make the recovery of that year short-lived.

Second, the Conversion Loan placed a tremendous strain on the bond market. Because the government refinanced too much debt in too short a period, the Bank of Canada had to support bond prices. When such support was removed, bonds plummeted in price (corresponding to increases in interest rates), disrupting the bond market and seriously hampering future government financing operations.

Third, by destroying confidence in the bond market the Conversion Loan interfered with monetary policy, since the government bond market is the principal *conduit* for the implementation of open-market operations of the Bank of Canada.

Finally, by increasing interest rates and interfering with monetary and fiscal policy the Conversion Loan played an important role in the government actions which led to the demise of Canada's fluctuating exchange rate, as described in episode 6 below.

5. perverse monetary policy

In the late 1950's and until 1961, the Bank of Canada pursued a restrictive monetary policy, irrespective of the state of the economy. In the expansionary period of the mid-1950's, such a policy was correct. However, the Bank persisted in its tight-money policy even when recessionary forces gained ascendancy in the late 1950's, and the 1960-1961 period witnessed the coexistence of a tight monetary policy and a 7½ percent unemployment rate.

Although the havoc wrought in the bond market by the Conversion Loan would have made monetary policy difficult to carry out in any event, the particular monetary policy adopted by Mr. J. E. Coyne, the Governor of the Bank of Canada, was primarily a consequence of his concern with the dangers of inflation and the deficit in the current account of the balance of payments. Unfortunately, the Governor's assessment of the situation was quite wrong. Economic statistics at the time clearly showed that the danger to the economy was a severe recession, not inflation, while the fluctuating exchange rate operating at the time automatically provided the equilibrating mechanism for the *over-all* balance of payments (current plus capital account). Moreover, the high interest rates that accompany a stringent monetary policy were likely to have a *perverse* influence upon the current account, by increasing capital inflows and appreciating rather than depreciating the exchange rate, thereby lessening the competitiveness of Canadian exports and import-competing goods.[29]

The monetary policy adopted by the Bank of Canada during this period was disastrous because (1) it exerted direct undesirable effects upon the economy; (2) along with the Conversion Loan, it temporarily paralyzed the bond market; (3) it contributed to the termination of the floating exchange rate (as discussed in the next episode); and (4) it inhibited the rational use of fiscal policy.

As mentioned above, the appropriate fiscal policy for the 1959-1962 period was one of expansion, which involves running a budgetary deficit. However:

> A deficit must be financed; and in the conditions that prevailed in the financial markets after the debacle of 1958, the debt management authorities found it necessary to add various premiums (almost like super-market trading stamps) to Government of Canada bonds in order to carry through the necessary financing at all. Until Mr. Coyne left the office of Governor, the Bank's policy remained strictly anti-inflationary and the government could expect no assistance in solving its financial problems through the route of monetary expansion. In the circumstances, not only was monetary policy seriously in error itself, but it limited the freedom of fiscal policy as well and made the Minister of Finance even more receptive to the argument that was being pressed strongly within the bureaucracy that the unemployment problem was structural in nature and should be attacked by non-budgetary means. Thus there were a variety of powerful forces which came to bear on [the Minister of Finance] Mr. Fleming in 1960 to induce him to abandon ... Keynesian economics.[30]

The lack of coordination between the fiscal and monetary authorities (the Department of Finance and the Bank of Canada) led to the resignation of J. E. Coyne and his replacement by L. B. Rasminsky. In his statement of August 1, 1961, Rasminsky stressed the need for coordination among monetary, fiscal, and debt-management policies, and to the time of writing (1969) the perverse and uncoordinated monetary policy of the late 1950's and early 1960's has not been repeated.

6. reversion to a pegged exchange rate

In the late 1950's the government became concerned with the relationships among the inflow of long-term capital, the exchange rate, exports and imports, and unemployment. The capital inflow (predominantly from the

---

29. True, Mr. Coyne was also concerned with American investment in Canada, as well as balancing the current-account deficit. However, in this respect he was making a *political* judgment, quite outside the purview of his position.
30. Gordon, *ibid.*, pp. 41-42.

United States) appreciated the value of the Canadian *vis-à-vis* the U.S. dollar, thus making exports more expensive to foreigners and imports cheaper to Canadians. Hence the balance of payments on current account deteriorated, output was adversely affected, and unemployment increased.

Rational policy under this situation would have been to counter directly the incentives for the capital inflow—simply by *lowering* interest rates. This policy was also called for by the domestic economic situation; lower interest rates, by encouraging domestic investment and consumer expenditure, would have helped to counter the recession and reduce unemployment. However, the Conversion Loan had the opposite effect on interest rates, and the "come prosperity or recession" tight-money policy of the Bank of Canada further served to keep interest rates high.

With fiscal policy constrained by the policy of the Bank of Canada (as discussed in the previous episode), the government resorted to special measures to limit the inflow of capital. In March 1960 the Minister of Finance sought to discourage Canadian borrowing abroad by remarking:

> However, those who undertake commitments in terms of United States dollars or other external currencies expose themselves to the risk of having to repay at a time when the exchange rate for the Canadian dollar may be quite different from what it is today. This is a risk which the borrower, whether personal, corporate, provincial or municipal must bear himself and is a danger which I clearly wish to stress.[31]

Ironically, this attempt at moral suasion indeed complemented the strictures of the Governor of the Bank of Canada against foreign investment in Canada. Thus in moral suasion—if not substantial policy—the monetary and fiscal authorities acted in concert!

The moral suasion had no effect, and on December 20, 1960 the government took substantive action. It attempted to discourage the long-term capital inflow by increasing the withholding taxes imposed on interest and dividends paid to non-residents. While these increased taxes on income transferred abroad had some retarding effect on the capital inflow,[32] they did not bring about a pronounced reduction in the exchange value of the Canadian dollar. Therefore the government decided to apply direct action to the foreign-exchange market. Thus on June 20, 1961 the Minister of Finance declared in another speech:

> No one can say today what the appropriate level of our exchange rate would be when our balance of payments is in a position better suited to our present economic circumstances. But the rate will certainly be

---

31. *Budget Speech, March 31, 1960*, p. 8.
32. See Lawrence H. Officer, *An Econometric Model of Canada Under the Fluctuating Exchange Rate* (Cambridge, Mass: Harvard University Press, 1968), pp. 73-81.

lower than it has been of late and it may well be appropriate for it to move to a significant discount. It will be government policy to facilitate such a movement. Accordingly the exchange fund will be prepared, as and when necessary, to add substantial amounts to its holdings of United States dollars through purchases in the exchange market. . . . Once an exchange rate more closely in line with Canada's economic position is achieved, the government will use the resources of the exchange fund to ensure that the rate is kept within a range appropriate to Canada's changing economic situation.[33]

Until this date, it was the announced policy of the government to let the exchange rate be determined solely by private demand and supply of foreign exchange, and this policy was pursued faithfully. The government used its international reserves (gold and U.S. dollars) only to iron out short-run movements in the exchange rate. Now the government had declared that it would manipulate the exchange value of the Canadian dollar downward to a new level and keep it there.

The new exchange-market policy

. . . unleashed forces of speculation in the foreign exchange market and the market was beset by uncertainties. Participants did not know what the government would do next. The government attempted to keep the dollar at an artificially low rate and its official reserves began to *decline* (rather than increase, as would occur under normal circumstances) because of fear on the part of the private sector of the market that the rate might fall even further. In the first four months of 1962 reserves decreased so substantially that continuance of the government's policy became intolerable. The government then had two choices insofar as exchange rate policy was concerned. It could withdraw as an extraordinary trader from the foreign exchange market, or it could formally terminate the floating rate. Obviously, to initiate once again a drastic change in exchange fund policy would entail still further bewilderment over sharp changes in governmental action. The return to the fixed rate was thus made almost inevitable.[34]

Finally, on May 2, 1962 Mr. Donald M. Fleming, the Minister of Finance, announced the pegging of the Canadian dollar at 92½ cents in terms of U.S. currency.

True, depreciating the Canadian currency was *an* appropriate policy (though not the *optimal* policy) from the standpoint of ending the recession in Canada. The new low par value of the dollar gave a substantial competitive advantage to Canadian export and import-competing industries. However, the price paid for this method of solving Canada's unemployment problem was the loss of the freely fluctuating exchange rate. The clumsy fashion in which the Canadian government reverted to a pegged exchange rate

---

33. *Budget Speech, June 20, 1961*, pp. 12-13.
34. Officer, *ibid.*, p. 89.

provides an incredible contrast to the courageous and clever action of a former government in instituting the floating rate some 12 years earlier.

7. the battle against inflation

During the 1960's the Canadian economy expanded rapidly and virtually without interruption. Between the first quarter of 1961 and the first quarter of 1969 real output in Canada increased by 60 percent, real expenditure on business fixed investment rose by 64 percent, and real personal consumption increased by 51 percent in the aggregate and by 31 percent on a *per capita* basis. Unemployment, which was 7.6 percent in the first quarter of 1961, averaged 4.1 percent in 1965-1968. In view of these gains it would have been astonishing if some distortions and excesses had not arisen, and these appeared in the form of a progressively worsening price and cost inflation which, at the time of writing (1969), had yet to be brought under control. Consumer prices, which rose at an average annual rate of 1.5 percent in the first four years of the expansion, increased at an average annual rate of 3.7 percent in the second four-year period, and at over 5 percent during 1968 itself.

Throughout most of this inflationary period monetary policy was the major policy weapon brought to bear on inflation, although most budgets in the 1966-1969 period called for tax increases in one form or another. In early 1965 the Bank of Canada began restraining the growth in the money supply and rising interest rates soon followed. This upward movement and a restrictive monetary policy continued well into 1966, when credit conditions were eased in anticipation of a slackening economic activity. However, this retardation was short-lived and by the spring of 1967 restraint was again applied, sending interest rates spiraling upward.

The rise in interest rates was sharply accelerated in late 1967 and early 1968 as the Canadian dollar came under attack following the British devaluation of November 1967. By June 1968 this attack had been thwarted and some relaxation of monetary policy was undertaken.[35] However, once more this relaxation proved to be premature and by autumn credit contraction was again underway, driving interest rates to historic heights. This restraint has continued to date *via* open-market operations, continual increases in the bank rate, and even variations in chartered-bank reserve requirements.

Despite this prolonged, if schizophrenic, restrictive monetary policy, which drove interest rates to historically astronomical levels (the government of Canada long-term bond yield reaching 8.30 percent in December

---

35. See L. Rasminsky, "Interest Rates and Inflation," a Statement before the House of Commons Standing Committee on Finance, Trade and Economic Affairs, July 3, 1969, pp. 8-9.

1969, and 7.60 percent in June 1969, compared to the 1967 average of 5.90 percent and the 1957 average of 3.80 percent), the inflationary spiral has not been lessened. A number of factors are responsible for this failure. First, the long period of continuous economic expansion during the sixties and the price increases of recent years have had a powerful impact on public attitudes, generating what might be termed an "inflationary psychosis." The almost continual economic growth of the last 25 years, interrupted only by a few relatively brief recessions, has instilled a confidence in many people that prosperity can be counted on to last indefinitely. Moreover, there is an increasingly held view that (1) inflation is a normal or even necessary concomitant of economic expansion; (2) public policies of restraint will not be carried to the point of dealing effectively with inflation (which has been true to date); and (3) almost any price or cost increase will soon be absorbed by the general rise in the price level. This attitude encourages various groups to try to improve their relative positions substantially, without worrying that as a result their services or products may be priced out of the market. This same psychology allows borrowers to tie themselves into contracts involving the payment of high interest rates for long periods ahead, and leads investors to insist on a relatively high interest return to cover the prospective erosion in the value of money.[36]

Second, Canada's inflationary problems by no means originate solely from domestic causes but are partially a consequence of international influences, since most Western countries have been experiencing the same general problems. However, although some inflation may be attributed to foreign sources, especially the United States, the generally poorer performance of the Canadian relative to the American economy in terms of inflation and unemployment rates during this period, indicates that Canadian policies may have failed to achieve potential capabilities.

Third, far too much reliance has been placed upon monetary policy, which has been virtually the government's sole stabilization tool. Despite the tax increases contained in government budgets during this inflationary period, a fiscal policy embodying deficits of $421 million and $808 million in the 1966-1967 and 1967-1968 fiscal years can hardly be called restrictive. Furthermore, their concomitant cash requirements in the vicinity of $550 million in each of these periods only compounded the difficulties for the monetary authorities. Greater attention to fiscal policy appears to be forthcoming at all levels of government, however, and a slight budgetary surplus is projected for the fiscal year ending March 1970. At the same time moral suasion, which had been rejected in the form of wage-price guidelines at the outset of the inflation period, has been reactivated in the form of a Prices and Incomes Commission to assist traditional monetary and fiscal

36. See *ibid.*, pp. 3-4.

policies. This concerted effort, unfortunately, was a long time in coming.

Finally, in all industrial countries there has been a very real fear of "over-kill," i.e., excessive contraction which would generate far more unused resources than the minimum required to combat inflation. This fear has been particularly prevalent in Canada, where unemployment during 1968 reached 5 percent despite the existence of a 5 percent rate of inflation. A protracted and all-out attack upon inflation by traditional techniques is likely to cause even further unemployment, and this is a very bleak prospect indeed. Yet one might speculate that it was the failure to embark upon such a confrontation earlier that is at least partially responsible for our present plight, and if we cannot find a way to stop inflation without a temporary (and limited) increase in the level of unused resources, then such an increase should be borne as the lesser of the evils.

The situation, however, is not without hope. As our survey has indicated, despite government reluctance to move sufficiently far in one direction (that of restraining inflation), stabilization policies are now coordinated, with fiscal and monetary policies moving in concert. At the same time special policies are also being used in harmony—policies such as the acceleration of the Kennedy Round reductions in Canada's tariffs so that they became effective in June 1969 rather than gradually until 1972, the establishment of the Prices and Incomes Commission, the rationalization of federal government expenditures, and the freeze on federal civil-service expenditures. These developments indicate that the government is now prepared to play both an active and an informed role in stabilizing the economy. A reversion to a floating exchange rate would make the government's macro-economic policies even more effective; but such an action is not in the cards—at least not in the foreseeable future.

the direct control of inflation

David C. Smith*
Queen's University

WHAT IS INCOMES POLICY?

The search for better national economic policies is influenced by the particular problems of the day and the types of policies in other countries. The failure in Canada to maintain desired levels of price stability has intensified demands for improved techniques for the control of inflation. But the persistence of inflation has been an international postwar phenomenon—the longer-term performance of the Canadian economy compares favourably by international standards—and foreign approaches to the problems have attracted considerable interest in Canada.

Economists' prescriptions that monetary and fiscal policies can maintain desirable movements in the general level of prices have not proved to be convincing or practicable to policy-makers. Pressures on domestic policies have inhibited a smooth expansion of monetary demand conditions in line with the objective of price stability. Particularly when a country has faced a deficit in its balance of payments and has been reluctant to use exchange-rate changes to assist in the necessary adjustments, monetary and fiscal policies have been viewed as imposing an unnecessarily heavy cost in checking inflation. Under these conditions interest has increased in many countries in measures that would directly control the rise of money incomes and prices.

Direct controls on general price movements have a long history; especially in times of grave national emergency, in Canada during World War II,

* Much of this paper has been taken from the author's *Income Policies*, Special Study No. 4, prepared for the Economic Council of Canada (Ottawa: Queen's Printer, 1966). Reproduced with the permission of the Queen's Printer for Canada.

for example—comprehensive systems of price controls backed by legal sanctions have been instituted. But under recent more normal peacetime conditions the search has been for devices that are based more on moral suasion than on compulsion. Measures that would bear on money incomes as well as directly on prices have been viewed as essential for curbing inflation.

A genus of policies, sometimes referred to as incomes policies or wage-price guideposts, has developed. The Organization for Economic Co-operation and Development defined incomes policy as follows:

> What is meant by an incomes policy . . . is that the authorities should have a view about the kind of evolution of incomes which is consistent with their economic objectives, and in particular with price stability; that they should seek to promote public agreement on the principles which should guide the growth of incomes; and that they should try to induce people voluntarily to follow this guidance.[1]

The policy, as developed in the early 1960's in countries such as the United Kingdom and the United States, involved three sets of problems:

First, there was the working-out of general targets for the whole economy of the appropriate development of money incomes and of prices. Most frequently, this took the form of targets for compensation to employees, which is the largest component of income, and for prices, since other incomes depend on the relation between prices and compensation to employees.

Second, there was the problem of translating these over-all targets into meaningful guides for individual wage and price decisions. Should the principles that guide compensation to employees in various sectors be expressed in terms of the national targets, or are there principles that should permit differentiation in the development of incomes by sectors? If the target is general price stability for the economy, what are the principles that should guide particular prices, and might it be desirable to add separate guides for some components of nonwage incomes?

Third, there was the problem of inducing people to follow these guides and thus behave differently than they would in the absence of incomes policy. Emphasis was placed on the use of moral suasion rather than direct controls, but some forms of persuasion are stronger than others. In countries that attempted an incomes policy for long, it became clear that various types of sanctions had to be developed for the policy to have much effect. Countries experimented, for example, with public exposure and condemnation of wage and price decisions inconsistent with the guides, prior notification and deferment of wage and price decisions, strong government pres-

---

1. Organization for Economic Co-operation and Development, *Policies for Price Stability* (Paris, 1962), p. 23.

sures through purchasing and stockpile policies, selective tariff or export-subsidy changes, and selective use of anti-restrictive-practices policy. A number of measures besides statutory powers were thus employed to limit wage and price changes.

Incomes policy can mean many things to many people. It can be a new name for some things governments have long practised. An incomes policy may have more than one purpose. Since it involves criteria for relative-income movements, the policy has been viewed at times as having a bearing on society's conception of an equitable distribution of income. Also, since the inflationary impact of a given rise of money incomes depends on the rate of increase of productivity in the economy, the policy, it has been argued, helps to focus on the importance of productivity change and may thus contribute to growth. But primary interest in the policy recently has centred on its contribution as an anti-inflationary measure; it has usually been conceived as a stabilization instrument that would help moderate general price increases at higher employment levels.

PRICE STABILITY AS A POLICY OBJECTIVE

The rate of general price increases has been one important economic indicator that has been combined with others in judging the success of government economic policies. An important feature of postwar economic-policy discussions has been the development of more specific quantitative economic goals against which to judge the actual performance of the economy. There have been both a large increase in available data on unemployment, prices, and growth that permit a constant testing of the direction of the economy in relation to the recent past and in relation to other countries, and also a more specific assignment of economic responsibilities to governments to ensure a satisfactory national performance in terms of these indicators. The economic goals have not emerged, however, as fixed, objective aims to which governments have rigidly committed themselves, and they have been strongly influenced both by the recent experience of the country and also by the recent experiences of other countries. Unemployment rates in some West European countries, for example, have been well below what was thought to be either possible or desirable at the end of World War II; but, given this experience in a country with low rates when other countries also have low rates, the scope for governments to allow rises in the unemployment rate in any one country is more limited. Thus the pressures from public comparisons tend to fix more specific limits to the variation in the main economic indicators that are commonly regarded, for reasons that are not always too clear, as important for economic welfare.

Most western governments have repeatedly professed a desire for greater price stability than has actually occurred, but none has been prepared to take the courses of action that would bring price stability. This objective has not in practice been easy to achieve for a variety of reasons:

—Attempts to curb price increases have usually, at least in the short run, conflicted with other objectives. Deflationary policies generally have some unfavourable effects on the unemployment rate. Direct controls impinge on freedom of choice and may suppress only the manifestations, not the causes, of inflation. Periodic short-run deflationary policies, often referred to as "stop-go" policies, have been opposed on the grounds that they are unsettling to growth processes.

—Price stability is a difficult objective for one country to tackle alone, particularly if the country is highly dependent on international trade. The rate of increase of prices in an open economy will depend heavily on price movements in countries with which it trades, especially if the exchange rate is kept relatively fixed. Clearly, in the case of the Canadian economy, for example, the rate of increase of prices in other countries, especially that of the United States, has a major impact on Canadian price increases.

—The meaning of price stability has not been too well defined. There is no single, perfect measure of the degree of price stability in a country. The coverage and biases in the construction of indexes, including the consumer, wholesale, and implicit (national-accounts) price indexes, need to be examined. Even then, if the source of concern about price stability is the balance-of-payments situation, it will be important to examine more specific indexes for the prices of internationally-traded goods, since experience has shown that these do not always move closely with the other major price indexes. Further, it is clear that a fixed absolute level of general prices would not be a desirable objective. Not only will a continual movement of relative prices be an essential mechanism for allocating resources, but also some movement of the general level of prices will be important for adaptation to changing internal and external economic conditions. While interest in the topic has waned, there were important debates not so long ago about whether or not there was some appropriate trend rate of increase of general prices.

—Since price stability must be viewed in the context of a number of economic objectives which may conflict, the emphasis placed on it in public preferences, particularly in relation to a low unemployment rate, becomes important. In most western countries a low unemployment rate has been a particularly important objective over the postwar period, and the general impression is that this objective has been given greater weight in many of the West European countries than in North America. Memories of the grave hardships suffered during the high unemployment of the 1930's have been an important factor in this postwar emphasis on low unemployment rates, and these may fade as a new generation assumes leadership roles. But earlier fears of the serious consequences from moderate rates of inflation, such as western countries have experienced in the postwar period, have also decreased. There has been no obvious evidence that moderate rates of price increase have been injurious to growth. Moderate rates of inflation have not automatically turned into runaway inflations. The general price increases have not caused large shifts in the distribution of incomes, such as from wages to profits, and government welfare measures have helped, in part at least, to compensate losers from inflation. But these points do not mean that concern about the dangers of inflation has disappeared. Depreciation in the value of money imposes costs on holding money. Varying rates of price increases are unsettling and costly to financial planning. Disruptive balance-of-payments difficulties may be encountered. An ingrained fear of inflation remains an important source of pressure on the formation of public policies.

The search for improved policies to deal with inflation thus remains important, and in recent discussions the search has followed a number of routes. One is to accept the present evidence of conflicts among economic objectives and to provide better information about them in order to aid in the difficult policy choices that have to be made. Considerable attention has been paid to estimating from the past both the apparent conflicts between price stability and other objectives, such as low unemployment, and also the relative costs to society of a slightly lower or higher performance on these objectives. Second, closer study of the mix of aggregative policies may reveal that there is room for reducing the conflicts that appear to have existed in the past between, for example, price stability and full employment. There are various ways through which monetary and fiscal policies may affect the rate of price increases, and not all will have the same effect on the relation between the unemployment rate and the rate of increase of prices. Third, improvements in economic adjustment mechanisms may not only modify the rate of price increases associated with given unemployment and growth rates, but also make the economy less susceptible to balance-of-payments difficulties at given rates of increase of prices. Improved commercial, competition and labour-market policies would be included in this approach. Fourth, some type of direct control of inflation through the specification of criteria to limit earnings and price changes may be proposed.

Interest in the last route will be influenced by the degree of public pressure to try to achieve a more ambitious set of economic policy objectives than seems to be currently possible with existing economic policies. The development of more specific quantitative policy objectives in the postwar period has increased the importance of a wider range and more skilful use of economic-policy instruments. But also, there have often been important constraints on the use of economic-policy instruments which may cause difficulties by increasing the number of objectives relative to the means for achieving them. For example, in western countries particular concern about moderating the rate of price increases has emerged when balance-of-payments difficulties have been encountered. The real adjustments that are required may be hampered by constraints on monetary and fiscal policy arising from public pressures for a low unemployment rate, public myths about the appropriate budget balance or level of interest rates, and an unwillingness to let an exchange-rate adjustment help, due to a belief in the virtues of an unchanged rate. Under such conditions there is an increased interest in searching for new devices. Various new ones may be suggested, but it has been under these kinds of conditions that much of the interest in incomes policy has been generated.

The suggestion that incomes policy can moderate the rate of price increases without offsetting costs to other objectives, and can thus make possible a more ambitious set of economic objectives, has an obvious appeal. But is it true?

INCOMES POLICY AND MORAL SUASION

Support for incomes policy has been based on the view that it can affect wage and price decisions through persuasion rather than through direct wage and price controls. The borderline between persuasion and direction is not always very clear, but several ways through which incomes policy might have an effect without an elaborate system of controls, have been suggested.

First, incomes policy may help to alter expectations. Wages and price decisions are influenced by what people think will be the changes in other wages and prices. General expectations about the future rate of increase of prices may become higher than the government feels is desirable. If incomes policy can bring about a smoother and quicker adjustment of expectations when restrictive monetary and fiscal policies are implemented, unemployment of economic resources will not be as large. The problem may prove in practice to be a recurrent one rather than a once-and-for-all one. Evidence of a waste of resources in the short run may lead to strong pressures on the government to revert quickly to more expansionary policies which will in turn justify previous expectations. But due, for example, to balance-of-payments difficulties, the government may soon bring in again more restrictive policies, and a pattern of "stop-go" policies can thus emerge. These abortive attempts to curb price increases can weaken the country's growth performance.

If incomes policy does have these effects on expectations, it will be useful in supporting changes in general policies. In this case, however, the use of targets and criteria for wage and price decisions is merely to emphasize the change of direction in government policy; and strong declarations of intent by the government, followed by action which showed it was not bluffing, might be sufficient. Incomes policy would thus not have the role many of its supporters have suggested for it, and there would not be a need for an elaborate machinery to implement it. The opportunities for incomes policy to have an effect in this manner are likely to be quite limited and confined mainly to the short run. If the forecasts of the government are not too accurate or the government does not back up its announcements with appropriate supporting policies, confidence in the relevance of the guides of incomes policy will soon break down.

Second, closely related to this idea of influencing general expectations, is the argument that much of the upward pressure on wages comes from a jockeying by unions to gain a better relative position in the wages structure for their members, and from the belief that it is necessary to bargain hard for wage increases to prevent profits from rising relative to wages. As a result of this struggle over relative incomes, both money wages and prices rise faster than they would otherwise and there is little effect on real wages. An incomes policy, it is argued, may reduce these sources of pressure on the wage side by convincing unions that the guides for relative wages will provide a fair wage structure and that the policy will cover profit movements as well as wage movements. Other people feel these points represent largely wishful thinking and have little chance of success on a voluntary basis, especially in the environment of aggressive economic opportunism that is characteristic of North American economic markets. If, in implementing the policy, it is not possible to contain some groups within the guides, an increased restlessness with the operation of the policy is likely to undermine it.

Third, recent discussions of incomes policy have emphasized the existence of a few key wage and price decisions in the economy that are subject to considerable discretion as to their timing and size, and which public opinion can influence. Thus R. M. Solow has argued:

> In our imperfect world, there are important areas where market power is sufficiently concentrated that price and wage decisions are made with a significant amount of discretion. When times are reasonably good, that discretion may be exercised in ways that contribute to premature inflation. (Institutions with market power may actually succeed in exploiting the rest of the economy temporarily or permanently, or they may see their decisions cancelled out almost immediately by induced increases in other prices and wages.) People and institutions with market power may, in our culture, be fairly sensitive to public opinion. To the extent that they are, an educated and mobilized public opinion may exert some restraining pressure to forestall or limit premature inflation.[2]

2. Robert M. Solow, "The Case Against the Case Against the Guideposts," in *Guidelines, Informal Controls, and the Market Place,* eds. George P. Schultz and Robert Z. Aliber (Chicago: University of Chicago Press, 1966), p. 44.

An important supplementary argument is that there are important institutional links which establish a fairly close relation between wage and price decisions in a few key sectors and pressures for wage and price movements elsewhere in the economy. The importance of this argument is that many of the problems of a comprehensive policy would be reduced—by focusing on a few key sectors, the administrators of an incomes policy could exert an influence on wages and prices throughout the economy. Many doubts have been raised about the significance of this point, however, and it will be important to examine it empirically.

Fourth, it may be argued that incomes policy will have some effect by exposing more clearly the impact of the vast array of special government policies on wages and prices, thus encouraging a more systematic review and better use of these policies. Through such measures as subsidies, tariffs, tax relief, and special expenditure programs, governments attempt to help particular sectors of the economy, but the encouragement these policies give to higher wages and prices in these sectors is often not publicly recognized. It may be argued that by reviewing the operation of incomes policy, the government will be in a better position to improve the economic basis of these other policies. On the other hand, critics of incomes policy may suggest that if the guides of incomes policy do not make much economic sense, it is not clear that much improvement will, in fact, be achieved through this route—that it should not require the mechanism of an incomes policy to supply a better economic basis for other government policies.

Other, stronger theoretical arguments than the ones mentioned here may emerge, especially with greater knowledge of the determinants of group responses. But incomes policy has not received a great deal of serious economic analysis so far, which is indicative, to some, of its shaky foundations and, to others, only of present weaknesses in the understanding of economic processes.

It would be very simple to dismiss the whole topic of incomes policy as complete fantasy, if it were clear that every attempt to implement an incomes policy had met with complete failure to influence the course of wages and prices. It might still retain some interest as a political device, but it would be of little interest for economic policy.

It is clear, however, that there will always be some form of sanctions that can make incomes policy have an effect, as wartime wage and price controls have demonstrated. And there is little doubt that controls on money incomes in the Netherlands over the postwar period have had an important effect at times. Nevertheless, recent interest in incomes policy has been based on the belief that only mild forms of persuasion techniques will be sufficient for it to have some effect. Is this true? There have been some failures. But have there also been some successes?

For a number of reasons, it is difficult to answer this question in quantitative terms.

Since incomes policy can take a variety of forms and can be implemented with different degrees of strictness, there is the problem of a quantitative measure for incomes policy itself. Also, to test for the effect of incomes policy it is necessary to estimate as accurately as possible what would have happened in the absence of the policy. An economic model that appears to provide an adequate explanation of past economic experience with earnings and price movements can be used to see whether the introduction of incomes policy makes a difference; but the results, of course, will depend on the confidence one has in the particular model used.

Finally, what are the criteria for measuring the success of an incomes policy? If the objective is to reduce the conflict between price stability and high employment, then the test is to see whether incomes policy had some independent effect on the rate of increase of prices. But there is also the time period to consider. If some success was achieved for a brief period but if there was then a reaction which led to an above-average rate of increase of prices for a time, is this evidence that the policy worked? Clearly, the answer depends on the objectives of the policy. If the policy had been conceived as one to add only short-run flexibility in influencing prices, the answer would be yes. But if the objective had been to have a longer-term impact on the rate of increase of prices, it would be no.

The success of the policy will also have to be judged in terms of its effects on other economic and non-economic objectives. Even if it did pass the test of having some independent effect on prices, it might be judged a failure on other grounds, such as those of impairing economic-growth processes, of diverting public support from other important types of economic policies, or, especially if control devices were used, of interfering with freedom of choice in economic markets. The hesitancy of most western countries in introducing more forceful measures to implement an incomes policy stems from the fear that the costs in terms of other objectives are too high.

The United States' experience with wage-price guideposts between 1962 and 1966 has been examined in several statistical studies.[3] In terms of the variables used to explain wage and price movements, a slower rate of inflation has been noted during this period than in earlier postwar years. Do the statistical studies show conclusively a significant effect from the guideposts? Alternative hypotheses have been advanced. Unlike Canada, which

---

3. See, for example, F. Brechling, "Some Empirical Evidence on the Effectiveness of Price and Incomes Policies," (paper read at the meeting of the Canadian Political Science Association, Montreal, June 1966); R. G. Bodkin, E. P. Bond, G. L. Reuber and T. R. Robinson, *Price Stability and High Employment: The Options for Canadian Economic Policy, An Econometric Study*, Special Study No. 5, prepared for the Economic Council of Canada (Ottawa: Queen's Printer, 1967); George L. Perry, "Wages and the Guideposts," *American Economic Review*, Vol. 57 (September 1967), pp. 897-904.

experienced a devaluation in 1962, the United States experienced during this period more severe price competition from abroad. In addition, the U.S. economy was moving gradually out of a period of considerable excess capacity and price stability. Yet, I think the evidence does point to the guideposts having had an effect before they began to crumble seriously in 1966.

In the United Kingdom, recurrent balance-of-payments difficulties over the postwar period have provided a major stimulus to a series of experiments with incomes policy. After the mid-1960's the form of the policy became much tougher. Some of the experiments appear to have had no significant impact, but the evidence is consistent with the policy having had at times some effect.[4]

While incomes policies cannot summarily be dismissed on the grounds that they have never had an effect, difficulties in sustaining the policies have been encountered in all countries. The criteria that have been used as guides for incomes and prices have not in fact proved to be meaningful for individual decisions for long. More economic research is required in this area and better criteria may be forthcoming. Economic arguments will not alone, however, be decisive in determining what a country does with this type of policy.

Incomes policy has the advantage of appearing to the public as a direct attack on inflation. Aggregative policies, such as monetary and fiscal policies, work more indirectly through market mechanisms; the economic benefits that can be expected from proper management of them have generally been difficult to explain to the public. Economic arguments about the appropriate management of monetary and fiscal policies have often not had the support from governments which economists had hoped for, because the arguments have not had the direct political appeal of more direct types of policies. To a public uneasy about inflation, incomes policy has the attraction that it appears to commit the government more strongly to the restraint of inflation. Such a policy makes it seem that the government is doing something about it. In addition, to a public suspicious of its exploitation at the hands of powerful economic groups, some direct pleasure may accrue from censure and sanctions against large businesses and unions that violate the guides of an incomes policy. As Edelman and Fleming argue in a study of the politics of wage-price decisions, incomes policy is frequently a political symbol that tends to yield some returns to a government because the people feel reassured about this evidence of the government's concern about inflation.[5]

---

4. See the author's "Incomes Policy" in Richard E. Caves et al., *Britain's Economic Prospects* (Washington: Brookings Institution, 1968).

5. Murray Edelman and R. W. Fleming, *The Politics of Wage-Price Decisions* (Urbana: University of Illinois Press, 1965).

There are also serious political risks to incomes policy. If the general guides for wages and prices are violated, repeated government intervention to attempt to gain adherence to them can adversely affect the government's popularity. On the other hand, allowing the guides to be violated continually can be politically embarrassing and can make the government appear weak. Given some limitation on the number of unpopular steps it feels it can take in the short run, a government trying to implement an incomes policy may be diverted from other measures of more basic importance to the economy. The implementation of criteria for wages and prices can involve a government more deeply in bitter disputes about appropriate wage and profit rates than it wishes. The stricter the form of incomes policy the greater the political risks, as the use of strong sanctions to implement it may bring sharp public criticism about interference with individual freedom of choice in economic markets. The hesitancy of western countries to venture far in the direction of control devices for implementing an incomes policy, except when it is felt crisis conditions make them unavoidable, reflects the general fear of the damage they will cause to other objectives of the society.

Incomes policy may also be viewed, however, as having some social advantages insofar as it moderates aggressive competition over materialistic gains and promotes greater harmony among labour groups and between labour and management. To many people, there is something very attractive about at least trying to work out a system where individual earnings will move according to some objective criteria, and thus in trying to reduce the struggle over appropriate relative-income positions. But the issues are immense. While economists have focused on the criteria for incomes that would make economic sense, it is clear that social and political factors are involved.[6] It will also be important to recognize that the alleged social advantages may turn out to be illusory. In transferring the development and implementation of criteria for incomes and prices from impersonal market mechanisms to incomes-policy administrators, social tensions over appropriate relative-incomes positions may be increased.

WHITHER INCOMES POLICY?

Historically, direct controls over inflation have had an appeal from time to time in most western countries, but enduring systems of controls have not emerged. The title "incomes policy" has embodied in the view of many people a new surge of interest in direct controls but in a more palatable form. Criteria for incomes and prices are used, but, instead of a comprehensive detailed set, fairly general guidelines are espoused by the authorities.

---

6. See Andrew Shonfield, *Modern Capitalism, The Changing Balance of Public and Private Power* (London: Oxford University Press, 1965), pp. 217-20.

Some sanctions to gain a significant measure of adherence to the guidelines are developed, but not a vast legalistic system through which all wage and price changes have to be cleared. This approach has incorporated a faith in changing through moral suasion the motivation of people in making wage and price decisions.

The tests of this approach in several countries yield some important results. The policy has had moderate effects on inflation, though not always in the desired direction. It has been easier to manage as a short-run policy instrument in times of national economic crisis than as a long-run instrument under relatively stable economic conditions.

Since acceptance and support of official criteria for incomes and prices have depended largely on moral suasion, the following factors have played, and can be expected to continue to play, a role:

—The apparent degree of conflict among the economic objectives of price stability, high employment, and a satisfactory balance-of-payments position will affect public interest in this type of policy. As a result it is not surprising that interest has varied within a country over time and among countries at any one time.

—Relations between labour and management organizations and the government, as well as general public confidence in the administrators of an incomes policy, will have an influence.

—If both union and management organizations are highly centralized, not only may the concentration of economic power make the policy more important, but also the potential of obtaining labour and management agreement on the criteria may be greater. The macro-economic implications of general violations of the criteria may be appreciated more fully by centralized organizations, and the leaders may in turn be in a better position to help implement the policy through their influence over members of the organizations.

—The degree of public support for a greater control over income distribution in line with the criteria will be important. Solidarity among workers on what is regarded as a more-just system of relative wages than that which market forces have tended to produce will influence support for a more central direction of the wage structure.

—If there is a general conviction in the country of the need to reduce the rate of general price increases, a strong opposition to increases in the unemployment rate, and a mutual confidence among economic groups that one sector or region will not benefit more than others from general wage and price restraint, the policy will be easier to implement.

—The degree to which governments are already involved in economic markets and the centralized power of the national government or the co-ordination of powers in a federal system affect the forcefulness with which governments can implement the policy.

—The openness of the economy to international influences on wages and prices affects the pursuit of an independent policy. High labour and capital mobility into and out of the country and close business and labour ties with foreign counterparts can reduce both support for and the effects of an independent national effort to develop criteria that modify relative wages, nonwage incomes and prices.

Difficulties in sustaining this type of policy have arisen from a number of sources. If the norms and criteria to guide wages and prices are kept very simple for easy public comprehension and are not frequently adjusted, they become increasingly inappropriate over time. For example, if a country introduces the criteria at a time of serious inflation, it is doubtful if the criteria will be credible unless they indicate only a marginal scaling down of wage and price increases. However, if the expansion of monetary demand is reduced at the same time, it may soon turn out that the criteria are leading to expectations of higher wage and price changes than are consistent with the slower expansion of monetary demand. Because monetary demand and productivity do not follow a steady path, fixed criteria become inappropriate and public support is weakened or expectations of wage and price increases are higher than they would otherwise be. In addition to this problem related to the stability of the economy, there is another problem in fixing on a simple set of criteria. It arises from the importance of an efficient allocation of economic resources. Relative price and wage movements help in the process of reallocating economic resources. If the criteria are not sufficiently complex to take into account the pressures on markets from changes in demand and supply conditions, they can inhibit important economic adjustment mechanisms or lead to serious evasion of the criteria. If the policy is conceived as only a short-run tool, neither the stabilization nor allocation problem may be viewed as serious. If the policy is conceived as a long-run tool, a search for improved criteria can be expected.

At the outset we recognized that the title "incomes policy" could be used to embrace a wide variety of policies. Our focus here has been on a very moderate form of direct control of inflation that has been widely discussed and occasionally tried in western countries during the past decade. It would be incorrect to conclude that all interest in this area has centred on some form of direct controls, however moderate. Many new measures may be proposed that could have an impact on wage and price determination indirectly rather than through the direct specification of criteria for wages and prices. Monetary and fiscal policies are the most important general instruments that operate indirectly through market processes, but they can be supplemented by others. For example, public support for an improved system of research, education and information on economic forecasts may assist in keeping expectations on wages and prices more closely in line with movements in monetary demand conditions. If public expectations on wage and price increases are higher than are consistent with government policy with respect to monetary demand conditions, the lags in adjustment may be shortened and the waste of economic resources reduced through better economic-information systems. Concentrations of economic power that influence wage and price decisions may be tackled in part through reform of economic institutions in factor and product markets. Government influences on general wages and prices, directly through its own wage negotiations and indirectly through governmental support measures for particular sectors of the economy, may be rationalized in a more comprehensive and interrelated form. Thus, an indirect approach might be based on improvements in the economic-information and coordination systems that would expose problem areas and provide a basis for modifications of the framework within which income and price decisions are made.

In December 1968 a White Paper published by the Canadian government pointed to difficulties in developing a formal incomes policy in Canada but suggested that new measures were necessary to promote price stability.[7] Two new bodies were proposed—a Price and Incomes Commission and a Joint Senate-Commons Committee to be known as the Standing Parliamentary Committee on Price Stability, Incomes and Prices. The direction these bodies take on new measures will provide an interesting case-study for the Canadian economy, which since the 1940's has not experimented with any form of a direct-control approach to inflation.

---

7. *Policies for Price Stability* (Ottawa: Queen's Printer, 1968).

the use of a normative model to analyze tax-reform proposals

John Bossons*
University of Toronto

1. INTRODUCTION

The tax system is one of the most important ways in which government policy interacts with individual decision-makers in the economy. It is important because of its size—$21.6 billion was collected in taxes and in social-insurance premiums from Canadian individuals and businesses in 1968, an amount equal to roughly 32 percent of Canadian gross national expenditure. It is also important because of its all-pervasive character. Few individuals or businesses are not directly influenced in their decisions by the effect of the tax system.

Given its importance, one might assume that proposals to change the tax system would be analyzed relatively closely by members of the public. Such an assumption would (in most cases) be incorrect, primarily because the tax system is complex. It is therefore of some importance to develop a normative tax model which can be used to clear away the complexities with which most tax-reform proposals become surrounded.

The purpose of this paper is to describe such a model. In doing so it is important to note that what is being described is a framework that can be used to simplify analysis of tax-reform proposals, rather than a set of "rules" from which a uniquely "ideal" tax system can be derived. No normative assessment of the desirability of policy changes can be made without specifying value judgements, and no normative model can be presumed to be a substitute for such value judgements. The purpose of a normative model is to focus on those issues in which value judgements are

---

* The author is indebted to Richard M. Bird for a number of useful comments and suggestions.

critical, and in doing so to define the issues clearly so that irrelevant value judgements of the type that confuse much public discussion can be excluded.

It is not a simple matter to state what the "best" tax system is, even assuming it were possible to obtain unanimous agreement upon the objectives of a tax system. Objectives conflict, and these conflicts have to be resolved. To know how to resolve them, it is necessary to determine the quantitative importance of the effects of a tax system upon the extent to which each objective is attained. Analysis of a tax system thus involves three separate problems: (1) defining objectives, (2) measuring the extent of any conflicts among objectives, and (3) determining how conflicts among objectives shall be resolved. These three problems are, of course, the essence of any policy problem.

This paper contains three principal sections. In the first (section 2), the basic objectives of government are examined in order to isolate those objectives which are of critical importance in designing a tax system. In the following section, the critical objectives thus isolated are discussed in greater detail in order to define how improvements in a tax system can be derived. Finally, section 4 provides a brief example of how this normative approach can be used in evaluating a specific set of reform proposals. The proposals analyzed are those made by the Royal Commission on Taxation (the "Carter Commission").

2. SOCIAL OBJECTIVES AND TAX POLICY

defining social objectives

The objectives of a tax system cannot be discussed separately from the basic objectives of any government. I shall distinguish among six basic classes of social objectives.

The first and probably oldest purpose of government consists of executing community tasks and providing "public goods"—things which cannot be financed or provided in amounts required by charging for them or by having people pay a price for them. These public goods include such things as irrigation canals, defence, education, anti-pollution measures, parks, and other community projects which cannot easily be provided by single individuals and have to be funded by a cooperative effort. The problem is generally not that it is impossible to organize cooperative ways of financing a project; for corporations and other vehicles of financial cooperation may be organized to serve as intermediaries to collect funds. The problem is that such intermediaries can collect funds by voluntary subscription only if they can generate a reasonably certain future profit for their subscribers or shareholders. A corporation can make a profit out of providing a service only if it can charge a price for the service. With most public services, it is either (1) impossible to provide optimal amounts of such services at prices which people will voluntarily pay, or (2) undesirable to charge a price for the service. Instead of being charged and paid for on a voluntary basis, these goods and services must instead be paid for on an involuntary basis, or by taxes.

A second social objective providing purpose for government is to regulate how people deal with one another. This involves such activities as the administration of justice, the establishment of a criminal code, anti-fraud laws, regulation of consumer information, and the like.

A third objective is the redistribution of the spending power of individuals in a society. Some part of the population will always need financial support; they may be chronically unemployed, ill or aged. How much redistribution should take place is, of course, a question of values. It is fair to state that there is a general consensus among Canadians that spending power must be redistributed to needy individuals from the more affluent.[1] Beyond this, most Canadians seem to be agreed upon the need for redistributive transfers among different regions of the country as well.

A fourth objective of government is fostering economic growth and maintaining economic stability. Governments must follow some basic economic goals aimed at ensuring that the country's economic growth is at the highest possible rate that is consistent with meeting other social objectives. These economic goals include establishing institutions that facilitate such growth, re-allocating resources to enhance economic growth, and maintaining economic stability through the elimination of fluctuations in the economy that cause price inflation and unemployment.

A fifth objective of government is promoting national unity. Why is the nation in itself so important? National unity, we may conclude, is a separate goal reflecting a social consensus that it is valuable to belong to a country and to owe loyalties to the larger group which is the nation. A government can foster an increased sense of pride among its people. This last purpose of government can be of importance even in the designing of tax policy.

A sixth social objective is concerned with the means of achieving the first five. Insofar as possible, a government implementing generally agreed-upon social objectives should do so in such a way that individuals' freedoms of

---

1. In a study prepared for the Royal Commission on Taxation, it was estimated that the net incidence of taxes and expenditures of all levels of government in Canada results in a significant transfer from upper-income families to families with lower incomes. Below an income of roughly $6,000, most families receive a net subsidy from all operations of all governments; for a family with an income of less than $2,000, this net subsidy amounts, on average, to in excess of 100 percent of their income. Cf. W. I. Gillespie, *The Incidence of Taxes and Public Expenditures in the Canadian Economy*, Studies of the Royal Commission on Taxation, Number 2 (Ottawa: Queen's Printer, 1967), ch. 4.

choice are not unnecessarily restricted and in a way that is generally regarded as fair. It is, of course, always difficult to define what is fair and what restrictions are truly necessary. But it is nevertheless safe to say that this sixth general objective has three components: (1) Individuals in the same situation should be treated by government laws in the same way; (2) the administration of laws should allow for appeal from and correction of arbitrary rulings that inaccurately reflect the principles of the underlying law; and (3) the choices made by individuals should be as close as possible to what they would be if no government existed.

conflicts among objectives

There are certain conflicts evident among these objectives. First of all, redistribution of economic spending power may lead to a slower rate of economic growth. As an example, consider unemployment insurance. The desire to ensure that no individual will be bereft of support while unemployed may lead a government to establish a system of unemployment insurance or benefits that will partially make up for lack of income. Such a scheme may fully reflect the social consensus regarding the way in which income should be distributed. But the effect of unemployment insurance is necessarily to reduce the rate of economic growth.

Suppose, as an example, that an unemployed individual is granted unemployment benefits equal to 100 percent of his previous salary as long as he remains unemployed. The effect of this benefit scale would be to increase the rate of unemployment in the country; for the unemployed would not actively re-enter the labour market as quickly. Removal of the benefit upon re-employment would act as a 100 percent tax on income obtained through becoming re-employed, and would reduce the speed with which many unemployed individuals would seek new employment. This disincentive could have profound consequences on the rate of economic growth. The redistribution objective thus, in this case, conflicts with the objective of fostering economic growth.

The design of an appropriate unemployment-insurance scheme affords examples of conflicts with objectives other than those of stimulating growth and redistributing purchasing power. One important effect of unemployment insurance is its contribution to economic stability. This contribution would be reduced if unemployment-insurance benefits were reduced in order to stimulate growth. If unemployment benefits were specified at a lesser rate, disincentives to enter the labour force would be reduced in time of purchasing power and thus national income would be reduced in time of recession, affecting economic stability unfavourably. A floor on the lowering of incomes during times of recession due to unemployment maintains purchasing power in the economy and is an important economic stabilizer.

Reducing this floor lowers the extent to which purchasing power is maintained. While the greater speed in looking for jobs would, to some extent, offset the unfavourable effect on purchasing power, there is necessarily a conflict between the stabilizing effect of unemployment insurance and its effect on economic growth.

These examples illustrate the necessary conflict between objectives of government policy. The problem of government policy-making is to see how all objectives are affected by government decisions and to try to resolve conflicts among objectives in a way which meets the social concensus that is reflected in the ballot box.

social objectives and the goals of tax policy

Public services use resources. If the government must provide public goods, then it must raise funds to cover the costs of transferring such resources from the private sector without inflation. The funds have to be obtained by some type of tax, since (by definition) people will not pay on a voluntary basis. (If individuals would voluntarily pay enough to make the provision of "optimal" amounts of certain public goods self-sustaining from a financial viewpoint, then there would be little justification for the government being in the business of supplying such goods or services.) A tax may be defined as any involuntary basis for collecting money, whether called a tax, an insurance scheme, or a "donation." We may assume that the nature and effect of the public service is unaffected by the form of taxation. The same may be said with respect to the function of taxation in financing the expenditures of government agencies concerned with the protection of individual rights. The function of the tax system is simply to provide the necessary funds.

Generally speaking, most Canadians seem to regard redistribution as calling for a floor under the incomes of the needy, but not for a ceiling on the incomes of those better off. One qualification should be made: namely, that while most Canadians view redistribution as concerned only with transfers to the needy, some citizens would want, in addition, to impose surtaxes on wealth transferred across generations.

The redistribution of spending power thus involves only the question of deciding to what groups of people transfer payments are to be paid. In assessing a transfer-payment scheme, it must be decided what payments will be paid to different individuals, conditional on their circumstances. The answer to this question is obviously dependent upon the total to be raised through taxes, but is not dependent upon the form of these taxes. As with the first two categories of expenditure, the function of the tax system is simply to raise money.

It may well be asked at this point whether it is very profound to say that the function of taxes is to raise money. Why should this statement be significant?

The important conclusion of what has been stated thus far is that, with respect to the first three social objectives underlying government goals, the form of the tax system is not a relevant factor. Because the purpose of taxes, given these three objectives, is merely to raise money, these objectives need not be considered in determining how the money is to be raised. This simplifies the problem of discussing how a tax system should be designed. As in many situations, the first step in analyzing the problem of how to levy taxes is to determine what is relevant to the problem and what is not. The fact is that much public discussion of taxes is confused because irrelevant considerations are introduced; such confusion is indicative of the crucial importance of determining in what way objectives of government have implications for the form of the tax system.

The fourth objective of government is in fact twofold: the maintenance of economic stability and the stimulation of longer-term growth. The economic stability of a country can be in part regulated by changes in the levels of expenditures of government and of taxes raised by government. Different methods may be employed in times of inflation or in times of recession to stabilize the economy.[2] As an initial generalization, economic stability is affected primarily by the relative level of government taxes and expenditures (i.e., by the size of the government surplus or deficit) rather than by the forms of the taxes and expenditures.

This irrelevance of the form of taxes does not hold so strictly when we turn to the objective of fostering economic growth. To foster economic growth, the tax system must raise funds in such a way that the result will be the best allocation of resources to bring about that economic growth. Taxes necessarily change the allocation of resources. The form of taxation affects this allocation, and so alters the rate of economic growth. To a considerable extent, the effect of the form of a tax system upon economic growth is the result of hidden subsidies built into the tax system that distort the allocation of resources away from what it would be in the absence of the tax system.

From the viewpoint of deriving what a tax system should be, it makes sense to separate such subsidies from the tax system and to make them explicit. Such subsidies may be used to encourage certain types of investment which are of strategic value in economic development and so engender a greater return to society than they do to the private investors making the investments. However, there is a greater likelihood of subsidies being

---

2. A very useful summary of these methods—together with a critique of recent government macro-economic policy—is provided in the *Report of the Royal Commission on Taxation* (Ottawa: Queen's Printer, 1966), Vol. 2, ch. 3.

made efficient if they are made explicitly than if they are hidden within a complicated tax system—one reason why most special interest groups prefer tax concessions to subsidies.[3]

Because subsidies should be considered as separate expenditures and evaluated simply on the basis of whether their effect is worth their cost, subsidies to promote economic growth can be regarded—like the provision of public services—as having only one implication for a tax system: namely, that the tax system will have to provide sufficient revenue to pay for those subsidies which are considered desirable in spite of their out-of-pocket cost to the taxpayer.

The essential effect of the fifth objective of government—the maintenance of national pride—is to engender additional expenditures that have to be paid for, and so is the same as that of the first three objectives. For the most part, then, this objective may be ignored in defining the ideal tax system. There is one exception: most countries have tax systems similar to Canada's in their complexity and *ad hoc* nature; the accomplishment of implementing a more rational tax system would necessarily foster national prestige. Whether many sacrifices should or will be made purely to foster such prestige is another question.

From the viewpoint of the first five objectives here discussed, the overall function of the tax system is simply to pay for transfer payments, public services, and subsidies provided by the government in meeting these objectives. The sixth social objective—that of implementing government programs in as fair a way as possible and in such a way as to minimize interference with individual choice—thus becomes the paramount objective governing how a tax system should be designed.

The important questions in designing a tax system thus become: How can the tax burden be equitably distributed across individuals? How can the burden of financing government spending be distributed equitably across the country? How can a tax system be administered fairly? What sort of tax system will interfere least with individual decision-making? There should be few significant conflicts of objectives in defining the tax system; for the principal objective to be met in designing a tax system is to achieve a fair distribution of the tax burden.

Objectives cannot always be fully met. A tax system must be designed so as to be administratively feasible, and this sometimes necessitates the use

---

3. This is not to say that it may not be administratively convenient to extend some subsidies through the tax system. The granting of refundable tax credits to students in postsecondary educational programs is a good example of a subsidy which can be most cheaply administered in this manner. However, such subsidies should still be subject to the same controls as other expenditures, including specifically the annual presentation to Parliament of data on the cost of such subsidies and on their distribution. The problem with most tax concessions is that their costs escape parliamentary scrutiny.

of arbitrary rules. Other constraints arise from the necessary (and desirable) structure of politics in a federal state. Nevertheless, insofar as possible, the objectives of fairness and non-interference with individual decision-making should govern the design of a tax system.

3. DEFINING AN IDEAL TAX SYSTEM

fairness in allocating tax burdens

Fairness is a word which can easily mean different things to different people. To some people, higher tax payments are necessarily "unfair," and an "unfair" tax system is one which raises taxes for the individual concerned. To be sure, few people are so self-centred as to think of fairness only in terms of whether they are themselves unfavourably affected. Nevertheless, it is difficult for anyone to talk about taxes without being concerned with what happens to himself.

Despite this difficulty in defining fairness to everybody's satisfaction, the quality of fairness is one which must underlie the tax system if it is to reflect the social objectives which we have defined as the purposes of government. There are two kinds of fairness between which we should distinguish: (1) administrative fairness, which is concerned with ensuring that individuals are fairly treated in the administration of tax laws, and (2) fairness in law, by which we mean that in the eyes of the law, individuals in the same situation should be treated in the same way. The Royal Commission on Taxation was concerned with both types of fairness, and its *Report* indicted the present Canadian tax system as unfair in both respects. It suggested (in the second half of Volume 5) that there were a number of respects in which the administration of the present tax system could be made fairer, through giving individuals more freedom to appeal and through eliminating opportunities for political intervention. While no one would question the competence and conscientiousness of the individuals administering the tax laws in Canada, it is inevitable that a searching examination could disclose opportunities for improvement, and the Carter Commission made a number of recommendations for changes in the administration of the tax laws.

More important, and more difficult to deal with, is the question of fairness in the eyes of the law. To define what is fair, it is necessary to divide government expenditure programs to be financed into two classes: (1) those for which the resultant benefits to individuals can be fairly easily defined and related to specific individuals, and (2) those which supply benefits that are of a sufficiently general nature to be difficult to apportion among individuals. The allocation of costs and benefits or even an evaluation of their allocability requires that government expenditures be budgeted and accounted for on a program basis. The allocability of costs in accordance with benefits is thus greatly aided by the current development of improved program-budgeting techniques in government.

the scope of benefit-related taxation

As an example of the first type of expenditure, consider spending on highways. A highway is clearly used by automobiles, trucks and so forth, and furthermore is used to a greater extent by people who drive more than others. It would consequently seem sensible to apportion the costs of highways among individuals roughly in accordance with the amount of use they make of the highways. Naturally, it is difficult to do this directly; for with very few exceptions it is impractical to levy tolls on the use of roads. However, the use of gasoline and diesel oil for fuel in cars and trucks is on the average fairly closely related to the use of highways, and so can serve as a fairly good proxy for the amount of such use. It consequently is reasonably equitable to finance highway construction and maintenance out of revenues raised from levying a tax on gasoline and diesel oil sold for this purpose— though only reasonably so, because fuel usage is not a completely accurate proxy for the benefit derived by individuals from highways.

Similarly, the provision of fire-protection service to individuals in the community is of benefit primarily to the owners of the property that is being protected. It consequently should be fair for such services to be financed out of the proceeds of a tax on property. One obviously has to pay for such services from a tax—one cannot impose a toll to be paid by the individual when his house is burning down—but it would make sense to make this service paid for by the individuals that are being protected, rather than by all individuals in equal amounts. In this case as well as the provision of highway facilities, a tax can be designed that distributes the financial burden of these services over individuals roughly in relation to the benefits received by the individuals who pay the tax.

Where the benefits of a government service can be clearly identified, and where it is not the purpose of the government expenditure program to transfer resources to the individuals who are receiving the benefits (as is the case with the family-allowance program, for instance, which is a pure transfer program), it is equitable to finance these services out of tax revenues that are related to the benefits. One class of taxes—and clearly a number of taxes fall in this category, because of the variety of ways in which benefits are distributed—is those taxes which are related to benefits received. As the examples discussed above may suggest, the majority of expenditures which can be financed by benefit-related taxes are made by provincial and municipal governments, and wherever possible, government services should be paid for by levying user charges.[4]

While some government services, some public goods, and some expenditures can be financed through taxes that levy charges on the individuals who receive the benefits, a substantial number of government expenditures cannot be related to specific individuals in this way. Some government services provide benefits which are impossible to allocate to specific individuals. The provision of public defence is one example. The provision of mass education with its general benefit to society as well as the individuals affected, provides another, though very different, example. In both cases not only is it impossible to charge a price voluntarily paid by individuals for such services which would cover the full cost of services, but it is also impossible to impose a tax which is clearly related to the benefits provided by these services. The difficulties associated with using benefit-related taxes to finance compulsory primary and secondary education should, however, not cause one to overlook the role such taxes can play in financing higher education. The benefits of post-secondary education specialized in the area of an individual's future vocation may more clearly be allocated to the individual being educated than can primary education. In particular, such benefits may include material increases in the individual's potential future income. Because of this difference between general, compulsory education and specialized post-secondary education, there is much merit in attempting to devise taxes for the financing of universities that are related to the benefits of higher education received by university students. One such scheme— a special surtax on the income of university graduates—has been proposed by Milton Friedman.[5]

Transfer payments constitute another large category of normal governmental expenditures which cannot be financed out of taxes related to the benefits they provide. It is obviously nonsense even to consider the idea of trying to finance family allowance payments or welfare payments out of taxes levied only upon the recipients of these benefits. Consequently, there are a large number of government expenditures which have to be levied out of taxes on individuals in general. How can this be done?

It has come to be generally agreed that all expenditures which cannot be

---

4. Contrary to a statement in the *Report of the Royal Commission on Taxation* that, "A careful examination of the goods and services provided by government or government enterprises does not suggest that greater emphasis should be placed on the benefit approach in Canadian taxation" (*op cit.*, Vol. 3, p. 3), the increasing strain on general taxation caused by expenditure growth at all levels of government necessitates a much closer examination of the feasibility of financing certain categories of expenditure through benefit-related taxation. Interurban expressways, university education, and health services constitute three principal areas where the potential role of user charges has been insufficiently examined.

5. Cf. M. Friedman, *Capitalism and Freedom* (Chicago: University of Chicago Press, 1962), ch. 6.

paid for by user charges or by taxes which are related to the benefits received from the expenditures should be based on ability to pay. The Royal Commission on Taxation came to this conclusion at a relatively early stage of its work. We thus have a second class of taxes—general taxes, in that they are levied on all individuals—which should be based on ability to pay. All that remains is to define what constitutes ability to pay.

defining ability to pay

While there are a number of ways in which different individuals might define "ability to pay," essentially all such definitions generally reduce to either what an individual has available to spend, or what an individual does spend. There are, in other words, two bases which are generally used as definitions of ability to pay—income and spending. In both cases, most individuals would define ability to pay as either one's income received in a year or as what one spends within a year.

It is worth immediately emphasizing that such definitions of ability to pay imply that there are only two taxes which can allocate fairly the burden of financing general expenditures which cannot be paid for by user charges: the income tax and a general sales tax. Other taxes, such as the property tax, may provide a means of allocating user charges to finance expenditures giving rise to specific, allocable benefits. However, such other taxes cannot allocate fairly the costs of general expenditures on education, welfare programs, or similar government activities. The current use of the property tax to finance education and welfare programs is indefensible from the viewpoint of equity.

A sales tax can be levied which is based on one definition of ability to pay. It is important, however, to point out that a sales tax can be based on ability to pay only if it is in fact a general sales tax, based on all expenditures on goods and services by an individual and not just on purchases of selected service and goods. In particular, a general sales tax must include services in the sales-tax base if it is to allocate taxes in accordance with ability to pay. The present federal manufacturers' sales tax and provincial retail sales taxes are not general sales taxes. Following the logic of basing general taxation on ability to pay, it was one of the Carter Commission's recommendations that the existing sales and excise taxes be replaced by a general sales tax levied on retail sales and on services.[6] A sales tax can be

---

6. *Report of the Royal Commission on Taxation, op cit.,* Vol. 5, Part A, especially ch. 27. The Royal Commission excluded the special taxes on liquor and tobacco from this recommendation. It goes without saying that arguments for the equity and necessity of special taxes on liquor and tobacco must be analyzed more from a sociological viewpoint than from the viewpoint of the logic developed in this paper.

made progressive, with progressive rates, exemptions and tax credits applied to total expenditures over an annual period.

More than anything else, income would be selected by most people as the thing which best measures ability to pay. Income, however, must for this purpose be defined to take in everything which an individual receives in a given period. The Carter Commission's *Report* stated this in words that have been widely quoted:

> We are completely persuaded that taxes should be allocated according to the changes in the economic power of individuals and families. If a man obtains increased command over goods and services for his personal satisfaction we do not believe it matters, from the point of view of taxation, whether he earned it through working, gained it through operating a business, received it because he held property, made it by selling property, or was given it by a relative. Nor do we believe it matters whether the increased command over goods and services was in cash or kind. Nor do we believe it matters whether the increase in economic power was expected, whether it was a unique or recurrent event, whether the man suffered to get the increase in economic power, or it fell into his lap without effort.[7]

If one individual has the money with which to buy a new automobile, and another individual does not, the first individual has a greater ability to pay—whether to pay taxes or to pay for a new car—and this is the case no matter from what source the individual has obtained this money. The tax system should not tax a man who has worked to get money at a lower rate than that applied to a man who has received the same amount of money as a gift. The tax system should not differentiate between an investor and a labourer. All individuals should be treated in the same way, regardless of the source or nature of their income.[8] A tax system based on ability to pay should thus be based on a comprehensive definition of income that includes all sources of income: wages, salaries, gifts from other people, capital gains, money won in gambling, dividends, interest paid by others, money received from the federal government in the form of transfer payments, unemployment-insurance benefits, family allowances, or any other receipt of income which increases an individual's economic power. For ability to pay to be the basis on which an income tax is defined, the tax base must include all forms of income.

A social consensus exists, I believe, that one's ability to pay is based not on income as such, but on what is left over after non-discretionary expenses

---

7. *Ibid.*, Vol. I, pp. 9-10.
8. The only possible exception to this statement results from one qualification made earlier with respect to the form of redistribution which is desirable. It may be considered desirable to impose special taxes on transfers of wealth (other than transfers between spouses), and so desirable to impose *heavier* taxes on income received in the form of a gift, bequest, or unexpected gain. The present tax system, of course, does exactly the opposite: lower rates of tax are imposed on all categories of unearned income.

are deducted from income. One has to live. One has to pay for the expenses of one's family. All individuals have certain non-discretionary expenses, and it consequently makes sense to say that ability to pay is related to what is left over after these non-discretionary expenses are deducted. It is, of course, difficult to define what non-discretionary expenses are. However, the following can be said: (1) For everybody there is some minimal amount of money which one needs to have in order to be able to survive in Canada. An ideal tax should consequently levy tax only on what remains after this amount has been subtracted from income, (2) non-discretionary expenses probably rise somewhat as income rises, but become increasingly less important as a proportion of income as income rises. In other words, non-discretionary expenses are a smaller and smaller fraction of an individual's total income as total income increases. This proposition implies that an ideal tax system should levy an increasingly high rate of tax on individuals as income increases. An income tax based on ability to pay must thus be a progressive income tax—that is, the tax rate levied on an individual's income must increase as that individual's income increases.

The concept of discretionary economic power—what is left over after non-discretionary expenses are deducted from total income, with income defined in accordance with a comprehensive definition of income—provides a very useful way for defining how taxes should be paid by different individuals. The important problem then becomes that of defining how individuals in different circumstances differ with respect to their non-discretionary expenditures. For example, in deciding what the relative tax rates should be on married individuals with two children compared to married individuals with five children or single individuals with no dependants, all of whom have the same income, the important consideration is, clearly, that of trying to define what the relative non-discretionary expenses are of the three types of families. Individuals may, of course, argue about what the non-discretionary expenses connected with a child really are. However, it is clear that such non-discretionary expenditures exist.

The effect of having another child on non-discretionary expenses may or may not be related to the income of the parents. If one accepts the proposition that the non-discretionary expenses of a second child are about the same as the non-discretionary expenses associated with a third child, and that these are a basically fixed amount (or should be so regarded in treating different families fairly), then one has accepted the proposition that an individual's taxes should be reduced by the same amount for each successive child and regardless of his income. (This is essentially the proposition the Carter Commission arrived at, which is to say that the fairest way of allowing for children is to allow a tax credit which reduces everybody's taxes by the same amount for each child.) It is interesting to note that under the present tax system in Canada, the effect on one's taxes of having another child depends very much on the income one has. The larger one's income, the more one's taxes are reduced. The dollar benefit of the exemptions for dependent children allowed under the present tax system is thus greatest for parents with incomes in the highest tax brackets.

To sum up what I have said on the subject of fairness, an ideal tax system would be established as follows. (1) Where possible, government expenditure programs with clearly definable benefits that can be allocated to specific individuals should be paid for by taxes related to those benefits. Such taxes would include user charges, property taxes, gasoline taxes, miscellaneous licence fees, and other benefit-related levies. (2) All other expenditures—and this clearly includes a large fraction of expenditures on education, welfare programs and other programs of general benefit to the community—should be financed by taxes based on ability to pay. Essentially there are two kinds of taxes which may be thought of as being based on ability to pay: income taxes and general sales taxes. (3) Because ability to pay is related to what is left over after non-discretionary expenses have been allowed for, a tax based on ability to pay must involve progressive tax rates. The rate of progression should depend upon the social consensus regarding the relationship between non-discretionary expenses on the one hand and income and family status on the other. (4) If either a sales tax or income tax is to be based on ability to pay, the tax base defined for each tax must be comprehensive. A general sales tax that is related to ability to pay must be based on all goods and services bought by individuals. Similarly, an income tax based on ability to pay must be based on a tax base that includes all forms of income, whether labour income, investment income, or any other form of income. In each case, from the viewpoint of ability to pay, a dollar is truly merely a dollar. There is no such thing as an investment dollar, a wage dollar, or a gift dollar. So far as one's ability to purchase goods and services is concerned, all dollars are interchangeable.

interference by a tax system in individual decision-making

The second major consideration affecting the design of a tax system is that a government implementing social objectives should do so insofar as possible in such a way as to minimize the extent to which individual choices are restricted. The very fact of taxing means, of course, that resources are diverted from some individuals to other individuals, thus changing the choices that would have been made by the individuals in the absence of taxation. Moreover, the essence of the purpose of the government is, after all, to divert resources to achieve those social purposes for which there is general support and which cannot be achieved through the private sector alone. Government, by its very nature, therefore, involves a change in the choices that otherwise would collectively be made by individuals on their own.

Nevertheless, given the objectives which a government is pursuing, the goal of least unnecessary interference in decision-making means that one prime objective to be kept in mind in designing a tax system should be that the taxing system should interfere as little as possible with individual decision-making. To put this in different terms, a tax system should be as neutral as possible from an economic point of view—that is, it should not bias decision-making. Such bias arises in a tax system when different types of income are taxed at different rates.

One of the most important non-neutralities in the present Canadian taxation arises from the differential taxation of corporate-source income. A shareholder may derive any or all of the following three types of corporate-source income from his investments in the common stock of a corporation: (1) cash dividends, (2) capital gains resulting from the corporation's retention of earnings, and (3) "pure" capital gains, arising from causes other than the retention of earnings. Income accrued after corporate income tax on investments in the common stocks of Canadian manufacturing corporations is, on the average, fairly equally distributed among these three components.[9] For corporate-source income before tax, this implies an average division of income as follows: 40 percent allocable to dividends, 40 percent allocable to retentions, and 20 percent allocable to "pure" capital gains.

At present, shareholders in a corporation are taxed in two ways. Income accrued by the corporation is taxed under the corporation income tax, which imposes a tax of roughly 50 percent of taxable corporate income. Dividends paid out of the income remaining after corporate income taxes are paid are then taxed again under the personal income tax.

To take an example, suppose an investor with a taxable income of $8,000 from sources other than dividends (and so with a marginal personal income tax rate of 30 percent under the current tax system) invests in the common stock of a company. The marginal tax rates paid on each component of corporate-source income would be as follows:

(1) On dividends: 50 percent at the corporate level, plus the tax on the dividends. The tax rate applied to the dividends would be his marginal tax rate of 30 percent, less the 20 percent dividend tax credit allowed on dividends from Canadian corporations. The total tax adds up to 55 percent of the before-tax corporate income.

(2) On retained earnings: 50 percent at the corporate level.

(3) On other capital gains: nothing.

---

9. Estimates of the relative importance of these three components of corporate-source income for large publicly traded companies are presented in J. Bossons, *Rates of Return on Canadian Common Stocks*, Studies of the Royal Commission on Taxation, Number 27 (Ottawa: Queen's Printer, 1967).

Since, for the average company, the first two components each account for 40 percent of corporate-source income accrued by shareholders, the marginal tax rate on this corporate-source income for our illustrative investor is 42 percent. For different investors, the marginal tax rate on income accrued on shareholdings in the average Canadian manufacturing company would vary with their marginal personal income tax rates as follows:

Marginal personal income tax rate of investor	*Actual marginal tax rate on income accrued on investments in an average manufacturing company*
10 percent	40 percent
20 percent	40 percent
30 percent	42 percent
40 percent	44 percent
50 percent	46 percent
60 percent	48 percent

As this table indicates, the present system of taxation favours the high-income investor at the expense of the low-income investor. Moreover, it is, of course, possible for the high-income investor to avoid even more tax by seeking investments which yield a larger-than-average proportion of their income in the form of capital gains.

The effect of the present system of taxation on investors' decision-making is both significant and severe. The discrimination against low-income investors exists only in the case of common stocks; it does not apply to income from fixed-income investments, such as mortgages and bonds. Consequently, most Canadian investors invest less in equities issued by Canadian corporations than they otherwise would. At the same time, high-income investors are put under substantial tax pressure to divert as much as possible of their investments into short-term speculation yielding income in the form of capital gains. The net result of the tax pressures on personal investment introduced by the present tax system's non-neutrality is a reduction in the supply of entrepreneurial capital.

Fortunately, tax neutrality and tax fairness are achieved by the same tax system: namely, a tax system that treats all types of income or all types of sales in the same way. It is therefore possible to obtain a tax system which interferes with individual decision-making as little as possible by obtaining a tax system which is fair.

4. ANALYZING A REFORM PROGRAM: THE CARTER COMMISSION PROPOSALS

the need for evaluating the Canadian tax system

The present tax system in Canada is an accumulation of the results of a number of historical accidents. It is really a misnomer, in fact, to call it a system; for it is anything but systematic. The Canadian income tax was hurriedly imposed in 1917 as an emergency income war tax, and has not changed much over the years. When introduced in 1917, it was very heavily influenced by the British tax system, which was in its essence first enacted in 1799 in a society which was very different from the society which exists today in Canada. At that time in Great Britain, parliament primarily represented large landowners, and it should scarcely be surprising if the income tax adopted to sustain a war against the French revolution should have reflected the attitudes and self-interest of the landowning class. It should likewise be scarcely surprising if an income tax essentially little different from this original 1799 version no longer fitted the needs of our society.

The complexities of our present Canadian system of taxation have been built in over the years, partly by judicial interpretation, partly by attempts to close loopholes, partly by *ad hoc* subsidies added to the tax system, and partly as a result of other essentially accidental developments.[10]

The present income-tax law in Canada contains a number of implicit subsidies that on examination cannot be regarded as fair and cannot even be said to satisfy the objective of fostering economic growth. Such subsidies are clearly undesirable from many points of view. An equitable distribution of the tax burden would eliminate such subsidies. Given the accidental way in which our tax system has developed, we need not look for villains to understand how such unfair subsidies have arisen. At no time in the history of the Canadian income tax has there been an organized, comprehensive examination of the tax system. The tax was imposed in an emergency, and changed only on a marginal basis over the years.

The Royal Commission on Taxation, headed by K. LeM. Carter, attempted to provide the organized scrutiny of the tax system which Canada has previously lacked. The Commission attempted to define what an ideal tax system would be for Canada, and from this derived a number of recommendations which would bring about as ideal a tax system as the Commission believed could be implemented and at the same time be administratively feasible.

---

10. A brief but instructive summary of the way in which important loopholes were first introduced as "temporary" expedients is contained in an address by J. Harvey Perry to the November 1967 Tax Conference; see *Proceedings of the Twentieth Tax Conference* (Toronto: Canadian Tax Foundation, 1968), pp. 7-21.

the Carter Commission recommendations

The essential recommendations of the Carter Commission were as follows:

(1) The personal income tax—the principal tax based on ability to pay in Canada—should be based on a comprehensive definition of income that would include all forms of receipts. (2) All other direct taxes on income (such as the corporation income tax and taxes on gifts and bequests) should be either eliminated or integrated with the personal income tax. (3) The tax unit whose income would be taxed should be defined as the family unit rather than the individual. (4) Sales taxation should be reformed by substituting a general sales tax on all retail sales and services for the present federal manufacturing sales tax and provincial retail sales taxes.

The recommendation to tax the family unit rather than the individual has some interesting implications. Any transfer between two individuals in the same family unit should not be taken into account for tax purposes. Moreover, the tax unit should be taken to survive as long as any member of it survives. If a husband dies and leaves money to his wife, that gift to his wife should not be taxable, since the family unit remains. A gift should only be taxable when it is a gift of money to somebody outside the family unit.

The taxation of gifts and bequests is substantially changed by the adoption of the family unit as the basis for taxation. The Carter Commission recommended that gifts made by a husband to his wife or to dependent children should not be taxed, since these would be transfers within a family unit. However, taxation should be applied to transfers, whether gift or inheritance, between parent and child, provided that the child is over twenty-one and so outside the family unit.

The Carter Commission's recommendations for taxation of gifts and bequests have been disputed widely. Much of this dispute can be regarded as a dispute about what constitutes a family unit. To some people, a family is a dynasty. Fathers, grandfathers, sons, grandchildren, nephews—all should be included within the definition of a family, at least when it comes to deciding whether transfers of income and wealth from one member of the family to another should be considered as taxable. To the dynasts, none of these transfers should be taxable—they are all between members of the same family. To others, perhaps concerned more about the results of aggregating incomes than about the results of not taxing transfers of wealth among family members, the family should be treated as consisting only of husband and wife. A son living with his family and earning money should not, such individuals believe, have his income added to the income of his parents in computing the family's taxes. The Carter Commission took a middle position in this quasi-sociological dispute, recommending that a family unit should consist of husband, wife and dependent children under the age of twenty-one. Under certain circumstances, the Carter Commission recommended that children could leave the family unit at an earlier date or, if students, could remain in it until the age of twenty-five.

A number of specific recommendations flow from the Carter Commission's recommendations for the adoption of a comprehensive tax base and integration of all income taxes. These include specific recommendations for the taxation of capital gains at full rates, the taxation of gifts and bequests received from outside the tax unit, the abolition of the separate gift and estate taxes now collected, the integration of corporation income taxes and personal income taxes for Canadian residents, and the elimination of many loopholes in the definition of the personal income tax base. Integration of the corporation and personal income taxes for Canadian residents would be achieved by treating the corporation income tax as essentially a withholding device, under which corporate income taxes allocable to a resident shareholder would be refunded to the shareholder while the shareholder would pay personal income tax on his share of the corporation's taxable income.

The integration method proposed for corporation income taxes by the Commission is a somewhat complicated mechanism whose purpose is to ensure that all corporate-source income by a Canadian resident is taxed at the same rate regardless of its form, and that it is, furthermore, taxed on the same basis as any other type of income. Essentially, it would work as follows: (1) The corporation income tax would be treated as a withholding tax; the income tax paid by a corporation on the before-tax income allocable to a shareholder would be refunded to the shareholder. (2) At the same time, the shareholder would have to bring his share of the corporation's before-tax income into his personal tax base; he would thus pay tax on this income in the same way as if it were any other type of income. (3) The shareholder would increase the "cost-basis" of his shares by the amount of after-corporation-tax earnings allocable to him which were retained by the corporation; in computing the capital gain taxable upon his selling his shares, he would deduct this augmented "cost-basis" from the proceeds of the sale. These three aspects of integration, together with the taxation of capital gains at full rates, would ensure that all types of corporate-source income would be taxable at the same rates upon realization.

impact of the Carter Commission's proposals on different individuals

If a tax system is unfair, it will contain ways in which taxes can be avoided on certain types of income. Studies prepared for the Carter Commission estimated that almost $5 billion in income received by Canadian individuals and corporations in 1964 either escaped taxation or were taxed at unduly low rates.[11] While some of this untaxed income was offset by some expenses not deductible from income under the current tax law (a situation particularly frequent among certain types of employees), a substantial amount of income would be added to the tax base if the income tax were defined in accordance with true ability to pay.

As a result, adoption of a fairer tax system would make possible a significant reduction in tax rates. The effect of this reduction in income tax rates is shown in Table 1, which shows the amounts by which a typical wage-earner's personal income taxes would be reduced under different income and family circumstances. Under the current (1967) tax system, a married wage-earner with two children and a salary of $8,000 per year would pay personal incomes taxes of $1,088, assuming standard deductions to be claimed. Under the Carter proposals, his taxes would be reduced by $230 to $858, a reduction of roughly 20 percent.[12]

Table 1.

REDUCTION IN PERSONAL INCOME TAXES PAYABLE BY A WAGE-EARNER WHICH WOULD RESULT FROM THE CARTER COMMISSION'S RECOMMENDATIONS

Gross income from employment	Single	Family status of taxpayer	
		Married no children	Married 2 children
$ 3,500	$ 20	$ 30	$ 67
5,000	46	78	86
6,500	98	156	137
8,000	139	255	230
10,000	196	371	344
12,000	305	543	442
15,000	585	943	828

Source: J. Bossons, **A General Income Tax Analyzer**, op. cit., Appendix J, Table J-4.

The extent to which an individual's taxes would be changed under the Carter proposals would depend upon the nature of the income received by the individual. Because wages and salaries are currently taxed at full rates and expenses of employment are currently non-deductible, most employees

---

11. Of this, $2.6 billion consisted of personal income which escaped taxes altogether, $1.2 billion consisted of gifts and bequests received from outside the family unit which was taxed in part through separate taxes on gifts and bequests, and $760 million consisted of corporate income not currently subject to corporation income tax. For details of these estimates, see J. Bossons, *A General Income Tax Analyzer*, Studies of the Royal Commission on Taxation, Number 25 (Ottawa: Queen's Printer, 1967), especially Table 7; and Vol. 6 of the *Report* of the Commission, especially Table 35-4.
12. These tax figures include Old Age Security taxes and are before deduction of federal income taxes abated to the provinces, but exclude the so-called "Social Development Tax," imposed in 1969.

are currently over-taxed, regardless of income. Under the Carter Commission's recommendations, employment expenses would be deductible and tax rates would be reduced. Most dividend income is likewise over-taxed as a result of being subject to tax both when earned by corporations and when distributed to shareholders. Gifts, capital gains, and certain other types of income are presently either under-taxed or not taxed at all.

Some estimates of the actual effect of the Carter Commission's proposals on Canadian individual taxpayers were made for the Commission by calculating how taxes would have been changed for each of 412,000 individuals whose 1964 tax returns were made available (without taxpayer identification) to the Commission. Based on these calculations, it was estimated that 3.8 million Canadians—more than one-half of all taxpayers—would have had direct taxes paid by or attributable to them reduced by more than 15 percent. At the same time, roughly 330,000 taxpayers would have had their taxes increased by over 15 percent.[13]

In addition to these changes in direct taxes levied on income, the burden of federal sales taxes would be reduced for all but high-income families by the Carter Commission's recommendations for changes in the sales tax. The combined percentage charge in income and sales taxes which would be realized by average families in different income classes is shown in Table 2.

Table 2.

AVERAGE PERCENTAGE CHANGE IN SALES AND INCOME TAXES FOR FAMILIES IN SELECTED INCOME CLASSES

Income	Average percentage change in taxes
Less than $2,000	−25.8%
$ 2,000– 2,999	−18.9
3,000– 4,999	−17.4
5,000– 9,999	−13.2
10,000–11,999	− 3.8
12,000–19,999	+ 0.1
20,000–24,999	+ 4.3
25,000–49,999	+ 7.8
50,000 and over	+26.3

Source: J. Bossons, **A General Income Tax Analyzer, op. cit.,** Table 17.

As Table 2 indicates, implementation of the recommendations of the Royal Commission on Taxation would result in a fairly material redistribu-

---

13. See J. Bossons, *A General Income Tax Analyzer, op. cit.,* page 61. By "direct taxes" is meant the sum of personal income taxes, corporation income taxes, and taxes on gifts and bequests.

tion of purchasing power from higher-income groups to lower-income families in spite of a large reduction in the top marginal rate of taxation. It is worth emphasizing that this was not the conscious aim of the Carter Commission, but is instead the result of the effect of income on individuals' ability to take advantage of tax-avoidance possibilities in the present tax law. It is not inevitable that an unfair tax system should prove relatively advantageous to wealthier individuals; it just happens that such is the case under current Canadian tax law[14]

evaluating the implicit subsidies of the current tax system

In proposing that the tax base be widened to include all sources of income, the Carter Commission recommended the abolition of numerous subsidies now hidden within the tax system. It should be immediately emphasized that it is not necessarily the case that subsidies are "bad." As was pointed out in discussing the implications for tax design of various social objectives, some subsidies may have beneficial economic or social effects that more than outweigh their costs. Nor is it necessarily the case that subsidies cannot be extended through the tax system; for it may prove administratively most efficient to extend certain subsidies in that manner.

From the point of view of designing an ideal tax system, the only important effect of subsidies is their cost. There are, of course, other quesions that need to be answered in order to determine whether a subsidy is justifiable, such as the evaluation of (1) whether a given subsidy is more efficient than alternative means of achieving the desired objective, and (2) whether the benefit obtained through the subsidy program is worth its cost. But for a tax system, the chief implication of a new subsidy program which has to be financed out of general tax revenues is that tax rates will have to be higher than they would otherwise be.

The most important fact suggesting a need to re-evaluate many of the subsidies presently contained within the Canadian tax system is that before the research undertaken by the Carter Commission was made available, there were no accurate estimates of their cost. The sudden availability of facts must necessarily change the nature of any debate, and this has cer-

---

14. The very sharp increase in taxes which would be experienced by families with incomes in excess of $50,000 is attributable to the continued progression of income tax rates between $30,000 and $100,000. Were the rate schedule recommended by the Commission to be modified to make the top marginal rate 35 percent, effective on incomes of $30,000 and over, the average increase in taxes of upper-income taxpayers would be reduced to roughly 10 percent, with little impact on total tax revenues. It should be noted that the rate schedule recommended by the Commission implicitly assumes that individuals' non-discretionary expenses continue to increase if their income rises above $30,000—a debatable welfare proposition!

tainly been the case with respect to public evaluation of a number of subsidy programs.

The cost estimates provided by the Commission for some major subsidies are presented in Table 3. This total cost is the equivalent of 16 percent of the total revenue which would have been obtained in 1964 from the corporation and personal income taxes by both federal and provincial governments under current (1967) tax law. To put this in other terms, the rates of personal income tax recommended by the Carter Commission would have had to be raised by an average of roughly 18 percent had the Commission not recommended the abolition of these subsidies.[15]

Table 3.

THE COST IN 1964 OF MAJOR SUBSIDIES CONTAINED IN THE CURRENT TAX SYSTEM*
(millions of dollars)

	At corporate level	At personal level	Total
Subsidies to mining industry	141	5	146
Subsidies to petroleum industry	19	1	20
Subsidies to life insurance industry	75	78	153
Subsidies to other financial institutions	25	—	25
Non-taxation of capital gains	100	209	309
Non-taxation of employee benefits	—	110	110
TOTAL	360	403	763

Sources: Report of the Royal Commission on Taxation, op. cit., Volume 6, Tables 35-4 and 37-2; J. Bossons, A General Income Tax Analyzer, op. cit., Table 10 and Appendix H.

* The cost of subsidies is defined as the amount of tax revenue forgone as a result of the tax concessions. The estimated cost of tax concessions effected through the personal income tax is based upon the net tax yield obtained through their elimination, assuming the rate schedule recommended by the Royal Commission. Their cost in the current tax system (i.e., valued using the current rate schedule) is, in fact, materially higher.

It, of course, does not necessarily follow just because these subsidies are expensive that they do not merit continuation. The Carter Commission recommended their abolition chiefly because (1) it concluded that these subsidies had to be justified on the grounds of their contribution to Canadian economic growth, and (2) it concluded, after taking into account the effect of these subsidies on general tax rates, that on balance these subsidies hindered rather than fostered national economic growth.

---

15. These calculations are based on data presented in J. Bossons, *A General Income Tax Analyzer, op cit.*, Table 5 and Appendix L, Table L-2.

over-all effects on economic growth

Certain changes which would be introduced by the Carter Commission proposals would have unfavourable effects on economic growth if taken in isolation. The abolition of the subsidies listed in Table 3 would remove incentives now encouraging particular forms of investment and saving. In addition, the redistribution of income from higher-income groups to lower-income groups which Table 2 indicates would be brought about by the Commission's reforms would mean a redistribution of income from people who save a relatively high fraction of their income to people who save less. The redistributional impact of the Carter Commission's proposals would thus tend in itself to reduce savings.

If the net economic effect of the Carter Commission's suggested reforms were a reduction in the level of savings and investment, the rate of growth of the Canadian economy would be reduced. It would then be necessary to ask whether such a reduction in economic growth were too high a price to pay for obtaining a fairer tax system. Analysis of the economic effect of the Carter reforms is thus of considerable importance.

A number of fairly exhaustive analyses of the economic effects of the Carter Commission's proposals have now been completed.[16] On the basis of these analyses, it is safe to say that the over-all net effect of the Carter Commission proposals would be a mild boost to the economy. The two objectives of increasing the tax system's fairness and of increasing the nation's rate of economic growth would be satisfied simultaneously by adoption of the Carter Commission's proposals.

The primary reason for the favourable economic impact of the proposed tax reforms is that the unfair aspects of the present tax system most heavily penalize the employees and entrepreneurs who contribute most to the maintenance of economic growth. Individuals who receive gifts for which they have not worked or who accrue short-term capital gains as a result of good fortune are favoured by the current tax system. Investors who risk capital in long-term investments in new ventures are currently penalized both if the venture fails and if it succeeds, since the capital loss resulting from failure is non-deductible under current tax law and since the income resulting from success is currently taxed twice. By taxing all income at the same rate, the Carter Commission's reforms would eliminate both penalties. Capital losses would become deductible from taxable income, thus becoming partially offset by a reduction in taxes. At the same time, the integration of the corporation and personal income taxes would lower the effective

---

16. For a review of these studies and integration of their findings, see A. R. Dobell and T. A. Wilson, "Overall Effects of the Proposed Tax Reforms: Savings, Investment, and the Balance of Payments," *IQASEP Working Paper Series* (Toronto: Institute for the Quantitative Analysis of Social and Economic Policy, University of Toronto, 1968).

rate of taxes imposed on the income produced by a successful corporate venture.

The removal of the present over-taxation of most corporate-source income would cause prices of company's common shares to rise, and this would in turn lead to increased saving and investment.[17] At the same time, other aspects of the Carter Commission proposals would engender an increased flow of savings through Registered Retirement Income Plans as well as increasing entrepreneurial investment policies on the part of the trustees of such plans. The buoyant effects of these two changes would more than offset the depressing effects of income redistribution and of the elimination of subsidies.

5. SUMMARY AND CONCLUSION

In examining the basis for designing a better tax system, the various objectives of government have been evaluated. While all government expenditures have to be financed (directly or indirectly) by tax dollars, only two objectives are of critical importance for the form of the tax system: that the tax system be fair, and that it interfere with individual freedom of choice as little as possible.

The goals of fairness and neutrality fortunately coincide to a very great extent. At the risk of some over-simplification, it is consequently possible to say—taking all of the varied objectives of government into account—that an ideal tax system is one which distributes the burdens of taxation as fairly as possible.

A fair tax system would be designed as follows:

(1) To as great an extent as is feasible, recipients of easily identifiable benefits of government expenditure programs should be taxed in accordance with those benefits. Too little attention has been paid in recent years (even by the Royal Commission on Taxation) to the possibility of financing important categories of rapidly growing expenditures through new benefit-related taxes, particularly at the provincial and municipal level.

(2) The expenditures which cannot be financed through benefit-related taxes should be financed through a combination of a general tax on consumer expenditures and a general income tax. Both taxes should be based on comprehensive definitions of sales and income.

---

17. It has been estimated that common stock prices would rise by an average of more than 15 percent, and that the attractiveness of common-stock investments would be increased especially for low-income investors. The result of these changes would be to bring about a broadening of the market for corporate securities, which would further aid in the enhancement of the rate of investments and economic growth. The estimates of the effects of the Carter reforms on rates of return on common stock are presented in J. Bossons. "The Effect of the Carter Proposals and of Alternative Proposals on Stock Prices," *Proceedings of the Twentieth Tax Conference, op. cit.*, pp. 133-152.

(3) The effective tax rates imposed on these two general tax bases should, after taking exemptions, tax credits, and nominal tax rates into account, be progressive. This progressivity should be based upon the relationship to the tax base of a taxpayer's ability to pay after allowing for non-discretionary expenses.

The Carter Royal Commission on Taxation attempted to design a general sales tax and a general income tax that would be both as fair and as neutral in their effects on decision-making as is feasible. Conflicts exist in some situations between these goals of fairness and neutrality and the necessity of designing a tax system that is administratively feasible. In general, however, the Carter report would provide a much more equitable basis for raising general tax revenues than does the present tax system.

The Royal Commission's proposals would, on the average, redistribute income from those better off to individuals with low incomes. As a general proposition, one would expect such redistribution to entail a social cost in the form of reduced economic growth in the private sector. This cost would not occur in the case of implementing the Commission's proposals, chiefly because these proposals would bring about redistribution through taxing most earned income more lightly (whether earned through labour or through entrepreneurial risk-taking) and at the same time taxing unearned income (such as gifts and bequests) more heavily. This fortuitous result is simply a concomitant of the inefficiency of the present tax system.

The *Report* of the Royal Commission on Taxation has justly been called a landmark in the annals of taxation. To a considerable degree, the Carter Report is such a landmark simply because it is based upon a logical approach to the subject of taxation. It would be an even greater landmark if the Carter Report were to result in a more rational tax system being substituted for the accidental accumulation of *ad hoc* tax-avoidance-prone provisions which constitute our current tax law. It is, of course, virtually impossible to conceive of political circumstances under which the recommendations of any Royal Commission on a subject of importance could be enacted without modification. No report can be so perfect that its recommendations cannot be improved. However, as the Commission itself stated, ". . . it is the basic ideas from which the proposals have been derived and not the details that are important." Adoption of a set of fundamental tax reforms based upon these basic ideas would be a landmark not only in the annals of taxation but in the annals of our country's progress towards a more just society in which individuals were not only provided for in accordance with their needs but also rewarded in accordance with society's evaluation of their productivity.

It is very difficult to forecast the likely extent to which the Carter proposals may be implemented in the short run. The influence of special interest groups is particularly difficult to predict. In the "mini-budget" of

October 22, 1968, the government implemented many of the Carter Commission's proposals for the taxation of financial institutions, while at the same time reaffirming its intention neither to implement the Commission's remaining proposals in full nor to avoid reform. In increasing corporate taxation on insurance companies and forcing policy-holders to pay tax on investment income allocable to them on policies when sold or cashed, the government adopted some of the Carter proposals which were most severely criticized on economic grounds in briefs submitted to the government. It may not be amiss to conclude that the need for new tax revenues caused by the introduction of new spending programs in recent years may be a paramount factor affecting what happens to the Carter proposals in the next few years.

No important reforms have ever been adopted immediately upon being proposed, and it would be wild optimism to predict that all of the Carter Commission's recommendations will become quickly accepted. Nevertheless, it is safe to say that the proposals of the Royal Commission on Taxation have become the standard against which any future government tax-reform programs will be compared. The Commission's *Report* has above all else widely disseminated a logical framework for evaluating a tax system, and this in itself cannot avoid affecting the way in which people look at taxes.

federal-provincial economic coordination

Jacques Parizeau
Ecole Des Hautes Etudes Commerciales

PRINCIPLES OF INTER-GOVERNMENT FISCAL STRUCTURE

The issue of federal-provincial coordination is, in Canada, the translation of a problem that is now raised in many countries and that pertains to the degree of centralization or decentralization of government decisions.

In highly centralized administrations, of the type that evolved from the Napoleonic system, the trend towards decentralization is supported by two main arguments. On the one hand, the considerable increase in the size of government operations implies that centralized administration becomes gradually less efficient, is subject to longer delays, and brings about considerable distortions in the allocation of funds, insofar as it is impossible to carry out from the centre all the rational choices that intricate and innumerable decisions require; on the other hand, a centralized government process has in the past tended to follow, and even to increase, the trends towards the centralization or the concentration of economic activities. Regional problems of growth have thus been enhanced, which may not have been tragic in terms of public finance or economic choices as long as social security hardly existed, but which became the source of huge public expenditures when welfare payments and agricultural subsidies were combined to buttress faltering regional economic development.

In countries where government processes are of the federal variety, decentralization has often been seen as the worst possible danger for coherent policies; and the greater the size of the public sector, the greater was the danger of incoherent policies.

Three solutions have been explored to avoid fragmentation. The *first* and most obvious was to change the constitutional framework so as to enhance the powers of the central government. The *second* was to shift actual financial powers to the centre and leave as little fiscal leverage as possible at the other levels of government. The *third* was to develop closer forms of coordination between the various levels of government.

When Canada emerged from the war, there was no doubt that, for all practical purposes, the federal authorities had become, during the emergency, the essential government process and the centre of all major decisions. Federal fiscal resources were equal to about three times those of provincial and municipal authorities. The federal debt was five times that of junior governments. While the constitution gave provinces exclusive powers in certain fields, such as education and social security, they could not carry out major expansions in these fields without obtaining equally important transfers from the central authorities.

There were, however, few chances for them to obtain such transfers. Embarked upon the organization of an extensive social-security program, strongly influenced, as all Western countries, by the Keynesian revolution, the Canadian government had little incentive to accept a type of fragmentation that would have complicated unduly the major reforms it envisaged and the responsibilities that it was now ready to shoulder. Indeed, in the White Paper on Employment of 1946, reference was made to the need for federal-provincial cooperation to set up anti-cyclical programs. But this was largely a pious wish and, in the context of those days, an unnecessary one.

In the years that followed, the financial requirements of provinces and municipalities increased. Not only did the cost of education rise enormously; but in the fields of health, road construction, housing renewal, community services of all kinds, provinces and municipalities were faced with rising needs that were outside federal jurisdiction in whole or in part, and for which they just did not have enough of the required resources.

No serious attempt was made by the federal government to amend the constitution so as to enter jurisdictions from which it had been originally excluded. Throughout the period, the only significant amendment to the constitution in this respect has to do with old-age security: the federal government was allowed to set up its own programs, without prejudice, one should add, to any other program that provinces might want to set up later on.

A transfer of resources to the provinces would take one of two forms. Either it raised the revenues of provinces without any indication as to how the money should be spent, or the senior government participated in new spending programs, provided that these programs were compatible with federal priorities and federal standards. The first procedure is unconditional transfers, while the second is, of course, of a conditional character.

Unconditional transfers can take all kinds of shapes or forms. They can, for instance, be the result of a change in the shares that each level of government raises in a given tax field, when it has been accepted by both sides that that tax field will be shared and that the total tax burden in that field is set at a certain level. Or, they can result in the complete evacuation by the federal government of a given tax field. Or again, they can be produced by the creation of a new tax field, accepted by both authorities as being allocated permanently to the provinces. Or, they can be straight financial annual transfers from the federal budget to the provincial treasuries. And, of course, there can be a combination of all these formulas.

A conditional transfer implies that the federal authorities agree to pay for all or part of a provincial program, as long as that program, its norms, and possibly its administration, have received federal approval or are subject to federal controls.

It should be pointed out that each of these two formulas is compatible with the present Canadian constitution. While one formula strengthens provincial autonomy and the second maintains federal control, both can be fitted to the same legal document.

Conditional transfers not only maintain federal control but they can also be used to expand it. Insofar as they take the shape of shared-cost programs, in other words, while the federal contribution is only a fraction of the total cost, the provincial contribution constitutes so much that cannot be allocated by provincial authorities to autonomous adventures. If the federal government opens shared-cost programs in existing fields of public expenditures, it can thus "freeze" gradually an increasing share of provincial budgets. At the limit, provincial authorities become more or less administrative agencies of federally initiated or federally financed programs, irrespective of how the legal documents distribute formal powers between the two levels of government.

The same sort of issue arises between provincial governments, on the one hand, and local authorities, on the other. The distribution of subsidies from one to the other can similarly be conditional or unconditional, and the effects of that choice will be similar to those noted in the previous paragraph. The rise of municipal needs in recent years and the expansions that are forecasted in the years to come, suggest that the sort of discussions that took place between the central government and the provinces in the last twenty years will find a similar echo in negotiations between provincial governments and local authorities.

The nature and extent of federal power is not, however, limited to fiscal or financial transfers. It also is an issue with respect to borrowing. In a federation several formulas are possible. A system can be set up according to which all governments borrow together through a common agency, under the guidance of the senior government and with the advice of the central bank. This is, more or less, the Australian formula, Or, at the other extreme, all governments — federal, provincial and local — borrow under their own authority, both at home and abroad, amounts they want, at the time they see fit.

Finally, two distinct possibilities exist with respect to the control or suasion exercised over municipal expenditures. Local authorities do not usually have, even in a federation, constitutional rights of any kind. In Canada they are creatures of the provincial governments. As local needs rise, they can be satisfied through provincial resources only (either conditional or unconditional), or they can be, in whole or in part, satisfied through direct financing by the federal authorities. The formula eventually chosen will have an impact upon the degree of centralization of decisions related to the allocation of public resources, that will depend, in turn, upon the relationships that exist between federal and provincial authorities. In other words, if the allocation of the provincial budget is frozen through shared-cost programs, then the degree of control of the federal government is not jeopardized if all transfers of resources to the municipalities are channelled through provincial budgets, as long as such transfers are conditional. If, however, a large part of provincial finances is not frozen, then direct federal-municipal shared-cost programs may be necessary to keep municipal spending in line with federal priorities.

To sum up all these relationships, it is possible to formalize them in a very simple model, or rather to write them in shorthand form. Such a presentation will help us to understand what has happened to inter-government coordination in Canada over the last quarter of a century.

Let A designate the taxation resources raised by a government in any field it wishes, a refer to taxes raised in all freedom but in certain fields only, and α refer to amounts obtained through formal tax-sharing arrangements.

Unconditional transfers from one government to another are denoted as b, and conditional transfers as β.

Free borrowing, that is, full and unconditional access to financial markets, supplies funds in amount c, while borrowing that must be authorized by a senior government or that is available only if conditions are met with respect to the use of proceeds, is γ.

On the basis of the above symbols, the financing of the federal government can be expressed in several ways:

$$R_1 = A + c \text{ or } a + c \text{ or } a + \alpha + c \qquad (1)$$

The financing of provincial governments is:

$$R_2 = [a + \alpha] + [b + \beta] + [c + \gamma] \qquad (2)$$

In turn, $[a + \alpha]$ is split in two parts: d_1 refers to provincial participation in shared-cost programs, and is thus the counterpart of β, while d_2 designates free funds. The same distinction applies to b and either c or $[c + \gamma]$.

The financing of local government can be expressed in the following way:

$$R_3 = [a + \alpha] + [(b' + b'') + (\beta' + \beta'')] + [c + (\gamma' + \gamma'')] \quad (3)$$

where $'$ refers to federal sources of funds or federal authorizations, and $''$ refers to provincial transfers or authorizations. The same division of $[a + \alpha]$, $[b' + b'']$ and c between d_1 and d_2 applies.

It will have been noticed that the possibility of A has been left out in (2) and (3). Otherwise, it would in effect be a peculiar federation, where provinces and municipalities would have complete access to all taxation fields, including custom duties.

Furthermore, depending upon the type of centralization or decentralization that is chosen by the political authorities, several of the terms of the last two equations can have a value of zero.

A fully centralized system could be based on the following formulas:

$$R_1 = a + \alpha + c \quad (1)$$
$$R_2 = d_1 + \beta + \gamma \quad (2)$$
$$R_3 = d_1 + \beta'' + \gamma'' \quad (3)$$
$$\text{or} \quad d_1 + [\beta' + \beta''] + [\gamma' + \gamma''] \quad (3a)$$

All other elements would be equal to zero. Realistically, however, a small amount of d_2 funds are required, if only to pay for the cost of administration. R_2 and R_3 should thus possibly be rewritten as, say, $.95R_2$ or $.95R_3$.

A highly decentralized system would be:

$$R_1 = A + c \quad (1)$$
$$R_2 = a + b + c \quad (2)$$
$$R_3 = a + b'' + c \quad (3)$$

Of course, between these two sets of formulas all sorts of other combinations are possible. It should be noted that they could be compatible with the same constitutional document, in spite of the fact that they are likely to produce very different kinds of countries.

THE CANADIAN EXPERIENCE

In the power play that has developed in Canada during the last 20 years, it does not seem obvious that the parties involved readily recognized what was at stake and, specifically, that different countries could be produced. Except for the Quebec government after 1960, the other participants wavered from one formula to the other.

For instance, until the late 1950's, unconditional financial transfers and fiscal abatements amounted to several times the amount of conditional transfers, to the point where in 1957-1958 the first two items reached

660 million dollars, as against 160 million for the third (including payments to universities). Conditional payments to municipalities were hardly significant.

The opposite trend lasted for a few years. By 1963-1964, unconditional payments and tax abatements were slightly above a billion dollars, while conditional payments, mainly through the channels of shared-cost programs, came close to 900 million dollars. Several attempts were also made to induce municipal works of various kinds, including the ill-fated winter-works program.

Obviously, a definite attempt was being made to link provincial and municipal expenditures more directly to the federal budget. But then came the crisis of 1964. Provoked by Quebec, it was essentially centred on two issues: shared programs and the Canada Pension Plan. Both of these issues are so important to explain present and explore future developments of the Canadian federation that they must be examined in some detail.

The Quebec government, for political reasons that are outside the scope of this paper, had decided to try to withdraw from several shared-cost programs. The recent tendency of federal authorities to control the administration of these programs in all their minute details was unfortunate. In fact, there was some sympathy for the Quebec outcry, even though other provinces were not ready to go as far. If, however, such a crisis could loosen up federal control, a number of provinces seemed to think so much would have been gained.

The second issue had to do with the financing of the Canada Pension Plan. In addition to universal old-age security, the federal government had proposed a pension plan applicable to all wage-earners and up to a certain limit proportional, both for contributions and benefits, to income earned. It was to be financed by contributions of both employees and employers on a pay-as-you-go basis.

The Quebec proposals retained the main features of the project, but suggested a funded plan that would bring about a considerable cash flow during the first phase of the plan, the proceeds being distributed to the provinces. Furthermore, irrespective of what would be offered to other provinces, Quebec was ready to organize a separate pension plan.

In the end the Quebec view prevailed, and the provinces thus obtained a windfall of a billion dollars of wholly unconditional funds, besides whatever else the federal treasury supplied.

The solution of the 1964 crisis wrecked whatever chances there were to set up in Canada a centralized process of government. A reaction towards strengthening the senior government was inevitable. But it took time to materialize. In fact, the fiscal conferences of 1966 and 1967 continued to increase the amounts of unconditional transfers, at least to the Eastern provinces, as the scope of fiscal equalization was considerably extended.

Furthermore, pursuing their attempts to avoid the emergence of a special political status for Quebec, the federal authorities first tried to induce other provinces to opt out from the social-security shared-cost programs, and when these attempts failed, suggested that they themselves should opt out.

Finally, as an ultimate gesture, the central government announced that, from then on, the abatement system that still ruled the sharing of taxation in the field of personal and corporate income as well as in the case of inheritance taxes would be abolished. There would be no more 100-points of these taxes to be divided between the two levels of governments. Each would tax as it saw fit and at the level that it wished. This decision at last stopped the power play, but it severed the main fiscal links that gave a semblance of coherence to the system.

During the fiscal year 1967-1968, on the basis of the previous tax-abatement procedure and of unconditional transfers, the federal government shifted 2.5 billion dollars to the provinces. More than a billion dollars flowed to them from the Canada and Quebec pension plans. Conditional payments of the federal government amounted to close to 1.6 billion dollars, but that amount included the compensation for Quebec related to the 29 shared-cost programs from which it had opted out, as well as the amounts that, according to the central government, would be remitted to the province when it opted out itself from social-security shared-cost programs. What would then be left in conditional payments would amount to a few hundred million dollars plus the cost of the federal contribution to medicare.

As for direct and conditional contributions of the federal government to municipalities, they still were very small and in terms of effective economic impact hardly significant.

These developments had to be detailed so as to give the full significance to the change that occurred in the respective financial "sizes" of governments in Canada. As of now, fiscal resources of provinces and municipalities amount to 55 percent of total fiscal resources collected in Canada. The public debt of junior governments is higher (at 24 billion dollars at the end of 1968) than the federal debt. More than 80 percent of all public investment is now the responsibility of junior governments and their crown corporations.

While federal control over provincial expenditures was considerably loosened, the same is not true of the extent of provincial control over local authorities. The impossibility for school boards to finance the rising cost of education through their share of the property tax, delivered all of them into the hands of provincial authorities who never thought of giving them unconditional transfers. In several provinces, education was reorganized by a ruthless practice of what amounted (without the name) to shared-cost programs.

In the case of municipalities, the situation is less clear. In a sense, one could suggest that provincial control is in inverse proportion to the size of the municipality. The largest cities still escape significant provincial influence to a great extent. Even the control exercised over their borrowing activities is largely nominal.

Be that as it may, the evolution of the Canadian federal system is in sharp contrast to what has occurred in the United States. Indeed, there also, a huge shift of resources has taken place towards the states and local authorities. But there has never been any doubt that such a shift should be based essentially on a rigorous system of conditional payments. This is particularly significant in the case of equalization. In Canada, the federal government has generally adopted forms of contributions to shared-cost programs that imply either a given percentage of average costs (the same for all provinces) or a given percentage of the cost in each province. Equalization was computed separately and paid unconditionally. In the United States, equalization takes place within the shared-cost program contributions: the percentage of federal contribution varies according to the relative wealth of the state, or, in other words, according to the yield of a standard tax structure.

Thus, while one can also observe in the U.S. that state and local authorities now spend as much or more than the federal government, the system has, in fact, through the "freezing process" become more centralized. It should also be noticed that, in any event, the U.S. system would tend to be more centralized than the Canadian. The largest states have, each individually, fairly small economic and financial weight in relation to the size of the federal budget. In Canada, at present, either Ontario or Quebec controls more public investment than does the federal government itself. If we assumed that New York State had 75 million inhabitants and that California had 60 million inhabitants, the American federal government might not be quite as powerful and so fully in charge of major operations. But this is precisely the situation in Canada.

When both factors are combined—relative size and unconditional transfers—one reaches the present situation of Canada: one of considerable decentralization where the possible efficiency of economic policies and their coherence must be questioned. In any case, it is obvious that the government variable of Keynesian models is surely not as homogeneous as textbooks imply that it must be.

The problem then arises as to whether forms of cooperation or voluntary coordination can replace the fiscal and financial links that have been abandoned. The record does not show that performance has improved on that count. There are obvious reasons for this. Clearly, the power play that developed over the sharing of resources has mobilized so much energy and has produced so much tension that it would have been over-optimistic to assume that coordination of economic policies could progress very much.

Thus was lost the lessons of 1956-1957. The boom of 1956 had been boosted carelessly by major federal and provincial investment programs, in complete opposition to the stabilization policies attempted by the central bank. In fact, total investment reached 27 percent of GNP. When the general recession came in 1957, the large investment programs of governments also came to an end, and there was not much left on the shelf to plug the hole. The recession that followed was thus unnecessarily severe. While there are several reasons (including overinvestment in plant capacity) that explain why the recession lasted so long, real income per head in Canada fell for four years. It was the only country of the industrialized world where this happened. Unemployment in Eastern Canada during the winter months reached as much as 14 or 15 percent of the labour force. There was not much that government had in reserve to step up investment.

The present fiscal structure is now more decentralized than it was then, and no real attempt has been made even to bring governments to coordinate their policies. A simple example is quite revealing on that count. As far as public investments are concerned, a fairly small number of public agencies are responsible for a large share of the total. Three major provincial hydro-electric companies, the Canadian National Railways, two or three highway departments, the Federal Department of Transport, two education departments, and, say, three or four large cities are really the major spenders.

Now, it is remarkable that representatives of such agencies have never met. No short-term investment plans have ever been set up or even attempted. Whether to expand against a reduction in the rate of growth of the rest of the economy or to contract when inflationary pressures are gathering, no official or unofficial program has ever been conceived for this group of major spenders.

In recent years, however, some attempts to coordinate various economic policies have been made and they should be briefly described, even though some of them were rather limited in scope. For instance, in preparation for the new fiscal arrangements of 1967, the federal and provincial governments set up a Tax Structure Committee that had as one of its major functions the establishment of coordinated five-year projections of the cost of existing public-expenditure programs and of tax revenues. This exercise was the first to have been made in Canada, and elementary problems of definition and compatibility of statistics had to be ironed out to start with. It seemed extraordinary that such problems should arise after so many years of federal-provincial negotiations, but in any event, at least that part of the exercise was completed. However, as the results were quickly used for bargaining purposes, they were shelved and forgotten.

A second area where coordination attempts were made is that of regional development. While actual results may not be spectacular, some area-development programs have been set up on the basis of a functional coordination between the governments. The so-called ARDA programs, the development project for the Gaspé Coast in Quebec, and that for north-western New Brunswick are indeed isolated cases, but it would not be fair to suggest that federal-provincial coordination failed in those instances. While some of these programs have been criticized, the issue usually had to do with their concepts or contents, but not really with the consultation procedures between the governments.

It is indeed strange that only such limited examples of coordination can be given, considering the large number of federal-provincial conferences that take place, or the huge apparatus of federal-provincial committees, particularly at the official level. Yet it should be recognized that, in recent years, whenever these conferences or committees have succeeded in achieving any results, they have usually been dealing with limited and technical objectives. Whenever the objective has been broader or whenever attempts have been made to enter the field of major economic policies, not much has come out of the conference. If their purpose was to help introduce a new federal plan, either fully paid for by the senior government or through a shared-cost formula, they could be useful to iron out marginal or technical details of application. But, by and large, as policy instruments these conferences have not been very fruitful. This is particularly noticeable in the case of the annual conference of finance ministers.

An interesting new development has taken place in recent months as the Prices and Incomes Commission was established by the federal government. The Commission is presently attempting to obtain from government, business and labour voluntary arrangements that would tend to reduce the rate of increase in the price level. As in all such similar operations, the main tool is to have business and labour agree to voluntary limitations. Yet there is an interesting by-product involved. Federal, provincial and municipal authorities actually control, or could by using existing powers control, various prices, wages and salaries. It is, of course, impossible to ask only one level of government to exercise its power and hold the line. All levels have to be part of the arrangement if it is to succeed. It is still too soon to foresee whether any arrangement is feasible.

Nevertheless, until now the record has not been impressive and coordination has not, and probably could not, replace the lack of cohesion in policies that the loose fiscal structure of the country has produced. It has been suggested in recent years, however, that perhaps the lack of coordination or the fragmentation of the fiscal structure was not really dangerous, at least as far as stabilization policies are concerned. The reasoning is based more or less on the following argument: stabilization policies operate at the margin. Even if all junior governments operated as private companies, it would still be possible for the federal government alone to change the size of either expenditures or revenues or both, to exercise the impact it wants on the level of economic activity. In other words, coordination could improve matters, but is not really necessary.

In a sense the argument is a valid one. In times of recession, there is no doubt that the federal government could increase its expenditures considerably, particularly with respect to current items rather than fixed investment. Yet, as far as taxes are concerned, the reduction of federal rates would, in present circumstances, probably be used as a windfall by provincial authorities, who would increase their own rates.

In times of inflationary pressures, the reverse is true. The federal government cannot really reduce its expenditures by amounts large enough to cancel a strong rise of expenditures of junior governments. The respective sizes of the two levels is now such that the impact of whatever contraction is possible at the federal level is fairly small in terms of what would be needed. On the other hand, the federal government can, of course, raise its tax levels as much as it wants to.

In other words, even in the present state of the fiscal structure in Canada and even without any coordination at all, the federal authorities can have some stabilization effect on the economy. How much they can actually have in relation to what a government can do in a unitary state is, of course, quite another question.

With respect to the rate of growth and to the shape of growth, present inter-governmental relations in Canada are, however, quite impossible to justify. And in that case, coordination just could not be relied upon to correct the central failure; in other words, it could not replace a system of centrally coordinated priorities and of a central system of allocation of resources. One cannot even rely upon the usual political process to give some orientation to the production and consumption of public and quasi-public goods. There is no way, for instance, to consult the voters on clear alternatives between, say, national defence and education, or between social security and funds for economic development, or between public transport and road expenditures. Even in a unitary state, such alternatives are not easy to present in an objective fashion to the electorate. But in a country where responsibilities are shared and truly shared, where no authority is in fact responsible for all major choices, the problem becomes hopeless.

It is in that sense that the Canadian situation is unique or, at least in the modern world, rather peculiar. Two main reasons seem to explain why corrective processes have not yet taken place and, in fact, have not even been fully explored. First, the massive impact of economic conditions and policies in the United States on the Canadian scene has tended to keep things in line and helped a sort of *de facto* coordination. In that sense,

Canada can probably afford a greater measure of disorganization in its public sector than can most countries.

Second, the political situation in Canada has not been conducive to a process of recentralization, or simply of redefinition of powers and responsibilities. But this is another problem, quite outside the scope of the present paper.

a theory of the economic council of Canada

Albert Breton*
Harvard University

1. INTRODUCTION

The analysis of the function, behaviour and performance of institutions such as private firms, commercial banks, households and competitive markets, though not always an easy task, can usually be carried out in a fairly straightforward fashion, largely because the goal or goals of these institutions and the constraints under which they operate have been operationally defined. Indeed, one can conjecture that the relative success of economists in analyzing institutions of this type has, to a large extent, been a result of their ability to discover and to impute to the relevant decision-makers empirically meaningful objectives and constraints.

The same success has not characterized the efforts that have been made to analyze the workings of other institutions, such as central banks, governments, universities, labour unions and corporations, mostly, one surmises, because of the economist's lack of fortune in defining empirically relevant objectives and constraints that could become the foundation of an integrated analytical framework. It is true that in recent years a large and growing volume of theoretical research has been conducted on the workings of these institutions and, as a consequence, our understanding of their modes of operation has been considerably enhanced. There exists, however, still

* What must be classified as an earlier version of this paper, though by now it bears no resemblance to the present product, was read in April 1969 at a Round-table on the Economic Council of Canada, organized by the Department of Economics at Carleton University. I wish to thank all those who participated in the discussion, particularly Jack Weldon and Roger Dehem, for their comments, which ultimately led me to the complete re-writing of the paper. I wish to express special thanks to Tom Rymes, who, outside the official discussion, helped me to focus on what I now think is the correct problem. This paper was written while I was at the London School of Economics.

other institutions—mainly offsprings of governmental and other types of collective action—that have a profound impact on the allocation of scarce resources, but nevertheless have received very little, if any, attention from economic theorists. These institutions, though they operate under a set of fairly definite constraints, do not pursue any obvious, well-defined and "permanent" objectives. Indeed, they usually re-define their goals and purposes as circumstances change and with every new chairman or board of directors.

In this paper, I am concerned with this third type of institution; more specifically, I will present a theory that makes it possible to rationalize the behaviour of these institutions and to understand that the absence of objectives, of definite and permanent purpose and of direction is the function that such institutions have been created to fulfill! Less paradoxically, I will argue that institutions of this type have the function of preventing the appearance of other institutions which, to some members of society at least, are strictly undesirable. And it is because they are, in a way of speaking, all things to all men that these institutions are able to fulfill their function.

Institutions of this type abound, but they do not all have the same importance and hence do not all receive the same attention. It is solely because of its importance and of the attention it has received and because of the consequent simplification in the task of exposition that this implies, that I have chosen to base the argument of this paper on the Economic Council of Canada. The added concreteness that comes from focusing on a particular case makes it possible in some instances to dispense with logical or historical proofs. This is a help in areas where proofs are notoriously difficult to come by, at least when models are first developed.

I will return later to the question of whether the Economic Council (henceforth, the ECC) is a "blocking-type" institution, but one can already point to the fact that a reading of the ECC's own *Annual Reviews*, of the various analyses that have been made of these Reviews and of other sundry papers on the Council[1] does not provide any help in answering such basic

---

1. E. Cape, *The Economic Council and Its Fifth Annual Review* (Canadian Trade Committee, 1969).

H. C. Eastman, *The Economic Council's Third Annual Review* (Canadian Trade Committee, 1967).

H. S. Gordon, *An Assessment of the Role of the Economic Council of Canada and an Appraisal of Its Second Annual Review* (Canadian Trade Committee, 1966).

G. Paquet, "The Economic Council as Phoenix," in Lloyd and McLeod (eds.), *Agenda 1970* (Toronto: University of Toronto Press, 1968).

D. W. Slater, "Wine or Vinegar? The Canadian Economy and the Economic Council of Canada," *The Canadian Banker* (Spring 1967).

D. C. Smith, "The Economic Council and Its Economic Plan," *The Canadian Banker* (Spring 1965).

J. H. Young, *The Economic Council's Fourth Annual Review: A Commentary* (Canadian Trade Committee, 1967).

questions as: "Why was the Council created? What are its functions? How has it performed in the past?" and "What are the tasks facing it?" This fact lies at the root of the complete lack of agreement among Council-watchers as to its nature.

As a preliminary to the task before us, it is important to recall that the ECC was created in 1963 after a period of five or six years characterized by high unemployment, a very slow rate of economic growth, inappropriate monetary policies aimed at combatting inflation, a plethora of inapposite commercial and domestic policies devised on the unverified (and wrong) assumption that the unemployment was structural and, but for a few notable exceptions, by a very low level of economic analysis and discourse—even on the part of many professional economists.[2] In addition, it must be recalled, this was a period when the economies of the Continental West European countries were growing at a very rapid rate and when mission upon mission of "experts" from the Canadian government and from various provincial capitals visited these European countries (except, of course, the German Federal Republic—the one with the highest rate of growth) to discover in the planning bodies that had been set up by the governments of these countries the secret of their economic success. These missions—and there were many—upon returning to Canada invariably declared that if Canada began to plan her economic activity as, for example, the French did, her problems would soon disappear. Round-tables, seminars, symposia, colloquia and public debates of all kinds were organized officially to clarify the issue, but also with a view to converting more people to the idea and also to force political parties and politicians to accept the idea of planning and to do something about it.

It is well to recognize that the concept of economic planning is not one that is easily defined. Whatever it was that the protagonists of planning had in mind in the early sixties, I will suggest a definition of planning which is easily integrated with the model developed below. The first thing to recognize about planning is that it is an activity of the public sector of the economy. This proposition does not deny that planning takes place in the private sector, as the advertising campaigns, the investment analyses, the tax planning (or, in less fancy language, the tax avoidance) and the host of other activities pursued there indicate. But economic planning proper is not an activity of private agents, because, unlike private planning, which typically involves a unit's own activities (the consumer plans his *own* purchases; the firm plans the level of its *own* inventories, the flow of its *own* sales, etc.), that kind of planning is always directed at someone else's behaviour and activities. This implies that economic planning always con-

---

2. For a discussion of these events, see the essay by Lawrence H. Officer and Lawrence B. Smith.

tains, at least when plans are initially implemented, some measure of coercion: it implies that some individuals are required to undertake actions
which they would not otherwise have undertaken and/or to adjust to constraints or circumstances different from the ones to which they would have
otherwise adjusted.

The degree of coercion imposed by a plan may be very small, but that is
more an indication of the extent of economic planning than a consideration
relevant to its definition or nature. This being so, assertions such as the
one that "bums are bums, because they do not plan" and the moral code
that is implied by such propositions are beside the point. It is true that we
face a difficult semantic problem, but we must recognize that planning one's
own activities and having these activities planned by someone else are
essentially and fundamentally two different things, though the word "planning" is customarily used to describe the two operations. In the first case,
planning does not involve coercion, since, by definition, decisions must be
assumed to be freely taken, while in the second, coercion is an integral
part of the activity.

Planning in the private sector, however, is not all voluntary and thus
coercion-free; in fact, one merely has to think of families, kindergartens,
corporations and universities to be reminded that when these institutions
engage in planning they also coerce individuals. There is therefore an additional factor that distinguishes private from public planning, and this is to
be found in the different channels, methods or instruments that coerced
individuals can use in their efforts to find redress from coercion. Just as the
methods open to a child who is coerced, that is, reprimanded, disciplined
or otherwise punished, differ from those that can be used by an employee
in a corporation or by a student in a university, the instruments that are
available to the citizen who is coerced by a plan or by parts of a plan are
also different. It is to an analysis of these various instruments that we must
eventually turn, but before we can do this we must examine briefly how
governing parties and governments work.

2. HOW GOVERNMENTS BEHAVE

The efficiency and hence the value of the instruments that coerced citizens
can utilize to improve their welfare is related to two factors: (1) the extent
to which governments respond to political pressure when they are subjected
to it, and (2) the costs of using the instruments at their disposal. I will
examine the responsiveness of governments first, and then, in the next section, I will analyze the characteristics of the costs of influencing politicians
and the political process.

To examine in a systematic fashion the extent to which governments are responsive to pressure, one must make some assumption about the objective that governing political parties and politicians pursue. In this paper I assume that the objective is re-election and that the rule of behaviour is the maximization of the probability of re-election. It is important to keep in mind, however, that the working of this rule is constrained by what we could call an "electoral production function" or, more simply, the electoral system. In the discussion that follows, I will examine the effect of two characteristics of the electoral system on the hypothesis that politicians and political parties maximize the probability of their re-election. These characteristics are: (1) the length of the election period or the length of time between one election-day and the next one, and (2) the set of decision-rules governing the number and choice of representatives.

To visualize the impact of a lengthy election period, begin by contrasting the above hypothesis with that of profit-maximization by competitive firms. Economic theory tells us that in this latter case the entrepreneur will equate marginal cost with the marginal price of output at every moment of time. Were he to lapse in this pursuit, he would begin to lose money and eventually he would go bankrupt. This is basically the meaning that one has to give to the concept of competition.

Governing political parties need not maximize the probability of their re-election on a continuous basis, since they run for office only at intervals of variable length, though seldom is that length less than two years, as is the case for members of the United States House of Representatives, but it can be as long as seven years, as for the President of France under the constitution of the Fifth Republic. Discrete maximization, as one could call the process to which this phenomenon leads, however, is not really maximization at all; but we can assume that at each point of time within the election period citizens use a positive rate of discount in calculating the value of each public policy to them and thus place a higher value on present than on future net benefits, while the governing party, which will run for office only in the future, places a higher value on the future than on the present reactions of citizens. Consequently, in the earlier part of the election period, the government uses a rate of time discount that is lower than that used by citizens, but as time goes on it discounts with higher and higher rates, so that toward the end of the period the rate it uses is equal to that used by the citizens. If we further assume that the distant past disturbs citizens less than the recent past, maximization of the probability of its re-election by the governing party is consistent with the implementation of policies that disregard the preferences of some or even of all citizens, at least for some time.

I do not intend to describe the various and multivarious possible decision-rules that exist, but only to illustrate the impact of this characteristic of the electoral system on the hypothesis that governing parties act in such a way as to maximize the probability of their re-election. Consider, therefore, the working of a simple majority, winner-take-all decision-rule applied to the selection of representatives in each electoral riding as well as to the choice of the party that will become the governing one. In such circumstances, it is possible *at the limit* for the governing party to remain in office by meeting the preferences of approximately only 25 percent of the electorate, if these citizens are distributed over electoral ridings in a "special" way. This follows from the fact that, with the postulated rule, only half (or marginally more) of the votes are required for each representative to be re-elected and only half the total number of representatives elected are required to form a government and to control the apparatus of the state. The above conclusion depends, as I have already intimated, on two things: (1) that the electoral ridings be of equal size (if they are not, the preferences of fewer citizens, as a rule, need be represented), and (2) that no votes be "wasted" in the riding, if a member of the governing party is not elected.

Given a set of decision-rules like the above, there can be little doubt that the governing party is able to implement many policies that do not receive the support of the bulk of the electorate. Alternatively, it becomes profitable for some citizens to organize themselves into small groups and to signal their preferences to the governing party, since that party has some degrees of freedom in meeting these preferences even if they do not receive the support of the entire electorate.

It should be at least intuitively clear now that the activities and behaviour of a party seeking re-election will be different if the election period is two years than if it is four or five years and if the preferences of half instead of a quarter of the electorate have to be taken into account. But in addition to affecting the basic behavioural hypothesis, the electoral system also allows the governing party some freedom in dealing with its bureaucrats. To put it simply, the governing party can allow its bureaucrats to engage in activities which are at variance with the preferences of citizens and even with the objectives of the politicians themselves, if the costs of managing and controlling the bureaucrats are too "large."[3]

3. HOW CITIZENS BEHAVE

Governing parties do not know who are the citizens coerced by policies such as the implementation of an economic plan. It is only as citizens engage in political action, that is, begin to use what I have called "political instruments," that this is revealed to the government. It will be sufficient for

---

3. In my forthcoming book *Decision-Making and Resource Allocation in the Public Sector*, I elaborate at length on the relationships between politicians and bureaucrats, but the above will be sufficient for the purposes of this paper.

the present discussion if I restrict myself to a list of these instruments without describing and analyzing each one of them.[4] They are: (a) participating in efforts to influence the activities of lobbies and large pressure groups, (b) engaging in actions to influence politicians directly, (c) joining in social movements, (d) regulating one's own private economic behaviour, (e) organizing the private provision of public and non-private goods, (f) moving from one jurisdiction to another, and (g) voting. One can engage in these activities only at a cost, which is measured in energy, time and/or money.

These costs, which are mostly organization, communication and information costs, will typically vary between instruments—the costs of operating a pressure group are different from those of participating in a social movement or of moving out of a jurisdiction—and also between citizens and groups of citizens if for no other reason than that the number of citizens who will be coerced in a like fashion by the implementation of a policy will be different from public policy to public policy and because organization costs are closely related to the size of groups. To put it differently, the costs of signalling their preferences to the government will vary between citizens, and as a consequence some of them will be able to influence the governing party, while others will not.

It is well to note that this state of things arises not because some individuals are dishonest, bad or otherwise undesirable, but exclusively from the operation of certain features of the electoral system and from the level and pattern of organization and communication costs. Whose preferences is the governing party going to satisfy? To answer this question, we must distinguish between three cases. The first arises when organization costs are at such a level that the number of citizens signalling their preferences to the government is equal to the number required for the government to remain in office. In this case the governing party will do everything in its power to meet the wishes and preferences of those citizens and of those only. The second case arises when the number of citizens effectively representing their desires exceeds the number required for re-election. In this second case the governing party has some freedom and can choose to satisfy only those preferences which are consistent with other sub-objectives, the main one being the maintenance of good relations with, and the management of, the bureaucracy. The third case arises when the cost of using the instruments is so high that the number who can reveal their wishes to the governing party falls short of the number required for re-election. The governing party in this situation will try by all kinds of means to learn about the wishes of the electorate, but basically it will be governing blindly and the task of retaining control of the apparatus of the state will be a difficult and almost impossible one.

---

4. I do this in detail in the above-mentioned forthcoming publication.

4. THE CASE OF THE ECONOMIC COUNCIL OF CANADA

As indicated in section 1, during the first years of the sixties, more and more Canadians began to focus on economic planning as a cure for Canada's economic problems. The idea gained ground with some speed, so much so that a number of persons found it profitable to become "professional" protagonists of planning. The seminars, round-tables and colloquia that were brought together to discuss the issue usually turned out to be meetings advocating the implementation of planning. Politicians of a class and variety that would not usually have been heard using the word, except to condemn it, were beginning to learn to live with it. Those who were opposed to planning were publicly defined to be opposed to progress, to be blind to its positive effects (as these could be observed in France, for example), and to be nothing but "nineteenth-century liberals" and hence to belong to a class of defunct moralists and philosophers.

In terms of the argument of the previous sections, the unemployment, the slow rate of economic growth accompanied by a forced re-adjustment in expectations and the steady flow of incompetent public policies were sufficient to induce new and old political and social leaders to meet the cost of engaging in political actions and thus to create a forum, and later a movement, that would impel others to meet similar costs. These efforts were eventually successful, because a sufficiently large number of individuals came to think that the solution to the country's problems could indeed be found in planning.

Many individuals, however, remained opposed to planning, whether of the French "indicative" variety or of any other variety. Such individuals were those who would have been coerced by planning; and there were those who were not willing to see private decisions curbed or modified to fit in an aggregate plan. In fact, it must be recognized that anyone who imagined himself to be a prospective victim of planning had reason to fear, if only because of the uncertainty that resulted from the lack of understanding and the lack of rigorous analysis surrounding the discussion of the issues.

Given their expectation of being coerced, the opponents of planning could follow one of two strategies: (1) oppose the introduction of any form of planning, or (2) favour the creation of an institution that would give the appearance of being a planning body, but which would be so structured that it would not be capable of any planning whatsoever. It is only necessary to list the two alternatives to recognize that the second is, from the opponents' point of view, much superior to the first. Indeed, the costs of the second are "low," since it involves only obtaining the acquiescence of the relevant politicians—usually a fairly low-cost venture, while the costs of the first must be "high," involving, as it does, the organization of competition with the groups of citizens who support planning.

The costs of the second strategy—that of promoting the creation of a "blocking" institution—were "lower" for a second reason. Since the proponents of economic planning did not have a clear idea of what they wanted in the way of a planning body, nor of what they wanted that body to do in specific terms, it was easy to satisfy their demands by suggesting the creation of any institution which had the appearance of being capable of doing what they wanted.

Given these circumstances, the most rational thing that the governing party could do was to propose the creation of an institution which would receive the general support of those who favoured economic planning as well as of those who opposed it. Thus was created the Economic Council of Canada. Through it, the governing party was able to silence the growing movement that was asking for a plan and at the same time not give offence to those opposing it, and thus maximize the probability of its re-election. There were, of course, some groups of citizens who were not satisfied with the ECC, citizens who knew what planning was and therefore were not duped by what had happened; but the electoral decision-rules in force, as well as the large number of citizens who had been able to reveal their preference to the governing party, made it easy for the latter to disregard those who were still unsatisfied. Furthermore, with the creation of a body which could be all things to all men, these citizens were not likely to attract much attention and could be left to grumble in isolation.

So much for this aspect of the question. But one may ask: "On what evidence is it possible to say that the ECC is a 'blocking' institution and not the real thing?" There is no direct evidence; but without a hypothesis such as the one suggested here, it is difficult to rationalize the awkward place that the ECC occupies in the structure of the Canadian government; it is difficult to understand the relatively minor role that the Chairman of the ECC plays in the formulation of economic policy in Canada compared to that of the other "senior" policy advisers; it is difficult to rationalize the nature and composition of the "Board," made up of representatives from all and sundry interest and pressure groups in Canada, representatives who must agree on the policy statements of the Council before they are made public and, being responsible to their constituents and not to economic principles, cannot but water-down all meaningful recommendations; it is also difficult to comprehend the relatively minor impact that the "basic" research undertaken by the Council or by scholars commissioned by the Council has on its recommendations and on its *Annual Reviews*; and, finally, it is difficult, if not impossible, to fathom why the ECC seldom, if ever, touches upon such basic Canadian policies as those related to the tariff and to business, and especially labour, monopolies.

It was an attempt to understand these various characteristics of the ECC, observed and discussed by a score of commentators, that has led me to the formulation of the above model. I have not drawn any normative conclusion from the analysis, nor will I, since this is a most difficult task; but the interested reader should try to find an answer to the question: "Was the creation of the ECC, as it stands, a good or a bad thing?"

II
International Aspects

The openness of the Canadian economy, insofar as it affects the operation of stabilization policy, has been discussed in the Officer-Smith essay in Part I. In Part II we are concerned with the fundamental aspects of Canada's place in the world economy. Specifically, we examine the economic relationships between Canada and other countries (particularly the United States) as these relationships manifest themselves in movements over Canada's borders—movements of capital, goods, and people.

A. E. Safarian's essay, "Benefits and Costs of Foreign Investment," surveys the entire range of issues associated with foreign investment in Canada. Safarian is concerned primarily with investment which results in foreign ownership or control of the Canadian economy, and over one-third of Canadian industry is owned or controlled by non-residents. The principal benefits of direct investment are seen as Canadian access to foreign capital, skills, and techniques, as well as the entrepreneurial (risk-taking) behaviour exhibited by foreign management. Safarian warns that unrestricted foreign investment does not necessarily provide *maximum* economic gain to Canada. Care must be taken to see that such investment results in an industry becoming more rather than less efficient and that the profits accruing to foreigners are taxed optimally. Furthermore, international investment gives rise to potential international conflicts, which could entail political costs to the recipient country. Many of these issues were studied by the Task Force on the Structure of Canadian Industry, of which Safarian was a member, and his essay closes with a summary of the recommendations of the Task Force.

Ronald J. Wonnacott's essay on "Tariff

Policy" reviews the various ways in which Canada can liberalize restrictions on the international movement of goods. Wonnacott strongly advocates freer trade as beneficial to Canada. He sees reductions of tariffs under the Kennedy Round as leading hopefully to further liberalization of international trade, though not necessarily by means of the same (multilateral-negotiation) process. In particular, Wonnacott argues that Canada has little to fear, and indeed much to gain, from free-trade competition with the United States. He recommends that Canada should endeavour to liberalize trade not only by supporting further "Kennedy Rounds" but also by entering into free-trade-area negotiations with the U.S. and other countries.

Lawrence H. Officer's essay on "Immigration and Emigration" sketches the history of migration into and out of Canada, and evaluates the immigration policy of the Canadian government. Officer criticizes traditional Canadian policy on both economic and humanitarian grounds, but stresses that the current policy marks a substantial improvement on both counts. He examines the role of the United States in attracting people from Canada. Throughout Canada's history, emigration to the U.S. has been a strong counterpoise to immigration from other countries, so that *net* immigration has always been only a fraction of gross immigration. However, regarding the much-publicized "brain drain" from Canada, Officer notes that the available evidence points to the fact that, on the contrary, international migration results in a substantial net "brain *gain*" for Canada.

benefits and costs of foreign investment

A. E. Safarian
University of Toronto

Few issues of Canadian economic policy in the past fifteen years can have aroused as much debate, and as little resolution, as those surrounding foreign investment in Canada. This uncertainty reflects not only the complexity of the topic, but the fact that the issues go beyond economics and eventually become part of the larger question of Canada's general involvement with the United States. The uncertainty also reflects the still limited number of systematic studies of foreign ownership of Canadian industry.

This essay is devoted largely to an analysis of the economic effects of foreign investment, particularly foreign business investment, in Canada. The restriction to economic effects is dictated not only by the subject matter of this volume, but also by the limited amount of research on the subject by other social scientists. Many of the non-economic effects are so conjectural, given the present state of research and understanding, that almost anything can be said on one side or the other—indeed, has been said—without fear of serious contradiction. The major exception is the important set of questions raised by extra-territorial extension of law through subsidiary firms, a subject which will be included here. Our approach will be, first, to consider macro benefits and costs, particularly as they relate to economic growth and the balance of payments. We must then disaggregate at least to the level of industry, in order to consider the dissemination of these effects through the efficient development of firms. After considering extra-territoriality, we shall briefly review Canadian policy to date regarding foreign ownership, and the rationale for various approaches to future policy.

A LOOK AT THE DATA ON FOREIGN INVESTMENT

A brief look at the data, and what they mean, is in order before considering the consequences. At the end of 1965 the book value of long-term investments in Canada owned by non-residents was $29.5 billion.[1] About $12.4 billion of this was portfolio investments, that is, holdings of bonds and stocks which do not carry with them foreign control (as defined below) of the Canadian enterprises involved. Little concern is expressed about such portfolio investments now, although in the thirties, when incomes and prices were falling, the heavy burden of fixed-interest debt (often payable in the highest of two or three currencies at the option of the lender) was the main source of concern regarding foreign investment.

More recently, concern has concentrated on foreign "direct" investment in Canada, which accounts for the remaining $17.2 billion. This represents the book value of stocks, bonds and other assets owned by non-residents in enterprises where the voting stock is controlled by non-residents. About 80 percent of the total represents investments by residents of the United States. Total direct investment was 60 percent of all foreign long-term investment in Canada in 1965, compared with 40 percent in 1945. The statistical concept of control used here, based on the undoubted legal powers of holders of voting shares, must not be confused with the question of the extent and manner in which the foreign shareholder exercises it. We know very little about the latter, except that there is a wide range of situations from a high degree of centralization to virtually complete autonomy, and that the outcome is determined by many other factors than the proportion of voting shares held.[2] Needless to say, the extent to which the owners and officers of the foreign parent and its Canadian subsidiary are free to decide on the use and disposition of their property is circumscribed also by private circumstance and public law. These circumscriptions vary in effect but are clearly important, ranging all the way from law and governmental influence to the degree of competition in the markets in which the agents of production are secured and those in which the products are sold.

We should also note that the statistical concept of direct investment itself covers four broad situations on stock ownership. This can be clarified by using estimates for the year 1960 and for all direct investment firms in Canada with assets of $25 million or more. These showed that 10 percent

---

1. A preliminary estimate suggests this figure was approaching $34 billion by the end of 1967. See Dominion Bureau of Statistics, *Quarterly Estimates of the Canadian Balance of International Payments*, Third Quarter 1968 (Ottawa: Queen's Printer, 1968), p. 16.
2. See Irving Brecher and S. S. Reisman, *Canada—United States Economic Relations*, Royal Commission on Canada's Economic Prospects (Ottawa: Queen's Printer, 1957), pp. 132-137; and A. E. Safarian, *Foreign Ownership of Canadian Industry* (Toronto: McGraw-Hill Company of Canada Ltd., 1966), ch. 3.

of the capital represented branch plants which are not separately incorporated under Canadian federal or provincial Companies Acts. Among the group incorporated in Canada, 36 percent represented subsidiaries whose stock was wholly owned by a foreign concern, and 40 percent in which the foreign concern does not hold all of the subsidiary's voting stock but generally has at least 50 percent of it. The remaining 13 percent of the capital of these larger firms reflects cases where there is no foreign parent with effective voting control of the Canadian firm, but at least 50 percent of the latter's stock is held by residents of a foreign country and they are believed to have control.

How much of Canada's *over-all* capital formation is financed by non-residents? Two approaches can be taken to this question. The first measures the extent to which Canada has drawn, on balance, on the resources of other countries for the savings used for all kinds of physical investment in Canada. This measure suggests foreigners financed 14 percent of net capital formation in the period 1950-1953, about 33 percent in 1954-1961, and 19 percent in 1962-1965. In 1926-1930 the comparable figure was about 25 percent. Not all of these savings were used, however, for investment in Canada. The second measure takes this into account and looks only at the extent to which non-residents directly financed net capital formation of all kinds in Canada. This figure rose from 29 percent in 1950-1953 to between 43 and 47 percent in succeeding four-year intervals to 1965. It was about 50 percent in 1926-1930.[3]

Our interest here, however, is in the more specific question of foreign ownership of Canadian assets and its consequences. Unfortunately, there is no comprehensive estimate of Canadian wealth and its ownership. We have no estimate for agriculture, which appears to be very largely resident-owned; nor of finance, which has always been largely resident-owned in some sectors, such as banks, but with significant foreign ownership in others, such as insurance; nor in many other service sectors or personal capital, much of which is, by its nature, resident-owned. We do have statistics for two major sectors. Social capital, since it is public, cannot be owned by non-residents, but they have supplied part of the funds to finance it. At the end of 1964, 5 percent of Government of Canada net long-term debt was held by non-residents (a sharp drop from earlier periods), as was 26 percent of each of provincial, municipal and railway debt. The other major sector is commodities (apart from agriculture) and utilities. The data for these are reproduced in Table 1. The distinction between foreign owner-

3. See A. E. Safarian and E. B. Carty, "Foreign Financing of Canadian Investment in the Post-War Period," *Proceedings of the Business and Economic Statistics Section* (Washington: American Statistical Association, 1954), pp. 72-79; and Dominion Bureau of Statistics, *The Canadian Balance of International Payments 1963, 1964 and 1965* (Ottawa: Queen's Printer), p. 75.

Table 1.

NON-RESIDENT OWNERSHIP AND CONTROL AS A PERCENTAGE OF CAPITAL INVESTED IN SELECTED CANADIAN INDUSTRIES, SELECTED YEAR-ENDS 1926-1963

Industry[1]	Non-resident ownership[2]					Non-resident control[2]				
	1926	1948	1957	1960	1963	1926	1948	1957	1960	1963
Percentage of total capital owned or controlled by all non-residents:										
Manufacturing	38	42	50	52	54	35	43	56	59	60
Petroleum and natural gas	—	—	63	62	64	—	—	76	73	74
Mining and smelting	37	39	56	60	62	38	40	61	61	59
Railways	55	45	30	26	23	3	3	2	2	2
Other utilities	32	20	14	14	13	20	24	5	5	4
Total of above industries	37	32	34	34	35	17	25	32	33	34
Percentage of total capital owned or controlled by United States residents:										
Manufacturing	30	35	39	41	44	30	39	43	44	46
Petroleum and natural gas	—	—	57	53	54	—	—	70	64	62
Mining and smelting	28	32	46	52	54	32	37	52	53	52
Railways	15	21	11	9	9	3	3	2	2	2
Other utilities	23	16	11	12	12	20	24	4	4	4
Total of above industries	19	23	26	27	28	15	22	27	26	27

Source: Dominion Bureau of Statistics, **The Canadian Balance of International Payments 1963, 1964 and 1965** (Ottawa: Queen's Printer), p. 127.

(1) A number of changes in coverage, concepts, and construction have occurred over the years. Components of the petroleum and natural-gas industry were included in other industrial groups until 1954. The total for all industries includes merchandising and (after 1945) construction; non-resident ownership and control of these two industries together was 9 percent and 11 percent, respectively, in 1961.

(2) The foreign-ownership ratios measure equity and debt capital owned by non-residents as a percentage of total capital employed in the industries. The foreign control ratios measure equity and debt capital invested by residents as well as non-residents in those companies whose voting stock is controlled by non-residents, all of which is taken as a percentage of the total capital employed in the industries. The ownership ratio for a particular industry will exceed the control ratio by the extent to which non-residents invest in companies they do not control, but will fall short of it by the extent to which residents invest in companies which non-residents control.

ship and foreign control should be kept in mind, as explained there, as should the distinction between ownership by all non-residents and by those of the United States only.

It will be noted that a substantial degree of foreign ownership already existed in 1926, the earliest year for which official estimates are available. Unofficial estimates indiciate significant foreign ownership of the industrial sectors shown, much earlier than this.[4] There has been a long-term increase in foreign-ownership and control ratios in manufacturing, petroleum and gas, and mining and smelting.[5] The ratios have fallen in railways and utilities. These changes are generally reflected also in the United States ownership and control ratios, which dominate those for all non-residents. It is well to add that, in broad industry groups where foreign ownership is high, there is considerable variation when one disaggregates. In manufacturing, for example, the extreme cases are automobiles and parts, and rubber, where foreign ownership is about 90 percent and control close to 100 percent. The ratios are much lower in industries such as pulp and paper and agricultural machinery, which are roughly evenly divided between resident and non-resident ownership and control, and lower still in primary iron and steel and beverages, for example, which are mainly resident-owned and controlled.

OVER-ALL ECONOMIC CONSEQUENCES[6]

At full employment the rate of growth of domestic production is determined by the increase in the supplies of the agents of production and by increased productivity. Increases in productivity depend, in turn, on improvements in the quality of the agents of production, greater efficiency in their use, and economies of scale. Foreign investment contributes to all these sources of economic growth by bringing capital, technology, access to markets, and entrepreneurship.

The contribution of foreign investment to economic growth can be measured by determining the extent to which foreign capital permitted an

---

4. See Herbert Marshall et al., *Canadian American Industry* (New Haven: Yale University Press, 1936), pp. 1-2 especially.
5. Comparable data are not available for petroleum and gas over the whole period. Between 1945 and 1955 the resident ownership of petroleum alone fell from 59 to 36 percent, and control from 43 to 20 percent. In this period the book value of investment in the industry rose nine times. See Dominion Bureau of Statistics, *The Canadian Balance of International Payments*, 1956, pp. 33-4.
6. The benefits and costs of foreign investments are analyzed in G. D. A. MacDougall, "The Benefits and Costs of Private Foreign Investment from Abroad," *Economic Record* (Melbourne, March 1960); Marvin Frankel, "Home Versus Foreign Investment: A Case Against Capital Export," *Kyklos* 18, 1965, pp. 411-432; and Donald T. Brash, *American Investment in Australian Industry* (Canberra, Australian National University Press), ch. 11. See also Privy Council Office, *Foreign Ownership and the Structure of Canadian Industry* (Ottawa: Queen's Printer), especially parts 1 and 2.

increase in the stock of Canadian capital that would not otherwise have taken place. In addition, we must take account of the technical change which accompanies capital investment and raises the productivity of the agents of production. Against these benefits to Canadian economic growth must be set the interest, dividends and business-service payments of various kinds which foreign owners earn in Canada. The measurement of net economic benefit at this aggregative level is a difficult technical exercise involving a number of assumptions. Such an estimate has been made for the period 1950-1956. It suggests that net foreign investment accounted for from 8 percent to 20 percent of the growth in *per capita* real income in that period, depending on the assumptions made. If it is assumed that a significant part of technical progress is implemented by additions to capital stock, as seems reasonable, then the most likely estimate is well above the minimum figure.[7]

No estimate exists for the period since 1956. Such an estimate would be complicated by the excess capacity prevailing from 1958 to about 1963, and the fact that Canada moved from a fluctuating exchange rate to a fixed rate during this period. Foreign direct investment was still clearly beneficial in economic terms, since much of the technical and risk-taking capacity involved probably could not have been matched internally. The same cannot be said for the heavy inflows of portfolio capital, given significant unemployment. The problem, however, lay not with portfolio inflows but with the failure to maintain full employment, and particularly with the inappropriate monetary-fiscal policies, which led to more borrowing abroad (and exchange-rate appreciation) than was necessary or desirable in that period.

To understand the full impact of foreign direct investment, however, one must disaggregate to the level of the industry and the firm. If a parent firm abroad establishes a new subsidiary in Canada, the effect is to increase the amount of capital working with the existing supply of labour and hence the wage rate, or to create new employment opportunities, or both. The consumer may benefit directly through lower prices or better quality, provided competition exists. Firms which are competitive with the new firms will find their profits reduced, or less than they might have been, given higher wage rates or lower selling prices or a reduced market share. These competing firms, of course, may themselves be foreign-owned.[8] A further impor-

7. Rudolph G. Penner, "The Benefits of Foreign Investment in Canada 1950-1956," *Canadian Journal of Economics and Political Science*, May 1966. This estimate is based on *net* capital inflow, after deducting Canadian investment abroad. The contribution of gross capital inflows would be larger. The estimate also includes both portfolio and direct investment.

8. Under dynamic conditions it is possible for the profits of competing firms to rise. The new entrant, for example, may introduce selling techniques which increase demand, or introduce cost-reducing innovations, and in each case be unable to restrict the benefits to itself. Or the industry may be a new one, and will attract domestic or other foreign entrants.

tant benefit arises from taxes levied on the profits of the firm. These taxes reduce the burden on other residents, except to the extent they are used to attract and subsidize foreign capital.

If the entry to Canada occurs by way of the takeover of an existing resident-owned firm, rather than the establishment of a new one, the initial effects do not differ assuming the recipients of the funds use the proceeds for real investment in Canada. The funds may be invested in Canadian securities, in which case they lower yields and help create other real investment.

It might be added that the growth of foreign-owned assets since 1945 has occurred largely while the assets were owned by foreigners. Takeovers as such have accounted for a relatively small part of the increase in such assets. In manufacturing, takeovers accounted for about an eighth of the increase in the value of foreign-owned firms from 1945 to 1961. The rest of the increase was due to growth of firms which were already owned abroad prior to 1945, growth after the firms had been purchased by non-residents, and the establishment and growth of new foreign-owned firms.[9]

These comments suggest that the benefits from foreign investment are similar to those from domestic investment. The question which remains to be answered, however, is whether the techniques which accompany such investment are similar. Unlike foreign portfolio investment, direct investment usually brings access to the parent's managerial and technical skills, research, patents and trademarks, and production and distribution techniques. For primary-resource products, which must often be exported in volume for efficient development, it may bring a guaranteed market in the parent. If a better technology is introduced to Canada, the important point in terms of net benefits to Canada is whether it or its results get outside the firm and have more general effects on real private incomes or tax revenue, as noted earlier, or, are simply reflected mainly in profits accruing to the firm.

Apart from access to capital and techniques, foreign direct investment brings a greater capacity to undertake certain kinds of risks compared with domestic firms. The result is that foreigners may undertake projects, at given rates of interest, which do not appeal to Canadian investors or do not appeal to them as soon. The foreign investor may possess a different body of knowledge and techniques from the Canadian investor when he examines investment opportunities. This can be of great benefit to Canada. For example, in a number of cases the long-term guarantee of the market in (or by) the foreign parent has been the critical reason for developing the resource in Canada, often far more important than the supply of capital

---

9. Grant L. Reuber, "Benefits and Costs of Foreign Investment in Canada," Canadian-American Seminar (Windsor, December 1968), pp. 4-5, mimeo. See also Grant L. Reuber and Frank Roseman, *The Take-Over of Canadian Firms, 1945-61* (Ottawa: Queen's Printer, 1969).

or technology. In many cases where foreign-owned firms now predominate they established the industry in Canada and developed the market, or were willing and able to wait for eventual returns. There are obvious advantages to having some firms with sufficiently long planning horizons to exploit longer-run investment opportunities. There can also be disadvantages. Such firms may take a longer-run attitude at times to exploiting resources after using them up, particularly since they have alternatives abroad, and it may take longer to correct mistakes of over-investment or inefficient investment given their staying power.

This difference in risk-taking capacity may reflect such factors as size and the greater degree of integration and of diversification in multi-national firms, readier access to capital within the global firm and (given its size) outside it as well, and the pooling of many specialized managerial-technical skills for use by the affiliates. The difference in risk-taking capacity may reflect also a broader spectrum of economic, sociological and psychological factors which determine the extent and quality of entrepreneurship. We do not know much about this, but some questions might be raised. Social mobility may have been less in Canada than in the United States, for example, with entrepreneurs (and perhaps other leadership groups) drawn from a more limited and more homogeneous segment of the population until recently.[10] The difference in the lengths of formal education of owners and managers in Canada and the United States is greater than that for almost all other major categories of the labour force.[11] Market horizons may have been limited by the tariff and private restrictions on trade. Canada has developed rather slowly the organizations which mobilize entrepreneurial capital, such as merchant banks, perhaps partly because for a century the banks were limited by law to a commercial-banking activity with emphasis on the security of loans and deposits. Foreign-owned firms have clearly supplied many managerial jobs and management training, both directly and indirectly, and to that extent have compensated for the limitations of the Canadian business environment. This is not all gain, however, for the inability to make some big decisions on one's own can impede the learning process.

It should be clear from the above that the nature and extent of the gain from any given direct investment depends crucially on two points. Firstly, it depends on the extent to which competition in the system diffuses the impact of new products and processes, increasing productivity or lowering prices. It depends, in brief, on whether the new entrant shakes up the exist-

10. There is no direct study of this, but the impression is left by comparing John Porter, *The Vertical Mosaic* (Toronto: University of Toronto Press, 1965), especially chs. 7-9, with studies of United States economic élites.
11. Economic Council of Canada, *Second Annual Review* (Ottawa: Queen's Printer, 1965), p. 62.

ing (relatively inefficient) pattern of production and distribution, or simply adapts to the existing pattern in order to avoid disturbing the market or perhaps monopolizes it further. The outcome will depend in significant part on government attitudes to the industrial policies which affect this outcome. Secondly, the extent of gain depends on the extent to which Canadian governments succeed in taxing profits accruing to foreigners, and doing so at an optimal rate. Tax policy in this, as in other respects, is a difficult exercise involving the need to balance a variety of objectives. It also includes the special need to ensure there is not overpricing on purchases from foreign affiliates and underpricing on sales, such as to reduce the tax yield due to the Canadian authorities.

THE BALANCE-OF-PAYMENTS EFFECTS

A continuing inflow of long-term capital leads to adjustments in the balance of payments which move the international current (goods-and-services) account to a deficit. This occurs because of the price and income effects accompanying the capital inflow, effects which lead to increases in imports relative to changes in exports. The current deficit is not a sign of weakness as such, but rather the real equivalent of the monetary capital flow. The historical evidence suggests that this mechanism of adjustment works fairly smoothly in Canada.

Our concern here is with two other questions. First, what is the *long-run* effect on the balance of payments of a continuing capital inflow? Second, what is the effect of such an inflow on the problem of maintaining internal stability?

The balance-of-payments effects of direct investment are more complex, and likely to continue longer, than those of foreign portfolio investment through bonds and debentures. Bond financing involves fixed interest payments, and bonds automatically come up for repatriation or refinancing at given points of time. Direct investment involves dividend and business-service payments (and earnings retained in Canada but accruing to the parent) which are indeterminate, depending on the degree of success of the firm. These liabilities rise to the extent the firm is successful, while the actual payments abroad are flexible depending on the needs of the parent and subsidiary, and such considerations as exchange-rate or taxation effects. While firms can be repatriated by acceptable bids, and often are, there is no fixed time or price, and many are so closely integrated with the parent that repurchase would be difficult.

The essential point in both cases is that the domestic and foreign-owned sectors together must generate, over time, a sufficient amount of foreign exchange to finance the income paid out and any repatriation of foreign investment. No systematic study exists for Canada of the effects of direct

investment itself on this process over time. We do know the actual contribution to the balance of payments by the larger foreign-owned firms in
Canada (with assets of $5 million or more) for 1964 and 1965. There
was a substantial deficit in the foreign trade of these foreign-owned firms in
secondary manufacturing industry, which was at least offset by a substantial
surplus by these firms in primary products and primary manufacturing.
These firms together had a substantial deficit in their trade with the United
States on the one hand and with all foreign affiliates on the other, but this
was at least offset by trade with other countries and non-affiliates abroad.
There was a net deficit on interest, dividend and business-services account,
so that their direct effect on the current account of the balance of payments was negative. Since they were net capital importers, their direct effect
on Canada's foreign exchange position in those years was probably close to
zero.[12] These data do not tell us what the indirect effects were on the
balance of payments, nor do they give us what we really need—a stage-by-
stage analysis of long-term effects.

Another way to look at this is to consider the actual burden of debt
acquired by Canada through the payments of income abroad. Interest and
dividends paid abroad by all firms and governments in Canada were $312
million in 1946. In 1968 they were $1,310 million, leaving a net deficit of
$971 million on this item after taking account of receipts of interest and
dividends. These absolute figures by themselves are not too meaningful
here, of course; for foreign investment has increased the Canadian capacity
to produce, to export, and to service debt. As a percentage of gross national
product, such payments have declined from 2.9 percent in the late nineteen-
twenties and 6.4 percent in the depressed 'thirties to 1.9 percent in the
period 1957-1967. As a percentage of sales of goods and services abroad,
they have fallen from 16 percent in the late 'twenties and 25 percent in the
'thirties to 9 percent in 1957-1967. These payments, it should be noted, are
for both direct and portfolio investment. The latest data for direct investment alone are for 1964, when $562 million was paid by such firms out of
total interest and dividends paid abroad of $1,010 million. In that year,
direct investment companies also reinvested $455 million of their profits in
Canada—a figure which does not show as payments abroad in the balance
of payments but does raise our foreign debt. In the first half of the 'sixties
such firms have retained from 43 percent to 52 percent of their income in
Canada after payment of income tax.[13] Unfortunately, we do not have a
complete historic or current measure of payments abroad by such firms for

---

12. Dominion Bureau of Statistics and Department of Trade and Commerce, *Foreign-
Owned Subsidiaries in Canada.*
13. Dominion Bureau of Statistics, *The Canadian Balance of International Payments:
A Compendium of Statistics from 1946-1965,* pp. 174-75.

engineering services, royalties, research, management fees, advertising and other business services. The larger foreign-owned firms whose balance-of-payments effects were described above paid $251 million for such services in 1965, with $153 million of this going to parent concerns. This figure probably understates the real value of such services, with the parent being reimbursed instead by greater profits and dividends than would be the case if full charges were made to the subsidiary.

The second point mentioned above is the effects on economic stability. An analogy can be made here to the case of foreign trade. Countries engage in foreign trade because specialization and exchange increases efficiency and *per capita* income. One qualification is that the markets for exports and the sources of imports must not be so frequently or substantially disrupted as to cancel these gains. Similarly, instability in the flow of capital can impose costs on a country which is developing with its aid. Short-term instability can usually be handled by the conventional instruments of monetary and exchange-rate policy or by more selective policies, but chronic instability or a fundamental change in direction would require more substantial changes in factor incomes, prices, and allocation.

The 'sixties raised some special problems in this respect, given the attempt by the United States to deal with her balance-of-payments problem by regulating the outflow of capital. The first attempt was by a tax on foreign borrowing in the United States beginning in 1963. Canada quickly secured an exemption from this tax so far as new issues were concerned. At the same time Canada agreed to a limit on her foreign-exchange reserves, so as to assure the United States authorities that this exemption would not be used to increase Canadian reserves at the expense of the United States balance of payments. Since the exchange rate had been fixed in 1962, Canada now found herself with both a fixed rate and an upper limit on reserves. This might not have been a problem for several years when reserves were below the ceiling, but at other times it may have increased the constraints on monetary policy. The specific limit on reserves was maintained until 1969, although Canada is expected still to avoid permanent and substantial increases in her reserves.

The United States government also attempted to place a ceiling on the combined new outflow of direct-investment capital plus the retention of earnings abroad, and also directed parent companies to deal with subsidiaries in other transactions in ways which would improve the balance of payments of the United States. These "guidelines" were at first voluntary and Canada was excluded. Canada was later included, in spite of protests about their effects on the Canadian economy. On January 1, 1968 a mandatory guideline was issued. An important factor in the strong pressure on the Canadian dollar early in 1968 was the expectation by direct investment companies, among others, that the mandatory guideline would have serious adverse effects on Canada's balance of payments.[14] In March the United States government agreed to a total exemption for Canada from all balance-of-payments guidelines. In return, Canada agreed to surveillance of exports of capital from Canada to ensure she was not used as a "pass-through" for funds from the United States destined overseas. No doubt this exemption was a recognition of the significant extent to which Canada depends on the capital market of the United States, combined with a realization that Canada could not sustain a large current deficit with the United States (given the smaller surplus overseas) without access to foreign capital.

THE PERFORMANCE OF FOREIGN-OWNED FIRMS

Does the fact that the firm is owned by foreigners reduce or increase the contributions it makes to the Canadian economy in other ways than those noted earlier? There has been a persistent criticism in Canada that decisions about Canadian-based facilities, made in the context of the global firm, may lead to something less than the maximum efficient development of Canadian resources. Charges that subsidiaries are biased against exports and against research, and for imports, because of their international affiliations, are among the types of criticisms frequently made.

Two *a priori* reasons are suggested to support this view. First, it is suggested that the centralization of some decisions in head office can work against Canadian interests because of poor information about or lack of interest in the Canadian operation. The other possibility is that even informed decisions at head office may conflict with Canadian interests, since a decision which is profitable globally may require sacrifices by the subsidiary. This second point raises the objection that an independent firm would be unlikely to make a different (i.e., less profitable) decision, if one can assume its information and costs are the same. The problem is complicated, however, by such factors as the need to take into account management and other pressures on behalf of competing facilities in the parent and its other affiliates, and maximization within different time horizons.

Specific examples can be quoted one way or the other on any of these issues, given the variety of Canadian industrial situations. Nor do data on the foreign-owned sector as a whole help much, since one cannot deduce from these whether the particular outcome associated with foreign ownership is due to it or to some other variable. Thus in considering exports and several other questions one should differentiate primary products from manufactures, and indeed go much further in distinguishing types of industries which, by their nature, give different results. Much foreign investment is in primary products or primary manufactures. The motive here is

---

14. For a discussion of this exchange crisis, see the talk by the Governor of the Bank of Canada, Mr. Louis Rasminsky, "Monetary Policy and the Defence of the Canadian Dollar," Victoria, October 17, 1968.

often to secure a source of supply in Canada, hence exports are substantial. In many other cases the major or sole motive is to serve the domestic market, and only future developments will determine what export markets (if any) are developed.

The more careful empirical studies which have been made suggest that, in the general or typical case, when like is taken with like to the extent possible, the economic performance of foreign-owned firms is as good (or bad) as that of their resident-owned counterparts.[15] This is the case for exports, where the performance of foreign-owned firms is similiar to that of resident-owned whether one considers all such firms, only the larger ones, or only those in manufacturing. The Canadian research performance of foreign-owned firms is at least as good as that of resident-owned firms, whether considered as amounts expended (percent of sales) or degree of sophistication. The profitability of such firms is also very similar in over-all terms to resident-owned firms.[16] Detailed industrial comparisons suggest that differences in productivity between Canada and the United States are not correlated with the degree of foreign ownership of the Canadian industries involved. Again, while both positive and negative effects appear when examining the relation of foreign ownership to industrial concentration and merger activity, the most general conclusion which has been drawn at an over-all level is that the extent of foreign ownership has not either clearly increased or decreased the degree of competition. One area of economic performance where a difference by nationality of the firm is evident in general empirical tests is the share of imports in purchases, which is typically higher for the foreign-owned firm.

Further doubt is raised about the relating of poor economic performance to nationality of ownership as such if one considers the experience of other countries which have received foreign direct investment. It is of interest that the European subsidiaries of the same United States parents are criticized for the opposite reason to that often advanced in Canada. Their performance in Europe is believed—often correctly, according to the data—to be superior to that of domestic firms.[17] This in itself does not rule

---

15. For exports, imports, research and profits see A. E. Safarian, *Foreign Ownership of Canadian Industry*, ch. 9, and also his *The Performance of the Foreign-Owned Firms in Canada* (Montreal: Canadian-American Committee, 1969). For exports and imports see B. W. Wilkinson, *Canada's International Trade* (Montreal: Canadian Trade Committee, 1968). These issues and concentration of production as well, are also dealt with in Privy Council Office, *Foreign Ownership and the Structure of Canadian Industry* (Ottawa: Queen's Printer, 1968), pp. 138-234.

16. Foreign-owned firms appear to have a somewhat higher return in secondary manufacturing. The profit estimates are the weakest ones in this list, however, because of problems of measuring profits both in general and between related firms, and because of insufficient disaggregation by industry.

17. See A. E. Safarian, *The Performance of the Foreign-Owned Firm in Canada*, for data on this. See also John H. Dunning, *The Role of American Investment in the British Economy* (London: Political and Economic Planning, 1969).

out the possibility that nationality is important, but it could suggest that subsidiaries adapt to the circumstances in which they find themselves.

Two important questions are raised by the evidence on Canada. Given that the foreign-owned firm has certain advantages in research, financing, and marketing because of its association with the parent, why is its performance typically not better than that of its Canadian-owned counterpart? Secondly, why is the performance of *both* sets of firms in many areas of secondary manufacturing typically so much worse than that of firms in the United States or of best-practice techniques elsewhere over considerable periods of time? This much would be suggested by the long-standing and substantial gap in productivity between Canadian and American manufacturing, as well as by direct comparisons of subsidiaries with their United States parents. There is clearly some common and overwhelming set of environmental factors at work to yield such a result for both sets of firms.[18] A number of theoretical and empirical studies for Canada, both of industry as a whole and of the foreign-owned sector, point to such proximate determinants as too many firms, too many products, and too short runs. Such studies also point to improvement in performance as size of firm, degree of specialization, and differentiation of product from the parent increases. In terms of ultimate determinants of inefficient industrial structure, emphasis is placed in these studies on the effects of Canadian and foreign tariffs and other barriers to trade, the lack of competition which tariffs help sustain, and inadequate government industrial policy in other respects. These are the main culprits. Canada's industrial policies may have emasculated the multinational firm in secondary manufacturing, and dissipated much of its potential gain in an inefficient structure of industry. Similar problems affect the resident-owned sector. A more explicit strategy of industrial development is required, geared to more scale and specialization however achieved, if the benefits of foreign and domestic investment are to be realized fully.[19]

One should not conclude from this that there are few significant differences between foreign-owned and Canadian-owned firms, once one passes from the typical case to specific problems. There are particular disadvan-

---

18. For studies in this area see H. C. Eastman and S. Stykolt, *The Tariff and Competition in Canada* (Toronto: The Macmillan Co. of Canada Ltd., 1967); H. E. English, *Industrial Structure in Canada's International Competitive Position* (Montreal: The Canadian Trade Committee, 1964); Economic Council of Canada, *Scale and Specialization of Canada's Manufacturing Industry* (Ottawa: Queen's Printer, 1968); and A. E. Safarian, *Foreign Ownership of Canadian Industry*, ch. 7.

19. This section should not be taken to suggest that the United States level of manufacturing productivity can be matched precisely, given the other determinants involved. The question is, rather, whether one can get closer, what degree of further integration with that and other countries is necessary to do so, and what consequences for Canada beyond the economic would follow. It should be added that a few scholars have questioned the degree to which the superior production and distribution characteristics of parent firms are in fact transferable to subsidiaries.

tages to be minimized and particular advantages to be exploited as policy is made in a number of contexts. As an example, the conclusion that export performance is similar may result partly from offsetting factors. A significant minority of subsidiaries have limited export franchises, which may impede exports in some cases, while others enjoy access to the parent's international distribution system, which may have favourable effects in some other cases. Our comments here are qualified because of the complexities in both situations: export franchises reflect the competitive power of the affiliates to some extent, and they may protect against imports as well as limiting exports; on the other hand, some of the pricing methods used in parent-company distributing systems can effectively bar competitive bidding by affiliates. Another example is the greater possibilities for tax shifting in a firm with foreign affiliates, a matter which merits close attention by Canadian tax authorities if the benefits from foreign investment are to be realized. There is also the access to superior technology in all its forms, if it can be efficiently utilized for Canadian needs. We know little about the decision-making process and the consequences for welfare in oligopolistic firms generally, including foreign-owned firms. More attention to specific problems or opportunities in specific industrial situations is likely to prove rewarding both for research and for policy directed to improving Canada's welfare.

SOME POLITICAL CONSEQUENCES

The issue of foreign investment is intertwined with political questions.[20] In a sense, the kinds of issues raised above are issues in political economy, raising questions of policy that involve fundamental goals which are more than economic in nature. But some further issues can be raised with more clearly political connotations.

The issue which has been most widely discussed is that of the extra-territorial extension of foreign law and regulation to Canada through the subsidiary. There have been a series of situations, particularly in the past decade, where United States law has been interpreted as extending to United States subsidiaries in Canada and elsewhere. These include regulations under the United States Trading with the Enemy Act which, by levying penalties on the parent, prohibit all trade by United States subsidiaries abroad with China, North Korea, North Vietnam, and (with some exceptions) Cuba. Canadian law includes no such general prohibition, although strategic goods are not exported to them. The two governments

---

20. For a discussion of political questions, with emphasis on extra-territoriality, see Privy Council Office, *Foreign Ownership and the Structure of Canadian Industry, op. cit.,* pp. 295-346.

have devised a formula whereby an exemption can be secured by the subsidiary if the transaction is economically important and if no non-American firm exists to fill a *bona fide* order from those countries. There is some question as to how well this works in practice, although little has been said publicly about its operations by the authorities.[21] An example of something which at least borders on extra-territoriality is the balance-of-payments guidelines of the United States, discussed above. These urged, and later required, parent firms to direct subsidiaries in ways which would worsen the operating performance of the subsidiaries, and could also limit the effectiveness of macro-economic policy in host countries. Canada now has an exemption from these guidelines. There are similar kinds of problems in the complex area of United States anti-trust law, which has on occasion been interpreted to apply to subsidiaries abroad because of the effects of the latter on United States trade.

In each of these cases there is a United States interest, as well as a Canadian one. On occasion also, the effect of the United States policy may be beneficial to Canada economically, as with some anti-trust decisions. Nevertheless, there is a serious problem of erosion of sovereignty for a country (as well as reduction in its ability to make policy) if it fails to assert the principle that its laws, regulations and policies take precedence over foreign insofar as its residents are concerned.

It will be noted that the problem here arises not because of foreign investment as such, but rather because of the unilateral extension of law abroad through the international firm, which then finds itself caught between two sovereigns with different laws or policies. It is, in effect, a problem of inter-governmental relations, and the optimal solution clearly involves inter-governmental negotiation and agreement.

There are still broader issues of a political nature which, at some point, merge with the larger question of Canada-United States relations generally. Clearly, these involve both benefits and costs, actual or potential depending again on how well policy options are exercised. For example, a larger economic base or higher *per capita* income is an important aspect of the increase in choices really available to a country, which in turn is an important aspect of policy; yet the increasing integration with other societies may complicate or limit the exercise of some forms of policy. But the proper consideration of these and still larger questions would take us well beyond the field of foreign investment.

---

21. In December, 1969, the United States government announced that foreign subsidiaries of United States firms, but not the parent companies themselves, would no longer be prohibited from exporting non-strategic goods to China. The prohibition apparently remains, however, for those commodities with components made in the United States.

SOME QUESTIONS OF POLICY

Canadian policy to date has been mainly directed to encouraging foreign direct investment in Canada, in order to enhance Canada's economic development and the higher living standards which go with it. All provincial governments and the federal government actively promote foreign business investment in Canada. There is no formal screening procedure of the kind which exists in many other countries for balance-of-payments reasons, or to ensure local participation. There are many regulations applying to new businesses and to business operations, of course, but in general they apply without distinction as to country of ownership.

There are three significant exceptions to this. The first is in industries considered as key sectors, involving some aspects of transportation for much of Canada's history but extended also to finance and communications media in the past 15 years. Thus in 1964 several acts were amended to retain Canadian ownership and control of federally incorporated insurance and loan companies by limiting the proportion of total shares which could be held by all non-residents to 25 percent, while any one non-resident (or resident) could hold only up to 10 percent. The revisions of the Bank Act introduced in 1965 extended these provisions to the banks. The one foreign-controlled bank was given the option of complying within a given period or accepting a ceiling on its deposits. Various limitations on foreign ownership of radio and television stations culminated in 1969 in a law stipulating that no more than 20 percent of the voting stock and 60 percent of the total investment of a broadcasting company could be owned by non-residents. Canadian firms wishing to advertise to Canadians in a non-Canadian periodical or newspaper were forbidden in 1965 to charge the cost of such advertising as a business expense for tax purposes, thereby inhibiting the sale of foreign publications to Canadians. The Canadian editions of two important foreign-controlled magazines were exempted, however. The rationale advanced by the government for these measures is that of the key-sector approach, in the one case to facilitate the exercise of Canadian economic policy and in the other to facilitate the expression of Canadian points of view. There have been echoes of this approach in one or two other cases, but it has not been extended to any other major sector.

Another policy approach is reflected in the legislation, announced in 1963, which has given modest tax incentives to those firms whose shares were listed on a Canadian stock exchange, whose voting stock was not more than 75-percent owned by non-residents, and one-fourth of whose directors were residents. Rather few firms have responded to this, perhaps because the advantages to the international firm of full ownership are too great to be offset by the size of the incentives. This approach, if pushed to the point of effectiveness, might also improve the capital market in Canada and provide more equity outlets for funds which might otherwise be invested in the United States. It would facilitate disclosure of information, since firms whose stock is held by a parent are regarded as private and do not publicly disclose their operations. The cost of the approach is partly reflected in the increased tax subsidies necessary to secure more share issues. The major cost might well be that Canadian equity capital would go into buying non-controlling minority shares in existing assets, with no necessary growth-inducing effects, particularly if the capital was then exported. The opportunity forgone by such a use of Canadian capital could be new growth-inducing Canadian-controlled ventures, or improvements in the quality of Canadian agents of production, as well as other alternative uses of the funds.

Finally, the Canadian government has from time to time attempted to meet specific issues arising from the extension of United States law or regulation to Canada through the parent-subsidiary relation. In 1966, largely in response to the balance-of-payments guidelines issued by the United States and the criticisms of these in Canada, guiding principles of good corporate behaviour were issued to foreign-owned firms. At the same time, voluntary questionnaires were sent to larger foreign-owned firms asking for information on various aspects of performance. In 1960 a formula was announced, as indicated above, in an attempt to provide a way of dealing with case by case exemptions from the United States prohibitions on trade with certain countries. Similar provisions were developed for consultation (or, at least, notification) on anti-trust and anti-combines policies as they extend to the other country. It cannot be said, however, that the government of Canada has a policy as such on the kinds of issues which arise from these and related problems, except, of course, for direct government-to-government negotiations when the pressures become severe, as with the securing of the exemption from the United States guidelines early in 1968.

Early in 1968 a federal task force of eight university economists reported in detail its analysis of the political and economic effects of foreign ownership, and briefly outlined a set of policies to deal with the problems it saw.[22] Its approach can be stated, briefly, as welcoming the contribution which foreign direct investment has made to economic growth, but urging measures to increase further the net economic gain from it, to reduce the political cost of extra-territoriality, and to stimulate private and public entrepreneurial activity in Canada.

22. Report of the Task Force on the Structure of Canadian Industry, *Foreign Ownership and the Structure of Canadian Industry*, prepared for the Privy Council Office, Ottawa.

The Task Force's first set of recommendations are concerned with improving the industrial policy of Canada in order to maximize economic gains and minimize economic costs associated with foreign investment (though not necessarily due to it). Thus it recommends that information on business operations be greatly increased for both private and public use; that stronger measures to increase competition be taken, both domestically and between countries; that rationalization of industry be encouraged by such measures as further multilateral reduction of tariffs, better research aid, and mergers of sub-optimal firms. These measures are generally directed to both foreign-owned and Canadian-owned firms, recognizing that the problems afflict both. The Task Force emphasized that rationalization on the scale envisaged involved complex questions of policy. It required, therefore, a close government interest, extending not only to the need to maintain full employment and labour retraining, but also to such questions as the effects on the decision-making procedure in subsidiaries and the international aspects of anti-trust as they affect rationalization mergers. A special agency on multi-national enterprises is recommended, since there are some special problems or opportunities presented by foreign ownership, and in view of the need for research on international firms and coordination of policies affecting them.

Its second set of recommendations deals with extra-territoriality. The Task Force indicated that the best approach was a multilateral, intergovernmental code on the treatment of international firms, as now exists for foreign trade, or at least bilateral negotiation between governments. In view of the limited success of past attempts at bilateral agreement, and the politicial threat involved, it recommended a number of "second-best" approaches. One technique recommended was an export trade agency which would ensure that export orders to communist countries were filled—on its own account, if necessary—when they conform with Canadian law and policy. The intrusion of foreign anti-trust law would be blocked by legislative means. The Task Force also recommended that American balance-of-payments guidelines be countervailed by Canadian guidelines.[23]

Its third major set of proposals concerns Canadian participation in the ownership of industry. One of the most troublesome things about the high degree of foreign ownership is that Canadian skills in entrepreneurship, capital and technology are apparently not up to undertaking more of our ventures, so that foreigners undertake them for us. As a policy approach the improvement in the quality of Canadian agents of production is attractive, because it largely avoids a conflict between growth in *per capita* incomes and Canadian ownership. Many of the things one might do to

---

23. The Report was presented on January 12, 1968, a few weeks after the United States guidelines were made mandatory and a few months before Canada was exempted from them.

improve growth also tend to make more of the newer ventures Canadian-owned, and thus to gradually reduce the degree of foreign ownership. These things involve costs, but also a payoff in terms of more resources for Canadians to dispose of as they wish. With respect to private entrepreneurship, the Task Force recommended better management education, a better organization of research and its industrial application in Canada, and improvement in the tax position of certain entrepreneurial groups. It suggested, however, that this would not be enough to match the giant international firm on a broad front. Some mechanism was considered necessary, in brief, to draw on the scarce entrepreneurial talent and capital which does exist and to bring it into continuing contact with its analogue in government. By concentrating these for certain purposes and using them as a catalyst, some new projects could be undertaken which would otherwise have to be undertaken largely by foreigners.

The Task Force's view of a Canada Development Corporation was radically different from those who saw it as a giant mutual fund (of which there are many) or to systematically buy back Canada (which, as a general approach, it opposed). Its version was a holding company with entrepreneurial and management functions. It would be closely associated with private groups in organizing consortia of investors, both domestic and foreign. It would undertake new projects beyond the capacity of smaller or less complex institutions, would play a supporting role in restructuring industry, and would maintain a clear Canadian presence throughout. The Task Force went on to recommend stronger incentives to encourage minority share issues. It noted there were costs to this approach as well as benefits—including as a cost the possible conflict with direct approaches to increasing Canadian ownership. Hence its final recommendation was that preference be given to finding ways to use Canadian capital for purely Canadian private ventures or for a Canada Development Corporation.

It should be added that the Task Force did not advocate a systematic policy to buy out foreign-owned firms. As noted, net economic benefits (some realized and some realizable) are secured through such investment. Moreover, the opportunity cost of such a program is large. It could involve watching foreigners finance the new ventures while we purchase the old, or, if we prevent that, considerable sacrifice of future growth and the uses to which we can put it. Nor did the Task Force recommend general control of new capital inflows as practised in a number of countries, given the present quantity and quality of Canadian agents of production. Moreover, such a policy would require a more precise specification of consequences, more accurate techniques for distinguishing desirable and undesirable flows, and clarification of the constitutional questions. These considerations become more manageable or less costly, of course, if considered in the context of selective repatriation or selective prevention of takeovers, particularly if there are other good reasons for undertaking them in any given situation.

The approach of the Task force essentially was that the multi-national firm offers too much to warrant rejecting it, so long as it respects our sovereignty, but we ought to try harder to match it and to increase the gain from it. If, moreover, the problems associated with foreign ownership are often of our own making, the solutions also lie in significant part in our hands.

tariff policy

Ronald J. Wonnacott
University of Western Ontario

A. INTRODUCTION

Historically, Canadian industry has developed behind a protective tariff. The argument has been that it could not otherwise survive the competition of the more efficient producers in the huge U.S. market. Increasingly, however, this policy is being questioned. Canada is now actively participating in the Kennedy Round, the name given to the negotiations for and implementation of a set of multi-national tariff reductions. These negotiations began in 1964 and resulted in widespread phased tariff reductions on many commodities beginning in 1968. In addition, proposals are being made for Canadian participation in free-trade areas involving various combinations of countries. The prospect for Canadian industry under freer trade has always been an important political question: the election of 1911 was fought on this issue, with trade reciprocity with the U.S. being rejected at that time. It has become an even more important question today with Canada an active trader in a world in which trade barriers are being lowered.

Tariff reductions such as the Kennedy Round have two effects on Canada, as on any participating country: its industry loses sales in domestic markets in exchange for gains in international markets. For all countries, the (international) gains will exceed the (domestic) losses and income will rise as a consequence. Moreover, what is true for all countries is almost surely to be true for any one country. But it is not so clear that it will be true for all producers in that one country. Specifically, a Canadian company that limits itself to the domestic market, and is not prepared to sell internationally, will find little of cheer in the Kennedy Round—or in the other changes likely to take place in the next 10 years. The performance of an industry, therefore, will be judged more by its success in opening international markets than by its success in retaining all of its present "domestic base."

There is a simple, fundamental reason why Canada has participated in the Kennedy Round, and why further initiatives for tariff reductions are now being sought: in a world in which tariffs are being lowered, a single country cannot stand aside without running the risk of becoming a high-tariff backwater, partially isolated in a world of rapid trade expansion. To illustrate, consider how the formation of regional trading blocks such as the Common Market puts pressure on the Canadian economy, and means that the "status quo" simply ceases to exist. Discrimination is established in Europe against Canadian exports: for example, Canadian exporters to Germany may now find they are losing this market to the French; although they may have been able to compete with the French on equal terms in the past, the French now have tariff-free entry into the German market—while Canadians do not. Thus Germany (and each Common Market country) discriminates against Canada, and in favour of its European partners. And if the British eventually do succeed in entering the Common Market, there will be an additional twist. There will not only be this discrimination against Canadian producers in the British market; in addition, Canadians will lose their Commonwealth Preference, the discrimination in their favour that has existed in the British market in the past. Thus Canadian producers find themselves at a disadvantage in Europe, not so much because the treatment they receive is less favourable, but rather because the position of their competitors is improving. This means that Canadian industry cannot ask Ottawa to opt out of world tariff reductions, in favour of the status quo. As long as other countries are reducing their tariffs, there is no status quo; Canada has little option but to participate.

Not only does the Common Market allow European producers to export to each other duty-free; it also tends to reduce their production costs. As Europeans scale up to service continental rather than national markets, they capture efficiencies of specialization and mass production. Cost reductions are by no means limited to the production side; in addition, in the larger more competitive European market, per unit selling and distribution margins may be reduced. For these reasons, Canadian producers find it harder to compete with the increasingly efficient Europeans—not only in Europe, but also in Canada and in third markets. (The one circumstance that has saved Canadian producers from even tougher competition is the fact that the Europeans have recently been cashing a large proportion of their efficiency gains in higher wages, rather than lower costs. This has happened less in Germany than elsewhere; and this is why everyone finds it difficult currently to compete with the Germans.)

This is, of course, the familiar argument of market size: it becomes increasingly difficult to prosper in a market of 20 million when the world is made up of markets of 100 million or more. This is the ultimate rationale of recent proposals for a North American Common Market (here markets available to Canadian producers would be well over 200 million) or the proposal for continued multilateral Kennedy Rounds (with the eventual objective of providing a "world" market for Canadian producers.)

This raises the question of what the prospects are for new trade initiatives. What would be the industry and region dimensions of any new scheme?

B. POLICY OPTIONS

further Kennedy rounds

At a single stroke, the Kennedy Round reduced tariffs of the industrial countries by an average of something like one-quarter to one-third; selected Canadian nominal tariff rates before-and-after[1] are shown in Table 1. One obvious route towards complete trade liberalization would be several more Kennedy Rounds. But such a step-by-step process of cutting all tariffs between all countries is by no means the only option. Another is to eliminate tariffs completely in one industry at a time.

single-industry schemes: the automobile experiment

The best known example is the 1965 Canadian-U.S. auto agreement. This allows manufacturers to ship autos and components across the U.S.-Canadian border duty-free, provided they satisfy certain production requirements in Canada. The objective is to provide a North American market for Canadian producers, allowing high-volume specialization on a limited number of models (such as the new Ford Maverick), rather than the previous low-volume production of a whole range of models. As a result costs have been reduced, allowing a substantial increase in Canadian auto wages and a considerable reduction in the price of autos to the Canadian consumer.

However, the Canadian price did not automatically drop to the U.S. level as one would expect under full free trade. The reason is that the auto

---

1. Although some of these reductions are of the order of one-quarter to one-third, many are not; this suggests that Canadian tariff cuts may have been more modest than those of other countries. Even more surprising is Melvin and Wilkinson's findings on effective rates of protection (i.e., the nominal tariff adjusted to take account of several factors, including the higher price that must be paid for protected inputs). They concluded that "in nearly 40 percent of the industries selected, the Kennedy Round changes have had very little influence on effective rates." See James R. Melvin and Bruce W. Wilkinson, *Effective Protection in the Canadian Economy*, Economic Council of Canada, (Ottawa: Queen's Printer, 1968), p. 38.

scheme is a peculiar mixture of free trade and protection: Canadian employment is protected by the provision that allows only manufacturers meeting specified production levels in Canada to import autos duty-free. Since the Canadian consumer cannot buy a car in Detroit and import it duty free, the auto producers are still free to sell autos in Canada at a price above the U.S. level, and it has been argued that the major weakness of the

Table 1

PRE- AND POST-KENNEDY ROUND NOMINAL TARIFFS
FOR 32 SELECTED CANADIAN INDUSTRIES

No.	Industry	Pre-Kennedy	Post-Kennedy
		%	%
5	Distilleries	20.0	20.0
9	Process cheese	5.9	5.9
11	Feed manufacturers	3.7	2.6
13	Fish products	7.1	3.6
22	Tobacco products	30.0	25.0
25	Shoe factories	25.6	23.3
37	Wool cloth	23.8	21.6
43	Foundation garments	25.9	23.4
44	Fur goods	24.5	22.0
45	Knitting mills	27.6	24.1
46	Hosiery mills	23.8	14.6
52	Sawmills	3.5	2.3
55	Veneer and plywood mills	16.1	11.4
57	Wooden box factories	20.0	15.4
60	Office furniture	22.0	17.0
65	Publishing and printing	1.4	1.4
73	Aluminum rolling, casting, extruding	3.0	2.2
74	Fabricated structural metal	16.8	13.5
78	Steel tubes and pipes	17.7	14.2
88	Shipbuilding and repair	15.2	15.0
89	Motor vehicle parts and accessories	3.6	2.6
90	Railroad rolling stock	12.3	10.6
98	Household radio and TV	19.2	19.0
99	Communication equipment	11.9	10.3
113	Clay products	9.5	7.8
115	Petroleum refineries	6.0	6.0
117	Other petroleum and coal products	9.1	4.6
125	Mixed fertilizers	.1	0.0
126	Broom, brush and mop	24.8	22.2
127	Clock and watch	17.6	16.2
129	Pen and pencil	21.1	17.4
133	Jewellery and silverware	22.5	17.0

Source: James R. Melvin and Bruce W. Wilkinson, **Effective Protection in the Canadian Economy**, Economic Council of Canada, (Ottawa: Queen's Printer, 1968), pp. 39-44. Reproduced with the permission of the Queen's Printer for Canada.

auto scheme is that no assurance was given for an eventual move to full free trade and price equalization.

Since the scheme was initiated, the price of autos has fallen[2] part way to the U.S. level. (All price comparisons, of course, must be made after account is taken of differences in excise taxes in the two countries; moreover, some initial price reduction is necessary simply to offset the government's loss of duty revenue previously paid by the auto companies). But this price reduction was not in response to the competitive pressure of low-priced U.S. autos that would normally result from full free trade, but rather in response to the pressure exerted by the public and the Canadian government. Although the issue of Canadian auto prices has not yet been resolved, the auto scheme has provided a preview of the economic gains that may accrue with increased market size in industries with economies of scale (i.e., in which costs fall with volume). These windfall gains have been distributed both to the auto producers (in substantial part in higher wages), and to auto consumers in the form of a lower price.

However, for several reasons this auto scheme may not prove to be a precedent for other industries. It is probably too complex to administer in most other industries. Moreover, it is unlikely that the U.S. administration would be at all enthusiastic about another asymmetrical scheme of this kind, since it provides protection to the industry in Canada, but not in the U.S. It would have to be sold to Congress—and it was tougher to sell the auto scheme than was generally expected. Instead, any future single-industry scheme would in all likelihood be multilateral and (unlike the auto mixture of free trade and protection) unrestricted free trade, with purchasers as well as manufacturers allowed duty-free access.

It has also been suggested that the first industries to be selected should be rapid-growth, high-technology industries. Since these are capital intensive there is less of a problem of potential unemployment; moreover, rationalization of the industry and its expansion in certain countries may be accommodated by the natural growth of the industry, rather than by its contraction in other countries; and finally, the more rapid the industry growth, the greater the future gain from trade liberalization.

regional trading areas

The other major option is a regional free-trade area. There are several variations on this theme: on the one hand, a free-trade area between Canada and the U.S. only; on the other, a broader arrangement to include the U.K., other EFTA countries, and possibly Japan. On political grounds, the

---

2. More precisely, Canadian prices have "fallen" towards U.S. prices by rising less rapidly.

Canadian view has generally been that the larger the number of participants, the better. However, a strong economic case can be made for an initial move to free trade with the U.S. only, as a first step towards a broader arrangement. Canadian exporters to the U.S. would receive relatively favourable treatment, since their products would enter the U.S. duty-free whereas competing European goods would still face a U.S. tariff. A key issue in evaluating these two options is: how many competitors do Canadians wish to take on at once? It has been argued that it is preferable not to engage all comers until a Canadian industry is established that is fully competitive with the U.S. Canada's long suit in competition with the U.S. is a substantial wage advantage. However, if Europe and Japan are also participants, Canada is no longer the low-wage country. It is true that Canada would still be an efficient location for producing many goods; but the problem is that it might initially be overlooked by firms preoccupied with deciding which activities to locate in the U.S., and which in Europe or Japan.

C. COULD CANADIAN INDUSTRY SURVIVE FREE-TRADE COMPETITION FROM THE U.S.?[3]

Regardless of whether Canadians consider a two-country North American arrangement, a broader multilateral arrangement (in either all or some industrial goods), or some option midway between, the key point is that the U.S. would be a participant in any case. The major benefits of free trade to Canada would result from the free exchange of goods over the 49th parallel; benefits from increased trade across the Atlantic or Pacific would be important, but secondary. The risks also lie to the South: could Canadian industry compete with U.S. producers in the North American market? Historically, the Canadian policy of protection has been based on a negative reply: "With free trade U.S. firms would load their subsidiaries on boxcars and ship them South." But this whole line of argument has now come under question. Since plants are already established in Canada, they probably won't be closed down; but this isn't much satisfaction. Unless Canada is a good place to produce, they will be closed down as they are fully depreciated. So the question becomes: "Under free trade, would Canada be a good place to produce goods for the North American market?"

The casual observation that costs are now higher in Canada than in the U.S. in most lines of manufacturing supports the traditional negative conclusion. But when Canadian costs are examined in more detail, it turns out

---

3. This, and other issues addressed far too briefly in this short chapter, are documented in more detail in Ronald J. Wonnacott and Paul Wonnacott, *Free Trade Between the United States and Canada*, Harvard Economic Studies CXXIX (Cambridge: Harvard University Press, 1967).

that these higher costs are to be explained (and in many cases, more than explained) by inefficiencies associated with the small Canadian market. Successful competition with U.S. producers, therefore, is not blocked by any inherent Canadian cost disadvantages; instead it has been limited by the tariffs (both U.S. and Canadian) that have backed Canadian producers into a low-volume domestic market. With the elimination of these tariffs, successful competition with U.S. producers would be contingent on Canadian scaling up to longer production runs; this would involve specialization, of the kind now being introduced in the auto industry. Thus, Canadian producers would typically drop many or most items in their broad range of products, and concentrate on high-volume production of selected items in which they enjoy some (e.g., labour or resource) advantage. The traditional U.S. advantage of operating in a large market would be equally available to producers in Canada. In such a common North American market, why would industry end at Detroit or Buffalo? Why would it not extend into Southern Ontario? With free trade, what would the North American economy look like?

D. NORTH AMERICAN INDUSTRY UNDER FREE TRADE

There is now a central industrial heartland in North America. This may be roughly defined by drawing a triangle from Chicago on the west to Boston and Washington, the two terminal points of the band of heaviest industrial activity along the eastern seaboard. This "Golden Triangle" represents only slightly more than five percent of the area of the United States, and about two and one-half percent of the area of the North American continent. Nevertheless, approximately thirty percent of the population is in this area, including ten of the fifteen largest North American cities: New York, Chicago, Philadelphia, Washington, Baltimore, Boston, Cleveland, Detroit, Pittsburgh, and Newark. In addition, Buffalo is on its border. This area includes only a small Canadian section—the southernmost strip of southwestern Ontario. Toronto and Montreal lie just to the north.

In terms of many of the influences determining industry location it is a superior region for several reasons. It is the area of heaviest central concentration of industry; as a consequence, it is attractive for firms seeking easy access to a wide variety of manufactured supplies. Because it is the area of heaviest industrialization, it is also the area of greatest concentration of employment and income. Firms seeking rich markets find it attractive as a consequence, with this region being one of the best areas from which to service North American markets at minimum transport costs. These advantages have allowed firms in this area, competing with firms less favourably situated elsewhere, to pay higher wages. As a result, its relatively high prevailing wage level now represents the one offsetting disadvantage of this area.

The same influences such as market proximity that make the golden triangle an attractive region for industry, also make the regions directly adjacent the next most attractive. In particular this includes the Windsor-Toronto-Montreal axis of present Canadian industrial concentration. But the Canadian axis has one great advantage: its lower wages. As a consequence, the prospects of the Canadian axis in a free-trade area cannot be compared to the U.S. triangle, because there are no firm guidelines for trading-off the Canadian wage advantage against U.S. market proximity. Hence only limited conclusions of the following kind are justified: if free-trade specialization takes place between these two areas, Ontario and Quebec may be expected to attract labour-intensive industries, whereas the U.S. areas will be attractive for industries sensitive to market influences.

Firmer conclusions may be reached in comparing the prospects of Ontario and Quebec with all U.S. regions *except* those lying in the Chicago-New York heartland. Ontario and Quebec are preferred locations because they provide lower wages, *and* better access to markets in the golden triangle. On the basis of this comparison, it may be predicted that the prospects of these two provinces in a free-trade area are likely to be at least as good as the prospects of those U.S. regions which do not lie in the Chicago-New York area. The proven ability of these U.S. regions to maintain prosperous conditions and high rates of growth within the U.S. "free-trade area" should provide grounds for considerable optimism concerning the (even more favourable) prospects of Ontario and Quebec. Because they would be good locations, the expectation would be for increased industrialization, and as a consequence wages rising sufficiently to just offset the initial advantages[4] of the area.[5]

---

4. One must be careful to avoid the following argument: "With free trade Canadian wages would automatically jump to U.S. levels, and with this one advantage lost, Canadian industry would collapse." The argument in this form is fallacious and tangled in contradictions; the labour market does not work this way. No-one (the unions included) could or would institute this cost of wage boost in the face of a collapsing demand for labour. If Canadian wages were to rise towards the U.S. level —as seems likely in the long run—it would be because of a buoyant demand for labour. But this could occur only if Canada proved to be a good place to produce goods efficiently.

It is true that a degree of wage parity (but by no means full wage parity) came fairly quickly in the auto industry following the 1965 free-trade arrangement. But this is not a free-trade precedent, because Canadian employment was protected by the agreement. Hence this was not a wage increase in the face of collapsing demand for labour; rather it was a wage increase in the face of guaranteed employment.

5. If Ontario and Quebec would be advantageous locations under free trade, why are wages there now low, compared to U.S. regions? The answer to a substantial degree lies in the existing levels of protection—and especially the U.S. tariff. Canadian products exported to the U.S. pay a tax at the border; were it not for this tax, wages and other factor payments in Canada could be higher. The same is true in Canadian industries that do not now export, but which would in the absence of the U.S. tariff; by blocking them out of their "natural" markets, the U.S. tariff reduces wages in these industries also.

The conclusion then is that Ontario and Quebec would be the best industrial locations in Canada under free trade—just as they are under protection. Because of its distance, Saskatchewan would be no bargain for industry under free trade—just as it is not under protection. In assessing the prospects of Saskatchewan however, the relevant question is not whether Saskatoon would be as favourably situated as Montreal; it would not in any case. The question is rather: "How would free trade affect Saskatchewan—would it leave it better off?" The answer to this question is a clear and unambiguous "yes"—in fact this judgement is made more easily for Saskatchewan than for any other province. Saskatchewan has essentially no industry to lose to increased U.S. competition; all it has is a protected industrial price level that would fall with free trade, raising real income. Thus the non-industrial areas like Saskatchewan would benefit, just like the industrial areas of Ontario and Quebec; but their relative position will not necessarily be greatly altered.

Another important question is whether the internationalization of industry will lead to the relocation of Canadian head office facilities of U.S. subsidiaries to the parent's location in, say, New York? To some extent, this may happen, since the present U.S. owner-Canadian subsidiary system involves substantial duplication of costly overhead facilities. To the extent that there are cultural and social advantages of having a group of senior corporate personnel in a community, this may be regarded as a national loss. But it's not quite this simple. If these are duplicate head office facilities, it means that this unnecessary but costly overhead is being paid for by the Canadian consuming public in the form of higher product prices; so the question becomes: "Is it worth it?" But an even more important consideration is this: once Canada is in the international market, cities such as Montreal should become contenders as the head office site, not for subsidiaries of international corporations located elsewhere, but for the international corporations themselves. Understandably, most international corporations have ruled out Canada in the past as a head office site because of the relatively small Canadian market. But when North American markets are opened, Canadian cities such as Toronto and Montreal would no longer be at a disadvantage vis-à-vis a U.S. city such as Minneapolis that does now have head offices of international corporations.

In summary, Canadian cities may well lose a large number of their present subsidiary head office facilities, in exchange for becoming potential sites for new international corporations; but in the long run this is not necessarily a bad trade.

It should be emphasized that Canada's favourable underlying economic situation cited above (i.e., relatively low wage rates, combined with proximity to markets) is only a necessary, but not a sufficient condition for free-trade success. An additional requirement would be a great deal of imagination, initiative and flexibility by both Canadian management and labour. Both would have to meet the standards of efficiency now prevailing in the U.S. Available evidence indicates that the Canadian worker can be as productive as the U.S. worker when he is put on the same sort of job, i.e., when he no longer has to turn around machinery as frequently as present short Canadian production runs require. And there is no evidence that Canadian management could not compete, when it is released from the confines of the Canadian market, but this question is still an open one.

In any case, there can be no doubt that free trade for Canada would bring an interim period of adjustment and reorganization; this could only be regarded as a long-run investment in getting the Canadian economy onto a competitive international footing. Moreover, the short-run dislocation would be less than often supposed, for two reasons. First, Canadian industry is already geographically in its best free-trade location. Second, most of the adjustment would occur within existing industries rather than between them. Thus the shift in labour and other resources between areas and industries would be less as a consequence.

Nevertheless, it should be recognized that some firms would undoubtedly fail, just as they fail as a result of normal, competitive economic growth. In fact, the costs and benefits of freeing trade are similar to those resulting from a very rapid and concentrated period of technological change. Those firms unable to adjust (i.e., meet foreign competition) fail; those flexible enough to take advantage of the new opportunities (i.e., for export) expand, in many cases receiving higher profits and paying higher wages as a consequence. The policy problem is to shift resources (especially human resources) from the former into the latter as quickly and painlessly as possible. The government's responsibility is to ensure that the free-trade market transfer is unimpeded, and if necessary provide adjustment assistance in the form of subsidized retraining of labour, and the like. The justification for having this paid for by the taxpayer is that it is the general public that benefits from this change; hence it should be paid for by the public rather than by the individuals temporarily unemployed as a consequence. As with technical change, in the short run there is a combination of costs and benefits; but in the long run, after resources are redirected, there remain only benefits.

E. THE GAINS FROM TRADE LIBERALIZATION

Two kinds of gain may be identified. First, a gain in real income would occur as each country specializes in its activity of comparative advantage. This would occur even if costs were constant in all industries. But the existence of economies of scale in many areas of Canadian manufacturing[6] means that there would be further substantial gains from specialization. Moreover, the importance of these economies of scale[7] indicates that these are likely to be the larger potential source of increased income in the Canadian case. Clearly, it is to be hoped that the classical gains from the selection of activities of comparative advantage would be added to this; but this is not a necessary condition for the success of trade liberalization—as it would be in a world of constant costs. To illustrate: the major gains from free trade in autos have come with the elimination of Canadian low-volume production of a whole range of models, with e.g., Ford now specializing in a very few models like the Maverick. It is this specialization *per se* that is important, rather than the selection of the particular model of Canadian comparative advantage (would this be the Maverick, or the labour-intensive Lincoln Continental?). This conclusion follows not only because economies of scale are important in Canadian manufacturing, but also because the relatively free mobility of factors of production (especially capital) reduces the thrust of the classical comparative-advantage argument.

These gains would be distributed as an increase in Canadian real income —in several ways. First, Canadian prices would fall as a consequence both of lower-cost imports and the reduced cost of domestic Canadian products. In a Royal Commission study, Professor John Young has estimated that this would increase Canadian *per capita* real income by about four percent This may sound like a modest figure; but in fact it is a very large sum. (This effect of lowering tariffs on the price level is now well-recognized; to curtail inflationary pressures the Canadian government in its 1969 Budget speeded up the introduction of its Kennedy Round tariff cuts.) Other potential benefits from free trade may come in the form of a Canadian wage rate closer to the U.S. level, and/or a Canadian dollar closer to parity with the U.S. dollar. While neither wage nor exchange parity can be assumed as a corollary of free trade, the best estimate is that free trade would allow some move towards both. To the degree that the attractiveness

---

6. For details on economies of scale in Canadian manufacturing, see (in addition to Wonnacott and Wonnacott cited above): H. C. Eastman and S. Stykolt, *The Tariff and Competition in Canada* (Toronto: The Macmillan Co. of Canada Ltd., 1967); H. Edward English, *Industrial Structure in Canada's International Competitive Position* (Montreal: The Canadian Trade Committee, 1964); and Cyril Hodgins "On Estimating the Economies of Large Scale Production: Some Tests on Data for the Canadian Manufacturing Sector," unpublished Ph.D. thesis, University of Chicago, 1968.

7. Note that economies of scale present in the Canadian case (roughly in the 10-20 percent range) imply a substantial source of increased income. But they are realizable over a remarkably large increase in volume: opening the U.S. market might raise volume by 500 percent or even 1000 percent in some Canadian product lines. Thus rapidly falling costs at the present margin of production need not necessarily be implied; costs may be drifting down so slowly at the margin that they appear to be almost constant.

of Canadian locations induces relatively rapid expansion of Canadian industry, one may expect an upward drift in Canadian wages in the face of pressure on the available labour supply; similarly this relatively rapid Canadian expansion also implies a more rapid increase in exports than imports, with resulting upward pressure on the Canadian dollar.

The total gain from both a lower price level and higher wage and exchange rate has been estimated at just over 10 percent of Canadian real income. In addition, there is a psychological advantage that is even more difficult to measure. Canada would emerge from such a period of reorganization with an industry tested in international competition, and ready to take on all comers—rather than a defensive industry, backed onto a high-cost domestic plateau. Competitively, Canadian industry would be in the international major league.

It is easy to illustrate the net benefits of free trade in a Canadian industry which would expand as a consequence, exploiting new export markets. But what is more instructive is to consider the net benefits in an industry which may not expand—and indeed may contract. To illustrate, consider the furniture industry: even with its present protection, it is under heavy pressure from imports, and its prospects under free trade are less exciting than many other Canadian industries. Only the more progressive and flexible Canadian firms would be likely to be able to meet free-trade competition from producers in the U.S. South. It seems likely, therefore, that this industry would face a relatively painful period of adjustment, with the prospect that some proportion of its present labour force might have to move to other expanding industries.

If these workers were hired by other industries at higher wages, they would gain from free trade. A more certain beneficiary would be the Canadian consumer, since the price of furniture would fall, on average, by about 18 percent.[8] In addition, with the greater exchange in furniture, the consumer would have a much wider choice of items, rather than the present relatively restricted variety.

The costs of free trade include the costs of retraining and relocation (which may be psychological as well as economic); sunk capital losses (which would be less for this industry than for most because of the age of much of its present plant facilities); and any residual permanent unemployment of trained personnel. The first two costs are once-and-for-all costs.

---

8. The lower price of domestically-produced furniture would represent a net gain. But, by and large, the lower price of imports would not; this gain to the consuming public would be offset by a loss to the taxpaying public, since the government would no longer be collecting duty revenue. For details on the furniture industry, see David E. Bond and Ronald J. Wonnacott, *Trade Liberalizaion and the Canadian Furniture Industry* (Toronto: Private Planning Association and the University of Toronto Press, 1968).

Weighing the last cost of permanent unemployment against one of the potential benefits (lower prices to the consumer), it has been calculated that, in the furniture industry, price benefits to the consumer from free trade would exceed the economic costs of unemployment unless over 40 percent of the present labour force in the entire industry became permanently unemployed. Not only is this sort of permanent unemployment contradicted by every historical precedent; even if it were to occur, its cost would fall (and eventually disappear) in the future as the unemployed grew older and retired from the labour force. At the same time, free-trade benefits to the consumer would necessarily increase with the future growth of furniture sales.

A significant point is that net long-term benefits of free trade to Canada may be associated with industries that contract as well as with those that expand. The problem is that it is difficult, politically, to explain this to those who lose their jobs—just as it historically has been difficult to explain the efficiency gains from new machinery to workers who have become temporarily unemployed as a result of technological progress.

F. FREER TRADE: WHAT KIND?

In evaluating any move towards free trade, Canadians should distinguish between three major institutional alternatives: a free-trade area, a customs union, and a common-currency area. Each has its own distinct political implications. To highlight political issues, suppose only Canada and the U.S. are involved; Canadians are more suspicious of the political implications of this sort of bilateral arrangement than any other.

a free-trade area

This arrangement would leave each country with a maximum of political autonomy; this is why the analysis above is limited to this case. The only loss of autonomy to each country would be its ability to set tariffs against the other. As a consequence of tariff elimination, trade flows would increase. This would not create Canadian dependence on the U.S.; but it would increase the high degree of Canadian dependence on the U.S. that already exists. But, paradoxically, Canadian vulnerability to the U.S. might be reduced rather than increased, since the U.S. would be committed by formal treaty not to raise tariffs against Canadian imports—a commitment much stronger than any now existing. Since the efficient scaling up of Canadian industry is contingent on entry into U.S. markets, Canadians should insist upon a long-term treaty guarantee that neither tariffs nor quotas[9] will be raised against Canadian goods.

a customs union

This would provide little in the way of further economic gains from Canadian-U.S. integration; the big difference would be in the treatment afforded third countries, with a customs union requiring a common external tariff by both partners whereas a free trade area allows each to set its own third-country tariffs. In a customs union, it is likely that Canada would exercise little influence in setting the common tariff against third countries. As a consequence, Canadian tariff policy would largely be made in Washington, and continued preference for Commonwealth imports would be out of the question.

If there is a self-conscious desire to move eventually towards political union, a customs union is preferred, since the participants are forced at an early stage cooperatively to determine economic policies. But if political union is not the objective, a free-trade area is preferred, since each participant retains a maximum of autonomy. Their economic effects, in the Canadian-U.S. case, would be very similar.

a common-currency area

This additional optional step up the scale of economic union would involve establishing a single dollar as legal tender in both countries. For Canada, there would be economic advantages and disadvantages which are hard to compare, but which would be of second-order significance. But the political implications would be important. There would be one central bank, or at a very minimum, extremely close coordination enforced between the Federal Reserve and the Bank of Canada; in either case, Canadians would lose most of their present limited autonomy over monetary policy, and as an indirect consequence some of their control over fiscal and debt-management policy. In the simplest case, suppose the Canadian government wished to run an expansionary budget deficit. It will clearly be limited in its ability to do so if a common North American monetary authority is

---

9. Although this essay has concentrated on the more easily analyzed effects of tariffs, it must be recognized that in a similar fashion quotas restrict trade and impose costs. Free trade involves the elimination of both; this is an obvious but important point, because any tariff concession can be cancelled by the application of quotas.

engaged in tightening money, and making it extremely difficult for the government to sell bonds to cover this deficit.

Countries wishing eventually to move to political union typically opt for a customs union followed by a common-currency area. The Common Market is following this path. Countries wishing economic benefits with a minimum of political implications, typically choose a free-trade area. An example is the European Free Trade Area; the absence of political commitment is evidenced by the willingness of several participants to abandon this arrangement in favour of the Common Market.

Two points are important. First, economic cooperation may take many alternative forms, but these should not be confused. Specifically, the discussion of a free-trade area should not be clouded with the pros and cons of other forms of economic union such as common markets, common currencies, common labour pools, and so on. Second, free trade does not necessarily involve the participants in an irreversible process of escalation, with the end result political union. Economics has no such controlling precedence. If it had, Canada would long since, with its enormous bilateral trade, have become part of the U.S.

G. CONCLUDING OBSERVATIONS

Two important points must be emphasized to keep this analysis in proper perspective. First, this discussion has focused on industrial, rather than primary products. The reason is that this is the more sensitive area of Canadian vulnerability. The traditional view that free trade would bring substantial advantages to Canadian agriculture and primary-materials production is essentially correct.[10] It is the premise that this would be at the expense of Canadian manufacturing that must be questioned, and this is why attention has been concentrated on this issue. The conclusion is that Canadians would not, in fact, become "hewers of wood and drawers of water." Instead, they would continue to do what they now do, only a good deal more efficiently. An important corollary is that although greater benefits would result if agricultural products were to be included, Canadians need not view this inclusion as a necessary condition; a scheme involving only industrial products would also prove beneficial.

The second important observation is that attention has been concentrated on the effects on Canada of bilateral free trade with the U.S. This is because it is the adjustment to competitive conditions *within* the North

---

10. For the favourable implications for Canada of free trade in primary products, see Bela Balassa, ed., *Studies in Trade Liberalization* (Baltimore: Johns Hopkins Press, 1957), pp. 55-60.

American economy that Canadians would find most diffcult. Some of the economic pros and cons from including third countries have been noted above; but there are also two political arguments favouring a broader scheme. Canadians are likely to prefer membership to be "balanced" by third countries to offset partially the dominant influence of the U.S. Moreover participation should be open to all, to prevent the arrangement from being regarded by non-participants as "a rich-man's club."

This leads, finally, to the following sort of policy prescription. While Canadians should be actively encouraging and participating in multilateral Kennedy-type Rounds, we should also now be prepared to negotiate with the U.S. and other countries on participation in an area free-trade scheme —an Atlantic Free-Trade Area. This should be open to all comers—with the medium-term objective being a cooperative arrangement with the Common Market. But regardless of whether area options are chosen and expanded, or whether the Kennedy Round is followed up with several similar multilateral rounds, the long-term objective should be the same: multilateral free trade between the developed countries—with tariffs being retained only by the less developed countries, who may be allowed free access in developed markets without necessarily being required to reciprocate. They would thus be offered "trade along with aid," with the eventual elimination of their own protection following attainment of an adequate level of development.

immigration and emigration

Lawrence H. Officer
Harvard University

INTRODUCTION

The United States has often been described as a nation of immigrants. So, too, is Canada composed of immigrants. The earliest settlers were the French, who began effective colonization of Canada in the 17th century. Their descendants constitute the majority of the population of Quebec today. Although Britain conquered Canada in 1763, British immigration to Canada remained low until 1820, and concentrated largely in Upper Canada (Ontario). The largest wave of immigration in Canadian history occurred in the decade prior to the First World War. In the period 1903-1913, 2.6 million immigrants came to Canada. Many of these people were neither French nor English but of diverse European nationalities, and settled in the Canadian West. The total gross immigration of 2.6 million in 1903-1913 is an impressively high figure (an average of 237,000 a year), compared to the Canadian population of 5.4 million in 1901. However, emigration *from* Canada amounted to over half the gross flow.

In the period since the end of the Second World War, say in 1946-1967, 2.9 million immigrants came to Canada. While this movement is an average of only 133,000 a year, barely half the pre-World War I figure, the loss of people due to emigration was much less than in the earlier period; so the net addition to Canada's population via migration in the postwar years exceeds that in any other period in Canada's history.

The composition of postwar immigration by country of former residence is of some interest. The principal sources of immigrants are Britain (28 percent), Italy (14 percent), Germany (10 percent), and the United States (8 percent). The French-speaking countries Belgium and France together account for only 4 percent of Canada's immigrants. Therein lies the source of the opposition of French-Canadian groups to immigration. Because of the low propensity of French-speaking Europeans to emigrate, French Canada had to rely on a high birth rate to maintain its proportion in Canada's population. In fact, in the past the natural rate of increase of the French-Canadian population was among the highest in the world. However, the drastic fall in the French-Canadian birth rate in recent years has accentuated the French-Canadian fear of gradually becoming a less and less significant part of Canada's population. This attitude is reinforced by the fact that only 21 percent of new immigrants settle in Quebec, as compared to over 50 percent in Ontario. Nor does the increased number of Catholic immigrants (predominantly Italian) assuage the fear. Most of these immigrants settle outside Quebec, and even those that do go to that province tend to be assimilated into the English-speaking minority.

The role of immigration in the relationship between Quebec and the rest of Canada, nevertheless, is secondary to other considerations of a political and economic nature. Furthermore, on the positive side, the immigration to Canada of various ethnic groups other than French and English over the years has given rise to a "third force" in Canadian society, one with a strong interest in preserving a united Canada.

IS IMMIGRATION GOOD OR BAD?

Canada is an underpopulated country. Its population—and hence labour supply—is low relative to its land expanse, natural resources, and potential for capital accumulation. Nevertheless, traditionally, labour unions (and even some professional groups, such as doctors) have opposed the entry of immigrants, because increasing the supply of labour in their occupational group would drive down the wage rate. It is true that this view has validity on a static micro-economic level. Increasing the quantity of labour input in a typical production process while holding constant the amounts of the other factors applied, would lower the real marginal product of labour, and hence, under competitive conditions, the real wage.

However, the static micro-view overlooks macro-economic effects of migration that are favourable to the receiving country. First of all, immigration has a demand as well as a supply effect. Increased population implies a rise in the demand for goods and services, and this in turn implies an increased demand for labour, hence an upward pressure on wage rates. The fact that not all immigrants are destined to the labour force but some are housewives and dependent children increases the importance of the demand relative to the supply effect.

On the supply side, it should be noted that the addition of workers in an industry beset by labour shortages will enable the expansion of production.

Furthermore, immigrants may carry with them factors of production other than (and in addition to) labour. Thus an immigrant might possess sufficient funds to be a source of financial capital. Coupled with this capital (or even apart from it), the immigrant might have entrepreneurial qualities, again involving favourable effects on production and income in Canada.

An immigrant might possess human rather than physical capital. In other words, he has received education and training in his country of former residence so that he is qualified as a professional or skilled worker in Canada. Not only is such a person likely to have an occupation that is in heavy demand in Canadian industry, but his very education and training represent a stock of "investment in human beings" that is a "free gift" to Canada. This attribute of immigration is referred to as the "brain gain." Needless to say, it is a "brain drain" for the country of emigration.

The unilateral acquisition of human capital is an opportunity gain to Canada, because no resources in Canada are devoted to the training and education of immigrants prior to their arrival. There is yet another advantage of immigration from a government standpoint, one that is perhaps even more important than the "brain gain." Canada is a country of vast expanse relative to its population. The level of social overhead capital—transportation and communication facilities, government agencies, schools, universities, hospitals, etc.—that is required to service the population increases much less than in proportion to this population. In other words, a country large in area such as Canada experiences increasing returns in its provision of social overhead capital, that is, lower *per capita* costs as population increases. In this respect Canada is underpopulated, and increasing her population, whether by natural increase or by immigration, must be economically beneficial.

CANADIAN IMMIGRATION POLICY

Historically, Canada's immigration policy has been a compromise between an open policy regarding total immigration but a restrictive policy with respect to the composition of immigrants. Canada has never imposed overall immigrant quotas by country or occupation (apart from inter-country agreements regarding the entry of immigrants from certain non-white countries). In this respect Canada's policy has been much more open than that of the United States.

Even apart from discrimination and preferences, however, Canada's open policy has been tempered by restrictiveness at various times. In the 1930's, under the impact of the great depression, all immigration was suspended with only minor exceptions. Furthermore, Canada traditionally has pursued a "cyclical" immigration policy—encouraging immigration in periods of high employment and economic expansion, discouraging it in times of high unemployment and economic recession. In 1966 this stop-go policy was questioned by the Minister of Manpower and Immigration: "If we were to promote immigration one year and discourage it the next year, turning the tap on and off in response to short-term economic conditions in Canada, we could not expect to get much high-quality immigration."[1]

What about the restrictive aspects of Canada's traditional immigration policy? Here three features are noteworthy: (i) country preferences, (ii) occupational preferences, (iii) racial discrimination. Preferred countries were the "white" Commonwealth countries—Britain, Australia, New Zealand, and South Africa—France, and the United States. Citizens of these countries were generally admissible to Canada, providing their health and character were satisfactory and they had means to maintain themselves until they found employment. To solidify this favouritism, most Canadian immigration offices were located in these "preferred countries," making it easier for prospective immigrants to apply for admittance to Canada.

No automaticity of entry into Canada existed for other countries. However, citizens of European countries could enter if they were in "preferred occupations" and had assured employment in Canada. Workers in primary industries (farming, mining, forestry) and domestic servants were the favoured occupations. As one commentator writes: "Again, before 1945, and even beyond that year, the Canadian government's criterion of a good immigrant was one with a strong back: farm labourers and servant girls were the preferred classes."[2] Even within Europe a country preference was applied as well: citizens of countries in northern and western Europe were favoured over others.

Racial discrimination was a distinct feature of Canadian immigration policy in the past. The devices to exclude non-white people were diverse, and included both covert and overt measures. Thus the preference given to British subjects served to bar black people (both in the West Indies and in Africa) by interpreting a Commonwealth country to be one inhabited principally by white citizens. In the late 19th and early 20th centuries, immigrants from Asia were discouraged by head taxes; later Asiatic immigration was prohibited by the order-in-council that an immigrant coming to Canada by other than a continuous journey from his home country could be excluded on that ground alone! This provision served to bar Asiatics, because their travel to Canada generally involved a transfer of vessel. The discriminatory racial policy was tempered (some might say, facilitated) by

---

1. Hon. Jean Marchand, *White Paper on Immigration* (Ottawa: Queen's Printer, 1966), p. 12.
2. Arthur R. M. Lower, "The Growth of Population in Canada," in V. W. Bladen, ed., *Canadian Population and Northern Colonization* (Toronto: University of Toronto Press, 1962), p. 57.

agreements with the governments of Japan, India, Pakistan, and Ceylon, to admit a specified token number of immigrants annually.

People of Oriental descent living in Canada even had their right to sponsor relatives restricted by government policy! Thus, as late as 1949, an Oriental had to be a citizen of Canada, and not merely a resident, in order to have the right to sponsor relatives; and the sponsorable class of relatives was limited to wives and unmarried children under 18 years of age. Neither of these restrictions applied to non-Oriental Canadians.

A quota applied to the West Indies was particularly heinous in its racism. An annual flow of 250 immigrants from that area was permitted (indeed fostered) by the Canadian government; but the only occupational class permitted was female domestic servants!

Finally, if these provisions did not suffice to bar the entry into Canada of a non-white (or indeed an undesired white) alien, the Minister responsible for immigration (and, through him, his subordinates and ultimately immigration officers themselves) could fall back on general exclusion principles first established by order-in-council in 1919 and later enacted into legislation. These provisions permitted the prohibition of entry of immigrants on the basis of such factors as "nationality, citizenship, ethnic group, occupation, geographic area of origin; peculiar customs, habits, modes of life or methods of holding property."

As late as 1947, the Prime Minister, Mackenzie King, expounded a discriminatory policy:

> With regard to the selection of immigrants, much has been said about discrimination. I wish to make it quite clear that Canada is perfectly within her right in selecting the persons whom we regard as desirable future citizens. It is not a 'fundamental human right' of any alien to enter Canada. It is a privilege. It is a matter of domestic policy. . . . There will, I am sure, be general agreement with the view that the people of Canada do not wish, as a result of mass immigration, to make a fundamental alteration in the character of our population. Large-scale immigration from the orient would change the fundamental composition of the Canadian population.[3]

It is fair to say, however, that the racially discriminatory aspects of Canada's immigration policy were gradually removed in the 1950's and 1960's. In 1966 the Minister of Manpower and Immigration took an unqualified anti-discriminatory stand:

> More will be done to maintain and improve international relations by removing the last vestiges of discrimination from immigration legislation and regulations, by continuing to respect the wishes of other

---

3. Quoted in David C. Corbett, *Canada's Immigration Policy* (Toronto: University of Toronto Press, 1957), pp. 3, 36.

countries as to the extent of our promotional activity, and by ensuring a high standard of protection and a ready welcome for all acceptable immigrants of whatever origin.[4]

Perhaps the most important feature of Canada's traditional immigration policy was its flexibility. Considerable scope was left to the minister responsible for immigration to carry out and even initiate policy. This authority extended to immigration officers themselves, *via* the administration of ministerial rules and regulations.[5] Even the basic policy of immigration was left to the cabinet itself rather than to Parliament—orders-in-council and departmental rules and regulations rather than legislation were the typical forms in which Canada's immigration policy was expressed and changed.

Is such flexibility in immigration policy a good or bad thing? Opinions differ. For example, one writer is quite sanguine: "It might be very difficult politically to obtain as liberal terms in formal legislation as it has been possible to adopt by order-in-council and ministerial regulation."[6] Other observers are more critical: "However, flexibility is not necessarily a value in itself. An Order in Council has resulted in a sound program for testing immigrants for tuberculosis, but an Order in Council has also been employed in the past to bar all Asians except relatives of Canadian citizens."[7]

A milestone in Canada's immigration policy occurred on October 1, 1967, when new immigration regulations—based on the White Paper on Immigration (1966) and recommendations of a joint committee of the Senate and the House of Commons—came into effect. These regulations mark a sharp break with Canada's traditional immigration policy. First of all, country preferences are eliminated. Favoured treatment is no longer given to a prospective immigrant just because he is a citizen of a particular country, such as Britain, the countries of northern and western Europe, and the United States. There is one qualification, however. Immigration offices and publicity can still be concentrated in certain countries, at the discretion of the Department of Manpower and Immigration. Nevertheless, it is fair to say that such concentration, for example, in favour of Britain, reflects a desire to attract immigrants in certain occupational classes (namely, professional and skilled) rather than immigrants of particular racial and national backgrounds for their own sake.

---

4. Marchand, *White Paper on Immigration*, p. 17.
5. In 1956 the Supreme Court of Canada in an historic decision ruled unconstitutional the delegation of authority to officers of the Department of Citizenship and Immigration (now the Department of Manpower and Immigration) and thus the scope given to their "individual notions."
6. David Corbett, "Canada's Immigration Policy, 1957-1962," *International Journal*, XVIII, No. 2 (Spring 1963), p. 170.
7. Donald R. Taft and Richard Robbins, *International Migrations* (New York: The Ronald Press Company, 1955), p. 352.

Second, racial discrimination is terminated. No country or racial restrictions on immigration exist in the new regulations. Furthermore, the racially-oriented geographical limitations on the sponsorship of dependents no longer exists. All Canadian citizens and residents are treated equally in the sponsorship of dependents. (However, non-dependent relatives nominated by a Canadian citizen are given a slight preference over those nominated by a resident. This provision is independent of the prospective-immigrant's home country.)

Third, the flexibility available to the Minister of Manpower and Immigration, and to immigration officials in particular, is greatly reduced. In a sharp break with past policy, a specific assessment system is set up to evaluate the qualifications of immigrants.

A prospective immigrant who is not sponsored or nominated by a relative must receive at least 50 points (called "assessment units") out of a maximum of 100 in order to be admitted to Canada. The grading scheme is as follows:

Factor	Maximum Points
Education and Training	20
Occupational Skill	10
Occupational Demand in Canada	15
Employment Opportunities in Area of Destination	5
Arranged Employment	10
Personal Assessment	15
Age	10
Knowledge of French and English	10
Relative in Canada	5

There are several noteworthy features of this assessment system. The scope given to subjective evaluation by the immigration officer is confined largely to an assessment of the immigrant's personal qualities, for a maximum of 15 points. It would be better to remove this last vestige of the traditional "flexible" policy of judging immigrants.

The emphasis on occupation and employment in the assessment scheme (60 points out of a possible 100) places Canada firmly in the race to be a recipient country of the "brain drain." The traditional preference for workers in primary industries and domestic servants has given way to a bias in favour of professionals and skilled workers.

In general, the system of assigning specific weights to desired attributes of immigrants is an excellent one. It makes Canada's immigration policy explicit to the Canadian community, to prospective immigrants, and to the world at large. It allows the establishment of objective criteria to judge immigrants, and it permits immigrants deficient in one desired quality to compensate by strength in another.

Presumably, the factors and their relative weights would be subject to change from time to time on the basis of experience in the quantity and quality of immigrants processed by the new system. Also, the evaluation scheme itself (the factors involved) might be altered to reflect changing preferences in assessing the qualities of immigrants on the part of the Canadian government.

As far as weaknesses of the particular scheme established are concerned, the system does not favour some types of immigrants who would generally be considered desirable. No points are given for the immigrant-capitalist, who brings funds with him to invest in Canadian industry. Nor are points given to entrepreneurial immigrants as such—those who would establish new products or techniques in Canada, using their own or borrowed capital—except insofar as they fit into the various educational or occupational categories.

Nevertheless, in general, the new immigration policy is a distinct improvement over past policies from both a "national-interest" and a "humanitarian" standpoint. While the policy favours explicitly the skilled and educated as immigrants, the racial and national discriminations inherent in past regulations no longer exist.

EMIGRATION FROM CANADA TO THE UNITED STATES

If Canada is a land to which streams of immigrants have been attracted, it is also a country from which large numbers of people have emigrated. In 1851-1945, a period covering nearly a century, 6,740,000 people immigrated to Canada. This is the gross flow. Balanced against it is a total of 6,239,000 persons who emigrated from Canada. In relative terms, emigration was 93 percent of immigration.

What is the explanation for the incredibly high emigration rate in Canadian history? After all, Canada was (and is) an immigrant-attracting country, and emigration amounting to 93 percent of immigration for such a country seems incongruous. The answer is that Canada has an even greater immigrant-attracting country as a neighbour—the United States.

We do not have data on the country destination of Canadian emigration. In fact, the over-all emigration series itself is only an approximation. The Canadian government makes no direct count of emigrants, and emigration is calculated as a residual in the population-balance statement. Nevertheless, there is no reason to doubt that an overwhelming part of emigration over the whole of Canadian history has been to the United States. While some immigrants to Canada returned to their native land, this could not have been more than a very small number. The United States was (and still is) the most preferred country among prospective immigrants, whether or not in Canada, and—if in Canada—whether Canadian or foreign-born. Once a person is in Canada, the other principal immigrant-receiving countries—Australia, New Zealand, South Africa—are far away compared to the United States.

Statistical evidence exists to support the assertion that the bulk of Canadian emigration has been to the United States. "The 1956 United Nations Demographic Year Book indicates that, based on censuses across the world, of the more than one million Canadian-born persons residing outside Canada, approximately 94 percent lived in the United States."[8] U.S. data on immigration of residents of Canada to that country are available since 1950. Comparing this series with the Canadian series on total emigration for the time period 1950-1966, yields the result that the U.S. was the destination of 81 percent of Canadian emigrants. Because the Canadian series is calculated residually rather than directly, this figure should be viewed only as an approximation.

The history of emigration from Canada to the United States is marked by two important changes in U.S. immigration policy—one in 1921, the other in 1965. Until the end of World War I, both Canada and the United States had fundamentally open immigration policies. This meant that people migrating to Canada could do so with the intention of treating Canada as a mere stopping-point en route to the United States. Thus it has been pointed out that immigration to Canada in the "open-immigration" era should be treated simply as immigration to North America. A subsequent movement to the United States by the Canadian immigrant was no more difficult than internal migration from one province of Canada to another. "The historical fact is that geographical mobility over the land border was about as easy as it was from east to west within the Dominion."[9]

In 1921, however, the United States instituted a system of restrictive immigration quotas allocated according to the country-of-birth of prospective immigrants. Later the quotas were made even more restrictive and discriminatory. Canada and the rest of the Western Hemisphere (except for colonial possessions) were exempt from the quotas. However, immigrants to Canada intending to re-immigrate to the United States were denied the free access still available to Canadian-born persons. Thus ended the role of Canada as an *entrepôt* for U.S.-destined immigrants from outside the Western Hemisphere. Of course, not all immigrants to Canada in the pre-1921 era intended to cross the border to settle in the United States. Some treated Canada as their ultimate as well as initial destination. Others, how-

8. Bruce W. Wilkinson, *Studies in the Economics of Education*, Occasional Paper No. 4 (Ottawa: Department of Labour, 1965), p. 59.
9. Brinley Thomas, *Migration and Economic Growth* (Cambridge: Cambridge University Press, 1954), pp. 135-36.

ever, while at first intending to remain in Canada, were "pulled" across the border by economic opportunities in the United States.

With the exemption of the Canadian-born from the U.S. quota, such persons were free to move to the United States as they had been under the U.S. open-immigration policy. As in the case of re-immigration by people who came to Canada, the "pull" of economic opportunities in the United States exerted a powerful influence on Canadian-born people. One important phenomenon was the mass migration of French-Canadians to the United States. This movement, again, can be viewed as internal migration within North America, based on unemployment and land shortages in rural Quebec contrasting with buoyant employment conditions in factories in the U.S., largely in textile mills in New England as far as the French-Canadian migrants were concerned. As Porter notes:

> There has, however, been a considerable French-Canadian emigra-
> tion to the United States. This net loss has been estimated at 800,000,
> most of it beginning around 1830 and coinciding with the first short-
> age of land in Quebec and continuing until 1930. Industrialization of
> the United States became a lure to the *habitant* denied access to land.[10]

Canadian-born, of both French and other origins, as well as new immigrants to Canada, were attracted to the U.S. not only because of the faster industrialization there but also because of the easier access to land for farming purposes. In fact, while the development of the Canadian West in the late 19th and early 20th centuries attracted new immigrants as well as some Canadian-born residing in the East, many people of like disposition emigrated to the United States to open up the American West.

In 1839 Lord Durham compared economic opportunities in Canada very unfavourably with those in the United States: "By describing one side and reversing the picture the other would also be described. On the American side all is activity and bustle. . . . On the British side of the line . . . all seems waste and desolate."[11] Canada's economic position, both absolute and relative to the United States, certainly has improved tremendously since that time. And in the postwar period, Canada comes out quite favourably in the migration "numbers game." In the period 1946-1967, Canadian emigration totalled 1,134,000 compared to an immigration of 2,922,000. In relative terms, emigration was only 39 percent of immigration, in contrast to the 93 percent figure in the 1851-1945 period.

On December 1, 1965 a fundamental change in U.S. immigration policy came into effect. As far as immigration from countries outside the Western

---

10. John Porter, *The Vertical Mosaic* (Toronto: University of Toronto Press, 1965), pp. 32-33.
11. Quoted in *Canada Year Book 1957-58* (Ottawa: Dominion Bureau of Statistics, 1958), p. 159.

Hemisphere is concerned, the new U.S. law had a liberalizing impact. The quota system based on national origins, which discriminated in favour of Britain and northern and western Europe, was abolished. Instead, an over-all quota of 170,000 immigrants annually was imposed, with a 20,000 maximum from any one country. On the other hand, for the first time in U.S. history a quota was imposed on Western-Hemisphere immigration to the United States. This quota is 120,000 a year, though with no country maximum, and came into effect on July 1, 1968. Immediate-family relatives (spouses, parents, unmarried children) of a U.S. citizen or resident can enter the country outside of the Western-Hemisphere quota.

While the quota certainly has the potential of restricting Canadian emigration to the United States, its effect in this respect cannot be nearly so powerful as another provision in the new U.S. immigration law. A Western-Hemisphere immigrant intending to work in the United States must obtain certification from the U.S. Department of Labor that he will not displace an American worker. Such a procedure allows considerable scope for "administrative" restriction and regulation of immigration on the part of the U.S. government. More important, the considerable time and effort required in obtaining certification tends to discourage Canadian emigration — both on the part of the people desiring to move and on the part of their potential employers in the United States. The red-tape certification procedure came into effect on December 1, 1965, and is the explanation of a drop in Canadian emigration to the U.S. from 50,000 in 1965 to 29,000 in 1966—the latter being the lowest figure since 1951.

Thus the "rules of the game" for emigration from Canada to the United States have undergone two drastic changes over time, each of a restrictive nature. In 1921 open immigration of foreign-born persons living in Canada was terminated; these persons could now enter the U.S. only under their native-country's quota. In 1965 the unrestricted immigration of Canadian-born people to the United States was replaced by a job-certification requirement, supplemented in 1968 by the U.S. placing Canadian emigration in general under a Western-Hemisphere quota.

Migration between Canada and the United States is by no means a one-way movement. While by far the greater part of the migration has been from Canada to the United States, there has always been some movement in the other direction. Some of this reverse flow has been politically motivated. The earliest such movement was the migration of Loyalists to Canada after the American Revolutionary War. Recently, there has been an influx into Canada of draft resisters and others opposed to United States policy in Vietnam, although the numbers involved might be smaller than one might expect from the publicity given to this movement.[12]

Most U.S. immigration to Canada, however, occurs for economic considerations, just as the Canadian outflow does. The strong corporate links between industries in the two countries promote two-way movements of personnel. Also, individuals in the U.S. may come to Canada of their own accord because of a better opportunity in their particular occupation. The U.S. red-tape and quota restrictions of Canadian immigration have not given rise to retaliation on the part of the Canadian government. U.S. immigration to Canada takes place under the assessment system described in the previous section.

BRAIN DRAIN OR BRAIN GAIN?

In the postwar period, Canadian emigration (which flows principally to the United States) has been less than half that of immigration to Canada (39 percent, based on data in the years 1946-1967). Yet the Canadian government—as well as Canadian industries and universities—are deeply concerned about the migration of Canadians to the United States. The reason is the concentration of emigrants in the professional and skilled-worker categories of the labour force. People who have received education in a profession or training in a particular skill embody capital that has been invested in them. If the education or training has been provided in their home country, a subsequent migration represents a unilateral transfer of human capital ("investment in human beings") from the home country to the country of immigration. If the education or training has taken place in a foreign country, say the country of ultimate migration, then there is an opportunity loss to the country-of-birth of the emigrant. In other words, the home country lost a potential gift of human capital from abroad.

Canada has experienced both types of losses of educated and trained people to the United States. The "opportunity loss" refers to Canadians who engage in graduate or professional study in the United States and choose to remain in that country. The Department of Manpower and Immigration considers the situation to be sufficiently serious that it sponsors

---

12. A figure of 5,000 draft resisters, as well as several hundred U.S. military deserters, living in Canada as at the beginning of 1968 has been suggested. See *The New York Times* (January 31, 1968), p. 3. Indications are, however, that the number of deserters admitted to Canada has increased considerably since May 21, 1969, when the Minister of Manpower and Immigration announced that a prospective immigrant would not be rejected because of active service in his home country's military forces. See, for example, *The New York Times* (October 5, 1969), pp. 1 and 58.

an "Operation Retrieval" to persuade Canadians educated in the United States to return to Canada.[13]

In a sense, the Canadian concern with its loss of brainpower is misplaced. The occupational composition of migration flows in general—not just that of Canadians emigrating to the United States—has changed drastically in the postwar period. In the 19th century, immigrants to North America consisted largely of peasant-farmers. In the 20th century until World War II, they were primarily unskilled workers, destined for factories. After the war, professionals and skilled workers constituted an increasingly important class of immigrants. "Instead of proletarian mass migration, . . . the scene is now characterized by professional elite migration."[14]

Thus, although Canada is losing educated native-born people to the United States, she is receiving professionals and skilled workers from abroad, principally from Britain. Furthermore, Canada also gains some trained manpower from the United States.

The flow of skilled and educated migrants is a general phenomenon throughout the world. One may speak of an international market for professionals and skilled workers. One aspect of the flow is from the underdeveloped to the developed countries. Another aspect consists of movements among the developed countries themselves, and, in general, this is descriptive of the Canadian situation. Quite analogously to its role in the period of unrestricted migration, Canada is both a "receiving" and "sending" country in the flow of human capital. And North America (Canada and the United States) is a sub-market in the international market for brainpower.

Countries throughout the world are aware of migrant flows of human capital, and seek to minimize their loss and maximize their acquisition of trained people. As the Minister of Manpower and Immigration noted in his White Paper: "If those entering the work force, whether native-born or immigrants, do not have the ability and training to do the kinds of jobs available, they will be burdens rather than assets."[15] The assessment system for immigrants introduced by the Canadian government in 1967 is strongly geared to attract educated people, professionals, and skilled workers, as noted above.

The Canadian government has shown a desire to maximize its net inflow of human capital, in several ways in addition to its new immigration regulations. In 1966 the creation of the Department of Manpower and Immigration linked governmental action in these two related fields. Previously,

13. For a description of "Operation Retrieval," see *The Financial Post* (March 16, 1968), p. 23.

14. Brinley Thomas, " 'Modern' Migration," in Walter Adams, ed., *The Brain Drain* (New York: The Macmillan Company, 1968), p. 33.

15. Marchand, *White Paper on Immigration*, p. 8.

immigration was the responsibility of the former Department of Citizenship and Immigration, and the manpower aspects were largely the concern of the Department of Labour. "Operation Retrieval," mentioned above, is a promotional effort on the part of the Department of Manpower and Immigration to help Canadian students in the U.S. find employment in Canada rather than in the United States. As far as the inflow of brainpower from overseas is concerned, both the federal government and several of the provinces maintain recruiting offices in Britain.

One would expect the change in U.S. immigration policy in 1965 to act to reduce the "brain drain" from Canada to the United States. However, in spite of its generally restrictive nature, the new U.S. policy may not significantly stem the flow of professional and skilled Canadian manpower to the United States. The reason is that the job-certification procedure does not apply to professionals and designated skilled workers. These people are preferred over other immigrants. So it is likely that, while reducing total Canadian emigration to the United States, the new U.S. immigration policy will alter the composition of this flow to be even more weighted in favour of people composing the "brain drain."

The question arises as to whether migratory movements have resulted in a net loss or gain in professional and skilled manpower for Canada. In other words, is Canada the recipient of a "brain gain" or the victim of a "brain drain?" All evidence points to the fact that, on balance, Canada benefits from a significant "brain *gain*." The fact that in the period 1946-1967, over-all emigration was only 39 percent of immigration indicates that, to produce a net "brain *drain*," professional and skilled workers would have to be weighted much heavier in the composition of emigration than in that of immigration. This, in fact, is not the case.

One researcher has gathered statistics to show that, in the period 1950-1963, the emigration of professionals and skilled workers from Canada to both the United States and Britain (the latter being the second most important destination of Canadian emigrants) was only 45 percent of the immigration of such people from all countries to Canada.[16] Another study considers the inter-censal period 1951-1961, and compares immigration to Canada (net of people who re-immigrate elsewhere) and Canadian-born emigration to the United States. Each flow is weighted by an estimate of the cost of the education and training embodied in the migrants, and the results show that the human capital in emigration is only between 17 and 29 percent of that in immigration, depending on the assumptions.[17]

---

16. Louis Parai, *Immigration and Emigration of Professional and Skilled Manpower During the Post-War Period*, Special Study No. 1 (Ottawa: Economic Council of Canada, 1965), pp. 1-2.
17. Wilkinson, *Studies in the Economics of Education*, p. 72.

III

Industry Problems

The macro-economic approach to an analysis of the Canadian economy provides many useful insights, as we saw in Part I. However, unless one at times escapes the framework of over-all aggregate economic variables, one is apt to ignore some aspects of the economy that may be as important as stabilization issues. In this part of the volume, we examine the competitive conditions, i.e., the market structures, of Canadian industries, with regard to both the selling of their products and their purchase of labour services (i.e., the union-management collective-bargaining process). Because of their importance in the Canadian economy and their unique features, the agricultural sector and the transportation industry are singled out for special attention.

Max D. Stewart's essay on "Industrial Organization" studies the market-structure aspects of Canadian industry and derives some policy conclusions. Stewart examines the geographic and ownership concentration of industry in Canada, interlocking directorships among corporations, the economic range of large companies across industries and regions, and the role of advertising. He urges that public policy emphasize the promotion of competition rather than the expansion of specific regulation of industry. In particular, Stewart suggests that (1) economic commissions replace legislation as the means of evaluating mergers, (2) interlocking directorates be curtailed more than they are at present, and (3) seller advertising be countered by the provision of direct total-information to consumers.

"Trade Unionism, Collective Bargaining and Public Policy" is the subject of John Crispo's essay. Crispo was a member of the Prime Minister's Task Force on Labour

Relations, and his essay draws on the *Report* of that body. Crispo recommends the broadest possible labour-force coverage of trade unionism and collective bargaining, greater discretion by labour-relations boards in reopening and realigning bargaining units, a careful balancing of individual-worker rights and union responsibilities, a scheme to accredit employer associations, the removal of impediments to the collective-bargaining process, a comprehensive picketing and boycotting code, the creation of a Public Interest Disputes Commission, and an updated legislation and administration of the collective-bargaining process on the part of the government.

"The Farm Problem" is the topic explored by D. R. Campbell, who notes the tremendous postwar decline of 55 percent in Canada's farm labour force. Campbell provides a survey of supply and demand conditions in Canadian agriculture and examines their effects—general overproduction, cycles of production, low average farm incomes, and rural poverty. Campbell reviews government agricultural programs to cope with these problems. In particular, he praises biological and physical research programs and advisory services to farmers, but criticizes the neglect of economic research, the dairy-subsidy program, and the lack of attention given to hard-core farm poverty.

The history and regulation of the transportation industry in Canada is the subject of W. J. Stenason's essay, entitled "Transportation Policy." Stenason reviews the development of railways and the subsequent competition offered by other forms of transportation (e.g., trucking, aviation). As far as government policy is concerned, Stenason indicates that only since 1959, with the appointment of the MacPherson Royal Commission on Transportation, has the government pursued a transportation policy based on efficient resource allocation within the transportation industry. Prior to that time, transportation policy was used, rather, to carry out other national objectives. Regarding an efficient transportation policy, Stenason emphasizes that in many cases it requires the planning of transport facilities ahead of the demand for them.

industrial organization

Max D. Stewart
University of Alberta

The Canadian economy is a mixture of some public and more private enterprises. Their economic decisions interact with each other and strongly affect both the direction of public affairs and the success or failure of business firms. Decision-makers are influenced in varying degrees by the particular environments in which they operate. Economic environments have many dimensions—resource location, geographic concentration of production, market dispersion, public policies and programs of federal, provincial and local governments, concentration of ownership or control of industry, and so on. The conduct of firms alters in turn their environment. The continuing interaction of market structure and market conduct gives rise to ever-changing market performances.

The interrelationships of market structure, market conduct and market performance are powerful factors in determining Canadian economic performance. Basic economic and social goals may be taken to be:

— full employment
— high economic growth rate
— viable balance of payments, and
— equitable distribution of rising incomes.[1]

The foregoing are the concerns of industrial organization. Its objective is to apply, with the necessary modifications, price theory so as to account for the specific conditions confronting various groups of firms. In order to keep a view of the forest and to avoid the confusion of single trees, it is most useful to arrange firms (or those related parts of firms that conduct

---

1. Economic Council of Canada, *First Annual Review: Economic Goals for Canada to 1970* (Ottawa: Queen's Printer, 1964), p. 1.

a range of unrelated activities[2]) in industries. The value of that procedure, followed by the Dominion Bureau of Statistics in its data collection and presentation, is by no means lost because of unavoidable difficulties in discerning the boundary between industries and some consequent vagueness.

Industrial organization cannot be fully examined within the confines of a single essay. A few illustrative aspects will be studied:
—geographic concentration of commodity-producing industries;
—ownership concentration in manufacturing and mining;
—interlocking directorates;
—the range of economic activities encompassed by large corporations; and
—advertising.

WHERE IS THE ECONOMIC ACTIVITY?

To achieve reasonable equity for all Canadians, it is necessary, though not sufficient, that many policies be formulated with due consideration given to the uneven geographic distribution of different economic activities. Although resource location is a powerful factor in the geographic concentrations of commodity-producing industries, public and private decisions may well be as important in determining the current levels of production of individual commodities and hence the level of income in different provinces or regions.

Where the economic action *can be* depends much upon resource location. Where the economic action *is* depends much upon public policies and private corporate decisions and their interaction.

The present conditions are shown in Table 1, which is based on 1965 census value added for commodity-producing industries.[3] It shows the importance of each of the eight industries and of the provinces and territories required to account for 80 percent or more of each industry and of the eight combined. Of the four provinces contributing 85.1 percent of the value added, three—Ontario, British Columbia and Alberta—have industry proportions relatively higher than their proportions of the Canadian population. All other provinces and territories have percentages of value added lower than their percentages of the population.

It would seem necessary that policies designed to affect the major por-

---

2. For example, a fertilizer plant and a meat-packing plant owned by the same firm would be considered as separate firms in their respective industries. A firm operating plants in four different industries would thus be subdivided into four "firms," all its plants in a single industry being counted as one "firm."
3. Dominion Bureau of Statistics, *Canada Year Book, 1968* (Ottawa: Queen's Printer, 1968), p. 1074 and elsewhere.

tions of each of the eight commodity-producing industries, be effective at least in the areas listed. For example, most (88.5 percent) existing forestry in Canada would be involved if policies were implemented in British Columbia, Quebec and Ontario; most (82.3 percent) of fisheries would be included in policies that covered Nova Scotia, British Columbia, Newfoundland and New Brunswick. That is not to say, of course, that policies concerning particular industries should ignore the interests of less important areas. It is a question of balance. For example, future developments could often be promoted in areas where a particular activity is currently relatively unimportant to Canada as a whole.

Table 1

IMPORTANCE OF INDIVIDUAL INDUSTRIES
AND MAIN AREAS OF PRODUCTION

Industry	Census Value Added, 1965 ($000,000)	Geographic locations of at least 80 percent of value added (in order of area's importance)	Actual percentage of value added in named areas
Manufactures	14,928	Ontario, Quebec	81.6
Construction	5,103	Ontario, Quebec, British Columbia, Alberta	81.7
Agriculture	2,535	Saskatchewan, Ontario Alberta, Manitoba	82.5
Mining	2,492	Alberta, Ontario, Quebec, Saskatchewan, British Columbia	84.7
Electric Power	1,036	Ontario, Quebec, British Columbia, Alberta	82.1
Forestry	603	British Columbia, Quebec, Ontario	88.5
Fisheries	160	Nova Scotia, British Columbia, Newfoundland, New Brunswick	82.3
Trapping	12	Ontario, Quebec, Alberta, Manitoba, Yukon, and Northwest Territories	82.0
Total	28,869	Ontario, Quebec, British Columbia, Alberta	85.1

The viewpoint of the importance of a province in each different industry, leaves aside two other important questions. How important to the area is a particular industry, say, mining? What kinds of mineral production make up most of the mining in a province or economic region? The composition of industrial activity varies considerably from region to region and the specific composition of the individual sectors also shows considerable variation. For example, mining is a more important part of over-all commodity production in the Prairie Provinces than elsewhere in Canada. The chief kinds of mineral production in that region are crude petroleum and natural gas in Alberta, and potash in Saskatchewan. If programs favouring mining were to have an impact upon Alberta or Saskatchewan, they would need to be planned with some care because they would likely be quite unlike those that would encourage Ontario mining, which is much more concerned with metals—nickel, copper, iron ore, gold and uranium. It must also be noted that Prairie mining is 44.2 percent of Canadian mining and accounts for 22.6 percent of value added by the eight commodity-producing industries on the Prairies. On the other hand, Ontario mining is the second most important, 22 percent of the Canadian total but relatively unimportant in Ontario, accounting for 4.9 percent of that province's commodity production. A policy adverse to mining would likely give rise to greater political outcry in Alberta than in Ontario or Quebec. Those are the kinds of situations shown in Tables 2 and 3, based on five economic regions for Canada.

Table 2
REGIONAL IMPORTANCE IN COMMODITY PRODUCTION

Region	British Columbia, Yukon and Northwest Territories*	Prairie Provinces	Ontario	Quebec	Atlantic Provinces
Percentage of Canadian Population (1965 Estimate)	9.3	17.2	34.6	28.9	10.0
Percentage of 1965 Industry Census Value Added In Each Region:					
Eight Commodity-Producing Industries	10.1	18.0	41.5	25.0	5.4
Manufactures	8.3	6.5	52.8	28.8	3.4
Construction	13.2	21.7	31.6	25.5	7.7
Agriculture	4.2	57.9	24.6	9.7	3.6
Mining	9.3	44.2	22.0	16.0	8.7
Electric Power	10.6	16.2	35.8	29.2	8.1
Forestry	48.1	1.9	16.1	24.2	9.4
Fisheries	30.3	4.3	4.0	4.4	57.0
Trapping	14.8	38.3	24.6	18.0	4.3

* It is convenient to include the northern areas with British Columbia because they presently account for quite small percentages of Canadian economic activity, although increasing expansion is now evident in some sectors. There is no intended implication that the two areas and British Columbia make up an economic region.

Table 2 depicts the relative importance in 1965 of each region in each industry total. The Prairies and Ontario, for example, account for 66.2 percent of Canadian value added in mining.

Whereas Table 2 shows where each type of economic activity is concentrated, Table 3 shows which kinds of industry are most important to each region of the country. From the two charts it can be seen that although Quebec is about twice as important as the Atlantic Provinces in the mining total (Table 2), mining value added is more than twice as important to the Atlantic Provinces as it is to Quebec (Table 3). More people in Quebec would be currently affected by mining policies than would be in the Atlantic Provinces because of the absolute employment difference; mining policies would have greater immediate impact on the economy of the Atlantic Provinces. Long-term changes could alter that geographic distribution. Ontario and Quebec are the chief manufacturing regions of the country (Table 2) and manufacturing is by far the most important activity in each province (Table 3). Turning to agriculture and mining, both provinces account for less of the Canadian totals than the Prairies (Table 2). Mining is somewhat more important than agriculture in Quebec; the opposite is the case in Ontario (Table 3).

Forestry is concentrated in British Columbia (negligible in the Yukon and Northwest Territories) and Quebec, with the British Columbia con-

Table 3

THE IMPORTANCE OF COMMODITY-PRODUCING INDUSTRIES TO CANADA AND EACH ECONOMIC REGION

(percentage of area 1965 census value added accounted for by each industry)

Region	Canada	British Columbia, Yukon and Northwest Territories	Prairie Provinces	Ontario	Quebec	Atlantic Provinces
Industry						
Manufacturers	55.6	45.9	20.2	70.7	64.1	35.4
Construction	19.0	25.0	23.0	14.5	19.4	27.0
Agriculture	9.4	3.9	30.3	5.6	3.7	6.3
Mining	9.3	8.5	22.6	4.9	6.0	15.0
Electric Power	3.9	4.1	3.5	3.3	4.5	5.8
Forestry	2.2	10.7	0.2	0.9	2.2	3.9
Fisheries	0.6	1.8	0.1	0.1	0.1	6.3
Trapping	—	0.1	0.1	—	—	0.3

tribution almost double that of Quebec. On the other hand, forestry is of equal importance (2.2 percent) in each of the regions. Merchantable standing timber is distributed across the country in different proportions than shown by forestry value added. British Columbia and the Prairies have greater stands available and Quebec and the Atlantic Provinces have relatively less available.

The eight broad industrial sectors fail to disclose the wide diversity in geographic concentration of individual commodity production. For example, the leading areas in non-metallic mineral production are Quebec, Prairie Provinces, and British Columbia, an order of importance quite different from mining in general. Individual non-metallics show further and different geographic concentration—asbestos in Quebec and British Columbia, potash in Saskatchewan, and sulphur mainly in Alberta. A final example from agriculture again shows the great variations from the over-all situation in Canadian agriculture. Ontario and Quebec account for more than 70 percent of the value of milk production and of butter; commercial fruit is chiefly in Ontario and British Columbia; commercial vegetable acreage is found mainly in Ontario and Quebec.

In brief, the geographic concentration of main industry groups varies widely from that of the over-all total and the geographic concentration of each individual industry varies widely from that of the major groups of which it is a part. The impact of a change in tariffs on manufactures would fall chiefly on firms in Ontario and Quebec. The effect in British Columbia would nonetheless be significant also because manufactures are much the most important sector of that economy.

Public policies that disregard the implications of geographic dispersion of industry in Canada will too often lead to results that were in part unintended and that prove to be undesirable. Private business decisions that pay too little attention to regional differences may well increase the divergence between private benefits and costs and public benefits and costs. A more elaborate version of the framework outlined in this section would serve to test, region by region, the probable effects of and responses to a variety of public programs and private business policies.

Geographic concentration of various kinds of output gives rise to specific problems, and, at the same time provides a possible vehicle for carrying forward regional development. However, although public policies, private decisions, and market locations continue to have their effect, areas of resource location and development remain powerful factors in determining the geographic concentration of commodity-producing industries.

WHO CONTROLS THE ECONOMIC ACTIVITY?

Ownership concentration concerns the number and size of firms in individual industries. Economic concentration is significant in the study of Canadian industry because it is an important determinant of market performance.[4]

Control in some industries is widely diffused. In others, it is highly concentrated with a major part of the entire industry output produced by a few firms. Ownership concentration is one important characteristic of the environment of firms, influencing in a number of ways their decisions and behaviour and affecting public policies about competition. If public policy regarding competition and regulation is to be made soundly, it will rely upon adequate information about such matters as ownership concentration, ownership residence or nationality, the relation between size and efficiency, mergers, price-fixing, advertising, trade marks, copyrights and patents. A reference from the Canadian Cabinet to the Economic Council of Canada to examine most of these subjects[5] is recognition of the value of obtaining sufficient evidence in advance of making decisions.

Who does control Canadian economic activity and how that control is exercised may have been influenced in the past more by private decisions than by public policies. Future changes in economic concentration and in the manner of exercising ownership control could be determined more by public policies than by private decisions. In the continuing interaction between the public and private sectors, it would seem likely that the balance between them will shift from time to time. What decisions are made depend upon interrelated public and private goals and attitudes and Canadian industrial structure.

Concentration is examined for two important industrial sectors—manufacturing and mining. Value of shipments and value of production were used to afford a useful comparison. The data are 1964 value of shipments of goods of own manufacture for each four-digit industry in *Manufacturing Industries of Canada*,[6] and 1964 value of mineral production of Canada (in a few cases capacity had to be used for the concentration estimation)

---

4. The field of industrial organization is thoroughly treated in the setting of the United States economy in: Joe S. Bain, *Industrial Organization*, 2d ed. (New York: John Wiley and Sons, Inc., 1968); Richard Caves, *American Industry: Structure, Conduct, Performance* (Englewood Cliffs, New Jersey: Prentice-Hall, Inc., 1964).

5. "In 1966, we received a new request from the Government to study and report . . . on the subject of consumer interests and the fields of combines, mergers, monopolies and restraint of trade, patents, trade marks, copyrights, and registered industrial designs." Economic Council of Canada, *Fourth Annual Review, The Canadian Economy from the 1960's to the 1970's* (Ottawa: Queen's Printer, 1967), p. 9.

6. Dominion Bureau of Statistics, *Manufacturing Industries of Canada*, Section A (Ottawa: Queen's Printer, 1967). The four previous subdivisions of dairy factories (butter and cheese, pasteurizing, condenseries, and ice cream) were retained and woodenware and cooperage were separate from miscellaneous wood industries, n.e.s. There were thus 181 industries instead of 176.

for 46 individual minerals given in *Canadian Minerals Yearbook*,[7] accounting for 96.7 percent of the total. The measure of concentration is an inverse one, the number of largest firms required to account for 80 percent of production in industry.

Establishment concentration in each manufacturing industry has been estimated from the size categories in individual 1964 *Census of Manufacturing* reports, following the procedure used by Gideon Rosenbluth.[8] The lists of establishments in each industry make possible an estimate of firm concentration.

Firm concentration has been estimated for each of the 46 minerals from individual mineral reports in *Canadian Minerals Yearbook, 1965*.

Three concentration categories are used: HIGH—up to 8 firms; MEDIUM—over 8 and up to 20 firms; LOW—over 20 firms. Where the degree of concentration is high, not more than 8 firms accounting for 80 percent of shipments, the firms likely recognize their mutual dependence and behave much as oligopoly theory would suggest. That tendency may be less marked in industries of medium concentration and may be absent in low-concentration industries, especially where many more than 20 firms are required to account for 80 percent. It may also be assumed that it is easier for a few to conspire than for many.

The level of concentration thus derived for each industry may in some instances understate the actual situation. No account has been taken of the over-all size of firms that operate in several manufacturing industries or in several industrial sectors of the economy. There also has been no attention

---

7. Department of Energy, Mines and Resources, *Canadian Minerals Yearbook 1965* (Ottawa: Queen's Printer, 1967). Too great difficulty in estimating the degree of concentration in the production of a few minerals led to their omission, amounting to 3.3 percent of the total production.
The 46 minerals, classified into three concentration categories, are:
HIGH: *metals* — antimony, bismuth, cadmium, calcium, cobalt, copper, iron ore, lead, magnesium, molybdenum, nickel, platinum group, selenium, tellurium, tin, uranium, zinc;
   nonmetallics — arsenious oxide, asbestos, barite, diotomite, feldspar, fluorspar, gypsum, lithia, magnesite and brucite, mica, nepheline syenite, potash, pyrite and pyrrhotite, salt, soapstone and talc and pyrophyllite, sodium sulphate, elemental sulphur, sulphur in smelter gases, titanium dioxide;
   structural materials — cement.
MEDIUM:
   metals — gold, silver;
   fuels — coal;
   structural materials — lime.
LOW: *structural materials* — clay products, sand and gravel, stone;
   fuels — crude petroleum, natural gas.
8. Gideon Rosenbluth, *Concentration in Canadian Manufacturing Industries*, National Bureau of Economic Research (Princeton: Princeton University Press, 1957), Appendix B.

given to intercorporate ownership or control relations[9] or to important intercorporate links established by interlocking directorates. To the extent they have an effect, greater size and intercorporate control arrangements, by shareholdings or common directors, tend to raise concentration and enhance market powers.

Although related products may not always be produced in the same manufacturing industry, as defined for statistical purposes, that source of overstating concentration seems probably to have been more than offset by concentration measures being calculated on a national basis, thereby seriously understating concentration in a number of cases. For example, among the forty leading industries nineteen show low concentration. Five of these, commercial printing, pasteurizing, bakeries, feed manufacturers and butter and cheese plants, are predominantly regional or local. Although some firms operate nationally, there are usually only a few firms in each regional or local market. Sand and gravel and, to a lesser extent, cement are similar situations among low-concentration minerals.

The over-all comparison of concentration in mining and in manufacturing is shown in Chart A. Canadian mining is more highly concentrated than Canadian manufacturing on the basis either of value or of numbers of minerals or industries in the higher-concentration categories.

The size of an industry as well as the number and size of firms affects the degree of concentration. It might be expected that larger industries would tend to be less concentrated. That expectation is not borne out by the levels of concentration existing among the 40 leading manufacturing industries on the basis of value of shipments. The number of leading industries of low concentration is, however, relatively greater than for all manufacturing industries. Omitting the five "regional" or "local" industries leads of course to higher concentration for the remaining 35 but not of the level found in mining.

Chart B shows the percentage of value of shipments of each major industry group that was produced in individual industries in the three concentration categories.

In only two groups, tobacco products industries and petroleum and coal products industries, 100 percent was produced in high-concentration industries.

There are no high-concentration industries in six of the major industry groups—metal fabricating, clothing, furniture and fixture industries, leather industries, printing, publishing and allied industries and knitting mills. There are also no medium-concentration industries in the last two groups.

---

9. Data collected under the Corporations and Labour Unions Returns Act on intercorporate ownership for 1965 provide much useful information, now available to the public in Dominion Bureau of Statistics, *Inter-Corporate Ownership* (Ottawa: Queen's Printer, 1969).

The value of shipments of the six groups accounts for 16.8 percent of manufacturing value of shipments. Nine of the 40 leading industries are in the six least-concentrated industry groups. The value of shipments of the six most-concentrated industry groups accounts for 22.7 percent of all manufacturing and eight of the 40 leading industries are included.

Chart A

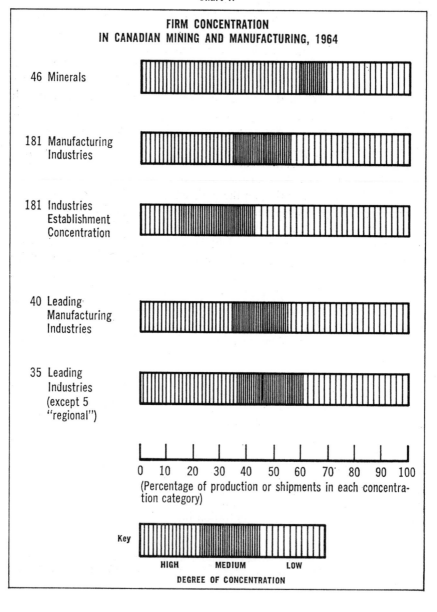

FIRM CONCENTRATION
IN CANADIAN MINING AND MANUFACTURING, 1964

46 Minerals

181 Manufacturing Industries

181 Industries Establishment Concentration

40 Leading Manufacturing Industries

35 Leading Industries (except 5 "regional")

0 10 20 30 40 50 60 70 80 90 100
(Percentage of production or shipments in each concentration category)

Key

HIGH   MEDIUM   LOW
DEGREE OF CONCENTRATION

Chart B

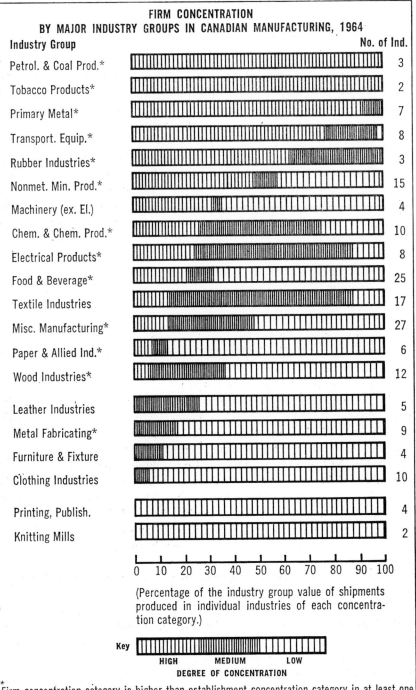

FIRM CONCENTRATION
BY MAJOR INDUSTRY GROUPS IN CANADIAN MANUFACTURING, 1964

Industry Group	No. of Ind.
Petrol. & Coal Prod.*	3
Tobacco Products*	2
Primary Metal*	7
Transport. Equip.*	8
Rubber Industries*	3
Nonmet. Min. Prod.*	15
Machinery (ex. El.)	4
Chem. & Chem. Prod.*	10
Electrical Products*	8
Food & Beverage*	25
Textile Industries	17
Misc. Manufacturing*	27
Paper & Allied Ind.*	6
Wood Industries*	12
Leather Industries	5
Metal Fabricating*	9
Furniture & Fixture	4
Clothing Industries	10
Printing, Publish.	4
Knitting Mills	2

0 10 20 30 40 50 60 70 80 90 100

(Percentage of the industry group value of shipments produced in individual industries of each concentration category.)

Key

HIGH   MEDIUM   LOW
DEGREE OF CONCENTRATION

* Firm concentration category is higher than establishment concentration category in at least one individual industry in the major group. (Detail from research findings at the Economic Council of Canada.)

MARKET STRUCTURE AND CONDUCT AND THE LAW

The Combines Investigation Act seeks to prevent certain private inter-
ferences with competition. A relatively ineffective provision (section 33)
regarding mergers detrimental to the public and an unused opportunity
(section 31) for a dissolution order subsequent to a conviction concern
market structure. Most provisions of the Act seek to restrain or prevent
specific forms of market conduct, that is, to change the behaviour of businesses. It is by no means a simple task to determine the force of criminal
law in curtailing or eliminating practices, which may be difficult to discover and which may be quite logical for self-seeking firms in their particular and continuing economic environments. If the market structure that
gives rise to undesirable conduct remains unaltered, it is far from clear
that modest penalties will end that conduct.

Unacceptable forms of behaviour are:

—conspiracies to prevent or lessen competition, with some exceptions
   (section 32);
—some forms of price discrimination and sales at unreasonably low
   prices (section 33A);
—discriminatory advertising allowances (section 33B);
—materially misleading representation concerning the "ordinary" price
   of an article (section 33C);
—resale price maintenance (section 34).

The ultimate goal of satisfactory market performance and acceptable
economic performance for Canada might be better served outside the
criminal law, which is less than ideally suited to assess economic considerations. An economic-commission approach, somewhat along the lines
followed in the United Kingdom, could possibly deal more adequately with
a number of industry problems. Some criminal offences might also be
retained to curb actions such as price-fixing. The constitutional process of
bringing about that sort of change might prove sufficiently complex so as
to require the continuation of the accustomed approach for some time. In
that circumstance, the merger provision might be overhauled.

HOW MANY COMMON MEETINGS GIVE RISE TO HOW MUCH COMMON PURPOSE?

Unlike the declaration of the United States Clayton Act (section 7)
prohibiting interlocking directorships on the boards of substantial and
otherwise competing corporations, the Combines Investigation Act is
silent on the question. The 1967 Bank Act, reflecting some policy changes,
has imposed limitations (section 18) on interlocking directorates that may

be held by directors of chartered banks. The new restraints do raise the question of opportunities provided to inhibit competition.

A study of concentration of economic power in Canada[10] has made clear that interlocking directorships link together many leading corporations. Recognizing that there is a continuum from "rubber-stamp" directors to active decision-makers, interlocking directorates nonetheless afford opportunities for directors and senior officers to become better informed of the viewpoints of their counterparts in other firms. The wider knowledge and better understanding can only be helpful, even in the absence of collusion, in raising the probability of corporate decisions being mutually "satisfactory" in the interdependent oligopolistic sense. Whether their accommodation of one another is greatly or slightly advanced by the interlocking device, it is unlikely that it will be hindered.

The kind of interlocking connections between Canadian corporations is illustrated by an examination of one set of interlocking directorates in 1964, as shown in Table 4—links through financial firms, and Table 5—links between non-financial firms.

The tables do not reveal whether the same individuals provide the intercorporate links. Interlocking directorships, however, do mean that, for example, the directors of Bank A sit together there and one or more of them are on a number of trust-company boards. Although it might be improper to assign villainy to their learning the operations of several trust-companies, this additional information of the decision processes of potential or actual rivals can only be useful in making bank decisions.

Which interlocking connections between corporations are associated with intercorporate ownership have not been determined.

Directors of four paper companies sit together at a chartered bank (2, 2, 1, 1) and directors of three of the four join together at a trust company (5, 1, 1). Directors of four banks sit together on the board of a trust company (17, 2, 1, 1) and of a metal manufacturer (3, 1, 1, 2); three of the banks are also represented together at a financial company (3, 1, 1) and a second metal manufacturer (5, 2, 2). Four insurance-companies' directors sit together on the board of a bank (17, 2, 2, 1). Life insurance companies have directors on the board of a single bank (6, 3, 2, 3, 4, 2). There are directors of four metal manufacturers sitting together on the board of a bank (5, 3, 6, 1) and three metal manufacturers are represented together at a trust company (4, 3, 4), an insurance company (3, 1, 3) and a financial company (2, 3, 1).

---

10. John Porter, *The Vertical Mosaic* (Toronto: University of Toronto Press, 1965), pp. 233-34, 589-60.

Section 18 of the Bank Act requires the elimination of interlocking directorships between chartered banks and financial companies accepting deposits from the public and confines interlocking directors with other companies to not more than one-fifth of their board members. There is implicit in the imposition of even these limited restrictions that there is a serious possibility of competitive market forces being impaired by links between firms that are otherwise independent competitors. Compliance with the new provision will not necessarily mean the end of such links as have been forged through common membership on the boards of manufacturing and mining companies.

Table 4

INTERLOCKING DIRECTORSHIPS: FINANCIAL AND OTHERS, 1964

		Banks				Trust Companies				Insurance Companies						Other Fin.
		A	B	C	D	E	F	G	H	J	K	L	M	N	O	P
Bank	A					17	2	2	1	6	3	2	3	4	2	
Trust	E	17	2	1	1			1	1	2	1	1	2	3		
Insurance	J	6		4		2	6					1				
Financial	P	3	1	1		3	1			2	1	1				1
Metal	U	5	2	2		4				3						2
	V	3	1	1	2	3				1						3
	W	6	1		2	4				3						1
	X	1														
Paper	Q	2		1	1	5				1						1
	R	2				1										
	S	1				1										
	T	1														
Flour	Y	3				2				1						1
	Z					1										
	ZZ	1				1										
Misc.	MA	7				7				4						4
	MB	1				2										
	MC	2				3										
	MD	3				3										
	ME	1														
	MF															1
	MG	1				1										
	MH	2				1										
	MJ					1										
	MK															1

The numbers in the matrix show the number of directors common to the company in the row and the company in the column.
Capital letters, such as E and MA, refer to specific companies.

There remains open the anti-competitive potential in those interlocking directorships and in the links solely between non-financial companies, illustrated in Table 5 for part of the same interlocking set as in Table 4. The assurance of competition between presumably independent firms is weakened by the election of common directors.

Some of the linked firms are in the same industry and some are suppliers to or buyers from the industries of other "related" firms. Others would appear to have no market contacts, leaving only the possibility of common meetings promoting common understanding.

THE ECONOMIC RANGE OF LARGE COMPANIES

Operating in several industries may reduce risk for a company and operating in different industrial sectors may improve a company's sources of

Table 5
INTERLOCKING DIRECTORSHIPS: NON-FINANCIAL COMPANIES, 1964

		Paper			Metal				Flour			Miscellaneous		
		Q	R	S	U	V	W	X	Y	Z	ZZ	MA	MB	MC
Paper	Q				3				2	1		3	1	2
	R					1								2
	S						1							
Metal	U	3				3	2		2	1		6	1	4
	V		1		3		1					3		1
	W			1	2	1			2			4		1
	X													1
Flour	Y	2			2		2			2		3	1	1
	Z	1			1				2				1	1
	ZZ													1
Misc.	MA	3			6	3	4		3				3	3
	MB	1			1				1	1		3		1
	MC	2	2		4	1	1	1	1	1	1	3	1	
	MD	1			1	1							1	
	ME								1					
	MF				1	1								
	MG				1		2							2
	MH	1					1		1					2
	MJ				1	1								
	MK	1												1

The numbers in the matrix show the number of directors common to the company in the row and to the one in the column.
Capital letters, such as R and MA, refer to specific companies.

supply or its distribution system. Advantages of market power may accrue to the firm. Gains in efficiency may benefit society. Private advantages are not always social gains. An appraisal of the effects, private and social, of wide-ranging activities by large firms would require a comprehensive and detailed study quite beyond the scope of this essay.

A survey of the operations of 50 of the largest non-financial Canadian companies, using details from Canadian Trade Index[11] and from private sources, gives the spectrum of their activities by establishments. It is presented in Table 6.

Table 6
LARGE COMPANY OPERATIONS, 1965

Number of Companies (descending order of number of establishments)	Average Number of Establish- ments[1]	Average Number of Regions* with Estab- lishments[2]	Average Number of Different 4-digit Manufacturing Industries	Average Number of Other Industrial Sectors[3]
50	23.1	3.8	4.2	2.1
6	74.2	5.0	10.3	2.5
6	34.2	4.8	5.2	3.5
6	23.3	3.7	4.2	2.8
6	17.7	4.2	4.7	1.7
6	14.3	3.8	2.8	1.7
6	12.5	3.5	2.5	1.2
6	9.5	2.8	2.7	2.3
8	5.0	2.8	2.2	1.2

* The five used in Table 2 — Atlantic, Quebec, Ontario, Prairies and British Columbia and the Northwest Territories.
1. The number of establishments varies from one to over one hundred.
2. The smallest number of establishments in a company that has establishments in each of the five regions is eight. Only two of the companies are confined to a single region.
3. Seven companies do not operate in other industrial sectors, such as mining, transportation, etc.

All but seven have establishments in more than one manufacturing industry. The 48 that have at least one manufacturing establishment would be counted as 212 "firms" in calculating the degree of concentration for individual manufacturing industries.

Twenty-two companies have establishments in all five regions and only twelve are confined to one or two regions.

ADVERTISING

Informed buyers and sellers are a necessary condition for effectively

---

11. *Canadian Trade Index* (Toronto: Canadian Manufacturers' Association, 1965).

competitive markets. Although the perfect knowledge of the theory of competition may not be required, the persistent price differentials that are observable in many consumer markets give some substance to the argument that there is a lack of sufficient information to sustain competition. Some possible defects are:

—difficulty in obtaining reliable information when it is desired,

—comparable information not readily available, and

—sellers' information, of which advertising is an important component, tends to be self-serving, that is, to be favourable to sellers.

As communication technology continues to advance at a rapid pace, there seems little doubt that we are close to adding to market information greater objectivity and comparability and timing appropriate to the preferences of buyers—all at relatively low cost. That is to argue not that advertising will vanish but that it will be supplemented by techniques of informing that are more directly responsive to the demands of buyers.

Recognizing that advertising is more likely to have importance in final-goods or consumer markets, it is of interest to examine the importance of advertising in various industries.

Using the concentration figures underlying Charts A and B and an earlier Dominion Bureau of Statistics compilation of industry advertising expenditures,[12] Table 7 shows the top twenty industries according to the importance of advertising within each industry and the importance of each industry's advertising.

The industries with a high dollar value of advertising are noticeably larger (by manufacturing value added) than those where advertising is high relative to industry value added. Nine of ten high-volume advertising industries that are below the top twenty on the basis of advertising relative to value added have value added of $82 million or more. The ten industries with high advertising to value added ratios that are not among the top twenty in volume of advertising are much smaller, $35 million or less of value added, and nine of them are of high or medium concentration.

That there is not a somewhat greater number of high-concentration industries may be explained by several points. The various outputs of such industries as miscellaneous food preparations, household appliances and confectionary are relatively poor substitutes, making for an understatement of concentration. In industries such as bread and bakery products, slaughtering and meat-packing, and dairy products, there are a few firms

---

12. Dominion Bureau of Statistics, *Advertising Expenditures in Canada, 1954* (Ottawa: Queen's Printer, 1956). A more recent study published in 1967 by the Dominion Bureau of Statistics — *Advertising Expenditures in Canada, 1964* — is not useful for this purpose because it lacks individual-industry detail, including advertising/sales ratios. Insufficient time prevented taking account of partially comparable data presented in *Advertising Expenditures in Canada, 1965* (Ottawa: Queen's Printer, 1968).

operating nationally along with many regional or local firms. The former tend to stress advertising more than the smaller firms. In each customer market, there are rarely large numbers of firms; concentration is understated by using a national basis because of data limitations.

It may also be noted that the effect of advertising depends to some extent on the frequency of messages and the medium chosen—that is, on the total cost. That is easily achieved in a large industry like motor vehicles with an expenditure total that is low in that industry but high absolutely. The use of advertising seems to be strongly determined by the type of product—differentiated and mainly consumer.

Table 7
ADVERTISING
RELATIVE AND ABSOLUTE IMPORTANCE, 1954

Industries in decending order of the ratio of advertising to manufacturing value added	MVA ($ millions)	Concentration Category		MVA ($ millions)	Industries in descending order of total dollar value of advertising
Toilet preparations	20	M*	L*	90	Misc. food preparations
Soaps, washing compounds	51	H*	H*	51	Soaps, washing compounds
Breakfast foods	15	H*	H	176	Motor vehicles
Misc. food preparations	90	L*	H	310	Petroleum products
Polishes & dressings	10	M	H*	104	Household radio, TV
Foundation garments	12	M	L*	83	Fruit & vegetables
Fountain pens & pencils	7	M	L*	66	Medicinal & pharmaceutical
Smokers' supplies	1	H	M*	71	Household appliances
Macaroni	3	H	M*	20	Toilet preparations
Medicinal and pharmaceutical	66	L*	L	210	Printing and publishing
Fruit and vegetable	83	L*	H	82	Distilled liquors
Paints, varnishes	52	L*	H	148	Breweries
Clocks, watches	6	H	L*	52	Paints, varnishes
Flour mills	35	H	M	158	Slaughtering, meat packing
Household appliances	71	M*	H	149	Rubber products
			L	120	Dairy products (except proc. cheese)
Fur goods	22	L		140	Bread, bakery products
Household radio, TV	104	H*	L	15	Breakfast foods
Oil cloth, linoleum	16	H	H*	19	Industrial machinery
Confectionery	46	L*	L	46	Confectionery
Batteries	15	H	L*		

* Industries that are among the top twenty on both bases — the importance of advertising re manufacturing value added and the industry position on total value of advertising.

CONCLUSIONS AND POLICY IMPLICATIONS

Most commodity-producing industries are concentrated in a few regions of Canada. The commodity production of most regions of the country is concentrated in a few kinds of output.

Two-thirds of Canadian mineral production is obtained under conditions of high or medium ownership concentration. High- or medium-concentration industries account for 55 percent of manufacturing shipments. Some major industry groups are much more concentrated than others.

If existing establishments are assumed to be roughly of minimum efficient size, establishment concentration may be considered to set an approximate lower limit to the level of concentration. A comparison of the second and third bars of Chart A shows that multi-establishment firms increase the percentage of manufacturing shipments in high-concentration industries from 14.2 to 33.8 percent. Chart B indicates which major industry groups show changes in concentration categories because of the effect of multi-establishment firms. Within the affected groups, a few individual industries account for much of the shift of manufacturing shipments from less to more concentrated conditions.[13]

It can be argued that specific public regulation of industry is costly and frequently rather ineffective. Regulation by competitive market forces seems to retain an economic advantage on grounds of responsiveness and efficiency.

The potentially most valuable role for public policy would seem to be active promotion of competition rather than expansion of specific regulation. The latter will, of course, continue to be necessary but a poor second-best wherever competitive forces are too seriously impaired. Some examples may illuminate that viewpoint.

New policies and programs should meet the test of equity across the nation by taking sufficient account of the geographic concentration of commodity production and of the specialized economic activity of most economic regions. An over-all assessment of the varying impacts of several programs is necessary even to attempt an equitable balancing of advantages and detriments between regions.

High concentration in Canadian mining calls for public policies designed to assure domestic customers at least as much benefit from competitive prices as foreign buyers enjoy.

Beyond the strong case that can be made for retaining *per se* offences for such conduct as price-fixing, there would seem to be a valid argument for a less legalistic and a more economic-commission approach to deal with

---

13. Details from basic research, much too extensive to be presented within the compass of this essay, that has been conducted at the Economic Council of Canada.

some questions such as mergers. For example, one might want greater justification (unit-cost reductions) for a merger in circumstances of high concentration. In some cases, lower costs from a merger might outweigh the anti-competitive potential. The net effect of commission decisions could well be less merger activity in some industries and more in others.

Interlocking directorates have sufficient anti-competitive potential to be curtailed more than is envisioned by Section 18 of the Bank Act. If a genuine shortage of qualified individuals is an important element, improved education and recruitment afford better prospects for sound management *and* more competition.

Until a more adequate assessment has been made of the various production and market effects of multi-industry companies, policy may currently have to be simply more resistant to their acquisitions where an anti-competitive aspect is evident and, at the same time, to promote research into the activities of such firms.

Ensuring that market information will effectively promote competition seems to require that a greater proportion of readily available information be more directly serving consumers. The technology is now at hand. Seller-oriented advertising would likely become relatively less important in the total-information system.

An effective Canadian "competition policy" will maintain competitive market forces as a major means of economic regulation. That will limit the areas where less objective and less responsive government regulation will prove necessary. Constitutional barriers, erected in days of old and now unsuited to modern economic conditions, may have to be removed. The importance of coordinating many policies and programs, both public and private, points to active participation at cabinet level.

The goals of competition policy are fewer private restraints on competition, government policies more clearly favouring competition and inhibiting monopolistic elements, less concentration of economic power (that is, less ownership concentration, including intercorporate ownership, fewer interlocking directorships, etc.), freer access to sources of supply and to customers (for example, elimination of captive markets), more easily available market information of an objective and comparable nature—in sum, an economy more responsive to consumer demands.

trade unionism, collective bargaining and public policy

John Crispo
University of Toronto

The purpose of this essay is to review Canadian public policy pertaining to trade unionism and collective bargaining. The challenge of conducting such a review at all objectively is heightened by the fact that the Canadian industrial-relations system is once again under severe attack.

Periodically the conduct of labour-management relations in any country is subject to severe criticism. In Canada, as well as in many other western countries, the attack on collective bargaining has been mounting in recent years. The result verges on a crisis of confidence in the present industrial relations system.

Why has the public apparently lost faith in the prevailing collective bargaining process? The rash of strikes which have caught the headlines in recent years provides much of the explanation. In many of these disputes the protagonists seem to suffer less than the public. Worse still, there is apprehension that the parties are using the public as their whipping boy while they work out their differences.

Many of these stoppages have interrupted services seldom before affected by collective bargaining. Strikes by professionals—even doctors, nurses and teachers—have disturbed the public. So also have shutdowns in what have long been thought to be essential services, notably school, hospital and postal services.

Public misgiving has been aggravated further by violence that has accompanied some recent labour disputes. Pictures of trucks being overturned and of pickets and police scuffling have not helped the image of industrial relations.

Nor can one minimize the damage done by corrupt and undemocratic practices which the Norris Commission revealed in the Seafarers' International Union of Canada. Added to earlier revelations of the unseemly conduct of certain unions in the United States, the publicity convinced many that organized labour was not the idealistic force for good that they had been led to believe.

To these events must be added a public predisposition to blame unions and collective bargaining for inflation which has plagued the Canadian economy in recent years.[1]

Before some of the salient issues are examined, it is important to have an appreciation of the place of trade unionism and collective bargaining within the total Canadian industrial-relations system and of the reasons why public policy in general now favours the development of these institutions among interested groups of workers and their employers.

TRADE UNIONISM AND COLLECTIVE BARGAINING WITHIN THE CANADIAN INDUSTRIAL-RELATIONS SYSTEM

The Canadian industrial-relations system is portrayed schematically in Chart 1. Briefly, the system may be described as the complex of market and institutional arrangements, private and public, which society permits, encourages or establishes within the prevailing set of environmental constraints to handle superior-subordinant relations growing out of employment and related activities. For present purposes the over-all operation of the system is not as significant as the role of trade unionism and collective bargaining within it. Important as they are in the total industrial-relations system, they are but parts of it, and not even essential ones at that, at least at the micro level. Nonetheless, public policy has for some time supported and encouraged the emergence and development of trade unionism and collective bargaining and the reasons for this commitment should be recognized.

THE RAISON D'ÊTRE OF PUBLIC POLICY IN FAVOUR OF TRADE UNIONISM AND COLLECTIVE BARGAINING

Trade unionism and collective bargaining stand at the base or pinnacle, depending on how one wishes to view it, of a hierarchy of values, policies and instruments which are fundamental to Canada's present way of life. These concepts require at least cursory treatment here as they are basic to the views which follow.

Underpinning the present Canadian way of life are certain cherished human rights relating mainly to freedom of the person, property rights, and freedom of thought and political action. These rights compose the liberal-

---

1. This quote, as well as most of the others in this paper, are drawn from the Report of the Prime Minister's Task Force on Labour Relations, of which the author was a member. See Government of Canada, *Canadian Industrial Relations: The Report of the Prime Minister's Task Force on Labour Relations* (Ottawa: Queen's Printer, 1969).

Chart 1

A SCHEMATIC PRESENTATION OF THE CANADIAN INDUSTRIAL-RELATIONS SYSTEM

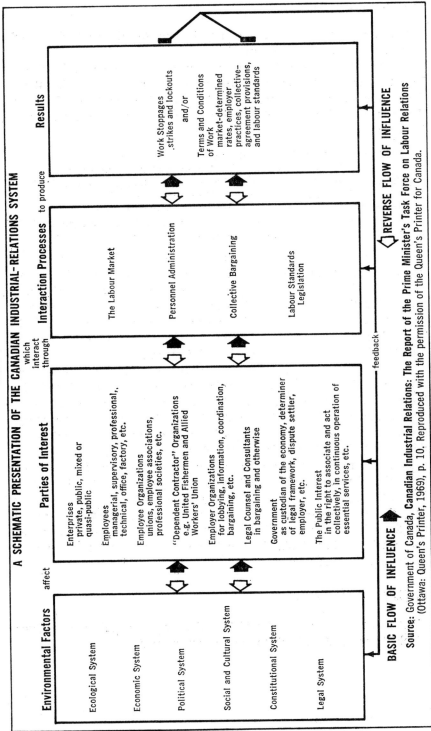

Environmental Factors — affect

Ecological System

Economic System

Political System

Social and Cultural System

Constitutional System

Legal System

Parties of Interest — which interact through

Enterprises
private, public, mixed or quasi-public

Employees
managerial, supervisory, professional, technical, office, factory, etc.

Employee Organizations
unions, employee associations, professional societies, etc.

"Dependent Contractor" Organizations
e.g. United Fishermen and Allied Workers' Union

Employer Organizations
for lobbying, information, coordination, bargaining, etc.

Legal Counsel and Consultants
in bargaining and otherwise

Government
as custodian of the economy, determiner of legal framework, dispute settler, employer, etc.

The Public Interest
in the right to associate and act collectively, in continuous operation of essential services, etc.

Interaction Processes — to produce

The Labour Market

Personnel Administration

Collective Bargaining

Labour Standards Legislation

Results

Work Stoppages
strikes and lockouts
and/or

Terms and Conditions of Work
market-determined rates, employer practices, collective-agreement provisions, and labour standards

⬆ **BASIC FLOW OF INFLUENCE**

⬇ **REVERSE FLOW OF INFLUENCE**

feedback

Source: Government of Canada, **Canadian Industrial Relations: The Report of the Prime Minister's Task Force on Labour Relations** (Ottawa: Queen's Printer, 1969), p. 10. Reproduced with the permission of the Queen's Printer for Canada.

democratic traditions of western society designed to enhance the free development of the human personality.

Elaborated and embodied in the concept of the rule of law, these rights have to date found their fullest expression and protection under liberal-democratic forms of government. In Canada such a government has taken the form of parliamentary democracy embracing essentially the following features:

> The sovereignty of Parliament and provincial legislatures in their respective spheres, in a constitutional monarchy under universal manhood suffrage; a court system with an independent judiciary; federal and provincial executives accountable respectively to Parliament and to the legislatures; and a Parliament and legislatures chosen by regular and free elections through a system of freely created political parties; and operating on the principles of responsible government.

Liberal-democratic political frameworks have for the most part given rise to modified capitalistic or mixed free-enterprise economic systems. Indeed, on the basis of past experience, one could argue, though hardly prove, that the two systems reinforce and in large measure complement each other. In any event, what has emerged as an economic system under Canada's parliamentary form of democracy is one basically the same as that found in virtually all other western liberal democracies.

It is at this point in the hierarchy of values, policies and instruments referred to above that the role of collective bargaining and trade unionism becomes so critical. Again, on the basis of historical experience, it is difficult to refute the fact that both go hand in hand with the type of economic system that has emerged in Canada. No such system has survived in anything resembling a free society in the absence of these institutions.

In a very real sense, therefore, one may cogently argue that the entire hierarchy of values, policies and instruments outlined above depends on the existence of an independent labour movement functioning within a free collective-bargaining system. Subject to certain constraints designed to protect the public interest, this is the rationale for a country such as Canada commencing and continuing in its public policies to favour trade unionism and collective bargaining.

CURRENT PUBLIC-POLICY ISSUES

What follows is a review of a highly selective list of public-policy issues which are now and are likely to remain controversial.

1. the labour-force coverage of trade unionism and collective bargaining

As traditionally conceived, trade unionism and collective bargaining have been holding to a non-agricultural labour-force coverage of about 33 percent for over a decade. Realistically, however, they cover a considerably higher proportion of workers. This fact becomes apparent when the many pseudo-union groups, including organized doctors, teachers and nurses, which take collective action to protect or enhance their economic position, are added to the total. Insofar as they are engaged in organized action to the same ends as the rest of the labour movement, it would seem reasonable to include them under the same legislation as that governing workers belonging to organizations forthright enough to call themselves "unions."

The more general point to be made is that if trade unionism and collective bargaining do have a valid role in Canada's socio-economic-political system, they should be equally accessible to all workers on as uniform a basis as possible and subject to as few exemptions as possible. Accordingly, coverage under the existing legislation should be extended to professional workers, junior supervisory and managerial employees, and agricultural workers, among others presently excluded.

Another facet of the same problem concerns the manner in which groups of workers gain entitlement to a certified bargaining agent when their employers decline to grant voluntary recognition. This issue raises a number of questions, only one of which bears mention here. That concerns the anomaly in the federal and in most provincial statutes whereby a union must secure a majority among those eligible to vote whether they choose to vote or not in a certification election. Suffice it to say that this requirement should be changed to a majority of those choosing to exercise their franchise.

2. determination and re-determination of bargaining units

Seldom appreciated is the significance of the power assigned to labour-relations boards of this country to determine appropriate bargaining units.

> The determination can be a crucial decision to collective bargaining, because the size and composition of the bargaining unit, the effective constituency of collective bargaining, determine to a significant extent the capacity of employees for being organized into unions; and hence the likelihood of organization, the potential bargaining

power of the union; and hence the point of balance it creates with the power of the employer, and the potential effectiveness of collective bargaining for dealing with different issues; and hence the substantive matters that are covered in a collective agreement.

The determination of bargaining units recently became a highly controversial issue at the federal level because of attempts by the Confederation of National Trade Unions to persuade the Canada Labour Relations Board to carve out regional units from existing national units in some of the major industries under federal jurisdiction. The controversy eventually led the Government to introduce Bill C-186 which among other things would have allowed appeals in such cases from the full Board to a smaller tribunal composed of its neutral members. Some of the heat was taken out of this issue by a labour-board decision in favour of a regional unit in a case where the circumstances seemed appropriate.[2]

Hopefully, labour-relations boards will be permitted to continue to exercise complete discretion in this area. Assuming they are, the chief need is to encourage them to make freer and more imaginative use of that discretion. Only in this way will it be possible

> to see collective bargaining liberated from any rigid bargaining unit patterns, in order that the system may be assisted to find its own level according to the interests of the parties. In contrast to the conglomerate of comparatively small units which prevail in many industries, [there should be] accessibility to wider bargaining units, company-wide units, multi-plant units, multi-employer units, multi-union units, and industrial as distinct from craft units in industrial plants. Similarly, where sound industrial relations call for a narrowing of units, the procedure for determining and re-determining bargaining units should be such as to facilitate that adoption.

In keeping with this emphasis, labour-relations boards should not hesitate to reopen and realign existing bargaining units at the initiative of any interested party where evidence supports the need for such change. Extensive use of such a power would mark a radical departure from past practice; but this is essential if any sense is to be made of industrial relations in industries such as construction.

3. protection of individual rights in unions

There was doubtless a time when unions could be equated with private associations in which the state had little or no interest or business concerning itself about the rights of their members or prospective members. That

---

2. Canada Labour Relations Board, *Judgement on the Application by Syndicat General du Cinema et de la Television (CNS) for unit of employees of the Canadian Broadcasting Corporation* (Ottawa, July 17, 1968). Mimeographed.

day ended when the concepts of certification and exclusive bargaining rights were introduced and when unions began to negotiate various types of union-security arrangements. To some extent the point that unions have become quasi-public bodies was further brought home by the Prime Minister's Task Force on Labour Relations when it recommended that compulsory dues deduction or the agency shop should come into effect automatically upon the consummation of the first collective agreement.

Despite the potential power of unions over their members, there is precious little legislative recognition or protection of any membership rights. Partly this is because few unions have abused their power. In addition, there are internal remedies in most unions and there is access to the courts. Because of lack of impartiality, delays or costs, however, these protections are not always satisfactory. Something more is clearly required both substantively and procedurally.

As for the former, there are several critical points of concern:

> There are four areas in which the individual is entitled to protection. The first relates to access to employment as it is affected by the operation of hiring halls, the regulation of standards of competency of job performance, and financial barriers to union membership. The second relates to the right to continuation in employment as that may be affected by continuing union membership. The third relates to the right to union membership to protect interests other than an interest in employment. The fourth relates to the rights of "union citizenship."

To provide adequate protection in each of these areas several changes are required: operation of all hiring halls by the Canadan Manpower Service; government determination and administration of minimum standards of competency where these are required to protect the public interest; reduction of initiation fees, dues and assessments where these are deemed unreasonably high; and a "bill of rights" for union members.

Procedurally, unions should be encouraged to establish public review boards similar to that in existence in the United Automobile Workers, which, after approval by the appropriate labour-relations board, would become ultimate and final appeal tribunals in each of the above areas. Failing the formation of such boards, meeting certain minimum standards, union members should have the right of appeal to the labour-relations board itself.

Changes are also required in connection with the obligation on the part of the unions to provide fair representation to all its members, in the conduct of ratification and strike votes, and in the use of union funds for political purposes. In each of these and the above areas, the problem is to balance membership rights and union responsibilities in such a way as not to handicap unduly the effectiveness and responsibility of the collectivity in the name of unnecessarily excess individuality.

4. employer associations and the balance of power

One of the underlying aims of most labour-relations acts is to provide for a reasonable balance of power between labour and management. In most situations this balance depends on the emergence of a union on the employee side. In some cases, however, the result is seriously to tip the scales in the other direction and to drive employers to band together to deal with a common union or group of unions.

Although employers who find themselves in such a position are permitted under the existing legislation to form associations for the purpose of dealing with unions, there is nothing comparable to the elaborate certification procedure for unions to protect employers in the exercise of any parallel rights. To remedy this imbalance, provision should be made for an employer-association accreditation scheme analogous to the union-certification procedure in those industries where the labour-relations board deems it appropriate and subject to whatever safeguards are required to preclude its use for anticompetitive purposes.

In industry in general there is a related need to ensure that employers are free to engage in collective lockouts where they have each legally acquired the right to lock out and to support each other through such devices as strike insurance.

5. freeing-up the bargaining process

Collective bargaining is often impeded in Canada by all sorts of legal restrictions. Some of these constraints arise from past policies and practices in the determination of bargaining units, remedies for which have already been suggested. It is more conventional to single out the delays occasioned by Canada's traditional two-stage compulsory conciliation procedure. It is wisely being curtailed to the officer stage in most jurisdictions, except where union and management jointly request a board or the government decides there is a special reason to appoint one. Although compulsory conciliation should be retained at the officer level, if only as a substitute for the morass of litigation accumulated in the United States on the "bargaining-in-good faith" issue, both parties should be free to take direct action as of the termination date of the outstanding collective agreement. This freedom would eliminate any serious delays except where the parties agree to postpone a potential confronation.

The collective-bargaining process could be further improved through various types of continuous bargaining and by the use of experimental clauses. Still further improvement could be derived by employing mediation as a distinct and separate step in the grievance procedure prior to resort to arbitration over in-term or rights disputes.

In these and other ways the disadvantages which often accrue from attempting to conduct effective employer-employee relations within a rigid legalistic straight-jacket could be partially if not fully overcome.

6. regulating the forms of industrial conflict

Inherent and essential to the operation of the present collective-bargaining process is the possibility of a strike or lockout if an impasse is reached.

> There is a basic characteristic of the collective bargaining system which is seemingly contradictory. Paradoxical as it may appear, collective bargaining is designed to resolve conflict through conflict or at least through the threat of conflict. It is an adversary system in which two basic issues must be resolved; how available revenue is to be divided, and how the clash between management's drive for productive efficiency and the workers' quest for job, income and psychic security is to be reconciled.

Although there is no effective substitute for the role of economic conflict within the collective-bargaining process, certain rules are required in order to prevent all labour disputes from degenerating into potential all-out class warfare. Aside from limiting the time when the parties may engage in a test of economic strength to the period following initial recognition or certification and to that occurring after the expiry of an outstanding collective agreement, the main problem is to regulate the normal weapons of labour-management conflict, including in particular picketing and boycotting.

The basic problem in this respect is to reconcile conflicting tendencies in the common law of civil wrongs and the statute law of collective bargaining.

> The juridical problem arises from the fact that the direction of the common law—and in this respect the judicial gloss on the civil law of delict or civil wrong, borrows much from the common law—is at cross purposes with the legislative policy of collective bargaining. Even in recent times it has been asserted judicially that the public has an interest in the entrepreneurial freedom which must prevail over the employees' private interest in collective action. Further, in determining whether there is a proprietary interest to be protected in an application to enjoin picketing, profits of enterprise have been equated with property, and the balance of convenience has fallen against the picketers. The policies and rules of the common law and those of the legislation are out of joint.

To remedy the situation, a comprehensive picketing and boycotting code is required, only the basic principles of which can be outlined here. The intention of such a code should be:

> to establish a code of employee and consumer primary and secondary picketing which effectively limits picketing, that can be respected lawfully by other workers, to plants lawfully struck in the course of a

negotiation dispute and to directly allied plants. In these circumstances it would become possible for workers, without fear of recourse under law or from their employer, to refuse to cross a picket line either to do work normally done by the strikers or to handle goods or transmit services produced by them or their replacements. In all other situations, such a refusal would subject workers to disciplinary action by their employer and would be cause for an order removing the picket line in question.

As important as the proposed new picketing and boycotting code would be the manner in which it was enforced. What is required is public enforcement of the law in this area, a marked departure from past practice. This change is essential if the role of law is to be re-established and preserved in this most troublesome field of industrial relations.

> One of the fundamental civilizing goals of the rule of law and the institutionalization of its enforcement is to get disputes off the streets and into the courts, where they may be settled on the basis of evidence and substantive law instead of by roving force of arms. The acceptance of picketing as part of the economic sanctions inherent in collective bargaining accommodates the return of industrial disputes to the streets, where the message of the labour interest in such disputes may reach the public. . . . This gives the public a special interest in enforcement of the law. Where the law is of general application, as in the law relating to the "how" of picketing, there is not . . . justification for providing machinery for enforcement unique to industrial conflict. Where, however, there is a special law as in the "why," "where," and "when" of picketing, particularly where the base of the picketing is broadened . . . the public interest in its enforcement ought to prevail over the parties' interest in law enforcement (or non-enforcement, such as where an employer may prefer to endure the harm caused by unlawful behaviour rather than run the risk of retaliation or general impairment to labour-management relations) should those interests conflict.

7. handling potential emergency disputes

Despite the need to accept the role of potential or actual economic conflict within the present collective-bargaining system, it must be recognized that there is mounting public concern over the inconvenience and hardship sometimes suffered by innocent third parties during the course of such confrontations.

Study of the issues involved in this dilemma lead to the following guiding observations:

> The expression of the public interest in being protected from the hardships of work stoppages takes many forms. Generally, they refer to protection of life and health, maintenance of public safety and order,

and preservation of the state. . . . Studies of Canadian experience and of events and experiments in countries with comparable industrial relations systems and social matrices [lead to] seven observations which are fundamental to the determination of a scheme for containing these disputes. First, it is extremely difficult to say with certainty or conviction in advance of actual events in what industry or service and at what time resort to economic sanctions ought to be curtailed. Second, the length of a strike or lockout frequently is a critical factor in making such an assessment. Third, there can be no one policy or procedure that works with uniform success. Fourth, flexibility of approach is essential lest the parties build the existing policy or procedure into their strategies. Fifth, a determination that a given stoppage of work ought to be terminated in the public interest is essentially a political decision. Sixth, the political element in a potential emergency dispute is an inducement to the parties to drive the dispute beyond any procedural device for settlement and into the political area. Seventh, circumstances may be expected to arise in the eventual course of industrial conflict in which disobedience to and defiance of the law will not be forestalled by that law.

One way out of the dilemmas involved would be to create a tenured part-time three-man Public Interest Disputes Commission, independent of any government department, reporting to the Prime Minister, and composed of public members only.

The Commission would have two major functions. The first relates to determining special procedures for resolving industrial disputes in industries in the federal jurisdiction which, because of their record of industrial relations, are prone to disputes which are likely to jeopardize the public interest. The second function relates to the handling of actual disputes in any industry under federal jurisdiction where the public interest is threatened.

With respect to the first function:

The Public Interest Disputes Commission would be charged with assisting the parties, in industries whose record of labour relations has been such as to make them prone to work stoppages likely to jeopardize the public interest, to negotiate special procedures for settling their disputes. In the event of a failure to agree to a procedure, or if the agreed procedure is deemed inadequate by the Commission, the Commission would have power to prescribe a procedure short of seizure, trusteeship, partial operation, statutory strike (full operation with complete or partial impounding of incomes and profits), or compulsory arbitration. Such a procedure would be subject to a three-year limitation in the first instance.

Where normal or special dispute-settlement procedures break down or are exhausted without affecting a settlement:

The Public Interest Disputes Commission [would] be available at the request of the government to advise on the dangers to the public of a particular work stoppage. In any dispute, whether or not it is covered by special procedure, the government should also have power, at a point which it considers timely, to request a report recommending a further *ad hoc* procedure for terminating the dispute in the event of an actual work stoppage. Here the Commission would be at liberty to consider the merits of seizure, trusteeship, partial operation, statutory strike and compulsory arbitration . . . or, indeed, anything else.

This report would be a public document and could contain alternative procedures. In any event the government would then act in the political arena as it saw fit, although in most cases presumably on the basis of the report's findings and recommendations. The final power to take any unilateral and arbitrary action would be limited to Parliament.

The advantage of the Parliamentary forum is that action would be taken by the main instrumentality of parliamentary democracy, with opportunity for debate and for all parliamentary parties to take a public position on the merits of the proposed action before it is implemented. An Act of Parliament promulgated after a public viewing and a full debate on the range of interests to be reconciled and alternative methods for solution may well be more conducive to acceptability than an executive order.

8. coping with the results of the system

Aside from periodic conflict, the collective-bargaining process generates results in the form of mutually-agreed-on terms and conditions of employment. Of particular interest are the possible consequences of these results in terms of their inflationary impact and hence their effect on the trade-off between stable prices and full employment. Although this subject is dealt with much more fully in David Smith's essay, a brief treatment of the problem would appear to be in order at this point.

One way of summarizing the available data and studies is as follows:

The role of collective bargaining in the inflationary process must be seen in the context of [a] review of the major theories of inflation. None of these schools explains everything; but there is an element of truth in each.

To the extent that demand pressures are the underlying cause of a period of inflation, collective bargaining tends only to serve as one of many possible mechanisms through which inflationary forces are transmitted. In such a situation, collective bargaining may help to retard the rate of inflation through long term agreements which temporarily hold wages below the level to which the forces of the market could drive them.

According to the cost-push theory of inflation, collective bargaining is one of many institutions which can exercise independent upward pressure on incomes, costs and prices. At the micro level it is difficult to refute the fact that there are situations where wages are driven up by individual unions beyond the rate which the existing constellation of market forces would have produced. Where this happens, however, it usually indicates that the employers affected either have some discretionary power in their product market which they are unable to exploit to the mutual advantage of themselves and their workers, or that they are confident of sufficient monetary expansion to take up any slack. In the absence of such market imperfections or demand expectations, the scope of independent union cost pressure would be considerably lessened. The existence of market imperfections allows those sharing the results of discretionary market power to appropriate to themselves most of the productivity gains that accrue in their particular sectors of the economy.

At the macro or total economy level it is more difficult to document the existence of cost-push pressure emanating from collective bargaining independent of any cumulative effect it may have at the micro level. Such pressure is indicated but not proved by the observance of substantial though lower wage settlements when cyclical economic indicators, such as the unemployment rate, show an absence of demand pressure. This was documented, though not fully explained by the Economic Council of Canada in its cyclical analysis of the problem. Barring a more definitive answer one cannot dismiss the possibility that collective bargaining has cost effects at the macro as well as the micro level. Indeed, depending on how extensively unions push up wages at the micro level, there may be some macro impact, since to a significant extent, it is the aggregation of a series of micro effects.

Another indicator of the potential impact of collective bargaining on inflation is to be found in the part that it plays in the demand-shift or structural model of the inflationary process. This theory draws heavily on the constantly changing composition of demand. As a result of older parts of the economy reviving, or new ones opening up, there are periodic sectoral booms which produce bottlenecks and excessive demand pressure. Like other institutions which find themselves in such a setting, unions can take full advantage of the opportunity to negotiate exceptionally large settlements. These, in turn, often serve as targets for unions in less buoyant parts of the economy which demand and sometimes win greater advances than would otherwise have been possible. Even stagnant or declining sectors of the economy can be confronted with settlements that would not take place in a competitive model. The result is a downward-rigid and upward-flexible wage structure that can adjust only to shifting labour force requirements by a ratcheting-up of wages.

As a cause of inflation, collective bargaining is only one of many institutional pressures that make it more difficult to maintain reasonable price stability while ensuring a high level of employment. In the short run at least, these pressures could be undone by sufficient slackening of aggregate demand but this would only work if the whole problem could be construed solely as a demand problem.

[These] conclusions about the causes of inflation, and particularly about the role of collective bargaining in the inflationary process, will disappoint those who seek a single culprit, and especially those who see the labour movement as the prime candidate for this honour. The problem is too complex for such a simplified solution.

Assuming both that this conclusion is valid and that price controls or guidelines are unworkable, one viable alternative suggests itself:

> If neither wage and price controls nor guideposts are in order, what should be done about collective bargaining and other private decision-making mechanisms that may aggravate the trade-off problem? [One] answer is relatively simple and consistent with all the potential causes of inflation and the trade-off. [That is] a strategy that focuses on the environment within which private decision-making takes place and that attempts to ensure that this environment is not conducive to inadequate or undesirable behaviour of incomes and costs.
>
> To this end, . . . an Incomes and Costs Research Board [could be created. It would be termed] an Incomes and Costs Research Board for two reasons. First, the title would make it clear that its terms of reference would embrace the performance of all types of incomes and costs and not only wages and prices. This reflects the fact that institutional pressures and market imperfections can emanate from all sectors of the economy. Second, the designation would underline the emphasis to be placed on research, although this should in no way inhibit the Board from making recommendations. Indeed, . . . its research should be policy oriented and should concentrate on remedies directed at particular problem areas. The Board would publish its findings, but would in no way involve itself in their implementation or in the actual income or cost determining process anywhere in the economy. In other words, the Board would be an educational and advisory body.

9. the role of government

Governments play a variety of roles in the industrial-relations system, from that of custodian of the economy to that of shareholder in a number of crown coporations. But the role of government that stands out in the present context is that of determiner of the framework of rules and regulations within which labour and management are to conduct their relations.

Two challenges confront governments in this capacity. First, within the bounds of practicality, they must strive to limit their intervention as much as possible. This poses some difficulty as the Prime Minister's Task Force on Labour Relations discovered:

> We seek to minimize the role of the state in the collective bargaining process and in places urge a reduction in state intervention; yet on balance we propose an increase in government involvement. Where we recommend more public participation in the industrial relations system our objective is to facilitate more constructive relations between labour and management and to protect the public interest. The alternative to this enlarged but still selective role for government could be greater state involvement on a broader basis in the future. This development

must be avoided if the parties are to be persuaded to continue to assume responsibility for their behaviour.

At the same time, without amending their labour-relations acts every time a flaw appears, governments must keep the statutory framework as viable as possible and ensure that it is upheld.

> If defiance of the law is not to lead to general disrespect for law and order, two steps must be taken. Laws must be kept under constant surveillance and brought up-to-date and clarified as changing circumstances dictate; and they must be administered and enforced fairly and impartially.

In keeping with these general principles, there is not only a need for a wholesale updating of the law, but an upgrading and major change in the composition and powers of the chief administrative instrument in this field, the Labour-Relations Board:

> In four basic areas of enforcement and administration of the collective bargaining law, [there is a need] for changing the roles and remedies of the [Labour Relations Board]: in the areas of bargaining-unit determination and redetermination, and in the regulation of internal union affairs, unfair labour practices, including unlawful strikes and lockouts, and picketing and boycotting. To bring the structure and powers of the [boards] into line with [their] changed roles, the [boards should] be reconstituted to consist of five persons who are representative of neither unions nor management and who are available for service on a full time basis. The [boards] should be authorized to sit in three-man panels and should have power to delegate quasi-judicial powers to commissioners located at its headquarters and across the country. The [boards] should also have a field staff to carry out administrative and investigatory functions.

CONCLUSION

The position taken in this paper might be described as a *status-quo*-plus approach. In many respects this is what it is. This reflects the fact that no-one has yet discovered a brave new world in this charged area of collective human conflict. Although there are many defects in the present Canadian industrial-relations system, and particularly in trade unionism and collective bargaining, there are no viable alternatives that promise a better future. But this does not mean that the existing system cannot be improved, and it was to this modest purpose that this essay has directed its attention.

the farm problem

D. R. Campbell
University of Toronto

A common feature of most western nations is the existence of "a farm problem." This problem is seen quite differently by various groups within a nation. To farmers themselves, the problem is that their incomes are low, and sometimes unstable, relative to those of non-farm people. To government officials, the farm problem is partly the low farm incomes and partly the cost of programs of trade protection, subsidies, and government-held surpluses which have resulted from trying to raise farm incomes. To economists, the low farm incomes indicate more deep-seated problems concerning the adequacy and allocation of resources, the mobility of labour, and the appropriateness of government programs.[1]

That there has been a farm income problem in Canada can be illustrated by the fact that the farm labour force declined by 55 percent between 1946 and 1967. The departure of workers on such a scale indicates that there must have been a considerable income differential between farm and non-farm employment even after all psychic forms of income had been included. The Economic Council of Canada described the problem as follows: "Measured in constant 1949 dollars, incomes in agriculture had increased by 13 percent while incomes in non-agricultural occupations had increased by 46 percent (1949-1963). If an allowance for a return on capital was deducted from farmers' incomes, the increase in current dollars was 21

---

1. For further reading on most aspects of Canadian agriculture, see the forthcoming report of the Federal Task Force on Agriculture. For special aspects see: *A Review of Agricultural Policy in Canada*, Agricultural Economics Research Council of Canada (Ottawa: Carleton University, 1966); *Conference on International Trade and Canadian Agriculture*, Economic Council of Canada (Ottawa; Queen's Printer, 1966); and D. R. Campbell, "Overcoming the Canadian Farm Problem — Theory and Practice," *Canadian Journal of Agricultural Economics* (December 1966).

percent, and in constant dollars there was a decline of about 10 percent."[2] The existence of the farm income problem has led to programs designed to increase or stabilize farm incomes; these programs have profoundly changed most marketing channels and institutions.

This chapter will discuss four topics related to the farm problem: the first two describe the underlying conditions of supply and demand in Canadian agriculture, the third deals with the result of these underlying conditions, and the fourth with government programs designed to deal with these results.

A. SUPPLY CONDITIONS IN CANADIAN AGRICULTURE

There are five particularly significant factors on the supply side.

1. *Large number of producers.* There were about 275,000 Canadian "commercial" farms[3] in 1966. Because of the special features of agricultural production in which close and knowledgeable acquaintance with animals, crops, and soil is necessary often on a day-by-day or even hour-by-hour basis, the most efficient size of farm is quite small relative to the industry. Even if all farms were of such a size as to be able to produce at the lowest possible cost per unit, the average farmer's output would be so small relative to total output that he could not, by himself, affect prices in any way.

2. *Rapid increases in supply.* Because of the competitive structure of agriculture and because of the rapid development of improved production techniques there is a constant tendency for the supply curves of various farm commodities to move to the right (that is, for the same price to result in ever-greater levels of output in succeeding years).

Producers of a particular farm commodity are in competition with one another; an effective new technique will normally be adopted by some because, if effective, it lowers their costs and increases their profits; then production is increased because of the profit incentive; the result is a decline in price, which exerts pressure on those who have not adopted the new technique and are therefore without its benefits in the form of lower costs; they must adopt it, or cease production, or suffer a decline in net incomes. Thus the competitive structure of agriculture encourages the widespread adoption of new techniques.

---

2. *Economic Goals for Canada to 1970*, First Annual Review of the Economic Council of Canada, 1964.
3. A commercial farm was defined as an agricultural holding of at least one acre and cash sales of $2,500 in the preceding 12 months.

Producers who are unwilling or unable to adopt an effective new technique, possibly because of their lack of appropriate facilities or credit or knowledge, find themselves at a permanent disadvantage if they continue to produce. Farmers in the Maritimes, for example, with small, stony and irregular fields which were quite satisfactory for horse-drawn equipment, find that they cannot use the new large tillage machinery that has lowered costs on the prairies and in Ontario.

There are two results arising from the rapid introduction of technology; first, there are such rapid increases in supply that prices decline, and second, the process throws up a steady stream of human beings who are unable to adjust to the new ways of production and who either remain in difficult financial conditions in farming or attempt to make the transition to non-farm employment, with the many psychological and social problems that such changes involve.

3. *Asymmetry of changes in output in response to changes in price.* When prices of farm commodities increase, farmers tend to produce more; but when prices decrease, output tends to decrease very little, at least in the short run. In this reaction, agriculture is quite different from most non-farm sectors, in which there is a symmetrical response of output to changes in price.

The reasons for what has been called this "rachet response" in agriculture arise largely out of the high proportion of fixed costs to total costs in farm production. Fixed costs are those which must be borne regardless of the level of production. When prices of farm commodities rise, producers tend to purchase new machinery, build buildings, and increase livestock numbers, all of which increase productive capacity. However, when prices fall producers must still meet interest and repayment charges, pay taxes and insurance, and take depreciation into account. Even their own labour may have no readily apparent alternative use. Their main possibilities of reducing costs lie only in a reduction in the use of hired labour and purchased fertilizer, pesticides, and so forth. Even for these latter "variable" costs, it is frequently the case that any considerable reduction in their use will reduce profits even more.

This asymmetrical response to price holds for agriculture as a whole and in no way rules out the tendency to shift resources from the production of one product to another in response to changes in their relative prices. This tendency to shift from one commodity to another has become less with increased specialization.

4. *Instability of output.* Output varies seasonally and among years because of weather and other conditions of nature. Local crop failures bear quite unequally upon individuals even when total output is stable. The federal government and several provincial governments have introduced crop

insurance programs to help offset the income problem arising from crop failures.

5. *Mobility of farm people out of agriculture.* Because the average income of farmers is considerably lower than that of non-farmers there has been a rapid decline in the farm labour force. Between 1946 and 1967 the Canadian farm labour force declined by 55 percent, a rate almost unprecedented in any sector of any economy. Yet the rate of decline was still not fast enough to match changing economic conditions! Many thousands of older people had no apparent alternative career or employment, and large numbers of those of appropriate age for other employment either saw no other attractive opportunities (perhaps because their farms and communities were geographically remote) or found themselves untrained for other employment. During Canada's "economic-stagnation" years from 1957 to 1961, when unemployment rates averaged almost 7 percent, it was difficult to find non-farm employment.

It is a measure of the remarkable technological change in agriculture that in the period 1946 to 1967 the farm labour force could have declined 55 percent, agricultural output increased 65 percent, and yet that still not enough people had left the industry. Whatever the cause—age, lack of training, lack of opportunities, social pressure to remain at home—the number of people moving out of agriculture has not been great enough to raise *per capita* farm incomes relative to non-farm incomes.

B. DEMAND CONDITIONS IN CANADIAN AGRICULTURE

There are four important factors on the demand side.

1. *Low price elasticity of demand for farm products in the domestic market* (i.e., a small percentage increase in quantity to be sold necessitates a large percentage decline in price and results in a decline in gross revenue). The demand for farm products at the farm level is a "derived demand"—derived, that is, from the demand for food at the retail level. To the extent that the marketing margin (the difference between price to the producer and price to the consumer) remains constant, the price elasticity of demand at the farm level will be much lower than at the consumer level.[4]

---

4. For example, assume the price of bread to be $1.00 per unit, the marketing margin to be $.75, and the price of wheat (per unit of bread) to be $.25, and assume that the price elasticity of demand for bread is −.5. If the price of wheat were to be doubled, that is, increased by $.25 per unit, the price of bread would increase only from $1.00 to $1.25, an increase of 25 percent. Since the assumed elasticity of demand for bread is −.5 (a one-percent increase in price is accompanied by a .5-percent decline in quantity purchased), the increase in bread prices of 25 percent will result in a decline in consumption of only 12.5 percent. Thus a doubling in the price of wheat results in a decline in consumption of wheat of only 12.5 percent, yielding a price elasticity of demand for wheat of −.125, or one-quarter that of bread.

Since the marketing margin for domestically produced – domestically consumed farm products in Canada is now about 60 percent of retail expenditures, and since the marketing margin tends to be relatively constant regardless of consumer prices, one would expect that the price elasticity of demand at the farm level would be less than one-half that at the consumer level. Most studies of Canadian consumption patterns indicate that the price elasticity of demand for food by Canadians is low.[5] Most Canadians are reasonably well fed and a considerable decline in prices of food would be necessary to induce them to eat more. The most that could be expected is that a decline in prices would induce them to substitute higher-priced foods for lower-priced foods and thus not reduce food expenditures very greatly.

The conclusion, then, is that the price elasticity of demand for farm products in Canada is very low, both because the elasticity of demand at the consumer level is low and because the "derived demand" at the farm level has a lower elasticity than at the consumer level.

The implication, in practical terms, of a low elasticity of demand is that an increase in output will result in such a large decline in price that gross revenue is reduced. Furthermore, fluctuations in levels of output will cause even wider inverse fluctuations in prices and usually in gross incomes.

2. *Higher price elasticity of demand for Canadian farm products in export markets than in the domestic market.* Because the exports of any one country are normally quite small in relation to total international trade in that commodity, the elasticity of demand for the exports of one country will be much greater than for the exports of all producers of the commodity. Thus the situation is somewhat analogous to that of a single producer who has a highly elastic demand for his own output whereas the industry has a much less elastic demand.

The major exception to this rule arises when a Canadian price decline (for example, in the price of wheat) sets off similiar price declines on the part of other exporters. This is likely to be the case only if Canadian exports represent a substantial share of world trade. In such a case, the elasticity of demand for the Canadian export would be about the same as for all exports of the commodity.

Thus, for many commodities, a lower limit on domestic prices is set by the possibility of exports and an upper limit by the possibility of imports. This situation is illustrated in Figure 1A opposite, in which AB represents domestc demand, DE represents domestic supply, BC represents foreign

5. See R. A. Holmes, *Estimation of Demand Elasticities for Substitute Foods*, Agricultural Economics Research Council of Canada (Ottawa: Queen's Printer, 1966); M. K. Emmery, "The Outlook for Poultry Meat in Canada to 1980," *Canadian Farm Economics*, Department of Agriculture (February 1968); G. Le Bel, *Effect of Price on Butter Sales*, Department of Agriculture, 1963.

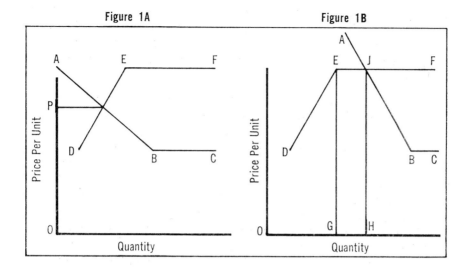

Figure 1A   Figure 1B

demand (i.e., the possibility of exports), and EF represents foreign supply (i.e., the possibility of imports).

The segments BC and EF are virtually horizontal, indicating very high elasticities of demand and supply for the small amounts of Canadian exports and imports relative to total world trade.

Figure 1A indicates that the price should be at P and that there are no imports or exports. Figure 1B indicates the position following an increase in demand relative to Figure 1A. Imports will amount to GH and price will be more or less stabilized at J.

One should recognize that, in a practical setting, it is possible for a country to export and import simultaneously. Some Canadians may be importing into British Columbia and others exporting from Nova Scotia. This complication is not considered in Figures 1A and 1B, which are based on the common abstraction of representing a country as one point in space. To explain simultaneous exports and imports, it would be necessary to produce separate demand and supply curves for British Columbia and Nova Scotia (and presumably for various points within and between these provinces).

Our conclusion is that the elasticity of demand for exports is undoubtedly very much greater than is the domestic elasticity of demand, and that for most farm products the possibilities of exports and imports set a minimum and maximum between which prices may range. Changes in world markets will affect the level of these minima and maxima.

The export demand for Canadian farm products varies greatly among products and little can be said in general terms. About 20-25 percent of Canadian farm production is exported—this is a remarkably high proportion considering the magnitude of surplus disposal programs of the United

States, protective tariffs and domestic subsidies of the European Economic Community, production subsidies of the United Kingdom, and the large farm labour forces and the amount of state investment in agriculture in the communist countries, and the fact that most Canadian farm exports receive little if any subsidy.

3. *Increases in demand through time.* The demand for food in the domestic market will increase from year to year for two main reasons—an increase in population and an increase in *per capita* real incomes.

One may assume fairly confidently that the annual growth in population leads to an approximately proportional increase in demand for food. The population of Canada increased by 37 percent between 1954 and 1968; this should mean an increase of about 37 percent in the quantity of food purchased, given no changes in incomes or prices.

In high-income economies, increases in real *per capita* incomes have only limited effect on the demand for food, and very little effect when demand is considered at the farm level, which is the appropriate level for any discussion of farm incomes. It has been estimated that the income elasticity of demand for wheat in Canada is −.53, for fresh fruit is .25, for beef is .6,[6] and that the income elasticity of demand for food in the United States and Canada combined is only about 0.16;[7] this means that an increase of one percent in *per capita* real incomes results in an increase of 0.16 percent in *per capita* expenditures on food at the consumer level. The increase in expenditures at the farm level would be very much smaller.

Thus increases in the demand for food in Canada depend largely upon the rate of growth of Canadian population; fortunately for Canadian agriculture, the growth of population in Canada has been considerably higher than in almost all western countries.

4. *Foreign agricultural subsidies.* Largely because of their own "farm problems," many western nations have conducted massive programs of subsidies and trade protection for their farm sectors. The European Economic Community in particular has instituted an agricultural program which adversely affects exporters such as Canada. The EEC establishes high target prices for farm products, imposes variable levies on imports in order to bring them up to the target prices, and then uses the proceeds for improving the structure of EEC agriculture or for subsidizing exports. Prices paid to EEC farmers in 1967-1968 exceeded world prices (in EEC ports) by 85 percent in the case of soft wheat, 100 percent for hard wheat, 297 percent

---

6. *Demand-Supply Projections for Canadian Agriculture — 1980*, Department of Agriculture, 1968. Appendix B presents data for many commodities.
7. *Agricultural Commodities — Projections for 1970*, Food and Agriculture Organization, Rome, 1967, Table 12.

for butter, and 338 percent for sugar. These high prices encourage output and reduce the export markets available to Canada. The sales price of French exports of wheat and barley is sometimes as low as one-half of the domestic price, with the balance made up by government subsidy.

The United Kingdom provided subsidies to British agriculture of about £280 million in 1968-1969; this represents a large share of the net income of British farmers, which was about £480 million in that year. The United States, too, has had extensive and costly programs of assistance to agriculture in the form of price supports, export subsidies, and land retirement.

All of these programs, and those by other countries, affect Canadian agriculture and contribute to the existence of a Canadian farm problem. Export markets for Canadian farm products are subject to protection or to the competition of export subsidies. Because 20-25 percent of Canadian farm production is exported, such competition is crucial. Canada cannot afford to indulge in an export-subsidy competition when agricultural exports represent a much larger proportion of national income in Canada than in the United States and many other western nations. As shown later in this essay, Canadian agriculture has received few subsidies compared with those of the EEC, U.K. and U.S.A., and the brunt of foreign-subsidized competition has fallen upon Canadian farmers rather than taxpayers. Canadian farmers have frequently found that they were competing not just against foreign farmers but against foreign farmers *and* foreign governments.

C. EFFECTS OF SUPPLY AND DEMAND CONDITIONS

The underlying factors affecting the supply and demand for Canadian farm products have some extremely important results.

1. *Level of output.* Because there are large numbers of farmers producing any one commodity, and because the production of each is largely undifferentiated from that of other producers in quality, timing, and location, each producer normally considers that he has an almost perfectly elastic demand curve for his output, i.e., he can sell all he wishes to sell without lowering prices. It is necessary, in the preceding sentence, to say "normally," because this assumption does not hold for sales of fluid milk and other commodities for which there are sales quotas.

The effect of there being a large number of producers each of whom produces a level of output which seems most profitable to him (and based on the generally accurate assumption that the demand for his output is highly elastic) is, in many cases, to produce an aggregate output for the industry far in excess of that which would maximize gross or net returns to the industry. Figure 2 on page 203 illustrates the situation for an industry.

The supply curve is ES, and the demand curve AD. For the relevant levels of price and output, the demand is inelastic.[8] Output is OJ, price is OP and gross revenue is OP times OJ. Total (gross) revenue would be maximized at output OH, and net revenue would be maximized at output OG.[9]

Why is output greater than OG or DH, the levels which would maximize net and gross returns? The answer lies in the difference in elasticity of the demand curve facing any individual producer and that of the industry. The demand curve facing an individual may be considered to be perfectly horizontal,[10] because the output of any one producer is not sufficiently large to have an effect on the market price. Thus, each producer considers that he has a demand curve at price P (from Figure 2 again) such that he can sell any amount at that price.

The sum of 20,000 or 50,000 individual decisions, each one of which may be entirely sound economically given the assumption of a horizontal demand curve, is a level of output for the industry which collectively is quite irrational and which results in reduced gross and net incomes.

2. *Cycles of production.* Resources can be shifted fairly readily to produce different commodities. A decline in the market prospects for wheat led to a decline from almost 30 million acres to 26 million between 1968 and 1969. A decline in the price of winter wheat would lead to a decline in winter-wheat acreage and a rise in the acreage devoted to corn or soybeans. In the case of livestock, there are cycles of production varying from a two-year cycle in poultry to a three-year cycle in hogs to a longer cycle of 6 to 10 years in beef production.

These cycles of production result in inefficiency, partly through the con-

---

8. For any output in excess of OH, the demand is inelastic. Those who have a background in economic theory will recognize AH as the marginal-revenue curve appropriate to the average-revenue curve AD. At output OH, where OH = HD, the elasticity of demand is unity. At output OG, marginal revenue = supply, or summed marginal cost of all producers.

9. There is a special assumption here that output would be so distributed among producers that the marginal cost for each producer would be equal to GL.

10. There are exceptions, the most notable stemming from the existence of quotas. For example, the demand curve facing an individual milk producer who has a quota of 1,000 pounds of milk for fluid consumption, the remainder to be sold for manufacture is like this:

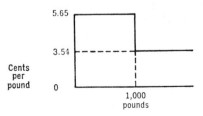

Figure 2

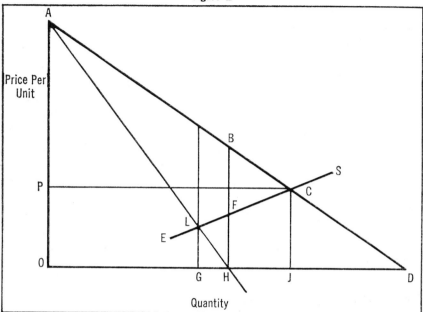

tinuing fixed costs of unused buildings, equipment and "know how" on the one hand, and partly through using productive resources to produce the wrong (i.e., unprofitable) products on the other. The number of hogs slaughtered in Canada increased by 34 percent in 1959 over the previous year; in 1960 they declined 23 percent from 1959, and in 1961 they declined 5 percent from 1960. Even greater changes occurred in the marketings of turkeys and broilers.

Investment committed to the production and processing of hogs, beef, turkeys and other products in boom times must lie partly idle and unproductive in periods of low production. The facilities and skilled labour force of food companies and packers have to be sufficient to meet the demands of peak production and peak marketing, but a return to subnormal or even normal levels of hog or beef production leaves excess capacity and unused investment throughout the whole industry. Canadian meat-packing plants had to be capable of handling 150,000 hogs in the last week of 1959; exactly one year later they slaughtered 82,000 hogs. These fluctuations have nothing to do with seasonal production, but are entirely a matter of cycles of production—heavy hog production for 18 months, then light for 18 months.

3. *Low average farm incomes.* Average net farm incomes are low rela-

tive to average incomes of most other occupations. While attempts to measure and compare incomes are difficult because of problems of pricing, income in kind, personal satisfaction, security, growth of asset values, off-farm earnings, and so forth, one point is clear and that is that the farm labour force has declined by more than one-half since World War II. This fact indicates the relative unattractiveness of farming, especially since there are no legal barriers to entry into the industry.

Per capita farm incomes are low because market offerings increase more rapidly than does domestic demand, and much of our exports must be sold in protected foreign markets or against subsidized exports, or in competition with highly efficient low-cost producers (e.g., New Zealand milk producers and American corn producers).

4. *The prevalence of rural poverty.* It is probably the case that the income discrepancy among Canadian farmers has increased substantially as a result of the technological revolution in agriculture. There is now a considerable farming elite with large investments, good management, and high incomes. There is also a considerable number of the very poor. In its *Fifth Annual Review*, the Economic Council of Canada estimated that in 1961 about 150,000 out of 275,000 farm families (55 percent) were below the poverty line, compared with 27 percent for the non-farm sectors.

Given their levels of production, management capacities, and availability of assets, many farmers could never make a satisfactory level of income from farming. If they were to be provided with the assets necessary to increase incomes, others would be forced out of farming because the increased production would lower prices, given the demand conditions for Canadian farm products.

Recognition has come gradually that neither of two fairly prevalent proposals is realistic. One of these is the laissez-faire position that: "If they cannot make a satisfactory income in farming, let them do something else." If this were amended to ". . . let us fit them to do something else," this attitude would be satisfactory. Poverty and frustration can exist for long periods even in an affluent society unless positive action is taken to eliminate them. A second solution proposed for the reduction of farm poverty has been action through the price mechanism, largely in the form of price supports. Because the basic problem for most such producers is that they produce too little, to increase the prices received will be of only marginal benefit to them. According to the 1966 Census there were 238,000 farms which had gross sales of $5,000 or less per year. These represented 55 percent of all farms in that year, had one-half of the farm labour force, 29 percent of farm assets, but produced only 14 percent of total farm sales. To attempt to increase the incomes of these people by price supports would be inefficient and costly, resulting in higher incomes for the larger producers and in surpluses and/or larger government outlays.

D. GOVERNMENT PROGRAMS IN AGRICULTURE

There are many good reasons why governments have devoted a considerable amount of attention to agriculture. It was the predominant sector in the Canadian economy until 1930; it still accounts for about one-fifth of Canadian exports; Canadian consumers allocate about one-fifth of their consumption expenditures to food; as an industry of many small competitive producers, agriculture tends to depend more upon governments for research, statistics, advisory services and credit than would be the case if there were only a few large corporations in the sector. A number of categories of government programs[11] are as follows:

1. *Programs to lower the cost of production.* Federal and provincial governments have provided free research (about three-quarters by the federal government), extension[12] (all by the provinces), credit (mostly by the federal government), farm gasoline-tax rebates, tariff-free imports of farm machinery and most farm supplies, and some minor price subsidies on lime and other inputs.

2. *Programs to improve marketing efficiency.* Grading and inspection standards are high; about 90 percent of Canadian agricultural exports are sold at a price premium in importing countries. Governments have supported some research, extension, and credit in marketing but far less than in production.

3. *Transportation and storage subsidies.* The Government of Canada provides two subsidies for the transportation of prairie-grown grain. The Feed Freight Assistance program subsidizes the shipment of feed grains from the Praire Provinces to other provinces. This program began in 1942 as an emergency wartime measure, and it has continued in spite of growing opposition from prairie livestock producers and Ontario corn producers. It costs about $20 million per year.

The Crow's Nest Pass Agreement has prevented an increase in railway freight rates over the rates of 1898 on grains moving from the Prairie Provinces into export channels.

The Government of Canada provides an annual subsidy to the Canadian Wheat Board to pay the cost of storing "surplus" wheat; this subsidy covers storage costs of all wheat in excess of 178 million bushels on hand on July 31, the end of the crop year. Averaging about $35 million per year this was the largest single subsidy in Canadian agriculture until the expansion of dairy subsidies in 1966.

---

11. For an excellent description and some analysis of government programs, see S. W. Garland and S. C. Hudson, *Government Involvement in Agriculture* (Ottawa: Queen's Printer, 1969).
12. Advisory service to farmers.

Minor subsidies are paid to encourage the construction of cold storage and other facilities for dairy products and fruits and vegetables.

4. *Tariff and import restrictions.* Canada has low tariffs for livestock and livestock products and higher tariffs for tobacco, some fruits and vegetables and for poultry products. Several dairy products have been protected by exclusion of imports rather than by tariffs. Canadian tariffs are generally much lower than those of the United States and the EEC.

5. *Export subsidies.* While the low transportation rates on grain destined for export markets may be regarded as a form of export subsidy, a more direct export subsidy is to be found in connection with gifts of wheat and other products under Canada's foreign-aid program. Such donations are partly to assist the recipient low-income economies and partly to remove embarrassing Canadian surpluses. Such donations have been relatively small, amounting to a total of $223 million in the period 1952 to 1963. By 1963 the United States was shipping about $1,500 million of farm products *per year* under her Public Law 480 program.

6. *Price supports.* The Government of Canada employs all three kinds of price supports. It operates an offer-to-purchase program for creamery butter, buying all of the butter offered to it at 65 cents per pound; it operates a deficiency-payment program for many products, making up the difference between market and guaranteed prices through the deficiency payment; it provides a direct subsidy on industrial[13] milk of $1.21 per hundredweight regardless of the market price of milk. Until 1966, when the Government of Canada expanded its subsidies to the dairy industry, the cost of price supports in Canada was extremely modest. Total cost to taxpayers was $450 million over the period 1946 to 1965; this was in striking contrast with expenditures in the United States, United Kingdom and many West European countries. Subsidies to the Canadian dairy industry now amount to about $130 million per year.

7. *The Canadian Wheat Board.* In 1935, during the period of depression and prairie dust storms, the CWB was created as an emergency marketing measure. It now markets all of the wheat, oats, and barley produced on the prairies and in northern British Columbia and entering interprovincial and international trade. The Board operates a system of delivery quotas to ration elevator space and it controls the movement and sale of prairie grains. It pools returns to producers so that every producer receives the same price during the crop year for the same quality laid down in the same

---

13. Industrial milk is that used for manufacturing into butter, cheese, and such products; fluid milk is the term used to describe milk sold for consumption in fluid form.

terminal. It is responsible to the Minister of Industry, Trade and Commerce of the federal government. *

8. *Provincial farmer-controlled marketing boards*.[14] In contrast to the Canadian Wheat Board, whose commissioners are appointed by the federal government and whose designated (geographical) area covers all or parts of four provinces, there are about 120 provincial marketing boards. These boards are created under provincial legislation after a favourable vote of those farmers who produce the commodity to be marketed by a board. Each board is limited in its operation to specified products produced within the province or within specified areas of the province. Some boards are responsible for several products; for example, the Ontario Vegetable Growers Marketing Board negotiates minimum prices with processor representatives for eleven different products. The majority of boards, however, are responsible for only one commodity. Ontario has 20 boards marketing 40 products; a considerably higher proportion of farm products is marketed through boards in Ontario than in any other province although Quebec has far more, but smaller, boards.

Boards have initiated many different kinds of programs. A few have done no more than conduct modest advertising campaigns; a substantial number have bargained collectively with buyers' representatives on minimum prices, maximum handling charges, grades and grade price differentials, and terms of sale; a smaller number have operated multi-price programs between domestic and foreign markets, sometimes pooling prices and sometimes merely subsidizing the export of supplies surplus to the domestic market. Some operate multi-price programs based on the form of utilization of the product. Some boards have taken legal and sometimes physical possession of products and directed them to market, receiving all revenues and making payments to producers. Some, such as the Ontario Hog Producer's Marketing Board, have developed highly sophisticated auction techniques based on simultaneous teletype installations in the premises of the Board and of the major buyers. Some have created their own facilities and become competitors with the trade (an unfair competitor, in the view of the trade, because operational losses may be met from deductions made by the board on all units of produce sold). In the case of several products boards have controlled production.

9. *Agricultural and Rural Development Act (ARDA)*. All eight of the categories of programs listed above are directed primarily at improving the efficiency and increasing the incomes of what may be called "viable" farms

---

14. For a more elaborate discussion of marketing boards, see the author's article "The Economics of Production Control — the case of Tobacco," *Canadian Journal of Economics*, II, no. 1 (February 1969).

—viable, that is, in the sense that they can produce a reasonably good standard of living for their operators. None of these programs have gone far in helping those producers whose incomes were well below the average of farmers generally; some of the programs, by increasing total output, have probably worsened the position of the lowest-income farmers.

In 1961 ARDA was initiated to assist low-income rural areas by consolidation of farms, creation of community pastures, retirement of land from farming, promotion of small local tourist attractions and industries, and by retraining of local residents largely for non-farm employment. Together with its later companion, the Fund for Rural Economic Development (FRED), ARDA has achieved some success in several areas. The existence of ARDA and FRED implies the recognition that two kinds of agricultural programs are necessary—one for viable commercial farms and another for the poverty or semi-poverty farms and areas.

E. SUMMARY AND EVALUATION

Rapid advances in management and in production technology since 1946 have permitted Canadian agricultural output to increase by 65 percent while the farm labour force was declining by 55 percent. In spite of increases in output per man exceeding the average for the Canadian economy generally, income of farm families continues to be lower than for non-farm sectors. The "farm problem" is seen in a different light by farmers, government, and economic analysts. It arises from the interplay of market forces and cannot be attributed to any perversity or obstinacy on the part of producers or of firms supplying inputs or purchasing outputs. With a large number of producers making sound economic decisions as individuals, producing for a domestic market that expands at a rate not much greater than the growth in population, with new labour-saving and output-increasing technology being made available at a rapid rate, and with foreign governments protecting and subsidizing their farm sectors, farm prices in Canada have fallen relative to other prices. Even a decline in the farm labour force from 1,186,000 in 1946 to 544,000 in 1966 has not been fast enough to overcome "the farm problem."

In 1966-1967 the federal and provincial governments spent a total of almost $450 million on agriculture—research, education, extension, price supports, credit, storage, and so forth.[15] In addition, farmers benefitted from quotas and tariffs applied on certain commodities, and they participated along with others in the general programs of education, welfare, and so forth.

---

15. Garland and Hudson, *op. cit.*, p. 330.

The areas in which governments have been most helpful have been in biological and physical research and in extension. These helped to reduce Canadian production costs faster than in most other countries. The *ad hoc* price supports, which for many years brought stability to farm prices and incomes, were beneficial to producers and consumers alike. Government action on grading and export promotion have been beneficial.

There have been serious weaknesses in government programs too. One has been the neglect of economic research, particularly in the field of marketing. Only 8 percent of agricultural research personnel were engaged in economic or rural sociology research in 1966, in spite of the fact that many of the pressing problems were in these areas. In 1969 the Canadian Wheat Board, responsible for all commercial sales of wheat, oats, and barley, employed only three marketing researchers. One result of the lack of economic and sociological research has been a failure on the part of government to anticipate problems and to provide guidance to farmers in meeting them. It was, of course, a politician's gambit that led one federal Minister of Agriculture to say: "We can market all the wheat you can produce." By contrast, the Federal Task Force on Agriculture estimated in 1969 that wheat acreage should be reduced from 30 million acres (1968) to a maximum of 20 million in 1980.

To be fair, however, it is true that part of the wheat-surplus problem could not be fully anticipated regardless of the amount and calibre of research. If the USSR, which produces as much wheat as the United States, Canada, Australia, and Argentina combined, has several consecutive good harvests, as she did, many good markets disappear. The recent development of new Mexican varieties of wheat promises (or threatens) to make India and Pakistan self-sufficient.

A second major weakness in government programs is that of the large dairy subsidies begun in 1966. These cost $130 million per year and support a sector in which Canada has a comparative disadvantage. This might be justifiable if the program were such that it would bring about structural readjustment. In fact it has been a series of one-year "holding actions" announced too late for farmers to make substantial changes in resource allocation.

The third major weakness in programs has been in regard to the hard core of farm poverty cases. Much has been said and proposed, but less has been done. Programs such as farm consolidation and community pastures are more resource-oriented than people-oriented; without special orientation it has been hard for the manpower training program to "reach" farm people; unemployment insurance is unavailable and welfare payments unacceptable to farmers.

In spite of these criticisms, it is fair to say that Canada's agricultural policies compare favourably with those in many competitor nations.

transportation policy

W. J. Stenason
Canadian Pacific

THE DEVELOPMENT OF RAILWAY TRANSPORTATION

It is only in comparatively recent years that Canadian transportation policy has been designed to achieve the objective of efficient resource allocation within the transportation sector of the economy, and not the objectives of economic development, correction of regional inequalities arising from location in relation to markets, or use of the freight-rate structure to achieve cross-subsidization of policies held to be in the national good.

Because trucking, pipeline, air, and highway transportation on a large scale are relatively recent, the evolution of transportation policy in Canada was, for the first eighty years of Canada's history, largely the evolution of railway policy.

Railway policy was conditioned by two factors. First, except for water transportation in central Canada, railways were the only effective means of transportation from the late 1860's to the period immediately following World War II. Thus, it was an effective monopoly and policies designed to regulate monopoly were required. Second, the creation of Canada as we know it today required the construction of railways, both a transcontinental railway and a railway between the Maritime Provinces and central Canada. The fact that railways played such an important role in the Canadian economy, combined with the fact that railways were monopolies, led to an inextricable mixing of transportation and national policy.

The oldest of the contemporary forms of land transportation are the railways. The process of railway merger to achieve full economies of scale in the United Kingdom in the late 19th century made it apparent that railway companies, to be efficient, had to be so large as to pre-empt the normal criteria of a competitive industry. This led to regulation of rates, terms and conditions of carriage, and control over entry into the industry. The regulatory system first established in England in the 1870's and 1880's was quickly adopted in the United States and Canada and in Western Europe. From the 1840's until the late 1920's, the railways had a monopoly over the movement of domestic freight and passenger traffic. During this long period, a sophisticated system of rate discrimination—the setting of rates on the basis of ability of the commodity to bear the transportation charge—was adopted and accepted by regulatory authorities. This system of pricing made it possible for the railways to finance many objectives of public policy in the provision of many services at a loss.

In the earliest days of the railways, freight rates were not based on well-defined principles, and it was not until publication of the first classification of commodities in 1874 by the Grand Trunk Railway that a more rational approach emerged. Basic to this classification and to railway pricing until the post-World-War-II period was "charging what the traffic will bear" or value-of-service pricing. The Canadian Freight Classification, made effective in Ontario and Quebec in 1884, was based on this principle but incorporated, in addition, an attempt at geographic equalization of rates with high rates on some lines averaged with low rates on others. Following publication of this initial classification, other policies became integrated with basic value of service. The requirements of national development, for example, led the railways, sometimes on the intervention of Government, to set low rates on raw materials and other low-value commodities, as in the case of rates for the movement of grain to export positions in Western Canada.

As pricing practices became more and more subject to complaint, a rationale based on the economics of price discrimination was developed. Essentially, this theory was that so long as rates on individual commodities covered the out-of-pocket or marginal costs of rendering a service, and were not in excess of a maximum above which the price of the service to the shipper could not go if movement was to take place, then total transportation volume and total utility from the service would be maximized. The value of the transportation service was affected to some extent by distance, use of the commodity, quality of service, and particularly by value of the commodity. The declining-cost nature of railway transportation led to lower average total costs of transportation than an alternative pricing system might have done.

Thus, the traditional theory of railway pricing was a sophisticated and complex example of price differentiation. Commodities of high value were charged a price high enough to compensate for the low prices charged to low-value commodities. With over-all revenue requirements in mind, rates were set to average out the differences in cost of service between easily accessible, more-settled regions and those more remote. Tapering of rates with distance resulted in assistance to long-haul movements. The accepted philosophy was that low-value commodities would not move except at a price which was little above the out-of-pocket costs of performing the services and that the assistance required for such traffic could be contributed, without harm, by high-value commodities.

There were many manifestations of this policy throughout Canadian history. In 1897 the government extended financial assistance to the construction, by Canadian Pacific, of a railway line through the Crow's Nest Pass area of British Columbia and, in return for this assistance, required fixed maximum rates for the movement of grain to export positions in Western Canada. Later, in 1925, these rates became statutory. The Maritimes Freight Rates Act (1927) was another example. This Act gave rise to 20 percent reductions in rates between the Maritime Provinces and central Canada. While the Maritime Freight Rates Act provided direct subsidy to offset the effects of location, its rationale was the added cost arising from location of the railway for strategic rather than commercial reasons.

Throughout this period, there was little attempt at defining a rational transportation policy. There were many public inquiries into railway problems, but generally transportation policy tended to take the form of reaction to railway crises.

The first of these had to do with the insolvency of the Canadian Northern, Grand Trunk, and Grand Trunk Western. When the Canadian Pacific Railway was built, it was granted a monopoly in certain parts of the Prairie Provinces. This led to substantial public outcry and to the chartering of two competitive transcontinental railways—the Canadian Northern and the Grand Trunk Pacific. Traffic density was too thin, and the properties heavily over-extended financially. Because securities of these companies were heavily held in foreign countries, and an adverse effect on Canada's international credit rating could have resulted, the Companies were acquired by the Government and formed into Canadian National Railways in 1919.

The Canadian National – Canadian Pacific Act of 1931, which required cooperation and elimination of competition between the two railways in a number of areas, similarly, arose from excess competition in the 1920's. This was a further reaction to a particular problm.

The Royal Commission on Transportation, 1949 to 1951, was concerned primarily with complaints of regional inequities in the freight-rate structure. It recommended a substantial change in the foundation of the rate structure and, particularly, establishment of a uniform equalized class-rate scale and uniform equalized commodity-mileage scales throughout Canada.

> It appears that Canada has reached a stage in its development when former methods of making regional rates must give way to a uniform

rate structure that, as far as may be possible, will treat all citizens, localities, districts, and regions alike.[1]

To assist further in equalization of freight rates between eastern and western Canada, the Royal Commission recommended that, "the cost of maintaining that portion of our transcontinental railway system which serves as a link or bridge between East and West be charged upon the general revenues of the country." This recommendation, which became known as the bridge subsidy, was enacted in 1951, and provided for an annual payment of $7,000,000 to the transcontinental railways to cover the cost of maintaining the bridge which was defined to be the unproductive traffic area in Northern Ontario.

THE EMERGENCE OF COMPETITION

Although the trucking and aviation industries were started in the 1930's, it was during the period following World War II that they had their fullest competitive effects.

The trucking industry, at least in its formative years, had very different economic characteristics from the railway industry. Entry was relatively easy, with licensing requirements in most Canadian provinces which, again in the formative years, offered few effective restraints to entry. Capital requirements were small, and frequently met by suppliers of equipment and petroleum products. The typical pattern in the industry was the owner-operator, concentrating on a limited geographic area. There were, at that time, few economies of scale and, in fact, some positive diseconomies.

Although a recent court decision[2] re-affirmed rights of the Federal Government in respect to regulation of interprovincial highway transport, and notwithstanding the fact that the National Transportation Act of 1967 provides for regulation of interprovincial highway transport in an as yet unpromulgated section, regulation of the trucking industry has been entirely by the provincial governments. Regulatory practices vary greatly between the provinces, with one province, Alberta, practising no entry or rate control, and other provinces, such as Quebec and British Columbia, practising relatively rigid entry and rate control.

Initially, the trucking industry developed on the basis of competition for traffic moved by the railways. Its initial success was largely a direct result of the value-of-service pricing policy followed by the railways, which, it will be recalled, had the effect of high rates on high-value goods to sub-

---

1. *Report of The Royal Commission on Transportation* (Ottawa: Queen's Printer, 1951).
2. *John D. Coughlin v. The Ontario Highway Transport Board et al.*, [1968] Supreme Court Report, p. 569.

sidize the movement of low-value traffic at low rates and the burden of national policy.

While, however, the railway rate structure had much to do with the early growth of trucking, many other factors explain the modern highway-transportation industry. Perhaps the most important single factor was a shift in the pattern of Canadian industry which reflected a decline in the importance of the primary-resource sector of the economy relative to that of manufacturing. The railways had been adapted in large measure to an economy largely dependent on the production of primary commodities. Substantial development of secondary manufacturing during and after World War II created a greatly increased demand for specialized transportation services such as pickup and delivery and for fast and flexible shipping schedules geared to meet the requirements of both shipper and consignee. Since much manufacturing industry is market- rather than resource-oriented, short-haul rather than long-haul movements became characteristic of their transportation requirements.

At the same time these developments were proceeding, the highway system was greatly expanded and developed, permitting much larger highway units. Developments in highway tractors and trailers and the changing nature of the markets served led to a subtle change in the nature of the trucking industry, which is still proceeding. Economies of scale developed, and a process of consolidation and merger commenced. Large freight terminals, extensive maintenance, and modern tractors and trailers imposed extensive capital requirements. Professional, computer- and control-oriented, management replaced the "seat-of-the-pants" approach of the owner-operator. Licensing requirements have become more rigid in many provinces. Lengths of haul greatly increased as the trans-continental highway system developed and as flexibility and speed of service by truck reflected themselves in the long-haul as well as the short-haul fields.

These circumstances contributed to a rapid growth in the number and size of trucking firms, and as these firms matured and their investment and standards of efficiency increased, the degree of competition that they were able to offer began to assume serious proportions for the railways.

A nation-wide rail strike in August 1950, tested the capabilities of the alternative forms of transport available, and provided clear evidence that the railways had finally lost the monopolistic position in Canadian transportation which they had maintained for almost a century.

At the same time that trucking was posing most formidable competition for the railways in the movement of high-value freight, commercial aviation in an eight-year period between 1948 and 1956 virtually eliminated long-haul railway passenger service. Also, immediately following World War II the discovery of oil and gas in Western Canada led to the development of the pipeline industry. Not only did pipelines lead to the direct loss of petroleum products and crude oil previously moved by railway, but they led to many secondary effects as well, such as replacement of coal, a commodity heavily dependent on rail transportation, by oil and gas which moved via pipeline.

The postwar period was one of steady rise in labour and other costs. This necessitated railway rate increases. While the railways had, since the 1930's, set competitive rates to meet competition in specific markets and had, since 1937, been permitted to contract with shippers for a specified portion of their freight through agreed charges, the effect of inflation *and* competition was to apply increases in rates on a narrower and narrower base of traffic—that was not subject to carrier competition. There were a number of other factors which impeded the railways in adjusting to the new competitive situation. Rates on grain and grain products moved to export positions and forming in 1956 some 27 percent of railway freight traffic were still pegged, by statute, at their 1899 level. Regulation remained more extensive in the case of the railways than in that of the competitors. Overcapacity was particularly serious, and it was readily apparent that the railways needed to make significant adjustments in the size of their plant to bring it into line with existing conditions. In this, they were handicapped not only by regulatory requirements, but also by public pressure which took the form of intense resistance to the dislocations occasioned by these adjustments. Such matters as removal of passenger services operating at a loss or the abandonment of unprofitable branch lines proved virtually impossible to decide solely with reference to normal commercial considerations. In effect, the advent of competition revealed a serious conflict of interest betwen commercial and national-policy considerations.

The long succession of postwar rate increases and the increased concentration of these increases on a narrower and narrower base of traffic led to the appointment of the MacPherson Royal Commission on Transportation in 1959.

FINDINGS AND RECOMMENDATIONS OF THE MACPHERSON ROYAL COMMISSION ON TRANSPORTATION

After a most exhaustive enquiry, the MacPherson Royal Commission on Transportation identified the substantial changes which had taken place in the transportation environment in the postwar years and, while it did not conclude that competition was sufficiently pervasive to take the place of regulation in its entirety, it did recommend that the extent and degree of regulation in the railway industry be substantially relaxed. At the same time, the MacPherson Commission identified a number of areas where public-policy requirements imposed a substantial burden on the railways, and recommended that these burdens be removed through direct subsidy by the federal treasury. Perhaps the most important finding and recommendation was that National Policy be separated from National Transportation Policy, and that the objective of National Transportation Policy be attainment of an efficient allocation of resources within the transportation industries.

The general conclusions of the MacPherson Commission were as follows:

1. The regulation of transportation should be minimized as much as possible, consistent with the protection of the public interest, and such regulation as is retained should bear in a reasonably equitable fashion on all carriers.

2. Where, for national-policy reasons, it is considered necessary to retain rail operations such as unprofitable passenger or branch-line services, the railways should be entitled to payment from public funds to cover their deficits on such services.

3. No particular form of transport should be singled out as an instrument of national policy if any burden is involved in the performance of the function, unless sufficient compensation is provided to that mode of transport to prevent distortions in the competitive transportation market.

4. Assistance to transportation which is designed to aid on national-policy grounds, particular shippers and particular regions should be recognized for what it is and not be disguised as a subsidy to the transportation industry. Moreover, whenever assistance of this kind is distributed through the transportation medium, it should be available on a non-discriminatory basis to all carriers.

To give effect to these general conclusions, the MacPherson Commission recommended that, in respect to rate regulation, the railways be permitted to price their services at rates at or above the variable costs attached to the service under consideration. Where monopoly conditions can be shown to exist, a maximum rate set at 150 percent over variable cost at standard carload minimum weights was also recommended. While the Commission recommended retention of the anti-discrimination features of the Railway Act, it rejected any attempt at equalization of rate scales between various sections of the country.

It identified the areas of burden imposed on the railways as a result of public policy shown below, and recommended the subsidies listed to remove their effects from the railways and from the freight-rate structure.

Passenger Train Service—Actual deficit geared to declines in service and deficit, with payments not to exceed $62,000,000 in 1961, declining to $12,400,000 in 1965.

Light Density Lines—An annual grant of $13,000,000 to provide compensation for losses incurred in the operation of lines the railways are prepared to abandon but which must be continued to meet requirements of national policy.

Export Grain Traffic—Loss on a variable-cost basis plus a contribution to constant cost of $16,300,000 per year.

These recommendations were largely enacted in the National Transportation Act of 1967. The National Transportation Act did much more, however. It grouped together under one administrative body regulatory agencies dealing with railway, air, water, commodity-pipeline and, to the extent that regulatory power is now or may in future be exercised by the federal government, highway transportation. It also authorized a vastly extended capability for research in the transportation industries in Canada.

CHALLENGES FOR THE POLICY-MAKER

The basic challenge faced by the policy-maker in transportation in Canada under the environment identified by the Royal Commission on Transportation and made the subject of the National Transportation Act of 1967 is that of achieving optimum efficiency in the allocation of transportation resources in Canada. This requires, under the Canadian transportation environment as it presently exists, primary reliance on the forces of competition and, particularly, the creation and maintenance of incentives which permit the competitive system to work effectively. Competition, however, is not an end in itself.

Beyond the challenge of efficient resource allocation in the transportation industries lies that of efficient allocation of public expenditure. Air, highway and water transportation involve substantial expenditure of public funds in the provision of airports and air-navigation facilities, highways, and port facilities. The challenge of planning these facilities in many cases in advance of demand for them requires exceedingly capable analysis of demand trends and technological innovation and adaptation. In many cases there are opportunities of influencing other developments in the public good.

In the field of air transportation, it is essential that airports and air-navigation facilities be planned sufficiently in advance of demand so that congestion and serious diseconomies do not arise. Should, for example, a large urban area be served by one airport or a number of airports? What location or locations make the greatest contribution to urban and regional development? To what extent will VTOL (vertical-takeoff) aircraft develop significantly in the next few years? What is the future of the SST (supersonic transport) and what are its implications for runway length, noise abatement, etc? Most important, how large a market—in passengers and air cargo—should be planned for?

In highway transport, similar questions must be asked in regard to the highway system. How much trucking is there likely to be between specific city pairs in ten, twenty or thirty years? What technological developments lie ahead in the field of highway transport? What should maximum length, weight, and height restrictions be on highway units? In this field, two challenges, perhaps, stand out above all others. First, what is the best method of charging for the use of public-highway facilities so as to best approximate the cost of the resources used in providing transportation? Second, what are the relationships between trucking and urban development? The cost of picking up and delivering traffic within urban areas, which is really the cost of congestion, is assuming ever increasing importance in the trucking industry. Should the industry charge less for pickup and delivery in the night than in the day, and more for pickup and delivery in the downtown core of the city than in the suburbs? These questions pose serious implications for urban planning and, particularly, for the planning of highway access which lies at its heart. Of equal importance to this are the questions posed by the efficient movement of passengers in urban areas. What method promotes greatest efficiency in the movement of people in urban areas? Should rapid-transit systems be developed? Should separate highways or separate highway lanes be provided for buses? Should the urban highway system continue to develop to provide a system to meet peak demands from all users, notwithstanding implications for land use?

In the field of water transportation, there are equally important and vexing issues. Overriding all other issues is the question of whether, in a period of unprecedented growth in international trade, Canada's ports make a maximum contribution of efficient resource allocation in the economy. Do they, for example, in an era of increased multi-modal activity in the transportation industries, make adequate provision for the handling of containers, and for their efficient transfer between water and rail or highway transportation? Are water depths adequate to permit use of vessel sizes now becoming standard in the international maritime industry for efficient transportation of Canada's bulk-commodity exports? The St. Lawrence Seaway System poses a whole new set of questions. Are water depths adequate? Would it be economic to make the system suitable for the use of larger bulk carriers in the Lakes trade? With increased containerization of package freight, and the need for more rapid turnaround of container ships, what is the likely future use of the system for package freight? What system of charges should be developed for use of navigation facilities provided at public expense, including use of icebreakers on the St. Lawrence in winter?

The private policy-maker in transportation faces equally interesting challenges. His greatest challenge is that of efficiency. How can the most efficient transportation systems be evolved? How can these transportation systems be shaped to make a maximum contribution to the public interest? How can institutional impediments to multi-modal operation—between, for example, rail and pipeline, rail and highway, highway and air—be removed? In an industry of extensive capital commitment, the size of the market to be served, and technological innovation and adaptation are even more important issues to the private than to the public policy-maker.

Transportation has been and will continue to be essential to Canada's growth and development. Provision of the most efficient and responsive transportation is one of the major ingredients in economic growth.

IV

Urban
Problems

Increased urbanization is a process that generally occurs in industrial countries, and Canada is no exception. There is a set of problems associated with the development of cities—for example, the creation of slum areas, the prevalence of poverty, etc. In this part of the volume, we are concerned with the Canadian urban problem in general, but we devote most of our attention to its most-publicized aspects, namely, poverty and housing.

Harold T. Shapiro provides a survey of Canada's poverty problem in his essay "Poverty—A Bourgeois Economist's View." Shapiro notes the astounding fact that approximately *20 percent* of non-farm families in Canada may be defined as living in poverty. He argues that households should be viewed as investing as well as consuming units. In this light, poverty involves under-investment in human capital. Thus poverty entails a loss to the economy not merely in direct welfare-assistance, but more important, in foregone output. The latter loss is analogous to the "brain-drain" phenomenon discussed in Lawrence H. Officer's essay in Part II. Thus Shapiro advocates *investment in human capital* as the principal form of anti-poverty policies.

"The Housing Market, the Housing Problem, and Government Policy" is the subject of Lawrence B. Smith's essay. In an important sense, this essay falls partially within the preceding part; for Smith is concerned with the *market structure* of a particular industry—residential construction. Contrary to the popular view that there exists a serious housing shortage in Canada, Smith argues that the extent of the housing problem has been exaggerated considerably. He suggests that, to the extent that a housing problem presently exists, it is largely distributional in nature and is an aspect of the general problem of poverty. Furthermore, again in contrast to widespread dissatisfaction with the government's role in the housing market, Smith shows that government policy has played a significant role in fostering housing construction. He notes, however, that the government use of this market for over-all stabilization purposes has often led to difficulties.

N. H. Lithwick's essay, "The City: Problems and Policies," examines the Canadian urban problem as rooted in the growth of cities and the allocation of economic activities within them. Lithwick agrees with Smith that an urban housing problem *as such* does not exist; Lithwick argues, further, that to a large extent the "problem" has been *created* by the government sector. More generally, he stresses the interaction of poverty, housing, transportation, taxation, and other problems of the cities, and criticizes government urban policies as misguided or non-existent. Policy-makers have treated urban problems individually in isolation from one another, with no understanding of their interrelationships.

poverty—a bourgeois economist's view

Harold T. Shapiro*
University of Michigan

1. INTRODUCTION

Canada is a rich country and getting richer. Her economy is sufficiently productive to assure all Canadians an adequate and continuing income. Nevertheless, one family in every five lives in poverty and many more face insecurity in employment and income. Thus, despite remarkable increases in productive capacity over the past few decades, poverty and employment (income) security are important continuing social and economic problems. The purpose of this essay is to provide a certain perspective on the problem of poverty in the industrially advanced, market-oriented economies of the twentieth century. The focus will be on poverty in Canada, but the framework developed to analyze this problem is easily adaptable to other economies where the generation and distribution of income is largely undertaken through some type of market system. The emphasis throughout is not on a detailed narrative of the characteristics of the poor, but rather on the general nature of the forces generating poverty in the economy. The

* In writing this essay I have been greatly influenced by the following works: A. B. Batchelder, *The Economics of Poverty* (New York: John Wiley and Sons, 1966); H. P. Miller, ed., *Poverty American Style* (Belmont, Calif.: Wadsworth Publishing Co., 1966); H. P. Miller, *Rich Man, Poor Man, A Study of Income Distribution in America* (New York: T. Y. Crowell, 1964); T. W. Schultz, "Public Approaches to Minimize Poverty," in L. Fishman, ed., *Poverty Amid Affluence* (New Haven, Conn.: Yale University Press, 1965); L. C. Thurrow, *The Economics of Poverty and Discrimination* (Washington, D.C.: The Brookings Institution, 1969); and C. Wilcox, *Towards Social Welfare* (Homewood, Illinois: Richard D. Irwin, Inc., 1969). I have also benefitted from extensive discussions with Gail Stewart and Barry Lacombe of the Economic Council of Canada. Despite intentions to the contrary, certain concepts may have found their way into this study without specific acknowledgement to their authors. To these authors I extend my gratitude.

analysis also leads naturally to some consideration of the appropriate direction and design of policies aimed at reducing the incidence of poverty. No attempt is made, however, to determine or designate an optimal set of policies. The study is divided into a number of sections. Section 2 attempts to put our rising social concern over the existence of poverty in historical perspective. Section 3 outlines the magnitude of the poverty problem (the incidence of poverty) in Canada today. Section 4 develops a particular notion of the *cost* of poverty (the economic consequences of poverty to society). Section 5 analyzes certain aspects of the generation of labour income in a market economy that bear on the issue of poverty. Section 6 deals with the consequences of poverty for the individual household. Section 7 contains some concluding remarks. Finally, although the causes and consequences of poverty are not simply an economic problem, but an emotional, cultural and political problem as well, it is the economic aspect of the over-all issue which is given primary attention in the pages below.

2. SOME HISTORICAL PERSPECTIVES

It has been noted, with some justification, that one of the outstanding facts about the problem of involuntary poverty today is our increased sensitivity to it. Clearly, involuntary poverty has always been with us, its extent at any particular time depending both on the level of *per capita* output and on its distribution. It is only recently, however, that we have witnessed the development of economies that are sufficiently productive to allow the elimination of poverty by a simple redistribution of national income (output). It is poverty amid general affluence that is a startling characteristic of advanced western economies such as Canada. The rising and spreading tide of affluence, however, does not itself explain why the elimination of poverty is "threatening" to become such a dominant goal of social policy. Although the present values of our society are such that we may assume that people would prefer to have fewer rather than more families in poverty, this is a recent development.[1] A brief consideration of society's changing views towards poverty, and some of the key events and philosophies which have shaped them, will help place our present concerns in a more useful perspective.

Attitudes in the nineteenth and early twentieth century were characterized by what we may call the *functional* view of poverty. According to this view, poverty of the working classes was a *necessary* condition for eco-

---

1. See T. W. Schultz, *op. cit.*; H. Vatter, "Some Historical Aspects of the Philosophy of Poverty," in N. Y. Glazer and C. F. Creedon, eds., *Children and Poverty* (Chicago: Rand McNally & Co., 1968); and R. H. Bremner, *From the Depths: The Discovery of Poverty in the United States* (New York: New York University Press, 1956).

nomic growth. This position was based on an appraisal of the nature of technological developments at the time and on certain now-discredited theories concerning the social motivation and habits of the lower classes. During this initial stage of industrialization, spectacular changes were taking place in the amount of capital equipment per worker used in production. The visibility of this phenomenon generally led people to the conclusion that the accumulation of plant and equipment was the principal (perhaps only) cause of the large measured increase in productivity.[2] Thus the state of technology was perceived as being characterized by the embodiment of technological advances in capital equipment. Growth in *per capita* output, therefore, was thought to be largely dependent on investment in plant and equipment. Further, it was the "burden" of the entrepreneurial class to carry on the socially productive role of saving (providing the resources for investment), as the working classes would only indulge themselves in "idleness and riot" the moment their income rose above the subsistence level. The ultimate release from this situation required both the protracted persistence of subsistence wages as well as some effort (thought futile by many) to teach the lower classes to limit their numbers.

There were, of course, other views at the time. To the socialists, poverty was an institutionally generated phenomenon related not at all to the prospects for economic growth, but to the level of exploitation of the working classes. The Social Darwinists, on the other hand, saw in poverty "the decrees of a large far-seeing benevolence" which gradually removed "misfits" from society. The growing slums of the larger cities were viewed simply as a refuge for the less virtuous and less able men. Both the Social Darwinists and those who held to the functional view of poverty often regarded the generous relief of poverty by public assistance or private charity as misguided benevolence. In general, public assistance was nonexistent during this period and although private charity has been an important aspect of Canadian social life for some time, its concern was largely with pauperism and not with the causes of poverty.

The second third of the twentieth century, however, is witnessing the culmination of a series of events which have swept away the basic cornerstones of the functional theory of poverty. First, the Great Depression together with the "Keynesian revolution," has revolutionized our thinking concerning the ability of government policy to modify the dynamics of the economic system. Second, technological advances are no longer so exclusively associated with investment in plant and equipment. Automation and the changing pattern of consumer wants (towards a demand for high-skill services) have greatly increased the importance (the rate of return) of

---

2. See H. A. Simon, "Decision Making as an Economic Resource," in L. H. Seltzer, ed., *New Horizons of Economic Progress* (Detroit: Wayne State University Press, 1964).

investment in *human* capital. The bulk of the productive wealth of an economy is no longer viewed as being embodied in factories and machines, but in the knowledge and skills stored in men's minds. Technological progress now depends as much on investment in human capital as on investment in physical capital. Third, the theory of population associated with the functional view of poverty has proved inadequate, as rising *per capita* incomes among all classes have led to a rationalization of family size. Now the existence of poverty, rather than being a necessary condition for economic growth, can be regarded as a hindering factor.

In a more technical sense, the existence of poverty together with a general excess demand for skilled labour, *even at peak levels of aggregate demand*, can be considered evidence that we have failed to allocate our resources in such a way as to equate the marginal yields from investment in human capital and investment in plant and equipment. Past policies of general underinvestment (sub-optimal investment) in human capital now produces a situation where the relative yield on investment in human capital is very high.

The causes of poverty are now clearly revealed as rooted in our underinvestment in human capital (education, health care, etc.) rather than in the personal motivation and habits of the poor themselves. The poor among us now represent *underutilized* resources which lower the potential *per capita* output of the economic system, diminishing our prospects for rapid economic growth. Thus the *dysfunctional* view of poverty is now replacing the more traditional functional theory. This new environment has critical implications regarding the nature of policies required to reduce the incidence of poverty. More important, the present environment provides avenues whereby poverty can be reduced in ways that need leave no one worse off while improving the economic condition of many. We can, by making appropriate investments in human capital, raise the productivity of the poor and share with them the extra output produced. This provides us with a set of policies which reduce poverty by creating new economic and human resources as opposed to policies that simply redistribute existing resources. Poverty can still be reduced (perhaps even eliminated) by direct income *transfers,* but as long as there are adequate net returns (as great as those on alternative investments) to investment in human capital, redistributive schemes by themselves are likely to be second-best choices, or simply avenues by which appropriate investments in human capital are made.

3. COUNTING THE POOR

In a complex urban society, there are many dimensions to the face of poverty and an equal number of relevant definitions. Thus, even the concept of poverty does not yield to any single "common-sense" definition. The definition of poverty, however, is an important matter, as it will affect the design of programs used to eliminate it. The definition used will also serve to help specify a measuring scale which will indicate when the job is done. For example, if poverty is considered to be a general lack of purchasing power, we might use income as a scale to indicate the progress we are (or are not) making. If, on the other hand, poverty is considered a complex of attitudes and behaviour patterns, it will be changes in these characteristics that we will have to measure. In any case, simple characterizations such as a level of family income and/or wealth are not completely adequate, as the availability of various public and private services, access to employment opportunities, and opportunities to participate in various ways in the society in which one lives, are often equally important elements to consider in any poverty calculus. In addition, family size obviously has a significant influence on the ability of the income-earner to provide adequately for his family responsibilities.[3] In general, however, we may consider a family to be in poverty when the amount of goods and services (of all kinds) available to it (from all sources) are insufficient to maintain an adequate (socially acceptable) level of participation in the economic and social life of the community.

The *Fifth Annual Review* of the Economic Council of Canada gave some indication of the extent of poverty in Canada.

> Poverty in Canada is real. Its numbers are not in the thousands, but in the millions.[4]

The actual extent of poverty, however, obviously depends on the standard that is used for its measurement. Poverty may be defined in relative or absolute terms. Although it is fashionable today to speak of poverty as a matter of relative deprivation, I think it is more useful to think of this latter concept as a problem of inequality rather than poverty. The problems of poverty are those that are created by serious deprivation and the misery that it entails. The standards by which poverty is judged ought to be stated as absolutes, with the obvious qualification that these absolutes may change over time as judgments about the minimal acceptable standard of living change. Only by using absolute standards will we recognize poverty as a serious social problem. A strictly relative measure (say, the bottom quartile of the income scale) cannot yield any measure of the

---

3. Any adequate long-run solution to the problems of poverty has to include a rational approach to family size.
4. See "The Problem of Poverty," in Economic Council of Canada, *Fifth Annual Review* (Ottawa: Queen's Printer, 1968), ch. 6, p. 103. Most of the basic data is available in J. R. Podoluk, *Incomes of Canadians*, 1961 Census Monograph (Ottawa: Dominion Bureau of Statistics, 1968).

progress that might be made in lifting people out of poverty. Under such definitions poverty cannot be eliminated as we cannot all get ahead of each other at once. We could, of course, commit ourselves to raising the bottom end of the income distribution faster than we otherwise would have. As noted above, however, this is a problem of inequality, not poverty. There may always be some Canadians richer and better off than others, but it need not follow that "the poor are always with us."

The most widely used and publicized procedure for measuring the extent of poverty is to establish poverty income levels, or "poverty lines." These lines are established by preparing family budgets that cover the costs of goods and services that are regarded as minimums to satisfy basic requirements. Families with incomes below these levels (known as poverty lines) are considered to be living in poverty. The definition of poverty developed in the *Fifth Annual Review* established a "poverty line" of $3,500 per year for a Canadian urban family of four. On this basis, approximately *twenty percent* of all non-farm families in Canada fall below the poverty line. This poverty line, however, is probably best interpreted as an irregularly contoured ridge or watershed falling somewhere within a fairly broad "poverty band." Despite the uncertainties about whether any such line slightly understates or overstates the particular number of families involved, it does serve the purpose of helping us isolate some of the characteristics of these families, and of generating an estimate of the over-all extent of poverty in Canada. Further, the data presented in the *Fifth Annual Review* revealed that, under any reasonable definition, the incidence of poverty in Canada was surprisingly and uncomfortably high. In addition, the data laid to rest many of our preconceptions concerning the profile of poverty in Canada. For example, more than half of all low-income families were found to be living in urban areas and the great bulk of them (83 percent) resided outside the Atlantic Provinces. Eighty-seven percent of these family units were headed by males, and seventy-six percent of these families had one or more income earners in the family. Table 1 opposite presents some further details concerning the nature and extent of poverty in Canada in the year 1961.

While there is little doubt that there has been some reduction in the total numbers of families involved since these data were collected (due largely to the record of growth in the Canadian economy, and somewhat to new schemes such as the Canada Assistance Plan), the problem is still one of very great magnitude reflecting many of the same characteristics. Further, these estimates simply reflect the fraction of families in poverty in a single year. The fraction of people that have known, or will know, poverty at some time during their lives would be considerably larger.

Table 1

SELECTED CHARACTERISTICS OF ALL NON-FARM FAMILIES AND NON-FARM FAMILIES
BELOW "POVERTY LINE." YEAR ENDING MAY 31, 1961

	Number of Families		Percentage of Total		
Selected Characteristics	All Families	Below "Poverty Line"	All Families	Below "Poverty Line"	Incidence of Poverty
					(Percent)
Total	3,626,964	916,050	100.0	100.0	25.3
Province					
Newfoundland	81,957	45,638	2.3	5.0	55.7
Prince Edward Island	14,269	7,017	0.4	0.8	49.2
Nova Scotia	144,003	58,029	4.0	6.3	40.3
New Brunswick	108,658	47,254	3.0	5.2	43.5
Quebec	988,307	275,505	27.2	30.1	27.9
Ontario	1,362,618	253,760	37.6	27.7	18.6
Manitoba	175,054	45,719	4.8	5.0	26.1
Saskatchewan	142,550	49,569	3.9	5.4	34.8
Alberta	238,647	54,710	6.6	6.0	22.9
British Columbia	368,116	78,359	10.1	8.6	21.3
Place of residence					
Metropolitan centres	1,901,221	314,540	52.4	34.3	16.5
Other urban municipalities	958,767	249,713	26.4	27.3	26.0
Rural	766,856	351,797	21.1	38.4	45.9
Age of head					
Under 25	149,134	43,179	4.1	4.7	29.0
25 - 54	2,508,658	553,891	69.2	60.5	22.1
55 - 64	491,119	109,026	13.5	11.9	22.2
65 and over	478,053	209,954	13.2	22.9	43.9
Labour-force status of head					
In current labour force	2,995,847	572,843	82.6	62.5	19.1
Worked during year (not in current labour force)	99,605	48,814	2.7	5.3	49.0
Did not work	531,512	294,393	14.7	32.1	55.4
Education of head					
No schooling or elementary only	1,680,323	625,040	46.3	68.2	37.2
Secondary 1 - 3 years	1,068,314	207,847	29.5	22.7	19.5
Secondary 4 - 5 years	551,095	62,160	15.2	6.8	11.3
Some university	137,234	12,727	3.8	1.4	9.3
University degree	189,998	8,276	5.2	0.9	4.4

Source: Statistical Tables in Economic Council of Canada, **Fifth Annual Review, op. cit.** Basic data are from the 1961 Census. See also J. R. Podoluk, **op. cit.**

4. THE COSTS OF POVERTY

Poverty has serious economic costs. Bluntly speaking, poverty impairs the poor as instruments of production and thus retards industrial output and impedes the over-all improvement in living standards.[5] The net output foregone by the failure to adopt policies to eliminate these effects of poverty is the primary economic cost of poverty. In principle, these costs could be either positive or negative. If the poor are composed primarily of those whom society feels ought not to participate in the labour force (the aged, the very disabled, etc.), or those for whom there is no known way to raise their net contribution to the economy's output, the cost of poverty may be close to zero or even negative, and the solution of the poverty problem consists of relief programs to guarantee these people a certain income. They should be ensured, without qualification, enough income to maintain what would be widely regarded as a decent minimum standard of living. Further, their incomes should be protected against inflation.

If, on the other hand, the poor are primarily those who have difficulty participating productively in the labour force because of *remedial disadvantages* (lack of education, training, health care, or an inadequate level of aggregate demand, etc.), the costs of poverty will be very high indeed. In this case, programs to relieve poverty should be aimed at helping these Canadians become productive citizens, rather than at a particular set of relief payments that simply guarantee a minimal income. Thus, in assessing the economic costs of poverty, it is important to distinguish between those poor who ought to remain outside the productive life of the economy and those who are poor despite their potential ability to participate in the labour force. The data presented in Table 1 on page 229 clearly indicate that in Canada, the poor are primarily composed of people and families in this latter group and the economic costs of poverty, therefore, are likely to be quite substantial.

Further, there are the secondary economic costs of poverty, which can be measured by the value of resources used up in trying to curb some of the social ills spawned by poverty. For example, the higher incidence of sickness among the poor involves not only lost output (through absenteeism from work) for the economy, but also an increased need for medical facilities. A more affluent society may choose to devote more resources to health care (as more affluent families do), but this must be distinguished from costs made necessary solely by the existence of poverty. There may also be increased costs (resource use) for the maintenance of charitable institutions, welfare programs, etc. The consequences of having a substan-

---

5. Conceiving of people as simply another form of capital goods has its obvious pitfalls; I hope the analysis that follows succeeds in avoiding these.

tial part of the population in poverty add an extra burden to the costs of operating nearly all our institutions.

The burden of poverty to society has yet another dimension—that of transfers of resources between persons. This is a flow of funds which simply passes through the government sector on its way from the non-poor to the poor,[6] and another analogous flow through private fund-raising activities, both of which reduce the potential spending (welfare) of those with higher incomes. These transfers include such items as family allowances, public-assistance payments, unemployment-insurance benefits and other government budgetary provisions designed, at least partially, to alleviate the hardships of poverty. While these payments do not represent real costs to the economy in a direct way because they do not use resources (except for some small administrative overhead), they do, however, involve a reduction in the potential spending of the non-poor.[7] Transfers of the same relative magnitude would have been unnecessary in the absence of poverty. It is important to note that quantitatively the most important income transfers carried out by explicit government policy either circulate solely among the non-poor or involve *a substantial flow of funds from the poor to the non-poor!* These are the transfers accomplished through the various tax-exemption and "loophole" provisions of the Income Tax Act. Curiously enough, the government gives no separate accounting of these in its budget!

Thus in a poverty-free Canadian economy operating at full capacity, there would be: (1) an increase in total output (a larger pie to share); (2) higher income levels for the poor; (3) relatively lower transfer payments from the non-poor to the poor; (4) resources freed from poverty-related activities for use in producing more desirable forms of output.[8] Poverty is thus not only a burden to those who experience it; it is a costly waste arising from our failure to conserve and develop the potential of our human resources. To cast it in the framework of a question of equity, of something to be resolved by more "adequate" income transfers, is a misconception of its nature. The central thrust of future policy must be directed towards expanding participation in productive activity. Only when assistance has been redesigned to become investment are we likely to succeed in eliminating poverty and reap the fullest benefits from doing so.

---

6. It is notable, however, that of total government transfers of $1.5 billion in 1961 only $.5 billion went to the poor. The remainder presumably circulated among the non-poor.

7. I have assumed here that tax-financed transfer payments have a negligible influence on the supply of labour. This implies that the incentive effects of taxation are not important.

8. The importance of maintaining a high and growing level of aggregate demand is discussed in detail below.

Unfortunately, public discussion of recent income transfer programs, such as the negative-income-tax proposals, has focused largely on such issues as incentive effects and administrative costs of these programs, rather than on the economically more critical issue of whether or not these programs are designed to allow those presently in poverty eventually to participate productively in our economic system. Hopefully, an optimally designed program of income transfers would make itself largely obsolete in a number of years.

5. THE GENERATION OF LABOUR INCOME

A careful study of some of the critical factors which determine the distribution of income is obviously a necessary precondition to an understanding of poverty and to the formulation of policies designed to deal effectively with the problem. In Canada, the generation and distribution of income is largely undertaken within the framework of a market system. In a market system, incomes are generated by the sale of land, capital and labour services. In any study of poverty, however, we may confine our attention to returns from the sale of labour services, as other sources of income are important only at higher income levels. We exclude from our analysis, for the moment, those among the poor who have voluntarily retired, or who society has agreed should not have to work.

If our economy functioned smoothly in every way, with perfectly functioning markets and without institutional rigidities that impede adjustment to an ever-changing environment, people would, by and large, earn pretty much what their skills and individual efforts were worth if they were added to the sum total of existing work effort. No market economy, of course, ever has or ever will function perfectly in this sense. However, the exercise of comparing a smoothly functioning but imaginary economic system having certain desirable characteristics with our actual system can sometimes serve a useful function. It may help us isolate certain aspects of our system that ought to be changed in order to bring us closer to some of the desirable characteristics of the abstract economic system.

perfect markets

In perfect markets, labour will be paid according to its marginal contribution to production. The marginal product of labour, given consumer preferences, will be a function of the amount and kind of physical capital each labourer has to work with, the skill and effort of the worker, and the stock of knowledge and skill with which the human and physical elements are combined. Perfect mobility of labour, equal access to employment opportunities, and perfect information are the elements that guarantee that workers with equal skill and putting forth equal effort will have the same marginal product and thus earn the same wage.[9] The distribution of labour income in this environment, therefore, is completely determined by the distribution of skills and effort (i.e., human capital). To earn larger incomes, one must either increase the quantity or quality of his human capital or the price he is paid for it. Education (formal or on-the-job) is the chief means of changing the quantity and quality of human capital. Mobility, improvements in information and the removal of other market imperfections is the main procedure for raising the price of the existing stock of human capital. In a world of perfect markets, therefore, government policy, if any, need only concentrate on schemes which alter the quantity and quality of human capital (i.e., it need concern itself only with the optimum level of investment).

Even in perfectly functioning labour markets, however, the over-all level of investment in physical and human capital (i.e., the trade-off between present and future consumption) may not be optimal if private and social rates of return differ. Examining this issue from the point of human capital, individuals will invest in education and training as long as the rate of return is greater than the rate of return from alternative investments. The individual, however, is interested only in whether discounted benefits exceed discounted costs, not whether output of society is increased. Given the limitation on individuals' budgets and the inability of capital markets to remove this constraint for private investment in human capital, the level of investment is likely to be sub-optimal.[10] The impact of imperfect capital markets is particularly harsh on the poor. The poor are less "well-established," usually have less information, will have few if any tangible assets, and therefore represent high risks. The market thus produces a set of incentives and constraints in which the least investment is done by the very groups that must invest the most if poverty is to be eliminated. Society therefore must alter this pattern of private decisions. There are a large class of public policies (a few already adopted) that can help accomplish this aim. I will list, without discussion, a number of examples: (1) income transfers—to relax the budget constraint on private investment (in human capital) expenditure decisions; (2) subsidization of educational and train-

---

9. Perfect markets, however, do not deal with the problem of varying family size among workers with similar productivity (income). This is an important, but separate, social issue. Neither do perfect markets, by themselves, guarantee the absence of poverty. They are simply an efficient way of allocating what resources we have. Needless to say, marginal-productivity theory has no nomative content. It does not tell us what people *ought* to get paid.

10. Perhaps a simple way to help relieve this budget constraint is to exempt all families whose incomes fall below the poverty line from income-tax liabilities.

ing programs; (3) a government insurance program for education loans; (4) improving knowledge of "payoffs" to education and training; (5) a set of inducements (perhaps tax incentives) to private business firms to invest in human capital (provide more training programs). This latter program is more difficult than inducing private investment in physical capital (through accelerated depreciation write-offs, etc.), as the private firm can never be sure of retaining the capital it has created.

This analysis also implies the desirability of at least a residual role for the Canadian federal government in education and manpower programs, despite the constitutional provisions in this area. Provinces and municipalities, just as private firms, run the risk of losing their investment in human capital through out-migration. Thus they too are likely to under-invest in human capital. The risk for the federal government, despite the highly publicized "brain drain," is less than that for any other level of government or industry.

imperfect markets

In actual fact, of course, in the real world there are a whole host of factors which work to produce imperfectly functioning markets and which disrupt, therefore, the relation between skill, effort and income. For our purposes, it is useful to distinguish two broad classes of market imperfections. First, there are various barriers to market adjustment which allow the generation of a wide range of marginal products (and hence a wide range of labour income) for workers of equivalent ability. When markets do not adjust properly, workers of the same ability will differ in the amount and quality of capital with which they work and in the efficiency of the organizations and/or sectors of the economy in which they are employed. The resulting variance of productivity (and hence income) for workers of equivalent ability breaks the connection between skill, efforts and income. Lack of labour mobility (between both jobs and regions) as well as lack of information about job opportunities are good examples of market imperfections that prevent adequate adjustment from taking place.[11] Much more important, however, is the situation created (only too often in Canada) when whole industries or firms are subject to tariff protection or special tax-loophole provisions that shield them from the necessity of using human and physical capital efficiently. In this situation, even though

---

11. In an environment characterized by rapid technological change, there will always be some disequilibrium in matching desired and actual skills, even if labour mobility were no problem. This, however, is an aspect of the problem of optimal investment in human capital. Technological change requires investment in *both* human and physical capital.

workers may be receiving wages equal to the value of their marginal product, they could, without any change in the distribution of skills and effort, have a higher marginal product if their efforts were combined more efficiently with the services of physical capital. To the degree that productivity (and hence income) of all workers depends very vitally on the way resources are combined and used, and on the gap between "best practices" and "actual practices," the poor as well as all other workers will be affected. Even if those imperfections noted above (mobility, information, etc.) were eliminated, and each worker was earning the value of his marginal product in production, inefficient industries or firms can cause an across-the-board shortfall below potential income for all workers and potential output for society. Without any need to upgrade skills or to expend greater efforts, workers could, other things being equal, earn higher incomes. Thus adjustment policies which assist firms to close the gaps between best and actual practices and the exposure of inefficient industries and firms to competition are not to be overlooked as devices to raise the level of incomes. This first category of market imperfections results in situations in which workers are still paid according to their marginal product, but the distribution of marginal productivity among workers is not solely determined by their distribution of skill and effort. In this type of world, if employed workers are in poverty, they do not possess enough human capital, or are not combined in employment with an adequate quantity or quality of physical capital, or are in inefficient sectors (regions) of the economy, or may suffer from some combination of these disadvantages. In order to reduce poverty, these disadvantages must be overcome, by an *additional* set of policies (other than those concerned with the optimal investment in human capital) designed to allow these markets to approximate as well as possible the desirable adjustment features of a perfectly functioning market.

The second set of market imperfections which I should like to isolate are those which break the link between labour's marginal product and labour income. In this world, the set of potential policies needed to reduce the incidence of poverty is further enlarged. Workers may not be paid their marginal product because of any one of a large number of factors. Two critical examples are discussed below.

1. *Unequal Access to Employment Opportunities (Discrimination).* We know very little in detail about the effects of discrimination on the poor,[12]

---

12. Where access to employment is regulated by publicly appointed boards, as it is in many occupations to ensure minimum standards of competence in the interests of public health and safety, restrictions on entry beyond legislated intent can (and often do) ensue, with consequent effects upon ease and equality of access to job opportunities.

except perhaps as it affects women, older members of the labour force, Eskimos and Indians. It is clear, however, that even in a world where the optimum level of investment (in both human and physical capital) was taking place, where mobility and information were perfect, and where markets were functioning perfectly, some workers might not actually earn the value of their marginal product, simply in consequence of the fact that equal access to employment was not available to all. Equally important are the negative-incentive effects of employment discrimination. One can hardly expect someone to prepare himself (by education or training) for a job which is not accessible to him even though he has the requisite skills. Unequal pay for equal work and unequal access to employment opportunities are forms of discrimination which intensify all the problems of poverty, lead to an inefficient allocation of resources, and thus lower the aggregate level of output for society as a whole. For example, any "quota" system of allocating jobs will very likely have the effect of lowering output. It is simply economically inefficient to allocate resources in this way. It is particularly important to note that those in poverty because of unequal access to employment opportunities (discrimination) are not likely to benefit from general economy-wide programs to reduce poverty. Special types of policies will be necessary to solve this problem efficiently. For example, although growth in aggregate output and general economic prosperity reduce both poverty and inequality, there is some evidence that these groups are not able to share proportionately in these benefits.[13]

2. *Market Power.* On both sides of the labour market there are degrees of monopoly power. Employers and employees are rarely in a relationship in which the relative economic power of each has no effect on the outcome of the price paid. In general, the assumption is that total employment will be lower, product prices higher, and wage rates divergent from their marginal products for a larger number of workers, the higher and more pervasive the concentrations of economic power on either side of the market.

stabilization and growth policies

Finally, the elimination of poverty depends very crucially upon the maintenance of a high and growing level of aggregate demand. The rate of return on investment in human capital will be negative if the level of aggregate demand together with the available capital stock provides no employment opportunities that make use of the newly acquired skills. Thus,

---

13. See W. H. L. Anderson, "The Relationship Between Economic Growth and the Extent of Poverty Among American Families," *Quarterly Journal of Economics* (November 1964).

as the productivity of labour depends crucially on the quantity and quality of the physical capital with which it is employed, policies to reduce the incidence of poverty *must* be pursued in tandem with policies designed for the stabilization and growth of aggregate output. The evaluation of programs to reduce the incidence of poverty through investment in human capital is critically dependent on the particular policies undertaken for economic stabilization and growth.

Historically, the growth of output has been the most significant factor in the reduction of the total numbers of low-income families; and to the degree that stabilization policies succeed in reducing the randomness of employment opportunities, they make a significant contribution to reducing as well the over-all magnitude of the poverty problem. Such unemployment as does exist, however, tends to fall with heavier impact upon the poor than upon the rest of society. Having a more marginal attachment to the labour force, whether by virtue of having lower levels of skill, more varied employment histories, more imperfect information, higher incidence of sickness or for whatever reason, when job opportunities are scarce, the impact weighs more heavily upon the poor. Although not necessarily designed to reduce the number of job openings so much as they are designed to reduce aggregate demand and thus check price increases, restrictive monetary and fiscal policies do nonetheless affect the level of unemployment. The phenomenon has become so much taken for granted that the concept of a trade-off (at least in the short run) between varying levels of unemployment and rates of change in price indexes is well developed. There is a serious question as to whether this situation is consistent with a determination to eliminate poverty. Stabilization policies place an inequitable share of the burden of maintaining price stability on the poor.[14] The tax system in Canada is highly regressive at low income levels and, caught between rising taxes, diminished employment opportunities and the diminished availability and increased cost of credit, many low-income families appear to have been most reluctantly forced to accept welfare assistance. There is a great deal of evidence to suggest that the lack of job opportunities is a central factor in this situation.

The investment in human capital which we believe should form the central thrust of policies to eliminate poverty and to increase output may be thwarted by unemployment. Further, it should be noted that appropriate investment in human capital will, among other things, improve the trade-

---

14. Evidence recently accumulated for the United States indicates that the poor may suffer less than the non-poor from inflation, particularly the non-elderly poor. It is the tax of unemployment not the tax of inflation that weighs especially heavy on the poor. See R. G. Hollister and J. L. Palmer, *The Impact of Inflation on the Poor*, Discussion Paper, Institute for Research on Poverty (Madison, Wisconsin: University of Wisconsin, 1969).

off between unemployment and inflation. As things now stand, once unemployment falls to the four-percent level we begin to generate price increases that policy-makers in Canada find unacceptable. An important contributing cause of this inflation is that the rest of the labour force may not be worth employing. Adequate training programs, therefore, may succeed in allowing a two-percent unemployment rate before we hit that "critical" rate of inflation. It should also be noted that at any given level of aggregate demand (or output), the larger the available supply of skills the less pressure there will be on prices.[15] In any case, a serious effort to explore the feasibility of a national commitment to full employment (voluntary unemployment approaching zero) should be undertaken. Such a policy would, of course, demand a reorientation of attitudes in a number of areas. For example, the relative size of the public and private sectors of the economy might vary more frequently and more widely than they have in the recent past, but there is no necessary presupposition that either would substantially grow or diminish in the long run.

To recapitulate, an examination of labour income of the poor has suggested that there is a need for both compensatory and general efforts of three kinds: public and private investment in human capital, public and private efforts to reduce or remove barriers to the smooth adjustment of labour markets to changing circumstances, and public policies to ensure full employment.

other factors—(psychology, sociology and all that)

At the same time that the importance of investing in human capital has been growing increasingly obvious to the economist, research in other disciplines has thrown new light on human behaviour. *Crudely* summarized, these studies have shown that once people have satisfied their basic physical needs, they are likely to feel the desire to participate more fully in the economic and social life of the community, and to maintain self-esteem. If the gap between these needs and their fulfilment is too wide, a loss of self-confidence and of motivation (may) result. Where lack of acceptance through discrimination, hostility or indifference is met, behavioural response seems to fork, choosing either a pattern of apathy and indifference, or of resistance and contentiousness. Such an unqualified summary is, of course, gross generalization, but is perhaps sufficiently indicative of the essential importance of taking into account what we know of human behaviour in designing programs for the poor.

---

15. Of course, unemployment will also be higher, but for an open economy the new situation may be advantageous. Although unemployment will be higher, *output will be no lower*, and the rate of price inflation considerably reduced.

6. POVERTY AND THE INDIVIDUAL HOUSEHOLD

By and large the economic significance of household units and families (as opposed to individuals) has been overlooked in the general analysis of poverty and in the design and delivery of most of our present social-development policies. Despite the fact that the household is our most common economic unit and operates in a fashion somewhat akin to a business firm in selling a product on a market, the importance of its economic viability has not been widely recognized. The economic and social consequences which flow from inadequate income to the family in poverty are directly analogous to those for the firm whose operating costs exceed its revenues from sales. Unable to enhance productive capacity through lack of access to credit, and unable in the long run to maintain even that level of maintenance costs which permits continued sales, it is forced to abandon the attempt. The economic and social consequences which flow to society are, however, quite different in the case of the firm and the household. While the firm may ultimately disappear, having sold its assets to others, the family remains. So too do its potential abilities for productive contribution. For society to allow revenues to the family to fall below the level of necessary maintenance expenses is clearly short-sighted. These should be maintained at a level which will not only allow the adults in the family to sell their services currently, but also to prepare their children to do so in the future. The long-run costs of providing families with inadequate assistance are very high. Inadequate assistance virtually ensures financial dependency of families, and failure of society to invest in their children simply perpetuates the problem. Thus, while our economy has provided a mechanism for a bankrupt firm's resources to flow to more productive uses (via mergers and sales), we have not provided a satisfactory analogous mechanism for families.

Where family income is more than sufficient to meet needs, we speak of a family having the ability to undertake some discretionary consumption expenditures—or to save—or perhaps to invest in itself or in one or more of its members. The uses to which discretionary income is put are not a matter of indifference to the rest of society, which stands to gain from the productive use of these funds. By the same token, the family which has no discretionary income and no access to savings or credit is not only unable to invest in itself but is likely to have negative effects on the rest of society. At a time when the pace of technological change is creating obsolescence in human capital at an ever faster rate, a family whose gross investment in itself is zero and net investment negative imposes a cost on others. At an early stage this cost may consist merely of foregone output, but may later entail a positive current resource cost of supporting essentially nonproductive services. Society may willingly assume these costs in the case of the aged or disabled, but it does not make much sense to provide them to a recipient family which would prefer to participate in a productive way in the economy. Thus *the concept of a minimum standard must be based on a definition of the family as a producing unit rather than merely a consuming unit.* Our aim ought to be to provide *family units* with sufficient resources for the basic necessities for productive participation in economic life.

A family's inability to invest in itself is likely to have particularly serious consequences on young children whose potential abilities may be largely shaped in the years of early childhood. Analysis of the data suggests that children of low-income families in urban Canada are most unlikely to have access to the broad variety of experiences in their early years, which is increasingly recognized as being essential to development of potential abilities. Beyond this, there is even an indication that lack of access to proper nutritional intake is a very real possibility. While more definitive statements can only be made after the results of minimum-budget studies and nutritional studies have been developed, the possibility must be taken seriously. It is now well-established that malnutrition in the early months of life will not only impair physical growth but may irreversibly damage mental development. In absolute-dollar terms, the poor appear most deprived of access to sufficient food, clothing, shelter, and transportation. However, if the expenditures of the poor are taken as a percentage of the expenditures which occur at poverty-line income levels, it is clear that the poor are most deprived, in a relative sense, of access to education, transportation, recreation, furnishings and equipment, clothing, reading, household operation, medical care, personal care, shelter, and food expenditures, in that order.[16]

7. CONCLUSION

If poverty is to be eliminated in Canada, a new approach to the problem is required. Serious efforts must be made to develop the potential abilities of both the poor and their children. A program of investment in human[17]

---

16. These latter statements are based on an analysis of Urban Family Expenditure data collected by the Dominion Bureau of Statistics. See D.B.S., *Urban Family Expenditures* (Ottawa: Queen's Printer, 1964). The analysis was carried out by B. Lacombe of the Economic Council of Canada. For further relevant literature see A. Breton, *Towards an Optimum Set of Policies for Combatting Poverty*, Special Planning Secretariat, Privy Council Office (Ottawa); and L. A. Ferman, J. Kornbluth, and A. Haber, eds., *Poverty in America* (Ann Arbor: University of Michigan Press, 1965).

17. On the research side of things, what is rather desperately needed is a series of careful studies to determine optimal investment (in human and physical capital) policies for future growth. This determination will, of course, require an assessment of the relative rates of return on investment in human versus physical capital. It is only after this information is assembled that an optimal policy plan can be constructed.

resources should assume *central* importance. A number of changes must occur if such an approach is to be implemented in Canada. The technical obstacles to change are not great, but institutional barriers are extensive. First, we must realize that our price system has failed to give the necessary signals which would lead to the most productive investments being undertaken. This failure can probably be associated, at least in part, with various institutional rigidities which affect the efficiency with which markets operate. But perhaps the most important of all barriers are simply those in men's minds—certain preconceptions about the causes or the methods of dealing with poverty embedded in our individual attitudes towards it. A willingness on the part of all involved to review and reconsider these attitudes and practices would seem to be an essential prerequisite to successful action.

the housing market, the housing problem, and government policy

*Lawrence B. Smith**
University of Toronto

The housing market plays an extremely vital role in the Canadian economy since it determines the housing standards of the nation, provides employment for almost 5 percent of the Canadian labour force, and has been an important medium for the transmission of government stabilization policy to the economy. This paper examines these roles in three sections. The first section describes the structure and operation of the housing market, the second section discusses the nature and magnitude of the Canadian "housing problem," and the third section examines the role of government and government policies in the housing market.

1. THE OPERATION OF THE HOUSING MARKET

The housing market is not really a market in the classical sense, but a series of overlapping submarkets differentiated by location, type of dwelling, type of tenure, age and quality.[1] Each of these submarkets is influenced by different institutional considerations and the behaviour of the participants in these submarkets often differs considerably, making it desirable to distinguish between submarkets whenever possible. Two major distinctions that should be made are between existing residential dwellings and those under construction or newly constructed, and between single-unit, primarily owner-occupied, housing and multiple-unit, primarily rental, housing. An indication of the differences that exist between these submarkets may be

---

* For econometric evidence of the model described in this paper, see Lawrence B. Smith, "A Model of the Canadian Housing and Mortgage Markets," *Journal of Political Economy*, 77 (Sept./Oct. 1969), pp. 795-816; and "A Bi-sectoral Housing Market Model," *Canadian Journal of Economics*, II (Nov. 1969), pp. 557-569.
1. J. Duesenberry, *Business Cycles and Economic Growth* (New York: McGraw-Hill Book Company, 1958), p. 135.

Table 1

SINGLE- AND MULTIPLE-UNIT DWELLING STARTS, AND PERCENTAGE CHANGES IN HOUSING PRICES AND RENTS

Year	Housing Starts (in thousands)		Multiple Starts as a percentage of total starts	Annual percentage change in		
	Singles	Multiples		Average Monthly Rents	New NHA House Prices	Existing (MLS) House Prices
1951	53.0	15.6	22.7	12.1	NA	NA
1952	60.7	21.5	26.2	8.7	7.1	NA
1953	70.8	51.6	42.2	7.2	3.1	NA
1954	78.6	34.9	30.7	9.9	6.8	NA
1955	99.0	39.3	28.4	3.0	7.1	NA
1956	90.6	36.7	28.8	6.1	10.7	3.5
1957	83.0	39.3	32.1	4.4	7.9	8.1
1958	104.5	60.1	36.5	7.1	.9	5.0
1959	92.9	48.4	34.3	.9	1.7	3.3
1960	67.2	41.7	38.3	3.4	1.0	1.4
1961	76.4	49.2	39.2	2.1	.7	2.6
1962	74.4	55.5	42.7	3.7	2.2	3.3
1963	77.2	71.4	48.0	2.3	2.8	3.1
1964	77.1	88.6	53.5	4.1	4.0	8.2
1965	75.4	91.2	54.7	5.2	4.5	8.5
1966	70.6	63.9	44.2	5.9	8.6	9.5
1967	72.5	91.6	55.8	7.7	8.1	9.9
1968	75.3	121.6	61.8	3.8	4.2	11.0

NA — Figures not available.

Sources: Column 1, 2 and 5, Central Mortgage and Housing Corporation, **Canadian Housing Statistics,** (Ottawa: Queen's Printer, 1968), pp. 7, 59 and 61
Column 4, calculated from worksheets at Dominion Bureau of Statistics based on Labour Force Survey results.
Column 6, calculated from statistics published by Canadian Association of Real Estate Boards, **The Canadian Realtor,** (Toronto).

gained from Table 1, which shows the different growth and cyclical patterns that single- and multiple-dwelling starts followed during the postwar period, as new multiple-dwelling construction rose from approximately 25 percent of total housing starts in the early 1950's to over 50 percent by the mid-1960's. During this same period, rents, the price of new government-insured (NHA) homes, and the price of existing homes (approximated by the average price of units sold through real-estate-board Multiple Listing Service (MLS)) followed quite divergent cyclical patterns, although their average annual rates of inflation were similar.

Perhaps the most fruitful way to view the operation of the housing market is in a stock-adjustment context which focuses attention upon the relationship between the existing stock or supply of each type of housing accommodation and the demand for each of these types. As in any market, the demand for each type of accommodation, together with its supply, determines its price or rent.[2] However, there are numerous frictions in the housing market which prevent quick and complete adjustments. Vacancies are common and housing prices and rents often differ from their equilibrium or perfectly competitive levels for considerable periods of time. This happens because consumer reaction in this market is slow as a result of the enormity of the housing decision, fixed tenancies, inertia, transactions costs, and the differentiated nature of the housing commodity, and because the supply of dwellings is essentially fixed in the short run, annual construction augmenting the housing stock by only 2 to 2½ percent. Over time, if the market were not subjected to random disturbances, housing prices, rents, vacancies, and new construction would interact so that prices, rents, and vacancies would approach their equilibria, given that some level of vacancies (usually assumed to be 3½ to 4 percent)[3] is required to enable people to change their accommodations without undue difficulty.

The volume of new construction undertaken in any period essentially depends upon a comparison of vacancy levels and prices or rents with construction costs, and upon the cost and availability of mortgage credit, since these determine the profitability and feasability of such construction. In the case of multiple dwellings, the greater the final or user demand for rental accommodation relative to its supply, the higher the rents and lower the vacancy rates, which increases the likelihood that developers will expect new construction projects to be profitable. Since developers plan either to sell their buildings once they are completed and rented, or to retain them for long-term investments, the profitability of a project depends upon the relationship between its expected selling price and its total costs, or upon the developer's expected yield on invested capital. Because real estate, like other investments, is usually purchased on a yield basis, the profitability of a project from either the "sale" or "yield" viewpoint depends upon the return on invested capital. This return will be higher the higher the rents, the lower the number of vacancies, the lower the construction cost, the lower the mortgage rate, and the more favourable the non-price borrowing terms (such as the amortization period and loan-to-value ratio).

A discussion of single-dwelling construction introduces an added complication because these homes both are built speculatively by merchant-builders (developers) for subsequent sale and are custom-built by owner-

2. Because only a small percentage of the housing stock is for sale at any time, the price obtained on those transactions is considered representative of the market as a whole, although it could not be realized if a large proportion of the stock were to be offered for sale at once.
3. Ontario Association of Housing Authorities, *Good Housing for Canadians* (Arnprior, Ontario, 1964), p. 80.

builders or contractors on a presold basis.[4] When the demand for owner-occupancy dwelling accommodation increases, the price of single-family dwellings increases relative to construction costs, and the speed at which homes are sold increases, generating an increase in the volume of new construction by merchant builders. Similarly, the greater the demand for owner-occupancy dwelling accommodation, the greater the volume of new custom-built home construction. However, since the volume of custom-building is not a consequence of the selling-price – construction-cost relationship, the mechanism influencing this type of construction is different from that influencing the volume of speculative building activity.

Mortgage credit influences the volume of single-dwelling construction somewhat differently than it does the volume of multiple construction, because the demanders of single-dwelling accommodations usually purchase their homes rather than rent them. Since the purchaser of a house assumes the responsibility for the mortgage on the house, the demand for single-family dwellings depends not only upon the nominal selling price but also upon the terms and conditions of the mortgage. Merchant-builders are, therefore, influenced by the availability of mortgage credit both directly, because they require this finance for construction, and indirectly, because the final demand for their product depends upon the cost and non-price terms of this credit. Commissioners of custom homes are also directly affected by the availability and cost of mortgage credit because this influences the affordability of their home. Consequently, although the builder of single dwellings responds to varying credit conditions, much of this is a derived response based upon an assessment of how variations in credit conditions will influence the ultimate demand for these dwellings.

From this discussion it is clear that the volume of residential construction is significantly influenced by the final demand for dwelling accommodations and the cost and availability of mortgage credit. However, these forces operate somewhat differently in the single and multiple markets. This is especially true in the case of mortgage credit, since it influences the profitability and feasibility of multiple-dwelling construction and the final user demand for single-dwelling construction.

The basic forces underlying the demand for housing accommodations are essentially the same as for other goods—population, income, prices, the cost and availability of credit and consumer preferences—with the demographic and income variables being most important in the long run. In the short run, population growth may be accommodated in a relatively fixed housing inventory by varying the intensity of occupancy, but in the long run, especially under conditions of rising real incomes, demographic

4. Royal Bank of Canada, *The Canadian Construction Industry*, Royal Commission on Canada's Economic Prospects (Ottawa: Queen's Printer, 1956), p. 52.

forces have been the strategic factors in determining the level of housing demand and residential construction.[5]

Demographic forces are not confined to population or family growth, but include such variables as age composition, family size and the number of first- and second-child births, which also play important roles in housing demand. Net family formation, net immigration and net non-family household formation (primarily single young persons who move out of their parent's home to live in separate dwellings, and middle-aged and elderly widows, widowers, bachelors, spinsters and divorcees) tend to generate demand for rental accommodations, while families experiencing first- and second-child births and families whose head is moving into the 25-35 age range often shift their demand from rental to owner-occupancy accommodations. Recently, completing the life-cycle pattern, there has been a tendency for families to move back to rental from owner-occupancy accommodations following the children's departure from the family home.

In assessing the relative strengths of these various demographic forces for the future, it is interesting to note that between 1951 and 1966 the number of doubled families in Canada (i.e., the number of families without the use of a dwelling unit of their own) declined by approximately 140,000 families (from 9.8 percent to 4.0 percent of all families), while the number of non-family households (60 percent of which consist of individuals over 55 years of age) rose by over 382,000. Since the number of family households in Canada rose by approximately 1,230,000 families between 1951 and 1966, undoubling and net non-family household formation accounted for 30 percent of the realized increase in housing demand.[6]

Variations in incomes also have a substantial impact upon the demand for housing accommodations by influencing the quality of accommodation desired and the number of families or persons who feel they can afford their own dwelling. Rising incomes stimulate demand for single-family dwellings by enabling families to afford higher-quality homes and enabling more families to afford the monthly carrying costs and downpayments required for home-ownership. Rising incomes also generate a net increase in the demand for rental accommodations, despite the fact that they enable some families to shift their demand from rental to owner-occupancy dwellings, by improving the quality of dwelling people desire and by facilitating net family undoubling, net family formation, and net non-family household formation.

---

5. L. Grebler, D. Blank, and L. Winnick, *Capital Formation in Residential Real Estate: Trends and Prospects*, National Bureau of Economic Research (Princeton, N.J.: Princeton University Press, 1956), p. 76; and K. Buckley, "Urban Building and Real Estate Fluctuations in Canada," *Canadian Journal of Economics and Political Science*, XVIII (Feb. 1952), p. 56.
6. W. M. Illing, *Housing Demand to 1970*, Economic Council of Canada Staff Study (Ottawa: Queen's Printer, 1964), p. 40; and Central Mortgage and Housing Corporation, *Canadian Housing Statistics, 1967* (Ottawa: Queen's Printer), p. 73.

Finally, credit variables have a strong influence upon the demand for owner-occupancy dwellings, since most families are quite sensitive to the downpayment and monthly payment requirements associated with a home purchase.[7] Larger downpayment requirements increase the minimum liquid savings that families require to enter the housing market and reduce the housing expenditure that a given downpayment would support, while larger monthly payments severely limit the number of households able to carry these payments out of current income. An indication of the impact of these variables can be seen from the Royal Commission on Banking and Finance, "Consumer Survey," which indicates that 15 percent of the families who purchased homes with mortgage credit during the 1957-1962 period would either have purchased no home (9 percent) or a cheaper home (6 percent) if downpayment requirements had been 10 percent higher, and that 32-40 percent would have purchased no home (20-25 percent) or a cheaper home (12-15 percent) if monthly payments had been 10 percent higher.[8]

The downpayment required for a home purchase depends upon the price of the home and the proportion of that price (loan-to-value ratio) that the mortgage covers. The amount of the monthly payment required depends upon the price of the home, the loan-to-value ratio, the mortgage interest rate, and the amortization period (the number of years required for the mortgage to be repaid out of monthly payments). Apart from reducing monthly payments by reducing the price or loan-to-value ratio (the latter, on balance, curtailing demand by raising the required downpayment), the monthly mortgage payments may be reduced by lowering the interest rate and thereby the interest portion of each payment, or by lengthening the repayment term, which spreads the capital repayments over longer periods and thereby reduces the principal portion of each payment. The relative importance of changes in the interest rate and amortization term upon the monthly payment may be seen from Table 2. This table indicates that rising interest rates can be substantially offset by an increase in the amortization term, for example, a 5-year increase in the amortization period of a 7½ percent, 25-year mortgage more than offsets a ½-percent increase in the interest rate, but that as the interest rate and amortization period increase, the extent to which an increase in the amortization period can be used to offset rising interest cost declines.

7. E. M. Fisher, *Urban Real Estate Markets: Characteristics and Financing* (New York: National Bureau of Economic Research, 1951), pp. 69-75; and R. Wood, "Credit Terms and the Demand for Residential Construction," in *Study of Mortgage Credit,* Committee on Banking and Currency, Sub-Committee on Housing, U. S. Senate, 85th Congress, 2nd Session, December 1958.
8. Royal Commission on Banking and Finance, *Appendix Volume* (Ottawa: Queen's Printer, 1965), p. 100.

Table 2

MONTHLY LEVEL PAYMENTS REQUIRED TO AMORTIZE $1,000 AT VARIOUS INTEREST RATES AND AMORTIZATION PERIODS

Interest Rate*	Amortization Period in Years						
	10	15	20	25	30	35	40
%	$	$	$	$	$	$	$
9.5	12.84	10.33	9.20	8.61	8.28	8.04	7.92
9.0	12.58	10.05	8.89	8.28	7.93	7.69	7.56
8.5	12.32	9.76	8.59	7.95	7.59	7.35	7.21
8.0	12.06	9.48	8.28	7.63	7.25	7.01	6.86
7.5	11.81	9.21	7.99	7.32	6.91	6.66	6.50
7.0	11.56	8.93	7.69	7.00	6.59	6.32	6.14
6.5	11.31	8.66	7.41	6.70	6.26	5.98	5.79
6.0	11.07	8.40	7.12	6.40	5.95	5.65	5.45
5.5	10.82	8.14	6.84	6.10	5.64	5.33	5.12
5.0	10.58	7.88	6.57	5.82	5.34	5.02	4.80

* Compounded semi-annually.
Source: **Monthly Amortization Mortgage Payments** (Boston: Financial Publishing Company, 1965).

2. THE CANADIAN HOUSING PROBLEM: FACT OR FICTION?

In the last few years, much has been written in the popular press about the severity of the Canadian housing problem, and in January 1969, a Federal Task Force on Housing and Urban Development concluded that, "if there was not an urban 'crisis,' there most certainly was a serious urban problem."[9] Yet, little evidence has been presented to demonstrate this, and even many of the Task Force "comments and conclusions stem as much from mental note or emotional impression as they do from proven fact."[10] Consequently, before turning to the role of government in the housing market, it is useful to place the magnitude of the "housing problem" into perspective and consider the present quality of the nation's housing standards.

Canada entered the postwar period with a very severe shortage of housing accommodation as a result of a sharply reduced building program during the depression and the war. Between 1931 and 1945 Canada averaged fewer than 39,000 dwelling completions annually, compared with an annual average of over 55,000 completions for the five years preceding this period and of over 77,000 completions for the five years immediately following this period.[11] By 1951, although the housing situation had improved sub-

9. *Report of the Federal Task Force on Housing and Urban Development* (Ottawa: Queen's Printer, 1969), p. 1.
10. *Ibid.*, p. 7.
11. Central Mortgage and Housing Corporation, *Canadian Housing Statistics* (Ottawa: Queen's Printer, 1967), p. 21.

stantially, 9.8 percent of all Canadian families and 13.0 percent of Canadian families in metropolitan areas did not have separate dwelling accommodations of their own. (See Table 3.) Moreover, many of the dwelling units that existed were of inferior or substandard quality, as the 1951 Census indicated that 13.4 percent of all dwellings and 9.9 percent of urban dwellings were in need of major repair. In terms of essential facilities, 29.3 percent of Canadian dwellings were without the use of flush or chemical toilets, 43.1 percent were without the use of piped hot and cold water, and 39.2 per cent were without the use of an installed bath or shower.[12]

However, owing to a strong building program, the situation rapidly improved, and by 1966 the percentage of families not maintaining their own households had declined to 4.0 percent over-all, and 4.5 percent in metropolitan areas. In terms of other measures of housing standards, the 1961 Census indicated only 5.6 percent of all dwellings were still in need of major repair, and by 1968 the proportion of dwelling accommodation without the use of flush or chemical toilets had fallen to 5.4 percent, without piped hot and cold water to 9.0 percent, and without installed bath or shower to 9.9 percent. Canada's housing standards are now sufficiently high to rank among the world's best, as Canada has the roomiest housing stock in the western world with an average 5.3 rooms per dwelling, is tied with the United States for the lowest occupancy density at 0.7 people per room, and is second only to the United States in the provision of basic equipment.[13]

Table 3
MEASURES OF HOUSING CONDITIONS

	Percentage of Canadian families not maintaining their own households		Percentage of Canadian dwellings without the use of essential facilities		
	All Areas	Metropolitan Areas	Flush or Chemical toilets	Piped hot & cold water	Installed bath or shower
1951	9.8	13.0	29.3	43.1	39.2
1956	7.7	10.0	20.4*	28.9*	28.5*
1961	5.7	6.8	12.8	19.8	19.1
1966	4.0	4.5	8.4	12.6	12.8
1968	NA	NA	5.6	9.0	9.9

NA — Figures not available at time of writing.
* — Figures are for 1957.
Source: Central Mortgage and Housing Corporation, **Canadian Housing Statistics**, 1968, pp. 64, 70.

---

12. *Ibid.*, pp. 84, 85, and 92.
13. *Report of the Federal Task Force on Housing and Urban Development*, p. 6.

Turning from measures of quantity and quality to measures of affordability, we find a similar pattern of improvement emerging over the last
decade, although the trend has been reversed recently in some metropolitan
areas. As shown in Table 4, the average annual increase in housing prices
and rents between 1957 (the first year that all our series were available)
and 1968 was probably between 3.1 percent and 4.8 percent, depending
upon the series selected, despite a much lower DBS estimate for rental
increases. In comparison, the average annual increase in personal disposable income per family was 5.1 percent and in personal disposable income
per person over 19 years of age, was 5.2 percent. Therefore, from the
viewpoint of nominal purchase price and rent, housing accommodations
became easier to afford during the 1957-to-1968 period. On the other hand,
dwelling accommodations became more expensive relative to other commodities as the consumer price index rose at an average annual rate of 2.3
percent and the GNE implicit price deflator at 2.4 percent.

Table 4

SELECTED PRICE AND INCOME AVERAGE ANNUAL RATES OF INCREASE, 1957-1968

	Percent
Housing Prices and Rents	
Cost of NHA Homes	3.1
Average MLS selling price	4.8
Home ownership index—DBS	4.0
Average monthly rents—labour force survey	4.1
Rental index—DBS	1.3
Downpayment and Monthly Payments on NHA Homes:	
Average downpayment requirements	1.6
* Average monthly gross debt service	5.4
General Price Indices:	
Consumer price index	2.3
GNE implicit price deflator	2.4
Incomes:	
Personal disposable income per family	5.1
Personal disposable income per person over 19	5.2

* Average increase for 1958-1968 period.
Sources: Bank of Canada, **Statistical Summary** 1968; Central Mortgage and Housing Corporation,
Canadian Housing Statistics, 1968; and Dominion Bureau of Statistics, **Labour Force Survey.**

Perhaps a more meaningful measure of the affordability of new homes
than the nominal purchase price is a combination of downpayment requirements and monthly gross-debt-service payments (consisting of monthly
mortgage payments and tax payments). Although this information is available only for new NHA homes, it does tend to substantiate our earlier findings since the average annual increase in downpayment requirements was

only 1.6 percent and in monthly gross debt service was 5.4 percent.[14] Hence, even by these measures which reflect not only the price of new homes but also the cost of mortgage credit and taxes, the affordability of new homes has increased during the last decade.

However, we cannot conclude on the basis of these aggregates that inadequate housing is no longer a major social problem without considering the relationship between current construction and new housing needs, the type of this construction, and the question of low-income housing standards. Present concern about the housing situation in Canada was spurred by a very rapid rise in housing prices and rents during the last few years, together with a rate of construction considerably below the Economic Council of Canada's five-year annual target of 200,000 units.[15] Extrapolating these recent price increases and low rates of construction, many people fear that a housing crisis is imminent, and that housing accommodation will soon outprice most family budgets. However, such fears fail to consider the cyclical nature of residential construction, which experiences major slowdowns in periods of rapidly rising interest rates such as 1966-1967, and the fact that rising rents and prices normally spark renewed building activity. This in fact has recently happened as housing starts rose from 134,500 units in 1966 to 196,800 units, just short of the Economic Council's target, in 1968 and to probably over 200,000 in 1969.

On the other hand, these figures say nothing about the mix between single-and multiple-dwelling starts, and the fact that during the last few years multiple dwellings accounted for over half our housing starts. Whether this should be viewed with alarm or not is quite subjective, but it does indicate that the Canadian dream of home ownership as opposed to rental accommodation may be becoming more difficult to attain.

Of more urgent consequence is the problem that even in periods of rapidly improving general housing conditions, the standards for lower-income families, and especially those with many children, may not be improving and may even be deteriorating. Although many more dwellings are being constructed, a large number of these are apartments which are unsuited for large-family living. Moreover, the construction of these projects often involves the demolition of poorer-quality housing, which reduces

---

14. It is interesting to note that most of this increase in monthly gross debt service was due to rising taxes, since monthly mortgage interest and principal payments rose only 3.5 percent per year, while taxes rose 10.0 percent per year between 1959 and 1967. See Central Mortgage and Housing Corporation, *Canadian Housing Statistics, 1967*, p. 70.

15. *Report of the Federal Task Force on Housing and Urban Development*, p. 1; and M. Wheeler, "The Housing Crisis and Public Policy," an address given to the Annual Conference of Mayors and Municipalities, Montreal, July 1967, and available from the Canadian Welfare Council, p. 4.

the availability of low-cost dwellings suitable for large families and maintains the cost of these accommodations. In addition, the fact that average incomes are rising faster than shelter costs is of little solace to the handicapped, elderly, unemployed, and families living on fixed incomes. Consequently, while general housing conditions are clearly improving, the housing standards for many low-income families may be deteriorating with little or no improvement in sight.

However, it must be stressed that these conditions are not purely the consequence of inadequate housing facilities or evidence of a housing problem, but rather are symptomatic of a more pervasive poverty problem. These conditions may be improved by working within the housing sector, but they would probably be better attacked within the context of an integrated poverty program. Therefore, although sectoral housing problems still exist, they are as much a consequence of poverty as of an inadequate housing stock. Moreover, considering that new dwelling starts in 1968 fell only 3,200 units short of, and that 1969 dwelling starts are likely to exceed the five-year annual target of 200,000 set by the Economic Council of Canada, the notion that we are about to experience a severe housing crisis seems to be more a fiction than a fact.

3. GOVERNMENT HOUSING POLICY

Government participation in the housing field has arisen for many different reasons—to improve the nation's housing standards, to reduce the cost of housing accommodations, to increase the availability of housing credit, to provide low-cost housing, university housing and housing for the elderly, and to combat general unemployment and inflation—and on many different levels—federal, provincial and municipal. This paper, however, will primarily be confined to an examination of the housing implications of monetary policy, the federal loan-insurance program and the federal direct-mortgage-lending program, which are designed to promote general economic stability as well as to stimulate the volume of residential construction in order to improve the nation's housing standards.[16] At the end, brief mention is made of federal assistance for low-cost housing and other sectoral programs.

Although monetary policy is usually not formulated especially to influence the level of residential construction, it does exert a tremendous influence upon residential-construction activity by affecting the availability of

---

16. Central Mortgage and Housing Corporation, *Submission to the Royal Commission on Banking and Finance* (Ottawa: Queen's Printer, 1962), p. 1.

mortgage funds and the demand for this credit.[17] Looking first at the supply side, the share of total credit flowing into competing sectors of the capital market depends upon the relative yields obtainable on alternative security investments. Monetary policy is able to influence the yield spread between mortgages and other securities because of the yield ceiling on NHA mortgages and the sluggishness and narrow range of conventional mortgage yield fluctuations.[18] When capital-market conditions tighten, bond yields tend to rise earlier and more rapidly than mortgage yields, increasing the relative attractiveness of bond investments. This induces institutions to invest more heavily in bonds and to reduce their mortgage-lending, making finance for new residential construction more difficult to obtain.[19] At the same time, mortgage interest rates will generally rise (although more slowly than bond rates) and non-price lending terms (loan-to-value ratios, amortization period, etc.) will become more stringent, reducing the desirability and feasibility of multiple-dwelling construction, and the affordability of single-family dwellings. Because over 80 percent of the finance for new residential construction comes from mortgage or other debt sources, higher borrowing costs, less favourable borrowing terms and reduced availability of mortgage credit will very significantly restrain the volume of residential-construction activity. Similarly, in an analogous manner, lower borrowing costs, more favourable borrowing terms, and increased availability of mortgage credit will significantly stimulate new residential construction.[20]

Apart from the indirect effects of monetary policy upon the housing market, the federal government first directly entered the housing field in 1935 when it introduced a guaranteed-loan program under the National Housing Act (NHA) to stimulate residential construction and employment during the depression. Since then the program has undergone many changes and now exists as an insurance program which insures the lender against almost

17. J. Guttentag: "The Short Cycle in Residential Construction," *American Economic Review* L1 (June 1961), p. 290, and W. L. Smith: "Impacts of Monetary Policy on Residential Construction, 1948-58," in *Study of Mortgage Credit*, Committee on Banking and Currency, Sub-Committee on Housing, U.S. Senate, December 1958, 85th Congress, 2nd Session, p. 260.
18. S. Klaman, *The Postwar Residential Mortgage Market*, National Bureau of Economic Research (Princeton, N.J.: Princeton University Press, 1961), p. 75, and J. V. Poapst, *The Residential Mortgage Market*, a working paper prepared for The Royal Commission on Banking and Finance (Ottawa, 1962), p. 122.
19. L. B. Smith, "Financial Intermediary Lending Behaviour in the Postwar Canadian Mortgage Market" *Quarterly Journal of Economics*, LXXXI (Aug. 1967), pp. 493-514.
20. For empirical evidence, see L. B. Smith, "A Model of the Canadian Housing and Mortgage Markets", *op. cit.*, pp. 795-816.

all losses associated with mortgage lending.[21] However, in order to qualify for this government insurance mortgage loans must meet certain specifications with respect to amount, loan-to-value ratios, amortization term, interest rate, and the relationship between the borrower's income and the gross debt service. By altering the maximum interest rate and other lending terms that qualify for insurance under this program, the government is able to influence borrower demand for and lender supply of mortgage credit.

For example, if the government wished to stimulate the demand for mortgage credit and thereby increase the volume of new residential construction either to combat unemployment or to put housing within the reach of more families, it could increase the minimum loan-to-value ratio and/or the amortization period that qualifies for insurance, thereby reducing the downpayment and monthly payments associated with a given mortgage. At the same time, to ensure that an adequate supply of mortgage credit would be forthcoming the government could, if necessary, increase the mortgage-rate ceiling (although not so far as to offset the complete reduction in monthly payments arising from the amortization-period extension), which would increase the attractiveness of this form of investment for lenders.[22] Therefore, by altering mortgage-lending terms, the government can alter the demand for and supply of mortgage credit so as to influence the volume of residential construction for general stabilization or long-run production purposes.

Variations in mortgage-lending terms and, in fact, the implementation of the insurance concept have had a considerable long-run influence upon the volume of residential construction.[23] The introduction of loan insurance, by creating a virtually risk-free investment and setting the insurance charge for absorbing these risks below what lenders would normally incorporate in their calculations for making an uninsured loan, has greatly increased the desirability of mortgage-lending and the availability of funds for housing finance. Similarly, the general easing of non-price lending terms has placed housing within the reach of many more families than would otherwise have been possible. Since both these developments stimulated the demand for housing services, it was important that the housing industry was capable of

---

21. For details of this program and a history of Canadian housing legislation, see Central Mortgage and Housing Corporation, *Submission to the Royal Commission on Banking and Finance, op. cit.,* pp. 60-64; J. Gillies, "Some Financial Aspects of the Canadian Government Housing Programme: A History and Prospective Developments" *Journal of Finance,* VIII (March 1953), p. 24; and J. V. Poapst, *op. cit.,* pp. 171-178.
22. Since this was written, the NHA interest ceiling on private lending has been removed, eliminating government discretion in the setting of this rate.
23. For a more detailed analysis see L. B. Smith, "Postwar Canadian Housing Policy in Theory and Practice," *Land Economics,* XLIV (August 1968), pp. 339-49.

meeting these demands; otherwise price rather than construction increases would have followed. However, except for the 1946-to-1951 period when the volume of residential construction was constrained by the availability of building materials and industrial capacity, this was not a problem.[24]

Since 1947 there have been only six major changes in the principal NHA mortgage-lending terms, demonstrating the policy-makers' reluctance to use such a politically sensitive area for stabilization purposes. This becomes even more apparent when we realize that five of these variations liberalized lending terms by increasing loan-to-value ratios and/or the amortization period that qualified for NHA insurance, while only one, a reduction in the loan-to-value ratio, tightened lending terms, indicating that some of these alterations were also for the long-run purpose of enabling more families to afford housing. Despite the infrequency of its use and its lack of reversibility, variations in mortgage-lending terms remain a potentially powerful stabilization tool, and one that has been used effectively in selected situations in the past. However, as may be seen from Table 2, failure to periodically tighten lending terms reduces the effectiveness of future liberalization changes since successive easements of lending terms cause smaller and smaller reductions in financial requirements. For example, a 15-year extension in the amortization period on a 10-year, 8 percent mortgage reduces monthly carrying costs by 37 percent, while a similar extension on a 25-year mortgage reduces monthly carrying costs by only 12 percent.

In addition to the above techniques for influencing the volume of residential construction, the government can influence the housing sector through the direct lending powers of the Central Mortgage and Housing Corporation (CMHC), a Crown Corporation established to administer federal housing programs. In 1946 CMHC was granted the authority to make residential-construction loans out of public funds to stimulate building activity when adequate private financing was not forthcoming, and since 1957 CMHC has used these powers with a vengeance. Between 1957 and 1968 CMHC financed approximately 296,000 new housing starts or over 17 percent of all new dwelling units constructed in Canada.

The general effects of a direct-lending program designed to provide additional funds to a sector are obvious, but the particular effects depend upon a number of special considerations. First, the degree to which a direct-lending program increases the level of activity in a sector depends upon the extent to which these loans satisfy demands that the private sector would otherwise have met. Since CMHC borrowers must, in most cases, demonstrate an inability, through at least two rejected loan applications, to obtain

24. Y. Dubé, J. Howes and D. L. McQueen, *Housing and Social Capital*, Royal Commission on Canada's Economic Prospects (Ottawa: Queen's Printer, 1957), p. 44; and Central Mortgage and Housing Corporation, 1959 *Annual Report*, p. 9.

private mortgage credit, CMHC lending is usually considered to be of a "residual nature," providing a net addition to the supply of mortgage credit and the volume of residential construction.[25]

Second, the method of funding a direct-lending program has a considerable bearing upon its ultimate impact. If funds are raised via government security sales to financial institutions, the ability or willingness of these institutions (which supply the vast majority of funds for new residential construction) to invest in mortgages may be diminished, since additional government security sales tend to raise bond rates relative to mortgage rates. If, on the other hand, funds are raised by security sales to the central bank, the housing sector also experiences indirect benefits from the general increase in the money supply. Finally, if funds come out of additional tax revenues or reduced spending on alternative programs, the incidence of the tax or nature of the foregone expenditure will determine the extent of the offset in the housing sector. Although we cannot directly measure the funding mix, which largely determines the magnitude of the financial offsets, we suspect the mix has been such as to have little or no effect upon the housing sector.

Third, direct-lending programs often have built-in pro-cyclical tendencies since private credit gaps arise only when funds are scarce because of excessive demands by other sectors or restrictive government policies, both of which occur in periods of accelerating economic activity.[26] A comparison of CMHC lending with general-economic and housing-market conditions indicates that CMHC has conducted its direct lending more with an eye on stabilizing the residential-construction sector than the economy in general. The appropriateness of this behaviour depends upon the marginal social gains to be realized from an extra degree of stabilization influence compared to the gains from an immediate increment in housing accommodations. Consequently, unless the nation is experiencing a severe housing shortage, the social benefits of general stabilization will probably outweigh those of additional housing expenditures and, therefore, CMHC must exercise extreme care to harmonize its lending policies with general stabilization policies and the over-all state of the economy rather than with the residential-construction sector alone.

Although other forms of government activity in the housing field have been limited, they have been far from absent. During the war and shortly thereafter, the federal government provided a large number of public housing units for war workers and veterans. The government has also been active in providing finance to the provinces and municipalities for low-

---

25. Royal Commission on Banking and Finance, *Report* (Ottawa: Queen's Printer, 1964), p. 273.
26. G. Break, *Federal Lending and Economic Stabilization* (Washington, D.C.: Brookings Institute, 1965), p. 7.

income housing, student housing, slum clearance, urban renewal, land acquisition and servicing, rental subsidies, limited-dividend housing and home-improvement loans. However, since the basic long-run objective of Canadian housing policy until recently has been to make every Canadian family a homeowner, it was inevitable that there would be some neglect of programs specifically directed to rental accommodation for low-income families.[27] This in fact has been the case as over the 1954-1967 period only 62,417 housing starts, or 3.4 percent of total housing starts during the period, were government-assisted low-income housing.[28] On the other hand, this situation has been improving recently with the greatly expanded program of Ontario Housing Corporation, and in 1967 there were 9,662 public housing starts, approximately 6 percent of total Canadian housing starts.

The above discussion indicates that government has played a substantial role in the housing market, initiating a variety of programs to increase the volume of residential construction while concomitantly using this market to promote general economic stability. Unfortunately, these dual objectives often conflict, creating uncertainty as to the government's response and demonstrating the need for a clearly defined set of priorities. At the same time, government preoccupation with the homeownership and middle-income rental market has led to a neglect of public-housing programs, which only now, spurred by Ontario, are beginning to tackle the low-income family housing needs. However, despite these shortcomings, in view of the tremendous progress made in the quality and quantity of the nation's housing standards during the last twenty years, the government's performance in the housing market must be considered to be quite impressive.

---

27. A. Rose, *Canadian Housing Policies*, a background paper prepared for the Canadian Conference on Housing by the Canadian Welfare Council, 1968, pp. 37-38.
28. Canadian Welfare Council, *Sourcebook on Housing in Canada*, a paper prepared for the Canadian Conference on Housing, 1968, p. 50; and Central Mortgage and Housing Corporation, *Canadian Housing Statistics*, 1967, pp. 48-49.

the city: problems and policies

N. H. Lithwick*
Carleton University

In the short space of less than two years, there has been what amounts to a revolution in national concern about the state of cities in Canada. This has both fostered, and been stimulated by, a number of major public events. The *Fourth Annual Review* of the Economic Council of Canada (September 1967) contained a sweeping introduction to urban problems and policies in Canada. Three months later, a Federal-Provincial Conference on Housing and Urban Development was held in Ottawa (December 11, 1967). In August 1968, the Federal Government set up a Task Force on Housing and Urban Development under Mr. Paul Hellyer, and its *Report* was presented on January 22,1969. The Science Council of Canada, in its Report No. 4, *Towards a National Science Policy for Canada* (October 1968) picked up the same theme, and included as two of the four areas for immediate planning of major projects, urban development and transportation. Transportation was also the theme of the First Canadian Urban Transportation Conference, sponsored by the Canadian Federation of Mayors and Municipalities in Toronto, February 9-12, 1969. Finally, urban poverty was more closely examined by the Economic Council in its *Fifth Annual Review* (September 1968).

There appears to be a general concensus arising from these activities that the problems of the urban unit have multiplied and intensified so greatly as to threaten the long-term viability of the city as we know it. Present methods for dealing with these problems have been judged to be inadequate, and comprehensive new approaches have been advocated.

* Many of the ideas expressed in this study have their origin in the teaching and research interaction between my colleague Gilles Paquet, and myself, although I alone am responsible for the particular formulation in this paper. Miss Cathy MacMillan helped in the preparation of this manuscript.

All this interest and excitement is probably to the good. There has for too long been insufficient awareness that we are a highly urbanized society and that the city, as it has evolved, may no longer be adequate as the environment in which an economically and technologically sophisticated society must operate.

Unfortunately, this conviction that we are faced with impending disaster in our cities is not based on adequate evidence. The data, when used, are often of questionable value and relevance; and even if this information revealed serious problems, there is little basis for understanding their nature and thereby dealing effectively with them. Few of the above-mentioned inquiries conducted or even drew upon meaningful research. Much was borrowed uncritically from other countries, and particularly the United States with its special racial problems and its particularly large urban conglomerates whose problems are quite different from those in even the largest Canadian cities. Finally, few of the grand new designs have any analytical content. Thus, to date the urban crisis is more an article of faith than a well-understood phenomenon. It is the intention of this essay to inquire rather deeper into the meaning, dimensions and roots of this so-called crisis.

At the very outset it is useful to clarify the notion of the urban crisis. It is generally viewed as a collection of particular problems typically found in larger urban centres: housing shortages, poverty, slums, congestion, pollution, violence. The convergence of these problems produces an increasingly inhospitable environment. The solutions generally offered derive directly from this view—solve each of these problem areas and the urban crisis will disappear. Needless to say, such a perspective is particularly comfortable for the specialist, for he is able to work within his own frame of reference.

An alternative perspective, and one that is pursued in this study, is to recognize that these problem areas are symptoms of a more fundamental process at work in the city. From a methodological standpoint, approaching each of the problem areas in isolation would then be quite inappropriate both for analysis and for policy-making.

Central to this basic process is the functional interdependence between the city and the national and international economy. All too often the urban unit has been viewed as a static environment within which economic activity takes place. Economists occasionally concern themselves with the effects of this environment on economic efficiency and growth—the city as a constraint —but rarely with the way in which the city fundamentally shapes and is shaped by the national economy. It is our intention to illustrate how much of the current spectrum of urban problems is directly attributable to the particular form of the relationship between city and economy, between urbanization and economic development.

Our approach will follow from these remarks. First we shall try to weigh the evidence on the growing urban problems in Canada. Then we shall attempt to provide an analytical framework which is capable of explaining these problems as symptoms of a more basic problem. Finally, we shall assess urban policy in Canada.

1. CANADIAN URBAN PROBLEMS

Before attempting to explain the major urban problems, it is necessary to clarify some misconceptions about them. These misconceptions arise largely from the lack of empirical evidence and careful analysis of such emotion-charged issues. While these are treated more fully elsewhere in this volume,[1] some specific points related to our analysis of cities in particular warrant further discussion.

(a) housing

There has been much concern voiced over the failure of the urban housing market. Rapid increases in the prices of new homes, in rents, and in costs of running older homes have been documented.[2]

The evidence provided by Professor Smith on housing[3] suggests that in terms of the facts the problems have been grossly exaggerated. Attempts to explain the presumed housing crisis have also been notoriously one-sided. Invariably the blame is laid on the supply function—the increasing concentration in the industry, the scarcity of land, the backwardness of housing technology, high interest rates and taxes, etc. Indeed, there exists much evidence on all these aspects in Canada. Thus, 34 large firms, constituting less than two percent of this regionally segregated industry, built just under one-third of all the new dwelling units financed under National Housing Act loans to builders in 1968.[4] As for land, most indexes show substantial price increases relative to most other commodities.[5] Compared to best practices elsewhere, including modular and industrialized construction, we appear to

---

1. See the accompanying essays by Lawrence B. Smith and Harold T. Shapiro.
2. Smith, *op. cit.*, Table 4.
3. *Op. cit.*
4. Large builders are those constructing more than 100 units per year. From Central Mortgage and Housing Corporation (CMHC), *Canadian Housing Statistics*, 1968, Table 87, p. 62.
5. With one major qualification, and that is the fact that the indexes typically include serviced and unserviced land. Preliminary inquiry suggests changes in the mix towards serviced land—usually through new municipal requirements—do bias the indexes upwards substantially.

lag significantly. Finally, the current trend to higher world interest rates and the 11-percent sales tax on building materials,[6] combined with a rapidly growing demand for publicly supplied urban services,[7] largely financed through the real-property tax, have added substantially to the cost of home provision. Not surprisingly, the bulk of the report of the Hellyer task force was devoted to correcting the supply side.[8]

Unfortunately, such moves are not costless—otherwise the approach would be unexceptional, a pure efficiency gain. The moment resources must be used to influence supply, we must begin to talk about benefits, and this gets us into the whole question of demand—so conveniently ignored in much of the current discussion.

There are two ways to ignore demand—either to assume it is inelastic with respect to price; or that it should be. Either way, all price changes can be blamed on the supply side and the conclusions already outlined can be drawn. The Economic Council and CMHC employed the first assumption. Their forecasts of housing demand are completely price free. They determine the demand for houses by calculating the number of households with some minor adjustments for vacancies and replacements.

Needless to say, such an approach to demand is highly questionable. It derives not from consumer preferences and their articulation in the face of a set of relative prices, but from a technocrat's perception of what they ought to have—their *needs*. If prices of houses were to go up, it is hardly reasonable to assume that the same number of units will be demanded— there will necessarily be some elasticity to the demand curve. Thus, to be useful, these forecasts require a projection of different quantities for each set of housing prices, a forecast of supply, and then an equilibrium price-quantity configuration. Independent of price, these measures of "demand" are quite meaningless and possibly misleading.

The alternative concept of demand is that it should be inelastic because of the belief that housing is a "right"—the view of the Hellyer task force.[9] This concept is essentially a philosophical one—the economic sources of such basic rights are impossible to determine. The economic consequences are less difficult to deal with. Once again the question of supply comes to

---

6. Implemented by the federal government in three stages—June 1963 (4 percent), April 1964 (4 percent) and January 1965 (3 percent). Economic Council of Canada, *Third Annual Review*, Nov. 1966, Chart 4-13, p. 111.

7. These are Baumol goods typically, since the majority of them are not subject to productivity increase and hence face rapidly rising prices. W. J. Baumol, "Macroeconomics of Unbalanced Growth: The Anatomy of Urban Crisis," *American Economic Review*, LVII, No. 3 (June 1967), pp. 415 ff.

8. *Op. cit.*

9. "Every Canadian should be entitled to clean, warm shelter as a matter of basic human right," *op. cit.*, p. 22.

the fore, and the role of the marketplace is to supply these basic requirements as cheaply as possible. Market failures are necessarily blamed on
supply and its determinants, and policies are hence supply-oriented—reduce
speculation in land, promote technological progress in construction, reduce
high taxes and financing costs, etc.; and it is just such recommendations that
occupy the entire report of the Task Force.

When the two issues of inelasticity and housing-as-a-right get built into
public policy, some serious consequences follow; but first, the evidence on
elasticity. Chung has found that over time the price elasticity of demand
for the housing stock is about −1.0.[10] His estimating procedures create
some difficulties in accepting this figure because of an adjustment for bias
—his initial estimate was −0.35 which, though less, gives little grounds for
accepting the zero-elasticity assumption.

With some further information, a related point emerges. Oksanen has
found, that for roughly the same period, the income elasticity of demand
(stock) is 0.5.[11] Winnick's analysis shows that it is possible to conclude
that there has been a shift of preferences by consumers away from housing
if the income elasticity is greater than that for price. He finds that for the
U.S. such was the case over a long period of time.[12] The Canadian estimates are not good enough to draw such a conclusion, but the debate is
highly suggestive. It may well be that there has been a change in the tastes
of citified Canadians away from houses and towards other goods and services. For example, between 1961 and 1966, despite similar trends in unit
prices, the volume of new cars sold increased by 55 percent as compared to
40 percent for housing, so that by 1966, the total outlay on new cars was
absolutely greater than that for new dwellings.[13] To the extent that this is
indicative of a change in tastes, failure to deal adequately with the demand
side is bound to lead to serious policy errors. Related to this question is
the changing nature of the commodity being sought, which is largely
explained by demographic and social factors. Thus, the growing number of
elderly people and of independent young people no doubt contribute to the
shift in demand away from houses as such to multiple-unit dwellings. From
constituting one-seventh of all new dwelling units built in 1949, the latter are

10. J. Chung, "L'analyse de la demand de logements—propriétaires: l'expérience
canadienne," *Actualité Economique* (Avril-Juin, 1967).
11. E. H. Oksanen, "Housing Demand in Canada, 1947 to 1962: Some Preliminary
Experimentation," *Canadian Journal of Economics and Political Science*, XXXII,
No. 3 (Aug. 1966).
12. L. Winnick, "Housing: has there been a downward shift in consumers' preferences?" in W. L. C. Wheaton, G. Milgram, and M. E. Meyerson, *Urban Housing*
(New York: The Free Press, 1966), p. 154 ff; and subsequent criticism by Jack
Guttentag, p. 162 ff.
13. Dominion Bureau of Statistics, *Canadian Statistical Review*; and CMHC, *Canadian Housing Statistics 1967*, Tables 1 and 15.

now more than half.[14] Part of this is no doubt due to the relatively greater increase in price of single units, although the sharp divergence in price trends has been apparent only recently. When we realize that this shift took place in the face of concerted efforts by the public sector, and particularly CMHC, to promote the purchase and construction of single detached homes almost exclusively, the source of the housing problem becomes clearer.[15] Rather than being faced with a clearly demonstrated taste for detached housing, the public sector promoted that taste and probably induced thereby an increase in the total demand for accommodation. Furthermore, that specific form of accommodation is extremely costly in social terms, raising very substantially the demand for scarce urban land, tying up larger quantities of capital per unit of dwelling, and compounding other urban problems. The housing crisis, then, is in large part a result of misguided public policy designed to cope with an issue that was only partially understood.

Thus far we have not come to grips with the question of *needs*, or housing as a "right." If society judges this to be a valid use of its collective resources in the light of full knowledge, then there is little one can do but indicate the costs and the possible allocational effects, including the impact of expanded social demand on price. There is certainly less than full knowledge on this issue, so the case remains tenuous. Furthermore, there is a tendency to confuse demand and even need with *wants*. It is judged that, because everyone wants a home, this constitutes a need; but this unanimity is neither surprising nor is it very useful. Wants differ from demands because they are unconstrained by income and price limitations. In addition, they are private, and hence provide no compelling reason to be accepted as needs. This three-fold confusion has plagued rational analysis of the housing market, and possibly serves to explain the strong preference for neglecting the demand side altogether, although at great cost in terms of useful policy-making.

(b) urban poverty

The second important area over which great concern has been voiced, particularly by the Economic Council of Canada, is the whole question of poverty. The Council found that three-fifths of all low-income non-farm families lived in urban areas in 1961, and 60 percent of these were in metropolitan areas. But the incidence of poverty was lowest in the largest

---

14. CMHC, *Canadian Housing Statistics, 1968*, Table 7, p. 7.
15. *Ibid.*, Table 14, p. 14. In 1960, publicly financed housing was 4:1 for single detached units, compared to 4:3 for privately financed. Only in 1968 was the emphasis on such units reversed.

cities, and indeed this group of urban poor amounted to less than 9 percent of all non-farm families in Canada.[16]

This evidence suggests that the magnitude of the problem of urban poverty is less than has been commonly believed—large cities tend to be middle class. Furthermore, more recent survey findings suggest that there has been a steady decline in the proportion of non-farm families classified as poor, from 26 percent in 1961 to under 20 percent in 1965.[17]

But the finding that poverty is declining and is relatively less prevalent in major urban areas, does not alleviate the problems of the poor. Unfortunately, there was no systematic attempt to cross-classify the data collected on the poor, with the exception of educational attainment, so that it is impossible even to describe the situation of the poor located in large urban centres.[18] Much of the Council's generalizations about the characteristics of the poor are not very relevant for our purposes, as a result.

This gap in our knowledge makes policies to alleviate urban poverty particularly difficult. Are they poor due to unemployment, to lack of a family head, to chronic illness, or what? A statistically unrepresentative sample, but an important one nonetheless, has been surveyed by the Canadian Welfare Council. In the four cities examined (Vancouver, St. Johns, Montreal and Toronto), 26 percent of the families had no male head, 43 percent of the households had a chronic physical illness in the family, 70 percent of the males and females had less than Grade 8 education, 46 percent were unemployed for a period greater than 10 weeks, and 36 percent for more than 21 weeks. As for their housing, it was judged to be unfit or bad in 48 percent of all the cases examined.[19] A more comprehensive understanding of the problems of the poor must await the publication of the 1971 Census.

At several points, the issues of housing and the poor converge. One is the question of slums. The general explanation of the emergence of slums relies largely on supply factors once again. Slums emerge because of an inadequate supply of housing. In the face of scarcity, the poor are least capable of competing in the open marketplace, and are thus forced to crowd into inferior dwellings, adding to their deterioration.

---

16. Economic Council of Canada, *Fifth Annual Review, op. cit.*, Table 6-3, p. 111. Data are from Jenny R. Podoluk, *Incomes of Canadians*, 1961 Census Monograph, Dominion Bureau of Statistics (Ottawa: Queen's Printer, 1968).
17. Gail Oja, "Problems of Defining Low Economic Status for Poverty Studies," *Canadian Statistical Review* (Sept. 1968), p. iii. The poverty line has been adjusted to account for price changes.
18. The evidence on education is suggestive—while less well educated than the urban rich, the urban poor are substantially better educated than the rural poor. *Ibid.*, Chart 6-3, p. 118.
19. Canadian Welfare Council, *Urban Needs in Canada, 1965*, A Case Report on the Problems of Families in Four Canadian Cities (Ottawa, 1965), pp. 6-11.

As we shall argue later, this neglects the central urban process which is instrumental in creating slums downtown where the poor are typically housed.[20] It also neglects the important question of demand. Given low incomes, the poor cannot afford other than inferior housing. Their problem may largely be one of inadequate income—i.e., poverty—rather than a housing problem *per se*. Attempts to solve the more basic problem by dealing with its symptom may be highly inefficient, and indeed inappropriate.

Consider the attempts to do so. It was felt that if enough houses were built, the "better-off" would move into newer units, leaving an adequate supply to "trickle down" to the poor. It is generally conceded that this was ineffective. The richer merely used more space and nothing to note trickled down. It was then felt that all that was needed was a push at the bottom. If slums were removed, the poor would have to improve their accommodation. This artificially created scarcity made matters worse, as slums merely spread, and the poor were exported where this was resisted.

The third solution, public housing, has also been questionable, because it identifies the poor by a most obvious symbol. Not surprisingly, it is resisted by some poor and most wealthier surrounding neighbours. Not once has there been a concerted attempt to deal with the demand side, despite the evidence that supply policies have not solved this persistent problem.

A second point at which these issues of housing and poverty converge has to do with the general inability of a growing segment of the population to afford accommodation.

> This housing market of relatively short supply and relatively high cost has made the quest for adequate accommodation a major problem for more than the lowest income groups. They have a problem, to be sure, but so do those in the next income brackets, the "average" wage earners of the $5,000 to $7,500 range . . . the home ownership dream of many Canadians is just that—a dream. Instead they are left to scramble in the rental market to obtain accommodation, *much of it ill-suited for family living* [italics mine, NHL]. . . . This is the group who, in many urban centres are increasingly earning the designation of the 'affluent' poor.[21]

It is not possible to trace accurately the relative movements of housing prices for various income groups. However, for the period 1961-1965 some crude estimates can be derived.[22] For the lowest third of the income distri-

---

20. For a graphic illustration of how the poor are concentrated in the core of Montreal and Toronto, see the 1961 Census of Canada, *Population and Housing Characteristics by Census Tracts*, Dominion Bureau of Statistics (Ottawa, 1963); Montreal Catalogue No. 95-519; Toronto Catalogue No. 95-530.

21. *Task Force Report, op. cit.*, p. 15.

22. Income data supplied by Gail Oja, Dominion Bureau of Statistics. Housing costs from CMHC, *Canadian Housing Statistics 1968*, Table 56, p. 44 and Table 66, p. 50.

bution,[23] their family income rose by 25 percent over this period while the price of homes they typically purchased rose by 35 percent. The next 50 percent of the income distribution[24] had an income increase of 25 percent, with the price of homes they tend to buy rising by only 18 percent. It would appear that in this period, the poor were indeed made worse off by the trend in housing prices. In addition, although our crowding indexes suggest no increase in scarcity in the aggregate, the absolute position of the poor regarding housing might have deteriorated, with improvements by the majority more than offsetting this in the aggregate. Certainly the position of the "affluent poor" does not appear to have deteriorated in this brief period. Over a longer period, 1961-1968, again the increase in the cost of housing for the lowest end of the income distribution far exceeded that of the middle groups.[25] Thus, our admittedly weak evidence does not tend to support the theory of middle-class immiserization regarding housing. Better longitudinal data would permit us to deal with this question more adequately, but in terms of over-all priorities this problem appears to be less severe than claimed by the Task Force.[26]

2. THE ROOTS OF URBAN PROBLEMS

In the preceding section, several key urban problems were examined largely from a public-policy perspective. The failure of public policy in dealing with the problems of housing and poverty was shown to be in part due to an inadequate perception of the issues involved. Thus, the demand for housing has been neglected, and the sources of poverty and the needs of the poor, not really known. Policy has therefore been based on a collection of myths, largely untested, and usually wrong when more carefully examined. Indeed, much public policy has tended to aggravate these problem areas—housing has been a major contra-cyclical activity with potentially great distributional effects; slums have been seen as a problem of ugliness, the elimination of which has been extremely costly for the urban poor, etc.

---

23. In 1961, they were found in the $0-4,000 income bracket, and in 1965, $0-5,000.
24. In 1961, they covered the $4,000-8,000 bracket, and in 1965, $5,000-10,000. These are presumably the "affluent poor" in the quotation referred to.
25. CMHC, *op. cit.*
26. It is true that all groups faced a very tight housing market after 1966, when housing starts fell to 134,000 from 167,000 the preceding year, and most of this decline was in urban centres. However, this is attributable to the tight monetary policy being pursued at the time. This shows up in the sharp rise in the interest rate on conventional mortgages from 6.9 percent in 1965 to 8.8 percent in 1968, and the increase in downpayments required. (*Ibid.*, Table 1, p. 1, and Table 53, p. 41). This cyclical phenomenon is well-known, yet the confusion over cyclical and secular patterns continues to plague much of the public discussion on housing. By 1968 housing starts were up to 197,000 and for 1969 the evidence suggests the 200,000 mark will be easily surpassed.

These perception and policy failures are not restricted to the areas discussed. For example, in the field of transportation, the problem has always been viewed as one of moving the extant population more efficiently. Rarely have innovations proven to be successful, however, for their introduction induced changes that were ultimately self-defeating. The public economy of the city has been almost entirely financed from a very weak tax base. Real estate is but one component of property, and property itself is a poor measure of ability to pay, and even of benefit from urban goods. Yet the property tax is the sole direct source of revenue of municipalities. Grants from provinces have kept these economies functioning, but the provinces do not have the most elastic revenue sources—the personal and corporate income taxes which are largely federal. Thus, a poor tax base and fiscal squeeze impose efficiency and distributional costs on the urban community that other levels of government have not adequately alleviated.

However, even if each of these problems were dealt with correctly, it is not clear that they would be solved. They are so interdependent that the effect of each on the others is more important than the mechanisms internal to any one in isolation. Partial analysis does not therefore provide the important clues as to the sources of these problems. Much more useful is an approach to the urban system as a whole. Yet even this approach can be misleading if the historical basis—the dynamics—of that system are not understood. More than most systems, the urban unit is dependent on its past development. The vast amounts of capital tied up in infrastructure and in private fixed investments dictate that changes are severely constrained. Thus the pattern as well as the location of most cities today is in large part a result of these historical developments. We intend to analyze only one dimension of these developments, namely, the emergence of an urban economy. Because the analysis is limited to the economic variables, the explanatory power must remain incomplete—geography, politics, social structure and accident all contribute to the emergence and functioning of Canadian cities. Nevertheless, the model we intend to develop is able to provide additional insights into the process of urbanization and the emergence of urban problems.

Early Canadian towns emerged typically as Central Places[27]—providing the predominantly rural export-oriented economy with goods and services. As such, they were little more than collection depots, and a view of such urban units as essentially spaceless would be fairly accurate.

In the course of economic development in this country, the technical

---

27. For a brief review of Central Place Theory, the gem of theoretical geography, see D. Michael Ray, "Urban Growth and the Concept of Functional Region," in N. H. Lithwick and G. Paquet, *Urban Studies: A Canadian Perspective* (Toronto: Methuen, 1968), Chapter 3, pp. 46-54.

linkages established by our successive staple exports were increasingly located in certain key urban nodes.[28] This was due not only to location advantages, particularly in the case of port cities such as Montreal and then Vancouver, but also to the fact that important inter-industrial linkages could be established in these units. For on the production side, the city provides a maximum degree of potential complementarity between industries. The role of final demand is also relevant here; for as incomes rose with successful staple exploitation, tastes shifted towards non-agricultural goods of the sort that are produced in cities because of the aforementioned economies. As a result, both supply mechanisms and demand pressures ensured the increasing relative importance of urban units, particularly as import replacement became feasible.

Furthermore, this process tended to become increasingly self-sustaining; for as demands for urban goods grew, the compensation of labour in the urban unit grew apace, attracting labour and hence urban population. The expanded scope of production permitted increasing specialization and hence greater productivity, higher incomes, and so on.

The expansion of varieties as well as quantities of job opportunities, together with an increasing spectrum of goods and services for consumption, made the city irresistible to the rural population, and more specifically, the young. Migration to the city of the rural population swelled the size of the urban labour force, kept wages relatively low, and induced further economic expansion in the city.[29]

Only a limited number of nodes could grow to become major urban units —economies of scale and transportation costs ensured that. Such factors as location, political vigour and often good luck determined which ones would be favoured. Within these, increased functional differentiation laid the basis for self-sustaining growth.[30]

This view of the urban unit as inextricably linked to the process of economic development, provides the first insight into the nature of modern cities as economically sophisticated production and consumption centres. The second relates the particular mix of economic activity to the spatial arrangements within the city. To understand the latter, a relatively simple but generally neglected aspect of urbanization must be taken into account. Early cities, as we have seen, were viewed as essentially spaceless. They

---

28. See M. H. Watkins, "A Staple Theory of Economic Growth," in W. T. Easterbrook and M. H. Watkins, *Approaches to Canadian Economic History*, Carleton Library No. 31 (Toronto: McClelland and Stewart, 1967).

29. In this view, urbanization is the necessary institutional form for development based on cheap labour of the sort analyzed by W. Arthur Lewis, "Economic Development with Unlimited Supplies of Labour," *The Manchester School* (May 1954).

30. In more technical terms, the off-diagonal elements in the urban input-output table became increasingly filled in. See W. Leontief, "The Structure of Development," *Scientific American*, Vol. 209, No. 3 (Sept. 1963), p. 148.

were small units using relatively small quantities of land relative to their hinterland. The large modern city cannot be so viewed; for increasing volumes of economic activity require increasing quantities of land as a direct input. Furthermore, the growing labour force requires land as part of its own housing input. This increasing demand for land conflicts with the limited supply that characterizes the urban unit.

Without transport costs, this problem would be nonexistent—the supply of land would be virtually infinitely elastic. But with present technology, distance does impose costs, and thus each land user is compelled to trade off distance against the quantity of land desired to minimize costs.[31] This would lead us to expect that market-oriented activities, such as retail trade and services, will be found near the Central Business District, while manufacturing and wholesale trade would be more typically located towards the urban fringe. Evidence by Loewenstein for the United States confirms these hypotheses,[32] although no comparable Canadian evidence exists.

We thus have two mechanisms to explain the growth and pattern of cities—one is macro-dynamic, relating urbanization to economic development, and the other is micro-static, allocating economic activities within the urban unit. The analytical device that can be used to relate them is the input-output table, where each activity is assigned locational and land-using coefficients. No empirical work on this issue has as yet been produced, but the barriers are largely imposed by the data rather than the theory. Thus, the analysis that follows is still in the form of hypotheses that remain to be proven, although casual observation suggests them to be valid.

How do these two mechanisms generate the Urban Problem? First, we have an economy that is undergoing rapid economic development. For reasons already cited, this takes place increasingly in an urban environment, and relatively more in large urban units. Evidence is available only for the demographic variables, and some of this is contained in Table 1.

It can be seen that the large centres, including the suburban fringes, have undergone the most rapid increases in population. In addition, family incomes in large centres are more than 50 percent higher than in rural areas, and 30 percent higher than small urban centres,[33] so that the economic

---

31. This process is more fully developed in Lithwick and Paquet, *op cit.*, Chapter 5.
32. L. K. Loewenstein, *The Location of Residences and Work Places in Urban Areas* (Metuchen, N.J.: Scarecrow Press, 1965).
33. Jenny Podoluk reports the following estimates of average family income in 1961 by urban type:

Metropolitan Areas	$6,442
Urban Centres: 30,000-99,999	5,848
10,000-29,999	5,477
1,000- 9,999	5,073
Rural	4,247

op. cit., Table 7.18, p. 174.

Table 1
LARGE-CITY GROWTH IN CANADA

	1871	1901	1921	1941	1951	1961	MA†
a) No. of Urban Complexes							
100,000 and over	1	2	7	8	15	18	
30,000 - 99,999	2	8	11	19	20	25	
5,000 - 30,000	16	43	70	85	102	147	
Total over 5,000	19	53	88	112	137	190	
b) Percent of Population Urban	18.3	34.9	47.4	55.7	62.4	69.7	
Percent of Population in PRMD's*	n/a	26.0	35.4	40.2	43.3	48.3	
c) Percent increase of Population over Previous Decade							
100,000 and over	n/a	n/a	32.2	9.8	14.2	28.2	45.4
30,000 - 99,999	n/a	n/a	27.0	12.2	33.2	33.3	37.4
Total over 5,000	n/a	n/a	31.8	12.0	18.7	28.5	40.9

Source: Leroy O. Stone, **Urban Development in Canada**, 1961, Census Monograph, DBS (Ott wa: Queen's Printer, 1967).
(a) Table 4.2, p. 72
(b) Table 2.2, p. 29
(c) Table 6.2, p. 132
* Principal Regions of Metropolitan Development
† Including Metropolitan Area Fringes

weight of the large cities is much greater than their simple demographic weight. Thus, the growth of Canadian cities in terms of economic activity and population has not only been an important source of our rapid economic development,[34] but a major consequence as well.

This rapid growth leads to a rapidly expanding demand for urban space. Given the fixed supply of urban land, price is driven up as fast as these demands rise. This increase in price leads to the exclusion of certain users with lower demands, occasioned by lower incomes or acceptable alternatives, from particular sub-markets. As they move into other sub-markets, prices there are forced up and the process continues to rebound throughout the urban system. Thus, the urban unit is the locus of a continuing struggle to acquire increasingly scarce land, and it is this struggle that underlies many of the Urban Problems.

3. URBANIZATION AND URBAN PROBLEMS

Consider, first, our housing problems. To the extent that urbanization makes sound economic sense because of consumption and production gains, we will expect an increasing level of demand for urban space. If to this we add the taste, manufactured by public policy or not, for land-intensive single detached dwellings, the demand will increase even more, and in the face of scarce urban land, prices will soar, as we noted above. But this will induce the population to seek land more remote from the Central Business District as distance is traded off against more land. This is the source of the pressure for suburbanization. However, moving farther out imposes increased travel costs, directly through greater distances and indirectly through the opportunity cost of time spent not working. Given a fixed transit system, congestion is also increased, so private and public pressures for more and faster systems increase. As new systems are installed, however, driving down travel costs, land farther out becomes more accessible and further suburbanization takes place, increasing demand on the system as more automobiles per family are required. This solution might not end the vicious circle but could at least prevent deterioration but for one difficulty, and that is the inability to expand the transportation system at all points. The greatest demands occur in the core, both in flow requirements and in storage needs, yet it is there that land prices are highest, streets are narrowest and alternative uses with large fixed investments already exist. This increases dramatically the cost of any transportation improvement in that

---

34. It is true that beyond some size cities may become dysfunctional and actually retard future growth—it is claimed that New York and Los Angeles are beyond that point. There is little accurate evidence on this, and even less grounds for believing that the major Canadian cities—Montreal and Toronto—have surpassed this level.

area; yet without it, congestion is inevitable. With concentration and congestion comes pollution, noise and general environmental decay.

The dilemma of problem interdependence is here starkly revealed. "Curing" the transit problem without regard to the locational choice of households is self-defeating, and housing policy without an eye to transit systems is as unpromising. Yet housing policy is conducted to this day as if the transit problem were nonexistent, and engineers design better transit systems, blissfully ignorant of the long-term impact on housing and urban structure. Both problems have their roots in the growth and structure of cities, and are not amenable to partial solutions.

More problematical, but strongly related to the central process of urbanization is the question of urban poverty. The characteristics of the phenomenon are familiar—slum housing near the core, endemic employment, high crime rates, disadvantaged children, and so forth. The role of urbanization in this is less clear and requires some elaboration. Families with low incomes have limited locational choices. Despite the high cost of land downtown, compensation can be made through crowding. The alternative of suburban living is just not possible, because for most low-income families the essential transit mode, the automobile, is inaccessible. Thus, in the absence of a low-cost rapid transit system these persons are forced into the fringes of the downtown area. Crowding invariably leads to a deterioration in the quality of the housing stock, and slums emerge. Similarly, employment opportunities in the core are typically for semi-skilled and clerical workers. Indeed, perhaps the most drastic change in the economy of the downtown area was occasioned by the move of manufacturing to the suburbs as technology introduced single-floor flow-operations that are land intensive, while concentration and specialization led to an increasing dependence upon national rather than local markets for the major firms. These developments weakened the locational advantages of the core and induced the migration of firms to the suburban fringe, where easier access to inter-metropolitan transportation routes is typical, where land costs are less, and where the increasing number of white-collar, and semi-skilled and skilled workers, required by modern technology, are domiciled. These groups, to preserve property values, try to keep out unskilled, low-income families through zoning laws that prevent both doubling up in single units and the construction of high-rise, low-rent units.

As a result, the poor are locked into their slums, increasingly without work, with prices and rents continually squeezing them as urbanization proceeds. Furthermore, the availability of urban services such as schools, hospitals and the promise of a better life continue to attract immigrants and those Canadians being squeezed off the farms and out of small towns as national economic development proceeds. Thus the slum population swells, increasing crowding and further driving up land values. This forces the slum to invade adjacent areas where possible, driving away further users of unskilled labour. Thus, the problem of urban poverty is not only serious, it necessarily deteriorates, creating a situation of hostility and violence in the downtown portions of most of our major cities. This is the most alarming of all our urban problems.[35]

4. PUBLIC POLICY FOR URBAN PROBLEMS

This review has attempted to place the major problems of the urban unit into a more comprehensive framework. It appears that they all stem in large part from the central facts of urban land scarcity in the face of a rapidly growing urban economy. The response of policy-makers has been to try to deal with each of these problems in isolation without understanding their central source, and thus their connectedness.

We have already examined several areas of public policy where this was apparent, particularly housing. The response to price increases, particularly for land, by Central Mortgage and Housing Corporation has been to attempt to direct more funds into the financing of housing, and until recently almost exclusively of the new single-unit, suburban type. This has, of course, stimulated the demand for housing and thereby land, driving prices up further, extending the urban population into the countryside and straining transportation systems.

As for transportation, there has been no national or even provincial policy. Individual cities have gone on major road-building sprees, capable of funnelling more persons into the core and extending the functional limits of the city, but with inadequate investment in the core area. Thus, parking is next to impossible in most cities and rush-hour congestion is increasingly costly, and indeed contributes to much of the air pollution in major cities. Yet air and water pollution control might well drive remaining industry out of the core, further exacerbating the problems of the poor.

With regard to the latter, policy has been particularly inappropriate. In general, the first solution to low-quality housing was to remove it. This not only reduces the supply of housing for the poor, but fails to take into account their specific needs—doubling up and proximity for self-help. As a result, even the rehousing requirement for CMHC urban-renewal schemes has been ineffective, because it is never at comparable prices. One solution has been public housing. Apart from the hysteria this form of housing appears to arouse, it has been only partially successful. All too often the new units are remote from potential work places and are poorly constructed and hence deteriorate quickly, so that the problem does not disappear. For

---

35. In the U.S., where the ghetto dwellers are typically black, the reaction has been more violent, reflecting the growing awareness of a clearly identifiable group.

those who pay urban taxes, this is evidence of the ultimate incorrigibility of the poor, and much opposition to this solution has been forthcoming.[36]

We have touched on only a few of the central urban problems that have become of increasing concern and the inability of public policy to deal with them. Other issues, such as the expenditure squeeze on municipal authorities as a result of a static tax base and rapidly growing urban needs, the increasing conflict between economic and political boundaries as cities spill out into the countryside, the merging of major cities into megalopolies all these have their roots in the pressures created by the interdependence between economic development and the spatial limitations of the urban environment in which most of this development takes place.

The long-term future promises new technologies in communication and transportation, construction, and pollution control, capable of ameliorating these many problems. For the foreseeable future, however, this remains beyond our tool kit. Yet the process of urbanization will continue, and each of these problems is bound to become increasingly aggravated. The reasons are clear. We have accepted to live in an environment that emerged to provide, very efficiently, private goods. This has, however, led to a growing collection of public ills which are difficult to constrain in a private marketplace, and which must therefore be handled largely by the public sector. But this new locus of decision-making has not emerged. Local governments do not have the resources for tackling the collective problems, and higher-level governments do not appear to have the will. This ultimately is the Urban Problem—the fact that our cities are growing quite autonomously because there is no attempt to discern what they are and to turn them into what they should be. There is, in other words, no Urban Policy in Canada.

---

36. The Report of the Task Force quite inappropriately uses the findings of a preliminary study to conclude that public housing is not the answer, *op. cit.*, pp. 54-5.

V

Social-Welfare Issues

Just as urban problems are an important feature of the Canadian economy in the postwar period, so are a host of other social issues which have come to the fore in recent years. Medical care and university education are two services which are increasingly viewed as the *right* of all Canadians—a value-judgment which fosters the role of government in the provision of these services. Quite a different problem is that of pollution, which is an undesired offshoot of an urbanizing and industrializing economy. Finally, social-welfare and economic-development problems in general are attributes of regional disparities of economic activity in Canada. In particular, the vast Northland is Canada's great underdeveloped area. All these issues—medical care, education, pollution, regional economic disparities, the Northland—are discussed in this final Part of the volume.

Canada's medical-care industry is evaluated by Robert G. Evans and Hugh D. Walker in their essay "Economic Issues in the Provision of Health Services." Evans and Walker note that both national expenditures on health services and government involvement in this industry have increased greatly in recent years. Yet, they argue, the medical-care industry is beset with misallocation of resources, and they make the following recommendations to mitigate these inefficiencies: (1) Proponents of plans to reorganize the industry should no longer have to show that their proposals would not deteriorate the quality of medical care; rather, opponents of the plans should have to prove that the recommended changes would in fact cause such deterioration. (2) Increased information on the cost, price, quality, and availability of medical care should be made available to the public. (3) Barriers to entry in the health-service professions should be tailored to serve public goals, not the well-being of the people in the professions. (4) Incentives in the medical-care industry should be altered so they encourage efficiency rather than inefficiency.

In his essay, "The Income-Redistributive Effects of Aid to Higher Education," Richard W. Judy notes that (1) public aid to universities in Canada has increased tremendously in the last ten years and (2) Canadian universities cater largely to the middle and upper classes in the income distribution. However, Judy's statistical results show that *both* the benefits and the costs of higher education are concentrated in these higher-income classes. Thus no significant income redistribution occurs through government financing of higher education in Canada. This means, in particular, that public expenditures on higher education do *not*, on balance, foster the education of children of poor families. Judy cautions against the abolition of tuition fees or the institution of student salaries as a means of achieving greater equality of education opportunity; rather, he advocates heavier taxation of the non-poor and greater subsidization of the poor.

"Pollution: a Problem in Economics" is the topic of Leonard Waverman's essay. While Waverman exhibits a sense of humour in his writing (for example, his reference to the migration of prehistoric man as dependent on the intensity of the stench from his accumulated refuse), he does not underestimate the seriousness of the pollution problem today. In addition to the detrimental effects of pollution on the health and aesthetics of human existence and the transfer of the costs of pollution to innocent parties, Waverman shows that pollution involves a misallocation of resources: firms that pollute the environment *overproduce* relative to the non-polluting firms in the economy. As for anti-pollution policies, Waverman argues that, to be effective, they must be *coordinated* among the various governments (municipal, provincial, federal) involved. The proposed Canada Water Act of the federal government is cited favourably in this light.

Regional disparities in output, employment, and income have long been a feature of the Canadian economy, and are the subject of T. N. Brewis' essay, "Regional Economic Disparities and Policies." Brewis notes that traditionally the Maritime Provinces have been Canada's most depressed region, but that economic growth in Quebec, too, is likely to lag substantially behind the national average in the future, in the light of political developments in that province. Brewis suggests that inter-regional migration in Canada would have to be encouraged, as one solution to the problem of regional disparities, and the decline of economic activity in some areas should be facilitated. He observes that provincial competition for industries is counter-productive, and he criticizes federal policies on aiding lagging regions as lacking in direction, foresight, and evaluation. Considerable expenditure of funds has occurred to date, but very little assessment of their results has been made.

Theodore W. Schultz's essay, "Some Economic Aspects of the Northland," is concerned with a topic that is rarely examined by economists, yet potentially of great importance to Canada's future economic growth. Schultz notes the economic characteristics of the Northland—a price system that does not reflect its true economic opportunities and heavy economic dependence on the developed part of the economy. He is not optimistic about the role of technological advances in developing the Northland—they will probably work to the relative gain of other areas of the globe. Nevertheless, Schultz emphasizes, direct measures to improve the economic development of the Northland can be taken, and should begin with a systematic research program.

economic issues in the provision of health services

Robert G. Evans
University of British Columbia   and

Hugh D. Walker
Ontario Hospital
Services Commission
and Indiana University

INTRODUCTION

It is a safe bet that this morning's paper contained an article on some aspect of the provision of health services, discussing at least one of the issues of rising costs, shortages, the quality of care, or the increasing role of the government in the health sector. These are the major issues as perceived by the man in the street. In this essay, we examine these issues to see why they have arisen, the public-policy implications of their continued existence, and possible solutions.[1]

A remarkable feature of western economies in the past twenty years has been the growth of the health sector. Expenditures for health have grown

---

1. The classic reference in this field, comprehensive but growing, alas, older, is H. M. Somers and A. R. Somers, *Doctors, Patients, and Health Insurance* (Washington: The Brookings Institution, 1961). H. Klarman, *The Economics of Health* (New York: Columbia University Press, 1965) is a detailed but somewhat uncritical survey of the literature down to 1964. A more up-to-date bibliography is given in M. L. Ingbar and L. D. Taylor, *Hospital Costs in Massachusetts* (Cambridge: Harvard University Press, 1968). A general survey of the field is S. E. Harris, *The Economics of American Medicine* (New York: Macmillan, 1964). An excellent, but somewhat technical, series of studies of the British National Health Service is M. Feldstein, *Economic Analysis for Health Service Efficiency* (Chicago: Markham, 1968).
   On the behaviour of the physician, K. F. Clute, *The General Practitioner* (Toronto: University of Toronto Press, 1963) is extensive and exclusively Canadian. H. D. Walker, *Market Power and Price Levels in the Ethical Drug Industry* (Bloomington: Indiana University Press, forthcoming) covers that industry. Finally, W. R. Scott and E. H. Volkart, *Medical Care* (New York: John Wiley, 1966) is a valuable and interesting collection of articles on medical sociology.

rapidly, in absolute terms, on a *per capita* basis, and relative to other kinds of expenditure; so that health expenses represent an increasing share of an increasing GNP. By 1968 this share was in the neighbourhood of six per cent or above for many countries.[2] By 1975 it is expected that the health-care industry will be the nation's largest single employer. Much of this increase in expenditure has represented exceptionally rapid price inflation in medical care—without being too specific, about fifty percent of the increase since 1950 represents inflation. But the real resource input has also been increasing.

This growth has occurred because of changes in both demand and supply. At the turn of the century, medical practice was relatively ineffectual. The average doctor relied on a supply of common sense and some manual skills, eked out with a few pain-killers and other putative remedies. The hospital was a place where paupers went to die. Thus care was cheap and access to care often made little difference. But the application of science to medicine has made medical care a highly desirable commodity, while rising incomes have expanded individuals' ability to pay. At the same time, the view has spread that access should not be conditioned upon income—reassurance and comfort might be luxuries for the sick rich but access to life-saving care should be open to all. However, while technological advance has widened the scope and effectiveness of medical care, it has also greatly increased its cost. Thus the resource outlay accompanying treatment of a given illness-episode, and the demand for that treatment, are both vastly increased because more can be done. This much is clear in the perspective of three-quarters of a century; but can the current rapidly increasing medical-care costs be offset by equivalent continuing gains in effectiveness? We must evaluate marginal performance relative to marginal costs.

The second issue, that of real or alleged shortages of care, is related to the first in that we may be seeing an equilibrating mechanism in action. Rapid advances in demand shift the demand curve upward while improvements in technology shift the supply curve upward. In the short run, prices will rise until markets clear; in the long run, new resources enter. Until markets clear, the consumer may occasionally find it hard to get a physician's appointment or a hospital bed for elective surgery. He may also be aware

---

2. U.S. data shows total health spending at 6.5 percent of GNP for the fiscal-year 1968; equivalent Canadian data are not available. *The Sixth Annual Review* of the Economic Council of Canada (1969) reports (p. 33) that in 1966 Canadian personal health expenditures were 4½ percent of GNP (this excludes government public-health programs, costs of administration and prepayment, and private voluntary agencies), compared with 4 percent for the U.S. Yet U.S. data (*Social Security Bulletin*, U.S. Department of Health, Education, and Welfare, January 1969) give a figure of 5.2 percent for 1966. In any case, the Canadian total-spending figure is about 6-7 percent.

that some sectors of the population are consistently unable to get care. This situation he interprets as a shortage; but a peculiar feature of the medical market is that a shortage means an excess of demand over supply in some absolute sense, not merely at existing prices. As a society we reject the notion of rationing the demand for medical care by price, and we argue that those unable to pay the going price should be subsidized. Rising prices will then eliminate the "shortage" only if the supply of services responds; but if elements of monopoly on the supply side inhibit the supply response, rising prices and observed "shortages" will be a feature of the medical market indefinitely, with benefit only to factor suppliers. If we add the additional complications that (1) in fact, a high proportion of medical care involves services which are optional and "nice to have" rather than essential to life or bodily integrity and these services *are* quite price sensitive, (2) buyer uncertainty and ignorance imply that certain sellers of services occupy a strategic position in determining the level of demand at any price, and (3) social policy is moving toward the logical-extreme implication of the view that price should not ration demand, i.e., that price should be zero; then we have a world in which demand for services and prices will rise without limit, but supply of services will react slowly and haltingly. Shortages will be endemic, expenditures astronomic, and discussions polemic. And the will-o'-the-wisp of satisfying the "medical need" of the population will still run ahead of us, never quite attained.[3]

The above discussion has been carried on as if medical care were some homogeneous commodity like wheat or newsprint; but, of course, in the medical field this common economic assumption is even more inadequate than usual. Everyone knows that there is good- and bad-quality care; but nobody can agree on what quality is, how to measure it, and how much to provide. Care-suppliers often argue and act as if the best quality of care currently available were the only type which should be supplied—in a world of scarcity this implies that it is better for some to go without than for any to have less than the best.[4] Consumers reinforce this approach by using supplier quality or reputation as a guide in selecting care. This is rational risk-aversion, given the consumer's uncertainty and ignorance; but it leads on the average to his trying to purchase care of far higher quality than he needs or would use if he had more information.

3. The best short reference on the role of suppliers in manipulating the medical market is R. A. Kessel, "Price Discrimination in Medicine," *Journal of Law and Economics* (October, 1958); reprinted in W. Breit and H. M. Hochman, *Readings in Microeconomics* (New York: Holt, Rinehart, 1968).
4. Thus in the fall of 1968, five dentists fleeing Czechoslovakia were prevented from practising in Ontario although they were planning to go to communities where no dentists were located. The Ontario Dentists' Association was implicitly judging no-care-at-all to be superior to care acceptable in Czechoslovakia. (See *Vancouver Sun* (October 10, 1968); *Toronto Globe and Mail* then and subsequently.)

Finally, the emotionally charged issue of government involvement in the financing and provision of health services touches on almost every issue of health policy. The "incompetent bureaucrat" and the "greedy and self-seeking physician" are emotionally satisfying but irrelevant stereotypes. The real issue is that increasing governmental involvement reduces the flexibility of the medical-care system, and both suppliers and consumers lose significant areas of choice previously open to them. This reduction of choice or discretion has consequences for the efficiency of delivery of health-care services as well as specific economic impacts on some individuals.

Why does this industry invite government involvement? To some extent, government participation arises from the peculiar mix of differentiating characteristics which, taken together, set medical care apart from most other industries.[5] Demand for medical care is irregular and unpredictable, and arises largely from illness or ill fortune. Thus the costs of care may vary enormously from individual to individual in any time period, leading to a demand for insurance. But, for some classes of people, actuarial risks make insurance prohibitively expensive, leaving government involvement as the only alternative to random bankruptcy or no care at all.

The consumption of care by one individual may confer benefits on others, either directly, as in the classic communicable-disease immunization case, or indirectly, as when saving the life of a family head prevents the members of his family from becoming public charges. Since the consumer cannot be reimbursed for the benefits his consumption confers on others, public intervention is required to assure optimal consumption levels.[6]

Uncertainty about medical care is perhaps more intense than for any other product, being present on both sides of the market but relatively much greater for the consumer. The consumer's uncertainty arises both because of his remoteness from the technical knowledge necessary for informed evaluation and because learning by experience is limited. One cannot try out care before purchase; and this uncertainty is accentuated by the suppliers, who often make little effort to inform the consumer and sometimes deliberately keep him uninformed.[7] The argument is that care is most effective in an atmosphere of low or neglible consumer uncertainty, thus it is necessary for the consumer to place his trust in the physician and rely on his integrity and responsibility. Information about the real nature of sup-

---

5. Klarman, *op. cit.*, p. 10, catalogues these characteristics and comments briefly on them.
6. This argument is theoretically sound, but tends to be overworked. Most medical care, in dollar or in physical-volume terms, has no external effects. Communicable diseases are now a small part of the health problem, and heads of households in prime earning years use less care than any other group.
7. Several articles in Scott and Volkart, *op. cit.*, bear on this issue; the network of peculiar social relations surrounding "the doctor-patient relationship" has interested a number of sociologists.

plier uncertainty must be kept from the patient lest his therapeutic trust and confidence be destroyed. The result is an absence of advertising and an almost complete refusal of physicians to give critical opinions of one another to the layman. This may maintain consumer trust, but it is as likely to promote even greater uncertainty and mistrust among consumers who are aware that information is being withheld. Public involvement by government or consumer organizations is thus encouraged to redress the information balance between buyer and seller or to mitigate its economic implications.

Many health factor markets are characterized by significant monopoly power maintained by control of entry, licensing, and direct control of practitioners. Private monopoly is backed by public legal sanctions; the suppliers have sought government intervention on the ground that restriction is needed to protect the public interest in care quality. At the same time, large government subsidies are paid to train many classes of health personnel.[8] In addition to monopoly elements, many health markets are largely insulated from the price mechanism. Third-party insurance payments lower the direct cost of care to the patient; non-profit industries do not compete to reduce costs; voluntary contributions of labour and capital are unrelated to need or demand. Thus normal market mechanisms cannot act to promote efficient resource allocation, and without public intervention nothing else will.

Underlying many of the above peculiarities is the problem that the output of the industry is indefinable—what is health? The World Health Organization definition, "a state of complete physical, mental and social well-being," is typical of the imprecise and operationally meaningless statements which surround the topic. Measures of mortality and morbidity provide some necessary fragments of information, but not much. We could administer tests to individuals, measuring a wide variety of physical and mental capacities, but how would we add up the results? And even if we could, how much "health" could be assigned to medical output as against cultural, environmental, and hereditary factors? Thus the industry output is intuitively clear but impossible to define precisely; the temptation thus becomes strong to use input measures as output proxies, a procedure which yields "outputs" that are meaningless for the evaluation of the efficiency of resource allocation.

Finally, there is a fundamental view that medical care is a "special" commodity because it relates to human life and bodily integrity. Thus even if all the above peculiarities could be removed—if market forces were able

---

8. Of course, medical-school graduates may have acquired a large personal debt. The subsidy element arises because the amount which they have paid for training is in general much less than its cost, and very much less than its asset value in terms of future higher earnings.

to produce a resource allocation which was "efficient" on the usual economic criteria—it is a widely held view that rationing access to care on a price basis would be inequitable or inhumane. In its extreme form, this view takes the form that economic variables are, or should be, irrelevant in health resource allocation. This view is clearly untenable. It is conventionally and falsely said that good health is valued above all else, so that no price is too great. But people smoke, they over-eat and drink, they take various drugs, they drive too fast—all activities which have some significant probability of reducing their health. They value the gains in satisfaction from these activities more highly than the expected health loss. The conclusion is that a finite upper bound (though not necessarily a consistent single value!) can be placed on each individual's valuation of his own health. "But you can't place a value on human life!" We can. We do.[9] Every time a level crossing is designed, an aircraft guidance system installed, an automobile tire constructed, trade-offs are made between cost and probability of failure with associated probability of loss of life.[10] In fact, no other approach is possible; because if we really set out to achieve for our population the best possible health that modern technology can produce, we would have to spend on health care all of GNP above that required for mere subsistence. If we are not willing to do this, then we are prepared to choose between allocating resources to health and to other goods and services. It is the inescapable allocation problem, combined with a dissatisfaction with practical or "best-potential" market solutions, which leads us as a community to fall back on the government.

THE NATURE OF GOVERNMENT INVOLVEMENT

The appropriate role of the government is sometimes specified as that of ensuring the highest-possible quality at the lowest-possible cost. It is this resolute pursuit of an inconsistent objective which has led medical care to be the policy jungle which it is. It is not possible to maximize quality while at the same time minimizing cost. The way to maximize quality is to spend as much of gross national product as can be spared from subsistence. The way to minimize cost is to stop providing any medical care at all. Thus all government health programs must strike a balance between these objectives.

---

9. See T. C. Schelling, "The Life You Save May Be Your Own," in S. B. Chase, ed., *Problems in Public Expenditure Analysis* (Washington: The Brookings Institution, 1968).

10. The role of probability is of interest here. We will as a society spend indefinite amounts to save a specific identifiable life (child trapped in well, aircraft down in mountains) but we place limits on spending for the reduction of a probability of death—decisions which may lead just as certainly to some death at some future time, but we don't know who or when.

For the moment, we will describe the general types of activities in which the government is involved; later we will discuss the appropriateness of the involvement.

The government supplies capital for the current production of health care. The major part of this contribution is for the construction of hospitals. The production of medical care requires the combination of labour, physical plant and equipment, and intermediate goods such as drugs and surgical supplies. For minor medical problems, the patient is seen in a physician's office. The doctor is the source of labour input, although he may be assisted by a nurse, and he is the supplier of the physical plant and equipment which is used for the treatment of the patient. For serious illnesses, requiring the hospitalization of the patient, the treatment becomes more capital-intensive. The physician again supplies his own labour; but in addition the hospital makes available, at no cost to the physician, personnel who will work under his direction in treating the patient. The hospital also provides the physician with capital equipment in the form of operating rooms, laboratories, hospital beds, etc., which the physician may use in whatever combination seems appropriate to him in the treating of his patient.

A remarkable feature of the industry is that the physician, a private businessman, has almost all of his capital equipment given to him.[11] The historical reason for this situation is that the organization of medical practice in the past was that of physicians practising by themselves. As medical technology progressed, and capital equipment became useful in the treatment of patients, it became uneconomical for each physician to provide the equipment which might be required for the treatment of his patients. It was necessary to develop a mechanism which would provide the necessary equipment for groups of physicians. If medical practice had followed the pattern of business, the physicians would have incorporated themselves into a firm and undertaken to raise their own capital. The prevailing view of medical ethics, however, prevented this. Physicians were, for a variety of reasons, committed to the individual practice of medicine, and the statutes of most jurisdictions contained explicit prohibition against the practice of corporate medicine. The conventional rationale for this has been that if the patient's physician is not the sole decision-maker, then there will be conflicts of interest between the physician who is looking after the patient's interest, and the managers of the corporation who are concerned with the profit-and-loss statement. (There are less charitable explanations of the physician's interest in preventing corporate medicine, but they require further discussion of physician motivation and are deferred until later.) As a

---

11. This partially explains the extraordinarily low rates of capital-equipment-per-doctor found by S. Judek, *Medical Manpower in Canada* (Royal Commission on Health Services, Ottawa: Queen's Printer, 1964), p. 16.

result of this prohibition, it was necessary to provide capital by methods other than the traditional ways which a firm would employ.

In addition, the first hospitals developed as charitable institutions. They were teaching centres for medical schools in which the sick-poor received treatment in return for being used as teaching material. As hospital care became more effective, local communities began to build and operate their own non-teaching hospitals. These hospitals were also run as charitable institutions in that money was collected from those who could pay, and those who could not were provided care at no charge, although in less comfortable surroundings than those enjoyed by paying patients. A tradition has thus grown up in which the physician expects the community-at-large to provide him with capital equipment and supporting labour. This has some interesting consequences. It means that the physician is interested in expanding his hospital's capital resources and supporting personnel, because the larger these supporting factors of production are, the greater will his own productivity be, and hence the larger the income that he can earn.

The government also supplies capital so that medical services can be produced in the future. It is financing the formation of human capital through the provision of facilities for the training of physicians, nurses and other paramedical personnel. Why should it do this? Physicians earn large incomes, and we should expect that they could finance their education out of anticipated future incomes. This does not mean that they would pay simply the tuition charged by the medical school, but rather they would pay their share of the total costs of medical education. Capital markets may be imperfect, so that medical students would be unable to find a financial institution willing to lend them as much as, say, $100,000 for their training. As well, however, borrowers may be simply irrational; they would be unwilling to incur this debt even though they could repay it and could insure against contingencies which would prevent them from repaying it. A further explanation for this type of government involvement is the public's belief that there is a shortage of physicians. To increase the number of physicians, it is thought that a subsidy is required in order to produce additional applicants. In reality, if there is a shortage of physicians, it is due not to any scarcity of applicants but rather to the unwillingness or inability of medical schools to expand their output.

The government also provides capital for the production of future medical services by financing medical research. The output of medical research provides information on how to treat illnesses more effectively than is now possible, or on how to combine resources more effectively in order to achieve the results which are now possible. Both of these activities affect the production function for medical services. In the first case we are changing the production function so that the level of feasible output is increased, and in the second case we are changing either the proportions or reducing the absolute amounts of the factors of production which are required to treat an illness. Government involvement in this activity is justified on the grounds that there is little or no private incentive to undertake the research. The researcher who finances his own effort and discovers useful results, finds that it is not possible to sell them. His results are information, and once he utters his information he no longer has any control over it and hence is unable to charge for its use. In research activities where the output is a new product, it may be possible to obtain patents and hence to recapture the research costs. In this case, explicit subsidies beyond those conveyed by the patent are unnecessary.

A further government activity is the operation of insurance plans for hospital and health services. There is no reason why the government should necessarily be involved in this area, other than the preconception that private insurance companies would be forced by competition to charge individuals according to their actuarial risk. The prevailing social opinion is that those people who are high risks—the aged and the poor—are least able to afford the corresponding high premiums. Hence, if all insurance plans are privately operated, the high-risk groups will not buy insurance, and will not have access to medical care when the requirement arises. The government could operate an insurance plan of last resort which subsidized the high-risk subscribers out of general tax revenues. To an uninformed public, however, the government plan looks as though it is being run inefficiently, and thus the government is subject to criticism. By making an insurance scheme mandatory, and by charging everyone the same premium, the low-risk persons are subsidizing the high-risk persons. This requirement could, of course, be imposed upon the private sector, thus eliminating the necessity of government involvement.

GOVERNMENT INVOLVEMENT AND RESOURCE MISALLOCATION

The preceding sketch of the governmental role in the health industry has referred at several points to the historical process of *ad hoc* public response to a series of problems peculiar to the industry. In this sense, there is not now and has never been an integrated and coherent public policy for health. Yet even the irregular formulation of piece-meal policy takes place with reference to some underlying set of public values; governments may act in response to an immediate and obvious crisis, but their response is usually conditioned by some implicit objective, however dimly discerned.

Faced with the extraordinary complexity of the allocation problem in medical care and the conceptual inadequacy of most available measurements, governments have tended to fall back on a medical-need objective. First, one establishes some basic standard of health services required by the population, often as crudely as in personnel/population or facilities/population ratios, by reference to appropriate health-industry authorities. Representatives of the suppliers are asked to determine the appropriate supply. Then one seeks to ensure that the industry will have sufficient capacity in the short and in the long run to meet this service level (within the constraints imposed by existing organizational patterns) and that the population will have sufficient resources, supplied perhaps by a universal insurance scheme, to enable them to purchase this level.[12]

However, this approach cannot help but lead to resource misallocation. Demand for service by the consumer and by the physician acting on his behalf is sensitive to a number of financial and non-financial costs; in the absence of any costs at all, it could be expanded indefinitely. Apart from the non-essential "nice-to-have" care components which bear directly on patient welfare, the doctor can always expand the amount of possibly beneficial work which he could do. Health is merely a state of inadequate diagnosis. In the absence of direct financial costs to the patient, which can be reduced to zero by insurance, the only deterrents to the patient are the time and trouble (discomfort, travel, income loss) of seeking care. Similarly, the doctor incurs time and effort costs in obtaining access to facilities for his patients, in booking hospital beds, lining up operating-room staff, etc. In the short run, these time and effort costs to both supplier and consumer may place an upper limit on the demand for care, although a level well beyond the point where the marginal value of the care justifies its resource costs; but in the longer run these costs generate pressure for even worse misallocation. The costs to the physician can be reduced if more facilities are available, so he will admit more patients. Hence the often-observed tendency for population use of hospital beds to expand whenever more beds become available, regardless of morbidity status.[13] More facilities and personnel will also reduce the non-financial costs to the patient; so over the larger run there is a steady pressure for excess investment in health care by the government.

Thus we reach the present situation in the Canadian hospital industry of provincial populations using from 1,500 to 2,200 bed-days of care per thousand per year. It has long been known that, with appropriate organization, high-quality health care can be produced with, depending on the popu-

---

12. Most of the work done by the Hall Commission reflects this approach. See Royal Commission on Health Services *Report* (Ottawa: Queen's Printer, 1964). This report speaks of ensuring "that the best possible health care is available to all Canadians."
13. See M. I. Roemer and M. Shain, *Hospital Utilization under Insurance* (American Hospital Association Monograph Series, No. 6, 1959); G. D. Rosenthal, *The Demand for General Hospital Facilities* (American Hospital Association Monograph Series, No. 14, 1964); and M. Feldstein, *op. cit.*

lation age-sex mix, 500 to 1,000 days of care per year.[14] These excess days of care thus imply too many hospital beds, each with too many under-utilized supporting facilities, scattered around the country in inefficiently small hospitals. The lengths of stay by case-type in Canadian hospitals run, on the average, 50 percent above similar U.S. averages; and U.S. authorities believe that *their* lengths of stay reflect over-utilization.[15] Moreover, Canadian hospitals run at about 80-85 percent occupancy, on the average, compared to 75-80 percent in the U.S. (this is claimed to represent a bed shortage) at costs per empty bed per day estimated variously at 75-80 percent of those of a full bed. It is argued that 85 percent represents hospital full-capacity under existing hospital organizations, ward structures, admission and discharge policies, etc. The answer is clearly not to build more beds but to change the organization. It is also argued that a percentage vacancy is a necessary stand-by to ensure that emergency cases never need to be turned away; but this argument must be applied to a region, not to an individual hospital. Our objective in providing stand-by is to ensure that not *all* the hospitals in an area will be full at any given time, rather than that none of them will be. The former requires a much lower vacancy rate.

Aside from excess utilization and too many facilities, Canadian hospitals also display a wide range of costs for performing the same service. The precise analysis of these differences is complex, particularly with existing data, but there appears to be a substantial inefficiency component. Personnel-to-bed-day ratios rise steadily with no measurable impact on patient welfare; the only apparent effect is to spread the workload more broadly and to inflate service costs.

Similar patterns of inefficiency exist in the supply of physician's services. The absence of financial deterrents to the patient under medical insurance leads him to seek care up to the point where the marginal utility of care to him equals the time-and-trouble cost of obtaining it, regardless of resource cost. If consumers systematically undervalue care-utility, of course, this could be optimal; but this result would be fortuitous. Traditional practices in the health industry weaken the consumer's ability to evaluate the utility of care by denying him information in the (often-mistaken) view that he will then accept the supplier's evaluation. (In other industries, the projection of sellers' product evaluations is achieved by advertising.) Thus hospital staffs habitually deny information or give false information to

---

14. Canadian data are available from the annual reports of the various provincial hospital plans; there are many studies on U.S. group-practice prepayment plans of which the California-based Kaiser Health Plan is the largest and one of the lowest hospital users.

15. For instance, New York State, *Report of the Governor's Committee on Hospital Costs* (1965); United States, *Report of the National Advisory Committee on Health Manpower*, Vol. I (November 1967).

patients; pharmacists may refuse to label prescriptions or may give misleading information on non-prescription drugs, and physicians debate (among themselves) the ethics of misleading the patient regarding the likely outcome of treatment.

But if the supplier's evaluation of care utility is accepted, then the way is left open for any amount of "over-doctoring," which, under the fee-for-service method of payment, rebounds directly to the benefit of the physician. The twelve-patient hour is a good way to build physicians' incomes, but not to supply health care. It is not known how serious physician-generated excess supply of medical (as opposed to hospital) care may be, and it is probably true that most physicians do not deliberately over-doctor. Still, it has never been denied that some physicians do so, and at present no one knows how prevalent a practice this is. Moreover, physicians generate excess demand for their own services in a more subtle and indirect way; by clinging to the fee-for-service predominantly solo-practice form of organization, they inhibit the use of less highly trained paramedical personnel, who could supply many of the services now supplied by physicians at much lower cost. The supply of medical services in Canada could be much more efficiently organized if groups of physicians, whose remuneration did not depend on their processing a large patient volume, directed the performance of the less technically demanding medical services by specialized and less broadly, less highly trained subordinates. However, this might reduce the demand for medical services supplied directly by doctors.

Yet another factor leading to high medical costs through inefficient resource allocation is the drug industry. This industry consists of a small group of large "ethical" firms producing brand-name drugs, surrounded by a fringe of small producers making many of the same drugs in unbranded form. The industry behaves as a classic oligopoly, with enormous mark-ups of price over cost to cover advertising expenses, which are estimated at 25 percent of sales revenue. Almost all of this expense is aimed at artificial product differentiation in the mind of the prescribing doctor, divorcing a branded compound from the same chemical under its generic name. In this way, a large part of this portion of medical expense is actually fed back into efforts to distort the flow of information to doctors. Some of this advertising expense has a social payoff in that some doctors might otherwise never learn about new drug developments. But its primary purpose is to maintain an artificial brand preference with the expected positive effect on oligopolist profits and negative effect on consumer welfare. It is argued that these profits are needed to finance "research," but most drug-company research is carried on by parent firms in the U.S., not in Canada. Even in the U.S., company research is a small part of the sales dollar, estimated at 6 percent, and is devoted to lines with a high private payoff ("molecule manipulation" to circumvent a rival's patent with a similar product) rather than a high social payoff (major but highly uncertain research breakthroughs). It is not obvious that the social interest in research which is primarily of private benefit justifies protection of the industry's oligopoly profits.[16]

THE MOTIVATION FOR RESOURCE MISALLOCATION

The reasons for this widespread inefficiency in the medical industry lie not in any uniquely evil disposition among the many and various suppliers of medical care. Nor are the members of this industry singularly incompetent in their allocation of the resources which they receive from governments and the public. Rather, it is a peculiarity of the medical industry that almost all of the incentives in the industry encourage excess spending and inefficient organization. The decision-makers involved have much to gain and little to lose by the waste of resources.

In the hospital, the decision-making triad is the board of trustees, the administrator, and the medical staff. Relative authority among these three varies from hospital to hospital, depending on past history and present personalities. Yet each has a distinct interest in the size and growth of the hospital, its level of slack or deviation from full efficiency, and its quality and community prestige. For the administrator, larger size means greater salary. The main determinant of hospital-administrator's salaries is institutional size; relative efficiency appears to have no influence at all. Quality and prestige may influence salary; they certainly enhance job satisfaction. But reduction in inefficiency means hard, careful management with much interpersonal conflict.[17] Under cost reimbursement, any savings yielded by greater efficiency accrue to the reimbursing agency, an arm of the government, but increases in costs represent expansion of the resources available to the hospital. Similarly, for the medical staff more beds mean more patients admitted, more cases treated, and more money or more service to suffering humanity, depending on how you look at it. Doctors use hospital facilities and personnel at no financial cost to themselves in treating patients, but excess availability reduces the time and effort required to mobilize these cooperating factors of production. Hence, they too have an interest in organizational slack. Excess nursing staff means, e.g., that someone is always available immediately to take orders. As for institutional prestige, this rubs off on the doctor and helps him in his practice. Finally, the trustee has an interest in inefficiency which reduces the interpersonal conflict in an

---

16. For this and following references to the drug industry, see Walker, *op. cit.*
17. On managerial slack in large organizations sheltered from competition, see O. E. Williamson, *The Economics of Discretionary Behavior* (Chicago: Markham, 1967).

organization for which he has final legal responsibility; while size, growth, and hospital quality or prestige enhance the sense of personal pride and/or community service which lead a man to become a hospital trustee. Thus, each of the key members of the hospital management team has an interest in expanding hospital expense; none gains by increasing efficiency. And so as long as the government agencies continue to reimburse on a cost basis, with no losses for the relatively inefficient or gains for the relatively efficient, costs will continue to rise.

As for the doctor, the incentives bearing on him from the fee-for-service method of payment have already been noted; but the relatively inefficient form of solo practice has several advantages for him. He is more independent; there is less professional scrutiny of his practice or of his income. His expenses may be higher, but they are tax-deductible, and in the tax bracket inhabited by the average doctor this means that the government pays most of his personal equipment costs. In any case, he can use hospital equipment to treat his patients at no cost to himself if he has a hospital affiliation. It is not immediately obvious, however, why solo fee-for-service practice has inhibited the use of less highly trained subsidiary personnel.

In the dental field, the expanded use of dental assistants, dental hygienists, dental nurses, etc., has taken place under the control of the practising dentist, who bills for a total-service package and pays them as employees. If the use of an extra employee increases his gross revenue by more than his wage and other variable costs, then he hires the employee, just as would any other businessman. In the process he increases his own profits, lowers the real-resource cost of producing dentist-type services, and reduces the share of the market for dentist-type services supplied by dentists themselves. Whether the absolute demand for dentist-type services *supplied by dentists* falls or not (at existing prices) depends on whether it was previously in equilibrium or whether a "shortage" existed.[18]

But in the field of medical practice, the shift from doctor as supplier of his own services to doctor as entrepreneur hiring and directing others and selling their services has not yet taken place. The reasons may be technical, in that one doctor does not perform enough lower-skill-level functions to spin-off work for a full-time assistant; or, alternatively, the spin-off which he generates is in a number of relatively specialized categories, so that several different assistants might be needed. Thus a solo practitioner could not support a patient-load large enough to provide work for all requisite assistants. Neither of these explanations is convincing. Alternatively, it may be that the service-package supplied by the doctor is too divisible. If private practitioners began spinning-off some visits to nurses,

---

18. See J. H. Weiss, *The Changing Job Structure of Health Manpower* (unpub. Ph.d. dissertation, Harvard University, 1966).

the public might become aware that immunization or regular examination of infants, etc., could be adequately performed by a nurse alone. The nurse could then set up as an independent practitioner in a way that a dental hygienist could hardly do. The importance doctors place in these simple bread-and-butter activities is evidenced by the regular opposition of organized medicine to free mass-immunization campaigns.

The problem of devising and applying more-efficient ways to supply physician's services is made more difficult by governmental insurance schemes which assume the private-practice fee-for-service system as given and embody it in nation-wide standards. The reason is that change to more efficient patterns of supply requires changing the motivation of both patient and doctor. If group practices supported by capitation payments turn out to be more efficient than fee-for-service solo practices in Canada, as they have elsewhere, the spread of such plans can be encouraged only if their subscribers are allowed to share in the savings this implies. If subscriber freedom-of-choice is extended to mean that all insured individuals pay the same premium regardless of whether they choose efficient or inefficient modes of medical-care supply, then the government is blocking the improvement of medical-industry productivity. Alternative ways of supplying physician-type services are badly needed, and any government policy which discourages their development or use by consumers is directly inimical to the objective of greater efficiency of health-resource allocation.

As for the pattern of incentives bearing on doctors relative to the over-supply of care, here too, doctors are in general better off to order more rather than less. Thus, if prevailing practice is to hospitalize seven days for a given condition, and a doctor leaves his patient in for nine, the cost to both doctor and patient may be minimal. If, on the other hand, he discharges the patient in five days, he is open to criticism for unsafe practice even if further hospitalization was clearly unnecessary. If anything should go wrong as a result of early discharge, the responsibility is the doctor's; the costs of excess utilization fall on society at large. As one doctor put it, "we protect ourselves by all agreeing to make the same mistakes."

As for the patient, his incentive pattern leads him to balance the costs of treatment, financial or otherwise, against the undesirability of being ill and the uncertainty and fear of future outcomes. Thus there are psychic costs associated with inaction as well as costs of treatment; and if the financial costs of treatment go to zero, the drive to "do something" will lead to an expansion of the patient's demand for service. To this is added a tendency for the patient to use price as an indicator of care quality if he has no other index on which to base judgements, thus encouraging consumption of higher-priced services at the expense of the insurance plan.

The motivation of private, profit-making drug manufacturers is clear enough; their primary incentive is to make a profit. The policy issues revolve around the extent to which the government should protect their oligopoly position through patent rights, in return for the social benefits of company research and dissemination of information to doctors. It has been noted above that both research and informational activities are (understandably) conducted with a view to private rather than public interest; the question is whether the "spill-out" of public benefit justifies the preferred profit position of drug manufacturers. Since their informational activities involve a heavy dose of advertising and thus inevitable distortion, it would appear that there is a much better case for direct governmental provision of information to doctors on relative drug purity, effectiveness, costs, side-effects, etc., including relative merits of branded and generic-labelled varieties. At the same time, if it is public policy to provide support for drug research, it might be more effectively supported by direct subsidy to researchers more interested in social payoff than competitive advantage— the type of research done would be significantly different. Moreover, if it is public policy to support the performance of research in Canada, direct subsidy could hardly fail to be more effective than the present pattern of almost all research done by foreign parent companies.

Finally, in the discussion of incentive patterns leading to inefficiency it is worth noting the incentives which bear on governments. There is more political credit in building hospitals than in not building them, even though the latter might be better policy. Still worse is the closing of a hospital, since the benefits in improved efficiency are widely scattered but the losses of revenue are localized and the losers are much more likely to give political expression to their dissatisfaction. Public ignorance in this area makes informed policy politically dangerous—Canadian newspapers appear to reflect a general feeling that hospital beds and personnel are in short supply rather than in considerable excess. Finally, health, like motherhood, is a bad thing to appear to be against; for it arouses deep emotions, which efficiency does not. The political payoffs from efficient government are, to say the least, unproven.

QUALITY OF CARE: THE ELEVENTH COMMANDMENT OR THE FIFTH AMENDMENT?

Any effort to improve resource allocation by public intervention in the medical industry is immediately challenged by the argument that it constitutes a threat to the quality of medical care. The charge is the easier to sustain because, like the concept of health, medical-care quality is almost impossible to define precisely.[19] It would seem that the obviously "correct" way to measure quality is by outcome studies—if the recipients of care are

19. A good survey is A. Donabedian, "Evaluating the Quality of Medical Care," *Millbank Memorial Fund Quarterly* (July 1966).

much improved, the quality is good. Thus we could look at infection and death rates at different hospitals or follow-up patients treated by solo practitioners and by group clinics, etc. The difficulties with the outcome approach are that there may be very long time lags before the effects of different qualities show up, and that the differences in the intrinsic health status of different populations due to cultural and environmental factors may swamp the influence of different care quality.

Going back one stage, then, one may measure quality by external review of error rates, rates of removal of healthy tissue, frequency of mis-diagnosis, medication errors, etc., by a detailed review of patient medical records. The problem here is that in a fragmented health-care "system" few patients have a single complete record. Often some of the record is in the family-doctor's head. Moreover, such review, particularly of the treatment patterns, must be in terms of "best-practice" standards (usually those followed at metropolitan teaching hospitals), and these are by no means absolute, eternal, and universally applicable.

At a still higher level of generality, some observers associate quality with physical or institutional environments—e.g., teaching hospitals, or hospitals with appointed chiefs-of-service, provide superior care; clinics provide better, or worse, care than solo practitioners, etc. This approach may begin with an intuitive notion of quality, find it associated with certain structures, and work out a possible causal connection. The alternative line of reasoning, which begins with the organizational framework and then argues that quality differentials *should* exist, shades into the fourth approach to output-quality measurement, that of adding up inputs. Thus more personnel and more highly trained personnel are assumed to produce higher-quality care than fewer or less-trained, regardless of the nature of the task.

This final "quality" definition is the most common argument against improved resource allocation in medical care, since clearly improved allocation with maintenance of existing care levels would imply a relative reduction in resources flowing to the industry. A definitional reduction in "quality" as measured by inputs results; but this sort of "quality dilution" is of no significance for public policy. A more sophisticated line of argument concedes that inefficiency exists in the industry, so that inputs could in theory be reduced; but the industry's own quality controls, based on professional attitudes and responsibility, would be gravely weakened by the kind of outside interference necessary to improve efficiency. Thus potential savings exist, but introduction of controls, incentive payments, or greater information flows would, in the process of achieving these savings, alienate members of the industry and destroy the self-policing process.

The second argument assumes that internal quality controls are both effective and fragile, and that they cannot be made more effective or supplemented with external controls under alternative institutional structures.

Yet it is not at all clear that solo practice of physicians, or cost reimbursement of hospitals, or protected oligopolies for drug firms, necessarily provide maximum or high-quality care. What *is* clear, however, is that as long as all proposals for improved resource allocation are required to demonstrate that quality will not be impaired, the defenders of the *status quo* will have an interest in prolonging the debate over quality definition and measurement indefinitely. For example, relatively detailed operating statistics are collected in a number of Canadian hospitals on the care received by each case treated. These data, machine-processed and tabulated, would be extremely useful (though hardly perfect!) for measuring quality of care provided across hospitals, physicians, or case types. Yet each hospital's results are kept secret from all other hospitals and from the public agencies responsible for purchasing and maintaining high-quality care!

It is hard to avoid the inference that the quality issue is being used as an economic weapon, as a smokescreen for the *status quo*. In a similar spirit, physicians have argued that medical schools cannot train more than X physicians and still provide "high-quality" training, thus restricting entry into the profession. Drug companies argue that brand-name drugs are "higher-quality" than their generic equivalents meeting the same U.S.P. or B.P. standards, in order to justify price differentials of 100 percent and more. The appropriate attitude for public policy in dealing with the quality issue would thus seem to be one of considerable scepticism. The issue should be turned around to place the burden of proof on the challengers—rather than requiring new proposals to prove that quality will not be diluted, it should be necessary for the opponents of change to prove that it will. This will have the dual effect of removing the quality issue as a roadblock to change and of encouraging more and better efforts at definition and measurement by health-care suppliers, who currently have an interest in keeping the issue blurred.

Finally, it should be noted that some reduction in health-care quality *may* be appropriate. To the extent that quality reduction implies reduction in patient comfort or convenience, it is possible that, depending on the savings involved, the reduction is justified. We have no objection to putting a price on comfort and convenience elsewhere in the economy. Even quality reductions which increase the risk to life and limb may be justifiable if the savings are large enough—not that we should cheerfully sabotage the health industry for possible savings! But we have pointed out above that in a world where resources are scarce there is some limit to the appropriate level of resource input, even for production of such an obvious "good thing" as high-quality medical care.

LONG-RUN PLANNING IN THE MEDICAL INDUSTRY

The policy problems which face us from year to year in the medical industry as elsewhere are in part the result of decisions made (or not made) over a number of years in the past. Once it is accepted that public initiative and control must continue to play a significant role in this industry, the question arises as to what are our long-run goals and objectives. Given a sufficiently long view, the whole industry is plastic and can be shaped by present decisions. These can be grouped into three areas of concern, and the issues are posed as questions because there are no very good answers as yet. The problems relate to physical investment in the industry, how many and what type of facilities will we need? What should we invest now? Going on from this, what sort of human-capital mix do we want? Who should be trained to do what? Finally, what is the appropriate level of research activity, what are the payoffs to research, how much should we spend now, and how should it be allocated? Lying behind each of these problems is the over-all problem of what will be the marginal return to health spending in a social sense, how big a health budget should our society have? But this cannot be determined independently of the evaluation of returns to individual medical-industry activities.

In the capital-facilities field, we can go on building more acute-general-hospital beds until no "shortage" is recognized, and then expand this level to keep pace with the population. We do not know how many beds this would take; but since the acute hospitals would find themselves with large numbers of geriatric and psychiatric patients, it would probably be about twice the beds-to-population ratios we now have. This would be equivalent to assuming a zero cost of capital in the medical industry, but it would yield a well-rested population. We can continue to focus on beds, but can build facilities with lower rates of capital equipment and personnel per bed, i.e., post-acute, extended care, chronic and convalescent facilities. Again, we would end up with many hospitals, but perhaps cheaper ones.

Alternatively, we can expand hospital outpatient and emergency facilities, putting higher priority on ambulatory care and keeping people out of hospital. We can build clinics and subsidize group practices, encouraging forms of physician payment which reduce rather than increase the incentives to over-utilization. These facilities may be hospital-based, or spread out through the community. The concentration of facilities provides scale economies and transportation costs—should we build facilities wherever people are, or move people to facilities? To what extent should the government take the initiative in coordinating regional use of facilities? "Regional

Planning" is a good word; but should the government dictate where facilities are and are not to be placed, should it require institutional cooperation or should it rely on financial inducements? And which government?

Should the government restrict itself to supplying funds and encouragement, or should it enter into the supply of medical services either in competition with, or as a substitute for, private activity? In general, direct government supply is becoming a less significant part of the industry, as veterans' and tuberculosis hospitals are reduced in scope. But it would be possible for the government to produce bulk drugs under quality-control standards at least as high as those in the private sector and to retail these at a margin over cost equivalent to that in competitive industries. From the point of view of social policy, this would be a pure and large welfare gain; but the political implications of such a blow at a powerful and wealthy industry and an extensive retailing system might be something else.

Finally, there is the question of whether public medical investment should focus on treatment or prevention. Is it better to build hospitals or to spend money on inoculation campaigns, mass screening for specific latent diseases, education, and environmental control? The payoffs to mass public-health activities are not well established, but the area is being, and will continue to be, widely investigated. Prevention, or early detection and treatment, of a given disease case is always much cheaper than treatment of the acute case; but if a hundred thousand people must be examined for each case prevented or treated early, the payoff may not justify the effort. Similarly, the cost of an anti-smoking educational campaign is or is not justified relative to the expenses of treating lung cancer, depending on the number of people convinced by the campaign and the change in their probability of developing lung cancer as a result of stopping smoking, adjusted for any change in the probability of their needing treatment for something else (even non-smokers get ill, and they have longer lives in which to get ill).

On the human-capital side, should we be making very heavy investments in training doctors, or would these funds be better spent on producing lower-level personnel so that the existing doctor supply can be used more efficiently? Should we be trying to keep up with the steady attrition of nurses into private life by training more and more, or would there be greater payoffs from substituting other forms of personnel? We could train non-nurses as operating room assistants, as anesthetists, as pharmaceutical specialists, along job lines which have been developed very effectively in military medicine—would these work in a civilian hospital? This is an area where policy initiatives are vital both in providing training facilities and in maintaining or changing the legal structure which defines professional codes and requirements.

Further, we must think about the sources of recruitment. Traditionally, the medical industry has had a sharply defined professional hierarchy, with each status level recruiting from outside through its own educational system. Movement from one rank to another is limited because one must go outside the system and re-enter at a higher level. Nurses must leave work and go to medical school to become doctors; they cannot rise through progressive on-the-job training. Characteristically, rich-men's sons become doctors. Similarly, an orderly or nursing assistant must go back through the regular school system to become a nurse, regardless of what he or she has learned at work. These "barriers to professional entry" are, of course, very useful to the professions themselves; but since government now provides most of the capital used in the training process, it must surely face the questions of who should be trained, for what, and how?

Finally, on the issue of medical research, there are three basic questions. First, what is the appropriate funding level? We do not know what research payoffs will be, but we do know that marginal payoffs are much lower than average payoffs. In any scientific field, most research is done by a handful of very good teams headed by exceptional men. These cannot be replicated, and the expansion of research activity by funding more teams does not, in general, expand output very much. For example, the boundaries of pure mathematics would hardly advance at all if a hundred times as many people as at present were trained and funded as mathematical researchers. The National Institute for Health experience in the United States suggests that this is true (to a lesser degree) of bio-medical research as well.

Second, should we put priorities on research projects? We may have social priorities—from an economic point of view, a cure for the common cold would probably have the highest payoff; but can research be thus guided? The chances of such a cure may at present be too small to justify investment. Can governments assign priorities better than researchers? Presumably governments know more about social benefits, but researchers know more about technical possibilities, and the proper course of policy is by no means obvious. And yet the funding process cannot avoid making some implicit decision as to how priorities are assigned.

Third, who should do research? We have argued above that providing subsidies through price protection to private companies doing research for their own ends is probably a minimally efficient approach. Should the government let contracts to private firms, universities, or hospitals for the solution of specific research problems? Should it operate its own laboratories? Should it simply fund non-profit research organizations and see what happens? These problems are of a level of generality which extends well beyond bio-medical research, but the answers may well differ depending on the type of research under discussion. We do not know the answers, but we must realize that any governmental decision taken in this area is assuming implicitly a set of answers, right or wrong, to these questions.

CONCLUSIONS

Is it possible to get better economic results from the health-services industry? What are the factors which are responsible for the current dismal
economic performance? The first problem is the inability to evaluate the
output of the industry. This causes proposals for change to founder on the
issue of "quality of care," and eviscerates efforts to formulate rational
and consistent objectives for the industry. Second, widespread public ignorance limits the scope of public policy. The inability to recognize that
choices must be made and that economic issues are inherent in decisions
about the use of resources in the provision of health services leads to the
selection of inappropriate policies. Third, there is extensive monopoly
power in factor markets, much of which is promoted by the government.
The regulations concerning licensing of personnel severely restrict entry and
inhibit the substitution of one type of personnel for another. Finally, the
structure of incentives in the industry almost assures undesirable economic
performance. Doctors earn fees only when their patients are ill. Hospitals
have no incentive to use resources efficiently. Consumers have no incentive
to reduce payments on their behalf by insurers, if these payments are
deductible from their income tax.

If the above diagnosis of the sources of poor economic performance is
accurate, what can we recommend as a course of treatment? First, we cannot delay treatment until the mystery of medical-care quality is resolved. If
we do, the mystery will never be resolved and the industry will never
improve. Thus we must take the position that quality deterioration must be
shown in criticizing any proposal, rather than that absence of deterioration
must be shown before a proposal may be advanced. The increase in debate
over quality issues which this approach would foster is consistent with a
second recommendation, namely, that public policy encourage the widest-
possible dissemination of information on relative prices, costs, qualities, and
availability of medical services, to producers and consumers of care. This
would make possible a more-open governmental decision-making process
and would broaden the set of politically feasible objectives, which is now so
circumscribed by public ignorance.

As for the degree of monopoly power in the health industry, few even
among economists would argue for free entry to the health professions with
no test of training or competence. Since barriers to entry are supported by
public legislation, however, they should be designed to further public purposes rather than private professional interests. In determining legal
requirement for entry, the state should not merely accept privately
determined norms, but should weed out those "professional qualifications"
the primary purpose of which is to block entry—particularly those which
apply to partially trained potential entrants from other health professions or

other areas. Professional bodies should be required to provide greatly accelerated "ladders of promotion" for such lower-skill groups in return for the high privilege of legally enforceable professional standards. This position can be generalized throughout the health industry—wherever public policy protects private monopoly, public rather than private ends must be served.

Finally, financial incentives industry-wide must be restructured to encourage efficiency, not waste. This will require much experimentation to discover how non-profit institutions react to different incentives. We could, for instance, pay hospitals by some suitably defined (there's the rub!) unit of output and let surpluses or deficits emerge. Alternative ways of supplying medical services, by reorganization of physicians and by substitution of machinery and less highly trained personnel, must be explored. Here the vital principle is not only that such experiments be encouraged, but that suppliers *and consumers* be able to share in any savings they generate. If Canada's Medicare policy requires that all enrollees in a province pay equivalent premiums whether they choose more or less efficient forms of medical-service supply, then it will represent one more aspect of governmental encouragment of waste and inefficiency. That would be an expensive pity.

the income-redistributive effects of aid to higher education

Richard W. Judy*
University of Toronto

1. INTRODUCTION

Canadian higher education has been in a period of rapid growth for more than a decade. University enrollment has tripled in the sixties. By 1975 it will nearly double again and by 1980 it may be roughly triple its present level.[1] Operating expenditures of higher educational institutions have increased even faster. From 1959-1960 to 1967-1968 university enrollment increased by 150 percent, while expenditures rose by 388 percent.[2]

Governmental support of higher education is placing mounting burdens on the Canadian taxpayer. From 1959-1960 to 1967-1968 government grants to Canadian universities grew by 440 percent. If trends of recent years continue, nearly 10 percent of all Canadian government expenditures will go to higher education. By 1980 as much as 17 cents of every tax dollar could go to higher education. This would compare with 1.1 cents in 1955 and 2.5 cents in 1965.[3]

The magnitude of the public subsidy to higher education prompts a series of questions. What are the net social benefits of this massive public investment in higher education? Do the increments in this investment bring greater social gains than those of comparable investments in other public programs? Is there a significant income-redistributive effect of public aid to higher educational institutions in Canada?

---

* This paper was produced as part of the research program on Systems Analysis for Efficient Resource Allocation in Higher Education, funded by the Ford Foundation.
1. See Appendix, Table A, page 316.
2. Dominion Bureau of Statistics, *Survey of Higher Education, 1967-68, Part II* (Ottawa: Queen's Printer, May 1969), pp. 17 and 19.
3. *Ibid.*, p. 19; *Canada Year Book*, 1968, p. 379; Appendix, Table A.

The first two of these questions are the kind that economists traditionally ask. Considerable evidence has been assembled in recent years to support the proposition that the social "purchase" of education is a sound investment choice. Investment in "human capital" is now regarded as an important source of economic growth.[4] A recent D.B.S. study indicated that the estimated lifetime earnings of a university graduate are 2.3 times those of a person with only a primary school education. The university graduate is expected to earn 1.6 times as much as a high school graduate.[5] The same study asserted that:

> The conclusion that the amount of education of the individual is the most important explanation of earnings differentials by occupations is now generally accepted.[6]

Despite the substantial research work that has been accomplished in recent years, we do not know the answers to a number of important questions about the social returns to investment in higher education. For example: What portion of the greater earnings of university graduates is due to superior innate ability or to cultural characteristics which, like the demand for higher education, are highly and positively correlated with parental socio-economic status? Given the present inventory and the rate of "output" of university graduates, what is the incremental (as opposed to the average) net social payoff to increasing the supply? Do the net private and social returns to higher education diverge? If so, specifically in what areas?

Significant through these questions are and important though it is to know their answers, this paper does not confront them. The focus here is on the income-redistributive effects of the present system of rendering public financial aid to higher educational institutions. Simply expressed, the question is whether, on balance, these public expenditures represent (1) a transfer of wealth from the poor to the rich, or (2) no transfer at all, or (3) a transfer from the rich to the poor. Redistributive effects of type (1) are said to be *regressive*, of type (2)—*neutral* and, of type (3)—*progressive*.

Every program of public expenditure has some kind of redistributive effects, although it is uncommon to find them explicitly considered. It appears frequently to be assumed that the redistributive effects are netural. Data which would permit rigorous analysis of income-redistributive effects

---

4. See, for example, Economic Council of Canada, *Second Annual Review* (Ottawa: Queen's Printer, 1965), pp. 71-95; Canadian Teachers' Federation, "Education as a Factor in Economic Growth—Some International Comparisons," Information Note 73, (Ottawa, 1965).
5. J. R. Podoluk, *Income of Canadians* (Ottawa: Queen's Printer, 1968), p. 86. Estimates are based on cross-section data from the 1961 Census.
6. *Ibid.*, p. 43.

are scarce; they are usually not collected. This is true even with those programs designed to achieve greater equality of opportunity and more-equal income distribution.[7]

It may be argued that examination of the income-redistributive effects of a particular public program is unjustified. Different programs are designed to benefit different social classes and, so the argument might continue, it is only the combined redistributive effect of all public programs taken as a package that can be legitimately analyzed.

Under some circumstances there would be merit in this argument, but when the issue is the expansion or contraction of a particular program, it is just as legitimate to ask about its marginal income-redistributive effects as it is to estimate its net contribution to national income. Two issues surrounding Canadian higher education compel our concern with the income-redistributive effects of public financial assistance thereto.

The first issue is simply the great expansion of public expenditures on higher education that will occur if present trends and financing arrangements continue. Under these circumstances, it would not be unreasonable to expect Canadian governments by 1975 to contribute $2.5 billion to higher educational institutions. This could exceed five percent of Canadian GNP and nearly ten percent of all governmental expenditures (see Appendix, Table A). Few Canadians will be indifferent to significant redistributive effects of an expenditure of such magnitude—especially if those effects are regressive.

The second issue concerns the proposals to abolish tuition fees and to institute "salaries" for all students. Implementation of these proposals could be expected to increase costs to taxpayers by from 25-50 percent above what they would be under the existing financial arrangements.[8] Student tuition fees have historically contributed about one-quarter of university operating revenue, although this has drifted toward one-fifth in recent years. The balance of university and college financial needs have been met largely by government grants directly to the institutions.

Proposals to abolish tuition fees and to pay student "salaries" are usually advanced as radical measures designed to benefit the poorer classes by

---

7. An example of this is the Ontario Student Assistance Program (O.S.A.P.). Designed in 1966 ostensibly to promote equality of educational opportunity. This program's effectiveness cannot be satisfactorily analyzed because neither the universities nor the Department of University Affairs has collected the necessary data. This is true despite O.S.A.P. grants exceeding $60 million in the first three years of the program's existence.

8. This estimate assumes that enrollment would not be affected by implementing these proposals. Alternative assumptions would be that enrollment would increase (because it would be financially more attractive to students to enter and remain in university) or that it would decrease (because, with given funding, it would be impossible to accept as many students as under existing financing arrangements).

removing financial barriers to higher education. It is not obvious that they would have this effect. All available evidence (e.g., Table 1) indicates that the children of relatively wealthy families are much more than proportionally represented among university and college students. Certainly, we know that the average subsidized recipient of a university degree is also the recipient of a valuable economic asset denied to those without university education. It is justifiable, therefore, to ask if increasing the subsidy to university education would not represent an increased net transfer from poor to rich (or, at least, to the offspring of rich and/or to the rich-to-be). What appears superficially to be a step toward progressive income redistribution may turn out to be just the opposite.

Table 1

MONEY-INCOME LEVEL—STUDENTS' PARENTS AND ALL
CANADIAN NON-FARM FAMILIES, SELECTED YEARS

	(Percent)					
	Less than $3,000	$3,000-$4,999	$5,000-$6,999	$7,000-$9,999	$10,000 and over	Total*
1956-57						
Students' parents	19.0	32.2	21.4	12.1	15.3	100
All Canadian non-farm family units	39.7	31.2	16.6	9.0	3.0	100
1961-62						
Students' parents	13.5	24.0	22.2	18.7	21.5	100
All Canadian non-farm family units	32.3	28.5	21.5	12.3	5.4	100
1964-65						
Students' parents	9.4	20.5	23.0	20.9	26.2	100
All Canadian non-farm family units	24.0	21.8	22.8	19.2	12.0	100

* Figures may not add to totals, due to rounding.

Notes to Table 1.

Students'-Parents' Income Data.
1956-57   Dominion Bureau of Statistics, **University Student Expenditure and Income in Canada, 1956-57** (Ottawa: Queen's Printer, 1959), p. 19.
1961-62   Dominion Bureau of Statistics, **University Student Expenditure and Income in Canada, 1961-62** (Ottawa: Queen's Printer, 1963), p. 25. This source did not provide the distribution of students' families by income groups for the totality of students but by individual faculties. These were aggregated using as weights the proportion of students in each faculty in 1961.
1964-65   Robert Rabinovitch, **An Analysis of the Canadian Post-Secondary Student Population** (Ottawa: Canadian Union of Students, 1966), p. 37. The four percent of students allocated in this study were spread proportionately over the various income classes.

All Canadian Non-Farm Family Units.
all years   Dominion Bureau of Statistics, **Income Distributions** (Ottawa: Queen's Printer, 1969), pp. 27-29. Family units included all families and unattached individuals.

2. THE ANALYSIS

The analysis reported here is a partial test of the hypothesis that the income-redistributive effect of public financial aid to Canadian universities is regressive. This hypothesis appears to be taken as an assumption in much recent discussion of higher education. Jencks and Riesman, for example, cautiously advance the hypothesis:

> Not only are colleges used by a minority, but they are mainly used by an affluent minority which is probably better able to absorb the cost than the average taxpayer. A scheme of the kind we have just outlined [a public program to pay all students subsistence and tuition allowances] might even have a regressive effect on income distribution. It might, that is, reduce upper-middle class expenditures on college more than it increased upper-middle class taxes, while increasing lower-class taxes more than it reduced lower-class expenditures.[9]

There can be little doubt that Canadian universities cater heavily to the middle and upper classes. In 1964-1965, for example, Table 1 indicates that nearly half of all students sampled said that their family income exceeded $7,000. This compares with less than one-third of all Canadian families in the over-$7,000 range.

To demonstrate regressive income redistribution, however, it is not sufficient to show that the services of universities are used largely by the affluent. It is necessary to show that the taxes that provide the public revenue going to universities bear less heavily on the affluent classes than do the benefits.

In general concept, the analysis is simple. It consists of four steps:

(1) Define several classes of income recipients.

(2) Determine what portion of the costs of publicly supporting higher education originates with each class.

(3) Determine what portion of the benefits derived from public expenditure on higher education accrues to the benefit of each class.

(4) Compare the incidences of costs and benefits for each income class.

In performing the analysis, it was necessary to make explicit some definitions and assumptions. It was also necessary to compromise certain features of the anlysis because of the limitations imposed by the available data. The next sections explain these aspects.

defining the income classes

The income classes in this study represent a compromise between those

---

9. Christopher Jencks and David Riesman, *The Academic Revolution* (Garden City, N.Y.: Doubleday and Co., 1968), p. 137.

used by W. Irwin Gillespie in his work for the Royal Commission on Taxation and those used by the Dominion Bureau of Statistics and Robert Rabinovitch in their studies of student incomes and expenditures.[10] The classes used here are as follows:

Up to $2,999
$3,000 – $4,999 $ 7,000 – $9,999
$5,000 – $6,999 $10,000 and over

determining the incidence of costs

The provincial and federal governments recently have borne the major share of the costs of higher education. The share of total university operating income contributed by all levels of government grew from 56.5 percent in 1961-1962 to 60.3 percent in 1965-1966. In the latter year, provincial governments contributed 43.0 percent, the federal government contributed 17.2 percent, and municipal governments contributed 0.1 percent. Student fees accounted for 25.9 percent of total operating income. The three levels of government contributed two-thirds of all capital income of universities in 1965-1966; provincial governments alone contributed 63.6 percent. For both capital and operating income, it is assumed here that governmental financial contributions derived from "general revenue."[11] The proportion of each tax or revenue source contributed by each income group was based on Irwin Gillespie's calculations.[12] Revenue data for all levels of government

---

10. W. Irwin Gillespie, *The Incidence of Taxes and Public Expenditures in the Canadian Economy*, Studies of the Royal Commission on Taxation, No. 2 (Ottawa: Queen's Printer, 1964); Dominion Bureau of Statistics, *University Student Expenditures and Income in Canada, 1956-1957, 1959* (Ottawa: Queen's Printer); Dominion Bureau of Statistics, *University Student Expenditures and Income in Canada, 1961-62, 1963*; and Robert Rabinovitch, *An Analysis of the Canadian Post-Secondary Student Population* (Ottawa: Canadian Union of Students, 1966).

11. Dominion Bureau of Statistics, *Canadian Universities, Income and Expenditure, 1961-62, and 1962-63*, p. 11, and *1965-66*, pp. 35 and 39. See Dominion Bureau of Statistics, *Historical Review of Financial Statistics of Governments in Canada, 1952-62* and *A Consolidation of Public Finance Statistics, 1963* (Ottawa: Queen's Printer, 1966).

Twenty-three general revenue categories are given in the source. The following categories were omitted from the present calculations:
Interest going abroad.
Motor fuel and fuel oil sales.
Motor vehicles.
Sales and services.
Contributions of federal and provincial enterprises in lieu of taxes.
Non-revenue and surplus receipts.
All intergovernmental transfers were also omitted.

12. For Gillespie's revenue categories, see W. Irwin Gillespie, *op. cit.*, p. 202.

in 1961 were used in the calculations.[13] Table 2 presents the results. The percent of general revenue contributed by each of the five family money-income classes is displayed for each level of government. The row marked "Total" in each year shows the weighted average of the other three rows for that year. The weights used were the proportion of total government grants to universities (capital and operating) supplied by each level of government for each particular year.

Table 2 indicates that about one-tenth of government grants to university capital and operating revenues was contributed by families with under-$3,000 annual money income. About one-fifth was contributed each by the $3,000-4,999 and the $7,000-$9,999 classes. The $5,000-$6,999 and $10,000-and-above classes contributed about one-quarter each.

The relatively regressive municipal tax structure has little impact on the total, because municipalities contributed little to the financing of universities. This is misleading to some extent, because few urban universities pay municipal taxes (or payments in lieu thereof) as high as they would if their land were owned and occupied by commercial or residential users. In the case of some universities located on highly valuable urban property (e.g., McGill University and the University of Toronto), this means a large municipal subsidy. Because alternative municipal revenue sources are

Table 2

PERCENTAGES OF GENERAL REVENUE CONTRIBUTED BY EACH OF SEVEN FAMILY MONEY-INCOME CLASSES, THREE LEVELS OF GOVERNMENT AND TOTAL* CANADA, 1961

Year and Level of Government	Family Money-Income Classes					
	Less than $3,000	$3,000-$4,999	$5,000-$6,999	$7,000-$9,999	$10,000 and above	Total†
1961						
(1) Federal	8.9	19.1	25.5	21.5	25.0	100
(2) Provincial	10.8	20.9	24.7	19.5	24.2	100
(3) Municipal	17.8	24.7	24.1	17.6	15.9	100
(4) Total†	10.4	20.5	24.9	19.9	24.3	100

* Figures in the "Total" row are weighted averages of the figures for the three levels of governments. Weights are the proportion of total government grants to universities (capital and operating) supplied by each level of government in the year indicated.
† Totals may not add to 100 because of rounding.

13. Dominion Bureau of Statistics, *Historical Review of Financial Statistics of Governments in Canada, 1952-62* (Ottawa: Queen's Printer, February 1966), p. 43.

very regressive, the subsidy to universities must likewise be considered to be very regressive. This factor has not been taken explicitly into account in the calculations reported here.

determining the incidence of benefits

Determining the incidence of benefits of public expenditures on higher education presents conceptual and empirical difficulties. The conceptual problems concern the *impact* and *shifting* of benefits. The empirical difficulties are caused by shortages of data.

Benefits of public financial aid to higher educational institutions can be grouped into three general classes:

1. *Direct benefits.* These are the benefits enjoyed by the recipients of the education, i.e., the students and their families. They include whatever consumption value higher education may bring (e.g., cultural values, greater intellectual acuity, improved social peers) plus the enhanced earning power brought by learning and academic degrees.

2. *Indirect benefits.* These are expenditures of students and their families which, because of the public subsidy, need not be made. They include that portion of the full cost of education borne by the public, subsidized subsistence, etc.

3. *External benefits.* These are benefits realized without direct payment by members of society other than the students and their families. They are extremely difficult to identify and measure. They may come about by way of more rapid economic and cultural growth. If public investment in higher education results in an increased proportion of the population with superior education, it is possible to argue that the rates of remuneration to these highly educated members of the labour force should decline relative to those with less education. This favourable (to the less-educated) shift in the "terms of the trade" would then result in increased real income to the uneducated segment of the working force. One way the external benefits may arise is from the contribution that greater and more dispersed knowledge makes to the solution of important social problems (e.g., improved health-care technology). The important point is that these benefits are realized by society as a whole without redounding to the direct benefit of the recipients of higher education.

In this analysis, we treat only the direct and indirect benefits. To which income class do the recipients of these benefits belong? Do they belong to the income class of the students' families or to the income class determined by the students' future earnings? We shall look at it both ways.

Future income-class of students. Here the focus of attention is on the income class which the university or college student will ultimately join after completing his post-secondary academic work. It is clearly impossible to know the exact distribution of the present generation of students among future income classes. What we can do is to use the present distribution of families by level-of-education of head and money-income class.

This involves a fairly complex assumption which deserves more careful examination. Let the following symbols be defined:

f^t — the total number of families at time t

f^t_i — the total number of families headed by persons with the ith type of education (e.g., a university degree) at time t.

f^t_{ij} — the number of f^t_i whose annual family money income at time t falls into interval j (e.g., \$7,000-\$9,000).

$a^t_{ij} = f^t_{ij}/f^t_i = f^t_{ij}/\sum_j f^t_{ij}$ i.e., the proportion of families of type i with annual income of type j.

Consider, now, the persons in the university-age generation, say, of 18-24 years. Suppose that each member of that generation is or will become either the head of or part of a family which will exist until its head dies, joins another family not as its head, or forms another family. A "family" here is taken to mean either (1) an unattached individual or (2) a conventional family.

y^t — the total number of persons in the age category 18-24 at time t.

Φ^t — the total number of families that will be formed by y^t.

Φ^t_i — the total number of families from among Φ^t which will be headed by persons with i^{th} type of education (e.g., a university degree).

Φ^t_{ij} — the number of Φ^t_i whose future average annual money income (defined for all years that each family exists) falls into interval j (e.g., \$7,000-\$9,000). Income of all future years is deflated by an index of personal income to remove the effect of secular and cyclical changes in real income.

$b^t_{ij} = \Phi^t_{ij}/\Phi^t_i = \Phi^t_{ij}/\sum_j \Phi^t_{ij}$

To use data on the present distribution of families among (1) annual money earnings and (2) educational level of family head as a surrogate for the distribution of student's future families by (1) future income and (2) education level of head is equivalent to using $A = \{a^t_{ij}\}$ as an approximation for $B = \{b^t_{ij}\}$.

Table 3

PERCENTAGE DISTRIBUTION OF CANADIAN FAMILIES* BY EDUCATION-LEVEL OF HEAD AND ANNUAL MONEY INCOME FOR 1959 AND 1965 IN CONSTANT (1961) DOLLARS

Education-level of Head of Family*	Family Money-Income Size in Constant (1961) Dollars						Average ($)	Median ($)
	Less than $3,000	$3,000-$4,999	$5,000-$6,999	$7,000-$9,999	$10,000 and above	Total		
No Schooling								
1959	69.8	15.4	10.4	1.8	2.7	100	2,543	1,723
1965	74.8	14.3	7.7	1.3	1.8	100	2,343	1,610
Some Elementary School								
1959	48.3	30.3	12.9	6.7	1.6	100	3,386	3,092
1965	43.4	27.9	16.9	8.6	3.3	100	3,883	3,485
Finished Elementary School								
1959	35.0	35.0	17.7	9.6	2.7	100	4,124	3,852
1965	28.2	27.7	24.3	13.3	6.4	100	4,975	4,618
Some High School								
1959	23.0	35.5	25.5	12.6	3.4	100	4,860	4,581
1965	19.5	25.3	26.0	21.9	7.3	100	5,648	5,377
Finished High School								
1959	22.6	29.6	26.0	14.4	7.4	100	5,352	4,865
1965	18.6	20.4	25.2	22.0	13.9	100	6,367	5,791
Some University								
1959	25.5	27.7	25.0	13.7	8.0	100	5,264	4,754
1965	16.0	21.6	23.0	26.2	13.0	100	6,339	5,892
University degree								
1959	14.8	19.0	19.9	24.3	22.0	100	7,804	6,681
1965	9.8	14.1	14.3	26.6	35.1	100	9,508	8,332

* Includes all families and unattached individuals.
Source: Dominion Bureau of Statistics, Income Distributions (Ottawa: Queen's Printer, 1969) p. 66.

The remarkably higher incomes earned by families whose head holds a university degree is apparent from Table 3 on page 311. More than 35 percent of those families whose head was a university graduate earned $10,000 or more in 1965. For all Canadian non-farm families, the percentage was 12 percent. (See Table 1 on page 305.) In other words, the probability of a family headed by a college graduate earning $10,000 or more was three times higher than for the average non-farm Canadian family. We need not interpret this to mean that the possession of a college degree is the sole cause of the higher income. For present purposes, it is sufficient merely to recognize the strong positive correlation between (1) the amount of education of the family head and (2) family earnings.

If we interpolate between 1959 and 1965, we can form an estimate of the distribution for 1961. Table 4 compares this with the distribution of public revenue going to universities in 1961. From Table 4 we see that families with money income of less than $7,000 contributed 55.8 percent of the public revenue going to support universities; some 47.1 percent of families headed by university graduates earned less that $7,000.

We can conclude that, so far as university *graduates* are concerned, the public subsidy of their study does represent a regressive kind of income redistribution. But not all university students actually graduate. The cal-

Table 4

COMPARISONS OF THE INCOME-CLASS ORIGIN OF PUBLIC AID TO HIGHER EDUCATIONAL INSTITUTIONS WITH THE DISTRIBUTION OF FAMILIES WHOSE HEADS POSSESSED UNIVERSITY EDUCATION, 1961

	Family Money-Income Class				
	Less than $3,000	$3,000-$4,999	$5,000-$6,999	$7,000-$9,999	$10,000 and above
(1) Public Revenue going to Universities (1961)*	10.4	20.5	24.9	19.9	24.3
(2) Family income of families whose head has "some university education"†	21.7	25.3	24.2	18.7	10.0
(3) Family income of families whose head has a university degree†	12.8	17.0	17.6	25.1	27.5
(4) "Blended family" to reflect a 35 percent dropout rate‡	16.1	21.1	21.1	23.1	21.6

* From Table 2, p. 308.
† Interpolated linearly from 1959 and 1965 data of Table 3, p. 311.
‡ A weighted average of the percentages for families whose heads had "some university education" (35 percent) and with "university education" (65 percent).

culation of the incidence of "benefits" must recognize that some beneficiaries will become heads of families with "some university education."
The distribution of these families is much more skewed toward the lower
end of the income scale than is the distribution of the public revenue going
to support higher education.

Suppose we assume that 65 percent of the "benefits" of public aid
to universities goes to those who graduate and 35 percent to those who drop
out before graduation. This would give us the "blended-family" distribution displayed as line 4 in Table 4. If we compare this with line 1, we see
that the incidence of "costs" is somewhat more progressive than the incidence of "benefits." The progressive effect is not strong, however, since the
percentages contributed and received by income groups earning more than
$7,000 are nearly equal.

Income-class of students' parents. Table 1 displays the distribution of
students' parents by income class for three different years. It was noted
above that the children of relatively wealthy families are much more proportionally represented among university and college students. We may
compare this distribution with that shown on line 4 of Table 2, which
shows the percentage of public funds going to aid higher educational institutions originating with various family income classes. Table 5 presents this
comparison.

Again, we see no remarkable differences between the distribution of
"costs" and "benefits." Some 44.2 percent of the costs of public aid to
higher education are borne by families earning $7,000 or more. About 40.2
percent of students' parents had family incomes of $7,000 or more.

Table 5

COMPARISON OF THE CLASS ORIGIN OF PUBLIC AID TO HIGHER-EDUCATIONAL INSTITUTIONS WITH THE DISTRIBUTION OF STUDENTS' PARENTS AMONG INCOME GROUPS, 1961

	Family Money-Income Group				
	Less than $3,000	$3,000-$4,999	$5,000-$6,999	$7,000-$9,999	$10,000 and above
Public funds going to universities (1961)*	10.4	20.5	24.9	19.9	24.3
Students' parents in 1961-62†	13.5	24.0	22.2	18.7	21.5

* From Table 2, p. 308.
† From Table 1, p. 305.

3. CONCLUSION

The hypothesis that the over-all income-redistributive effect of public aid to higher education is regressive is not supported by the findings reported here. This is true whether the recipients of the benefits are taken to be the students themselves (in their capacity as earners of future income) or their parental families. The slight over-all redistributive effect measured is in the progressive direction. In view of the approximations of data and analysis, however, it is not to be accorded much significance.

If we had more and better data, we could look at the redistributive effects for graduates and non-graduates in specific faculties and fields of study. In Medicine, for example, the costs and public subsidies are particularly high, a high percentage of students graduate, the distribution of parental family income is more skewed upward than in other faculties (except for Law), and expected lifetime earnings for doctors are much higher than for the average university graduate. There is little doubt that public subsidization of some fields of study (e.g., Medicine and Law) produces a markedly regressive income redistribution irrespective of how it might be measured.

The basic conclusion, restated, is that no appreciable over-all redistribution of wealth among income classes takes place through the medium of public financial-assistance programs to higher educational institutions in Canada. The people who benefit from these programs are, or will be, heavily concentrated in the higher-income brackets—but so are the people who pay the taxes that create the revenue from which comes the aid to universities.

Consider, now, the proposals to abolish tuition fees and to establish salaries payable to all students. Would the net incidence of these programs be the same as the net incidence of public aid to universities in the early sixties, i.e., approximately neutral? The answer depends upon (1) the impact these programs would have on the level of enrollment and the class distribution of students and (2) how the revenue would be raised to fund the programs.

It seems reasonable to anticipate that the requests for admission to and continuation in university would be greatly increased with no tuition fees and/or student salaries. If there were not sufficient public funds to accommodate all requests, then some applicants would have to be refused. This would mean the rationing of places in university, i.e., selective admission. If the criterion for admission were academic performance in secondary school, then we could expect the student body to be more heavily weighted toward the upper-income brackets than it is now. This is because high-school academic performance is highly and positively correlated with family income. The resulting change on income redistribution would tend to be regressive.

If enrollment were allowed to grow to meet the increased demand for admission, then the quantity of funds required to operate the universities would increase greatly. How might these funds be raised? If they came at the expense of other public programs, then the incidence of benefits of the sacrificed programs would have to be taken into account. If programs with progressive, neutral, or less-regressive incidence of benefits (e.g., public-health programs) were sacrificed, then the net tax results might be regressive. If the increased expenditures were met by net increases, then the incidence of those increases would heavily influence the nature of the resulting income redistribution.

It seems counter-productive, in any case, to attempt to create greater equality of educational opportunity and income distribution by abolishing tuition fees or instituting student salaries. A better way to achieve these objectives would be to tax more and subsidize less those who are or will be affluent and to subsidize more and tax less those who are poor.

(Appendix, Table A follows on pages 316 and 317.)

Appendix, Table A

SOME ACTUAL AND PROJECTED VALUES OF SELECTED INDICATORS
OF CANADIAN HIGHER EDUCATION, 1955-56 TO 1980-81

	Actual 1955-56	Actual 1960-61	Actual 1965-66	Forecast 1970-71	Forecast 1975-76	Forecast 1980-81
1. Total population in the age group 18-24, Canada, millions	1.56	1.69	2.04	2.58	2.93	3.20
2. Post-secondary enrollment in Canada, thousands	72.7	113.9	205.9	374.6	619.8	966.4
3. Expenditures per post-secondary student in Canada, in constant (1965) dollars	$1,651	$2,520	$3,317	$4,740	$6,775	$9,680
4. Total expenditures on post-secondary education in Canada, in millions of constant (1965) dollars	103	287	683	1,776	4,199	9,355
5. Percent of Canadian Gross National Product devoted to higher education	0.35	0.72	1.36	2.75	5.26	9.49
6. Percent of all Canadian government expenditures devoted to higher education	1.1	1.4	2.5	4.9	9.5	17.1

Notes to Appendix, Table A.

1. **Total population in the age group 18-24, Canada, millions**
   Data for 1955-1975 are from E. F. Sheffield, **Enrollment to 1976-77 in Canadian Universities and Colleges**, 1963 Projection (Ottawa: Canadian Universities Foundation, 1964), p. 14. The 1980 figure was estimated by the author's demographic model.

2. **Post-secondary enrollment in Canada, thousands**
   It was assumed that participation rates in Canada as a percentage of the population in the 18-24 age group change as follows:

   1955 — 4.7 percent
   1966 — 10.6 percent
   1967 — 11.4 percent
   1970 — 14.5 percent
   1975 — 21.2 percent
   1980 — 30.2 percent

   In 1966 the participation rate for the same age category in the United States was 27.4 percent. This compares with 15 percent for 1955 in the United States.
   Figures for the United States were computed from data in U.S. Department of Health, Education and Welfare, **Projections of Educational Statistics to 1976-77** (Government Printing Office, 1968), pp. 13-15; and the **Statistical Abstract of the United States** (Government Printing Office, 1967), pp. 8-9 and p. 34. Canadian figures are from Dominion Bureau of Statistics, **Survey of Higher Education**, Part I (Ottawa: Queen's Printer, 1968), p. 11.

3. **Expenditures per post-secondary student in Canada in constant (1965) dollars**
   Costs per student rose from $1,508 in 1954 to $3,317 in 1965; this is a rate of increase of 7.4 percent per annum. Data were deflated from Dominion Bureau of Statistics, **Canadian Universities, Income and Expenditure, 1964-65** (Ottawa: Queen's Printer, 1967), p. 27. The deflator was developed from information in Dominion Bureau of Statistics, **Survey of Educational Finance, 1964** (Ottawa: Queen's Printer, 1968), p. 11; and **National Accounts, Income and Expenditure, 1967** (1968), p. 8.
   It was assumed, for the purpose of Table A, that the 7.4 percent annual rate of increase would continue until 1980-81.

4. **Total expenditures on post-secondary education in Canada in millions of constant (1965) dollars**
   Figures are the product of rows 2 and 3.

5. **Percent of Canadian GNP devoted to higher education**
   Based on the assumption that GNP will grow at the average annual rate of 4.3 percent per annum in Canada.

6. **Percent of all Canadian government expenditures devoted to higher education**
   Based on the assumptions that government expenditures in Canada will continue to account for one-third of GNP and that Canadian governments will pay 60 percent of all expenditures on higher education.

pollution: a problem in economics

Leonard Waverman
University of Toronto

Down the river one million toilet chains,
Find my Hudson so convenient a place to drain,
And each little city says "who me?"
Do you think that sewage plants come free?

My Dirty Stream, a song
by Pete Seeger

1. THE NATURE OF THE PROBLEM[1]

The Oxford Dictionary defines the verb "pollute" as: "destroy the purity or sanctity of, make foul or filthy." Whenever an environmental factor—air, water or land—is described as polluted, an implicit comparison is therefore being made between the polluted factor and some *standard of purity* for that factor.

Each of us has a subjective standard for the environment. (The standard, of course, depends on how the environment is to be used.) A swimmer might find Lake Erie acceptable to him (i.e., unpolluted) while a commercial fisherman would consider the lake as seriously polluted. A firm which

---

1. An interesting collection of readings on the pollution subject is: M. I. Goldman (ed.), *Controlling Pollution: The Economics of a Cleaner America* (Englewood Cliffs, N.J.: Prentice-Hall, Inc., 1967). Water pollution is well discussed by A. V. Kneese and B. T. Bower, *Managing Water Quality: Economics, Technology, Institutions* (Baltimore: Resources for the Future Inc. by Johns Hopkins Press, 1968). A book of articles on air pollution, H. Wolozin (ed.), *The Economics of Air Pollution* (New York: W. W. Norton & Co. Inc., 1966), has some informative papers. In 1966 a Canadian national conference "Pollution and Our Environment" was held. A. Devos (ed.), *The Pollution Reader* (Montreal: Harvest House, 1968) is a compendium of 22 papers presented at that meeting.

used water as a cooling agent only, would accept a degree of impurity of that lake which would be unacceptable to both the swimmer and the commercial fisherman.

There are several attributes which all pollutants have in common. First, pollution is a "bad," as opposed to a "good" (clear air). It is a product which individuals would not pay for in a market. It is, in fact, a product which those whom it offended would pay to remove. At the same time, the group that wishes to remove the pollutant may not be the same group which supplied the pollutant. Second, pollutants are generally joint products. They are produced in conjunction with goods which are desired. No factory exists which produces pollutants alone. For example, a pulp and paper mill can be considered as producing two classes of products—paper and wastes. Pollution is not caused by evil demons who wish to destroy the environment. It is caused by firms and individuals who are trying to minimize their costs. The conflict between polluters and non-polluters is therefore not a conflict of evil against good. It is a conflict between well-intentioned people, each having his own subjective standard of purity in mind.

There are three unanswered questions to consider in discussing pollution. Since pollution is a "bad," (as opposed to a normal good), how is it that those who do not want the pollutant and who did not supply it, end up paying to remove it? Second, if the term "pollution" means "all things to all men," how is society to set an objective level of pollution, thereby weighing the differing demands of each individual in that society? Finally, once this level is established, how can the supply of pollutants be kept below the level?

The standard role of economics is to answer these types of questions. No two people in a society necessarily have the same subjective desire or use for any good produced, be it a Cadillac or an orange. Yet, it is not necessary either to vote or to legislate on the number of cars and oranges produced. A rationing scheme exists which weights the relative desires of people who wish to consume and firms who wish to produce these goods. This rationing scheme is based upon a price mechanism.

The three unanswered questions exist because our environmental factors are unpriced scarce resources. Whenever a scarce factor is underpriced, some rationing scheme must be introduced. The nature of the rationing scheme introduced for clear water is that those who wish to use the resource for technological purposes which exclude other uses can do so.[2] For example, a firm which uses the water to dump toxic wastes can exclude the demands of swimmers for that same water. The purposes to which swimmers put the water cannot technologically so exclude others. Economic

---

2. This point was made by John Dales, in his *Pollution, Property and Prices* (Toronto: University of Toronto Press, 1968).

theory states that such a rationing scheme will lead to a misallocation of resources.

Before the difficulties and benefits of establishing a market price system for the environmental factors are discusssed, a further explanation and definition of the problem along with a description of the extent of the destruction of clean air, water, and soil follow.

2. DEFINITIONS OF POLLUTION

objective definitions

Since the existence and extent of pollution have been discussed in such subjective terms some authors have tried to define objective scientific measures. Unfortunately, these are all misleading.

Some, for example, have suggested that the objective standard of purity should be the pure chemical form of the environmental factor. This is unworkable. No pure chemical form exists for soil. If the purity standard of water were defined as two atoms of hydrogen connected to one atom of oxygen, with *no* other elements, this standard could not be met in nature. All natural water flows contain some other elements either suspended or dissolved in them.

Another standard sometimes used, is to define pollution as the release of substances into the environment as a result of man's activities. Under this definition, all living creatures are polluters. One wouldn't want to legislate against emissions of carbon dioxide (i.e., breathing) by human beings; it is only levels of emissions which are harmful, which concern us.

All living creatures can tolerate in their environment a presence of most substances. Fluoride dissolved in water at a level of less than one part per million is apparently beneficial to the structure of teeth in humans. Fluoride, above the level of 10 parts per million, consumed for a lengthy period, causes fluorosis—a fatal disease involving bone decay.[3] Nitroclycerine in minute quantities alleviates the distress of patients with cardio-vascular attacks. In large quantities, nitroclycerine has a far different impact on the environment.

Life-sustaining activities place in the environment substances which in sufficiently large volumes can be harmful to life. The process of breathing

---

3. For a discussion of fluoride pollution, its effects, and a controversial case study, see *Report of the Committee Appointed to Inquire into and Report Upon the Pollution of Air, Soil and Water in the Townships of Dunn, Moulton, and Sherbrooke Haldimand County* (Ontario, September 1968). This Report deals with the C.B.C. film, "The Air of Death," which "reported" cases of fluorosis resulting from the activity of the Electric Reduction Company at Port Maitland, Ontario. The Report discounts the C.B.C. story.

or burning displaces oxygen from the air with carbon dioxide. If two people were on a picnic in the open air, neither would consider the other's breathing as harmful, i.e., as pollution. If the two were in a small enclosed room, the breathing of either would after a few hours produce pollution for both of them (as would the burning of a candle). Any definition of pollution for a specific element must therefore take into account the level of that element already in existence and the additional increment resulting from an activity.

These definitions are too general. What is more, they do not help in explaining the nature of the problem.

a definition in economics

The nature of the problem is that people who neither produce nor desire pollution end up paying for it. All urban dwellers, for example, pay for the emission of unburned hydrocarbons in the air through higher cleaning costs for houses, cars and clothes, less lovely flowers and more nose blowing. An appropriate definition of pollution is contained in these descriptions. *Pollution is the addition by man of materials to the environment to such an extent that costs are imposed on other men and where no recourse exists to receive equitable compensation for these costs.* If equitable compensation is paid, then no-one is hurt, no *net costs* are imposed on others.

This is a most important point. An example will make it clear. Imagine an industry which produces (in addition to a good) a single, readily identifiable waste product. This waste is deposited by air currents on the land of one farmer who does not consume the good produced by the industry. These wastes contaminate the farmer's land, and his production of food cannot be sold. If the farmer is not compensated for his loss, this is a clear example of the imposition of costs by the industry on an individual. The individual farmer pays the costs of the industry's waste disposal even though he does not consume the good that the industry produces. The individuals who consume the good do not pay for waste disposal. If the farmer is adequately compensated, no costs which should be borne by the industry are imposed on others. The farmer, instead of producing food, uses the land for waste disposal. He receives the same profit with either use of his land. In this latter case of full compensation, *no pollution exists.* The farmer is as well off with the waste-emitting industry as he would be without it. The industry is paying the full costs of the production, including waste disposal.

In real life, the costs imposed on others are not so easily measured. How can the costs be estimated of a swimmer's inability to use certain polluted areas of Lake Ontario? It is conceivable but difficult to impute to this pollution the costs of public and private swimming pools and the costs of travelling to distant clean lakes. Besides being forced to swim elsewhere, the swimmer does not have the legal right to receive compensation for his additional costs.

The inability to receive compensation is generally due to the inability to single-out the individual who caused the specific damage. An urban dweller cannot identify *the* automobile whose unburned hydrocarbon emissions settled on his flowers. Where such identification is possible, the courts have upheld the right of the person who suffered damage to be compensated by the polluter. The Electric Reduction Company of Canada plant at Port Maitland, Ontario has paid $86,206.44 in 1965 and $122,126.79 in 1966 for crop damage and losses in the surrounding area.[4] On May 5, 1969 the federal Department of Fisheries closed an 800-square-mile area in Placentia Bay, Newfoundland as polluted for fishing. The federal government granted loans to stricken fishermen as an advance against compensation from the suspected polluter—the plant of Electric Reduction Company of Canada at Long Harbour.

Pollution as it has been defined here involves the transference of costs from a firm to a set of individuals (or other firms). In so doing, the polluter has imposed on society costs greater than the costs to the polluting firm. The case where social costs are greater than private-firm costs is known as a technological external diseconomy. A polluting firm does not itself bear the entire costs of its production. At any positive price, it would therefore be willing to supply a greater amount of output than if it paid all the costs of its production. The existence of technological external diseconomies will lead to an oversupply of the good which the polluting firm produces, at the expense of other goods. Pollution is accompanied by a misallocation of resources. Polluting firms overproduce and thereby attract too many resources. Non-polluting firms underproduce and too few resources are committed to their production.

3. AN EXPLANATION OF POLLUTION—SCARCE RESOURCES AND "INAPPROPRIABILITIES"

The amounts of most products produced are a result of a market decision involving a price. This market decision can be made because the ownership of Cadillacs and oranges, for example, can be traded in this market. Land ownership can also be traded in markets. However, the ownership of air and certain large water areas cannot so be traded.

It is because of this *inappropriability* of the ownership of air and, to a lesser degree, water, that a market price for these factors does not exist.

---

4. *Ibid.*, p. 9.

Figure 1

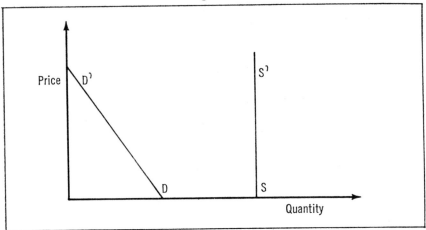

Because a price does not exist, it does not mean that these elements are worthless.

In Figure 1 the horizontal and vertical axes are, respectively, the quantity of good X and its price. The curve D'D represents the demand schedule for X. The curve S'S is the supply schedule of X. The diagram shows that there is an excess supply of that good at a zero price (X is a free good).

If air and water, which are inappropriable goods, were also free goods, no problem of pollution would arise. In this case, clean air would be inappropriable yet no costs could be imposed on others, since at a zero price the natural supply of clean air is greater than the demand for clean air.

Pollution—the imposition of costs on others—can exist only when the natural supply of an inappropriable factor is, at a zero price, less than the demand at that price. Pollution is a problem which arises when scarce resources cannot be priced in a market.

Land is appropriable. Examples of soil pollution do exist, however. This does not mean that the entire reasoning so far has been inaccurate. It is not possible to divide real-life examples of pollution into neat little categories of soil or air or water. Water and air are in contact with soil. The build-up of lead in the farmland around major highways is an example of air-pollutant residue. This type of pollution is not caused by the inappropriability of traded land in a market. Its cause is the inappropriability of air around the farm. Neither the farmer nor his customers can receive compensation for their costs from passing motorists. Many other examples of soil pollution are residues of either air- or water-borne elements.

The case of pesticide build-up involves two different problems. If a farmer in spraying his land could not deposit pesticides on anyone else's land or water, pesticide build-up would *not* be an example of pollution in the definitional sense given above. The use of pesticides to yield more grain to the farmer imposes costs of illnesses on customers. Presumably, the consumer could sue the producer for compensation. The producer placed the pesticide on his land. He is therefore liable for any ill effects. If it becomes known that a farm has large amounts of pesticide residue, consumers will stop purchasing products of this land. The producer will then bear all the costs of this pesticide build-up himself; no net costs will be imposed on others. Clearly, this is not the case in the real world. A farmer in spraying his land inadvertently sprays other land and water. Rain washes the pesticides from one land area to other land and water areas. Pesticides such as D.D.T. do not easily decompose. Scientists have shown that the fatty tissues of fish, fowl and animals collect D.D.T. residues to the point where life is threatened. Because of the movements of air and water, fish and fowl, the identification of the specific polluter is impossible. Pesticide poisoning does fall under the definition of pollution. The extent of this pollution can be seen in the high concentrations of D.D.T. found in animals and humans in areas where no pesticide spraying has ever occurred—the Arctic and Antarctic.

Air and water in the case of oceans and certain bodies of inland lakes (the Great Lakes, for example) are *collective* goods, not subject to private ownership. They are owned and enjoyed by the community at large.

Land is considered a collective good not subject to private ownership, in certain societies. An example from such a society will show the costs imposed when an inappropriable collective resource is in scarce supply.

The Commons areas of feudal England belonged, in common, to all residents of the fief. No one could be excluded from using the common pasture for his cattle. No one could buy or sell the rights to use this commons for his cattle. As long at the commons was large enough to support all who wanted it, no problem existed. No one could impose costs on anyone else as long as the right to pasturage was *a free good.*

Overcrowding, however, did become a problem. Since no price existed for the land, the incentive always existed for an individual to put one more cow into the commons. The consumption of grass by this one additional cow decreased the supply of grass for all other cows. But if this cow ate and survived, the owner was better off, even though all other cow-owners were worse off.

The costs to society of placing one more cow on the common pasture were far greater than the private costs to an individual of that one cow's feeding. The private costs were zero (no price paid for the use of that land), while the costs imposed on others (the social costs) were positive.

If a farmer were allowed to appropriate the land, i.e., fence off a portion for himself, this technological external diseconomy would vanish. On an individual plot of land, the farmer could impose costs only on himself by overusing the pasture. He would therefore be reluctant to overcrowd. A supply of better-nourished cattle would be ensured. If the land were appropriable, it could also be traded. Each individual would have a different estimate of the value of the land to him, depending on his ability as an entrepreneur and the use to which he intended to put the land. The bidding for land among alternative users would establish the price which ensured that the land went to the individual who valued it most (could get the most out of it). The allocation of land so as to maximize the product of that land was ensured.

The enclosure movements in medieval England were a direct response to this "cow pollution." The range wars in the western USA between sheep-herders and cattlemen resulted from the inappropriability of public land and the imposition of costs by one type of grazing animal upon the other.

Before investigating whether an enclosure movement or a range war is an appropriate answer to the problems of air and water pollution, the severity of these problems must be discussed.

4. EXTENT OF POLLUTION

Pollution is mainly the result of the use of the environmental factors for waste disposal. As such, it is not a new problem but has been with man since he climbed down from the trees. Caveman would move when the stench of accumulated refuse became too strong.[5] The Roman aqueducts and viaducts were the products of necessity, the need to remove large amounts of human waste. With the introduction of water as a waste-removal agent, water pollution becomes a problem in the Western world (the Ganges was a problem before Rome rose from the seven hills). The problem worsened. The accounts of the plagues of the middle ages and eighteenth-century Paris and London bear stark witness to the costs of water pollution in those days.

Water, air and soil can assimilate the presence of a great number of harmful substances by *decomposing* them into less harmful elements or by *diluting* them such that their level in the total environment is harmless. Agents also exist which replace the toxic by-products of man's existence with beneficial elements. (For example, plants take in carbon dioxide and expel oxygen). These regenerative properties of the environment are, however, dependent on the volume of toxic substances and their rate of introduction into the atmosphere.

---

5. For a humorous yet educational treatment of pollution, see G. R. Stewart, *Not so Rich as You Think.* (Boston: Houghton Mifflin Co., 1968).

The earth is a totally closed environment (identical to the closed room of the above example). As a closed environment, future life depends on the recycling regenerative properties of this spaceship earth.[6]

Today the problem is different and more complex than in those days. The water-supply systems of most modern cities can cleanse polluted lakes and rivers so that water is fit for human consumption. In a sense, then, water pollution is not as major a problem as it was in the middle ages. The cost imposed on others is rarely their lives, but rather the quality of their lives.

The style of living has changed. The spread of civilization across the continent has altered the nature of the problem. What was once concentrated in a few urban areas is now a nation-wide problem. Jack Davis, the Minister of Fisheries and Forestry, recently reported that the Ottawa and lower St. Lawrence Rivers were badly polluted, as was the St. John river in New Brunswick.[7] A lake in Algonquin Park, far from civilization, has been closed to swimming. There are also reports of the contamination of herring off the coasts of Labrador and Newfoundland, and the closing of certain shellfish areas in the eastern oceans due to the presence of toxic elements in clams and oysters. The deaths of large numbers of bay seals in the Gulf of St. Lawrence near the Straits of Belle Isle were believed caused by oil pollution in that area. In some cases of water pollution, bodies of water have been polluted to the extent that their natural restorative properties have been destroyed. Certain chemical wastes poured into lakes are oxygen absorbing. This absorption of oxygen destroys the environmental balance of the lake, eliminating high-oxygen-demanding fish. Lake Erie is an example of this type of pollution. What was once a source of pike and trout for commercial fishermen now yields only carp. The difficulty in coordinating the divergent municipal, state, provincial and federal bodies which have jurisdiction over this dead body of water makes restoration improbable.

Even the oceans are not immune to pollution. In the earlier decades of this century, the largest ships were in the order of 25,000 tons. If they broke up on an uninhabited coastline, the volume of foreign matter which they added to the water could be assimilated (diluted) by that water. Today, oil tankers of up to 400,000 tons displacement are common and versions of up to 1,000,000 tons are on the drawing board. If these tankers break up near a coastline, these volumes of oil cannot be diluted by the water to

---

6. K. Boulding, "The Economics of the Coming Spaceship Earth," in H. Jarrett (ed.), *Environmental Quality in a Growing Economy* (Baltimore: Resources for the Future Inc. by Johns Hopkins Press, 1966).
7. *The Globe and Mail* (Toronto, August 7, 1969).

a degree which makes them harmless to aquatic life. The break-up of the *Torrey Canyon*, a 118,000 ton oil tanker, off the coast of Cornwall in 1966 destroyed thousands of migratory birds, polluted the once-white sand beaches, and cost the British and French governments nearly $16,000,000 to clean up.[8] The costs of the oil leak in the off-shore well off the coast of Santa Barbara, California in April 1969, have been estimated at nearly *$2 billion.*[9]

The air in and around urban areas has been found to contain elements in a high-enough proportion to be toxic to man, besides increasing his cleaning costs. An automobile in Northern Alberta does not pollute. The air dilutes the possible toxic wastes of the automobile to render them harmless. The nature of the problem is the multiplication of these elements to a level and a rate of introduction which are harmful. The air that we can see and taste and smell is a product of combustion. The unburned hydrocarbon emissions of the automobile are an obvious source of air pollution. Less obvious but possibly more dangerous are the emissions of lead and rubber which are building up in the soil of our urban metropolies.

The problem of air pollution in a major city perhaps is not of the same magnitude as the problem of water pollution in Lake Erie. The body of air surrounding a city apparently has not had its restorative powers destroyed. A reduction in the rate of new emissions would restore a cleaner standard of air.

Combustion, besides emitting these secondary products, replaces oxygen with carbon dioxide. The ability of this planet to compensate for this increase in the level of carbon dioxide is being seriously threatened. In 1965 the Environmental Pollution Panel of the President's Science Advisory Committee (USA) reported that if the rate of increase of carbon dioxide emissions continued at the 1960-1965 rate, the level of carbon dioxide in the atmosphere of earth would increase by 25 percent by the year 2000. The impact of changing the atmosphere to such a degree is highly conjectural. The seriousness of the consequences of conjectures such as the flooding of all coastal areas as a result of the melting of the polar ice-caps make this change in the atmosphere an important area for further research and possible remedies.

Clean air and water have long been considered as collective free goods. Yet, in the extent of the problem of pollution, it is evident that they are scarce resources in some areas of this globe.

---

8. E. Cowan, *Oil and Water, The Torrey Canyon Disaster* (Philadelphia: J. B. Lippincott Co., 1968).
9. *Business Week* (April 19, 1969).

5. REMEDIES: THE POLICY ALTERNATIVES

Pollution results from the utilization of inappropriable and underpriced scarce resources. Those who bear the resulting external diseconomies cannot readily identify the specific source of these externalities.

The possible remedies are threefold—an enclosure movement for air and water, government regulation, and a market price system. These will be discussed in turn with the difficulties of each described. It will be found that no single policy alone can solve the problem of pollution.

enclosures

While the enclosure movement eliminated the problem of "cow pollution," enclosures are not a viable remedy to eliminate air and water pollution.

Under the existing scheme of property rights, enclosures could not solve the problem of water pollution. Lake Erie has many private beaches. Some polluted rivers are entirely owned by a number of individuals. For private property rights to end water pollution, *the entire water system* would have to be owned by one individual. For example, assume that the entire St. Lawrence system (i.e., including the Great Lakes) were owned by the government, except for a small one-mile right-of-way on Lake Superior owned by a sulphuric-acid company. If the ownership of this right-of-way gave the company the right to dump factory wastes in the Lake, the entire system could be polluted. Land does not have such flows. It is difficult for a firm to use its land in such a way to pollute all the neighbouring land for miles around.

With only one owner of the water system, no externalities would be possible, no costs could be imposed on other users without being imposed on himself. One means of ending water pollution is for the government to confiscate all water systems and to sell the water to customers. Any use which imposed costs on other users would reduce demand and therefore government revenue. The government (assumed to be a profit-maximizer) would either clean the water or force the polluter to do so.

This is a politically impossible and administratively costly proposal. Beaches would have to be sealed off and tolls instituted. Enforcement would be difficult.

The complexities of "nationalizing" air are even more absurd. Such a scheme would involve (among other things) attaching a meter to each resident's lungs. Before one went jogging or indulged in any oxygen-using exercise, the price of air would be studied in order to estimate the costs and benefits of such exercise.

Enclosures certainly cannot help solve the problem.

government regulation

Governments can affect the level of pollutants in the environment in two other ways. They can introduce laws which make a specific form of pollution illegal. Automobile-exhaust controls are an example of this form of government control. Governments can allow the emission of wastes by private firms and provide abatement devices which remove these pollutants. Municipal sewage-treatment plants are an example of this type of service.

When a government legislates against a specific pollutant, it implicitly must be weighting the subjective standards set by the voters it represents. Laws, however, unlike the standards of individuals and the composition of political parties, are inflexible and difficult to change. Government legislation does not solve the problem of weighting, it merely disguises it. A more obvious and flexible system (if available) would be preferable.

The use of removal devices provided by the government can be a method of pricing an environmental factor if the polluter alone pays for the installation and maintenance of the device. Funds for such abatement controls should not come out of general tax revenue.[10] There may be valid reasons why a firm or group of firms would prefer to have a government remove its waste emissions from the environment. There may be economies of scale in the installation and operation of abatement-control equipment. In this case of scale economies, the costs for a single firm would be lower if equipment would be installed for a number of firms. There is little data available which allow one to assess whether this is, in fact, the case. Government-provided abatement equipment operates after the environment is polluted. It is easier to remove the toxic elements from a firm's wastes before it enters the environment. The economy-of-scale argument for government provision of services may well be a fiction devised by firms who do not care to provide in-house abatement controls.

So far in this discussion, it has been assumed that *a* government exists which has, first, the legal jurisdiction over the environmental factor and, second, the desire to prevent pollution. This may not be the case in the real world. There are three levels of government which have an interest in pollution—municipal, provincial, and federal. The municipal level, which has the jurisdiction over air and of some water resources, rarely has the desire to end pollution. The federal government, which appears to have the desire to end pollution, rarely has the legal right to invade the jurisdictional preserves of the municipalities and provinces in order to do so.

Municipalities are engaged in a struggle for the industrial property tax

---

10. If the public pays for these devices out of their taxes, then the externality is costing them directly in higher taxes rather than in indirect ways such as cleaning costs, etc.

dollar. Business tax assessments averaged 46.1 percent of all real-property assessments for all Ontario municipalities in 1961.[11] A single municipality *alone* is therefore unlikely to institute environment charges which will reduce the desirability of its location for industry when a neighbouring municipality does not introduce similar charges. The results of this competition can be measured by the small number of municipal controls on air and water polluters. Municipally provided services for removing toxic elements from wastes are not far advanced, either. Of the eighteen largest metropolitan areas in Canada in 1969, only eight provided full treatment of all waste water.[12]

The provinces have also been slow to introduce pollution controls. The reasons may also be the fear of frightening business away. Pulp and paper mills "use up more than 80 percent of all the water consumed by industry in Canada."[13] Yet it was not until 1969 that Ontario introduced measures to force pulp mills to clean their wastes, even though "half a dozen pulp mills have all but destroyed the lower Ottawa (river) insofar as healthy aquatic life is concerned."[14] The desire of provincial bodies to reduce pollution can be seen in the recent proposal by Ontario Hydro, a provincially owned company. That company suggested that it would reduce the pollution emanating from its thermal plants by building a higher smokestack! From the many heated discussions, it was not obvious that the public believed that a higher smokestack would allow greater dilution of the smoke rather than just a wider dispersion.

Because of this competition between jurisdictional bodies, controls on the municipal and provincial level have been lacking. The federal government is not competing for tax dollars.[15] It, however, does not have the jurisdiction over all air and water ways. In the areas where the federal authorities have jurisdiction, some controls have been established. For example, the Department of Fisheries has control over the dumping of wastes into bodies of water which fish frequent. Up to this point, this control has been exercised only with respect to ocean fish which use provincial rivers and lakes to spawn. Consequently, the pulp and paper mills of British Columbia, which are located on salmon runs, clean their wastes to a far greater extent than the pulp and paper mills of Ontario. Another government agency, the

11. The Ontario Committee on Taxation, Volume 2, *The Local Revenue System*, p. 105.
12. Department of Health and Welfare, *Survey* (September 1969).
13. Jack Davis, Federal Minister of Fisheries and Forestry, article in *The Globe and Mail* (Toronto, August 7, 1969).
14. *Ibid.*
15. In effect, if factors of production are mobile between countries, pollution controls established in Canada but not elsewhere could affect the international location of industry. (The pulp and paper industry, a major polluter of water, exports over 90 percent of its newsprint production).

Central Mortgage and Housing Corporation, has an influence on the amount of water pollution near urbanized areas. All loans which it administers under the National Housing Act have strict requirements as to the type and size of sewage-treatment plants that must be installed. In the late summer of 1969, the federal government announced a plan to coordinate and extend government control over the pollution of this country's water resources. The proposed Canada Water Act will require provincial collaboration in establishing a uniform code across Canada. Each separate river and/or lake system would have a single agency whose jurisdiction would be over that entire system. A detailed plan of the proposed act was not available at the time of this essay's writing. The intention of the act appears to require strict conformity, with very broad definitions of pollution. Any refusal to follow the regulations established by an agency would result in fines and charges which equal the government's costs in removing the pollution. Whether or not the provinces agree to this proposed Canada Water Act remains to be seen. It is a sensible proposal to try to have a uniform code established by each province. No individual province could then claim that the regulation of pollution by it alone would merely drive polluters to others provinces.[16]

There are problems in using government legislation as the means of ending pollution, besides the issue of the weighting of individual standards mentioned above. Under legislation, pollution becomes a crime. The notion of fines for offences makes pollution appear an evil anti-social act, which it is not. Legislation which prohibits completely the dumping of wastes in any area favours recreation users of the environment over all other users. In so doing, it may induce for some firms and for society as a whole, costs far greater than the benefits of purifying all wastes. Imagine a lake in northern Saskatchewan, a lake used by a few boaters and recreational fishermen. A factory decides to locate on that lake. It is told that no waste can be dumped into that lake. All waste must be recycled at a cost of $1,000,000 a year. Are the benefits of a clean lake worth $1,000,000 a year? There is no market which can compare costs and benefits.

a market price system

A third possible way of reducing pollution is to introduce a market, and therefore a price, for water and air. The property rights to land now give *free*, certain rights to the air and water that abut that land. The government could legislate that such rights do not in fact exist but must be purchased.

---

16. However, it may be in the interests of each province to stay *out* of the proposed Act. If only one province does not introduce this law, it perhaps would attract all the polluters and their tax dollars.

The quality of air and water can be controlled by making them independent of the property rights of land. The government would create a new commodity called *pollution rights*,[17] the right to decrease the quality of the air and water. Before a firm could dump refuse into the environment, it would have to bid against other firms for this right. A price would be established. If a firm thought the price was too high, it would then undertake a cheaper alternative, cleaning its wastes.

If a firm wanted to locate on a lake outside Montreal, it would have to bid for the water against the recreational users. If the firm bid higher, the water was more valuable for industrial use than for pleasure, i.e., the costs of cleaning the wastes for the firm were greater than the costs of finding another swimming and boating area for the recreational users. Water would be allocated to its best use.

As we saw, the use of government legislation to reduce pollution favours recreational users of the environments. The market price system favours *industrial users* at the expense of recreational demanders.

For recreational users to outbid a firm for pollution rights, the recreational users would have to organize and be able to exclude non-members of the group. Imagine a group which did outbid industry for the right to a specific lake. That recreation group would have to prevent other swimmers, who did not pay for the right, from swimming in the lake. If the lake is sufficiently large, so that exclusion is improbable because it is very difficult and costly (barriers and armed guards around Lake Superior), it is a wise policy for any individual swimmer to stay out of the group. The swimmer who did not pay to join the recreation group still gets to swim in the lake.[18] A positive price for the right to consume a good, such as a lake, which is enjoyed in common, will lead to a less than optimal supply of that good. "No individual is willing to pay for the services [of the collective good] because he knows that his willingness to pay will not result in the services being produced if other persons are not willing to pay, and if the services are provided he will benefit from them whether he pays or not."[19]

---

17. An interesting point of Professor Dales, *op. cit.*
18. This large lake is a collective good—its consumption is enjoyed in common by a large number of people and it is extremely difficult (costly) to exclude any one individual from enjoying that good.
19. J. F. Due, *Government Finance: Economics of the Public Sector*, 4th ed. (Homewood, Illinois: Richard D. Irwin, Inc., 1968), p. 8. The student interested in the problems of externalities and collective goods can extend this knowledge by reading: W. J. Baumol, *Welfare Economics and the Theory of the State* (Cambridge, Mass.: M.I.T. Press, 1965); P. A. Samuelson, "The Theory of Public Expenditures," *Review of Economics and Statistics* (November 1954); "Diagrammatic Exposition of a Theory of Public Expenditure," *Review of Economics and Statistics* (November 1955); and "Aspects of Public Expenditure Theory," *Review of Economics and Statistics*, November 1958 (all in Joseph E. Stiglitz (ed.), *The Collected Scientific Papers of Paul A. Samuelson* (Cambridge, Mass.: M.I.T. Press, 1966)).

The ability to exclude individuals from enjoying the environment is feasible but very difficult and costly, for water resources. In the case of air, one wouldn't expect recreational users of air (everyone who breathes) to band together and outbid industrial users. The possibility of excluding life for not paying is a possibility not considered here.

There is another attribute of certain forms of pollution which a real-life market price system cannot be expected to handle. For prices to lead to an optimal allocation of the environment, a great deal of foresight must be assumed. Many forms of pollution are irreversible. The destruction of a glorious mountain range can never be reversed. For recreation users to outbid industrial users for picturesque land in the far North of Quebec requires foresight that in the year 2000 such land will be a scarce resource as picturesque land. Such foresight also requires the existence of a capital market which would lend the money to buy this land now as a recreation site for the year 2000.

If oil companies had the foresight of the phenomenal riches of Alaska as an oil reservoir, they might have been ready to forego the drilling off the coast of California, drilling which has led to great damages. Ten years from now, a solar cell may be the cheapest form of energy. At that time, the grandeur of Alaska may be gone forever. Ecologists are worried about the impact of supertankers on the temperature of the polar ice cap. The tankers which will carry oil from Alaska will carry hundreds of thousands of tons of warm East Coast water as ballast which will be dumped off the Alaskan coast when they are filled with oil. Little knowledge is available which helps to evaluate these dangers.

Each of us can dream up many conjectures such as this. If pollution were reversible, if hydro dams could be built on the Frazer or Hudson rivers and later dismantled so that no damage remained, the price system would work with a minimum of other restrictions.

Such foresight is impossible, such reversibility a dream. A price system alone is not the answer. Some flexibility of price is needed, however. Firms should have a guide as to whether the costs of cleaning wastes are greater than the benefits. Since the costs of recycling vary greatly from firm to firm and from product to product, firms should be given the choice as to which will recycle and which will dump.

6. SUMMARY

Three questions were asked in the introduction to this paper. The answer to the first, the reasons for the existence of pollution, has been given. The questions of how to weigh the standards set by each individual and how to reduce the amount of pollution are not so easily answered. For two reasons, the most desirable allocative mechanism, the market price system, *by itself* cannot answer these questions. First, air and to a large extent water are goods enjoyed in common. Second, the real-world capital market operating under uncertainties and imperfect foresight cannot be expected to prevent irreversible pollution which future generations might have been willing to pay to prevent.

Adequate knowledge is unavailable to judge the irreversibility or even the extent of most pollutants. The cumulative effects of pesticides on higher forms of life are just being investigated. Our knowledge of the effects of a combination of pollutants is negligible. Even information on the patterns of air and water currents is rudimentary. The first task for serious scientific investigation in this area must be to quantify the harmful effects, the costs imposed on others, and to establish who is paying.

Once this knowledge is available, a coordinated group of policies among responsible government agencies must be worked out on a feasible systems basis. It does little good for a single municipality on a river system to impose pollution controls. If other municipalities on that river system do not enforce similar policies, the water will remain polluted.

For certain forms of pollution, where the costs are obvious yet enforcement via a price mechanism unwieldy, government legislation is necessary. It is difficult to conceive of the situation where before one used the car, one phoned up to discover the price of hydrocarbon emissions for the day.

Industrial users of the environment whose wastes are identifiable should be allowed to bid for the right to emit wastes, the total volume of wastes being determined by the government. A limited pure system would ensure that among these firms there is a means of weighting the costs and benefits of recycling or dumping wastes.

In the case where costs are not obvious, such as the irreversible destruction of mountain ranges which are in excess supply now, the decision is not an easy one, and must be political. I, for one, would vote for the mountains to retain their grandeur.

regional economic disparities and policies

T. N. Brewis
Carleton University

THE NATURE AND MEASUREMENT OF DISPARITIES

No observer of the Canadian scene in the 1960's could fail to be struck by the surge of interest and concern with regional economic problems, problems associated particularly with disparities in growth rates, levels of unemployment and income. The disparities have been seen as a source of injustice and a threat to national unity. Efforts to attack their causes have been described by the present administration as one of its major priorities, and among the first measures of the newly elected government in 1968 was the establishment of a Department of Regional Economic Expansion with comprehensive responsibility for planning and coordinating action for regional development.[1]

As is well known, such disparities are nothing new. Some have persisted over several decades, and for many years the federal government has distri-buted tax revenues in favour of the poorer provinces. But transfer payments have done little to strike at the causes of inequalities and new approaches are being introduced.

Regional disparities among the more- as well as the less-developed nations are a world-wide phenomenon, and even the smallest countries,

---

1. Speaking in Moncton, N.B., May 31, 1968, the Prime Minister stated: "Les habi-tants des régions moins favorisées du Canada sont souvent dissociés de notre vie nationnale parce qu'ils n'ont pas l'occasion d'y participer pleinement. Et j'ai la con-viction que le besoin de s'attaquer aux causes premières de l'inégalité régionnale cons-titue l'une des grandes priorités de n'importe quel gouvernement canadien. Je crois fermement, le parti liberal le croit également, que l'unite canadienne ne pourrait être vraiment assurée que lorsque tous les Canadiens, d'un océan a l'autre, auront le sentiment de posséder cette égalité de chances qui leur permettra de participer pleinement a une societe juste."

such as Switzerland and Luxembourg, display concern over regional differences in prosperity within their frontiers. It is not surprising that such differences exist. Declines in the prospects of many rural communities, constant changes in technology and world demand, the discovery and depletion of natural resources contribute to a never-ending variation in the fortunes of particular areas.

What is surprising is not that disparities manifest themselves or that they tend in many cases to be self-perpetuating, for poverty tends to beget poverty, but that economists at least in the English-speaking world have devoted so little attention in the past to spatial factors in their analysis of levels of unemployment and income or the structure of industry. Discussions of income determination, price stability and the policies associated therewith are rarely examined at a sub-national level.[2] Though changing locational patterns of economic activity with concomitant effects on population distribution are matters of obvious import, economists have tended to ignore them.

In contrast to the relative dearth of inquiry on the spatial aspects of the economic landscape and their implications for policy, there has been a phenomenal output in the literature on economic growth, concerned with the more- as well as the less-advanced countries. This literature has contributed in some measure to an understanding of the problems besetting lagging regions within a country.

Regional disparities can take a variety of forms and their measurement depends not only upon the criteria selected but also upon the delineation of the boundaries themselves. Although wide differences in income occur between provinces, still wider differences appear within individual provinces, between urban and rural areas, for example, or between one locality and another. The choice of different time periods and variations in the statistical techniques employed may also have a significant bearing on the picture presented.

The following tables and figure draw attention to some of the spatial characteristics of the Canadian economy which have been the subject of public concern. Table 1 opposite indicates the net shift in population by province between 1946 and 1966. It will be noted therefrom that Ontario, Alberta and British Columbia have shown large increases; Quebec has remained about average and the Atlantic Provinces, Manitoba and Saskat-

---

2. One facet of this issue is that depressed areas of the country contribute little or nothing to inflationary pressures, yet policies designed to stem these pressures are introduced at the national level with scant regard for their regional implications. This is a matter which merits much more study than it has received. The implications of provincial and municipal budgets for stabilization policy are discussed in an exploratory paper by T. R. Robinson and T. J. Courchene, "Fiscal Federalism and Economic Stability—An Examination of Multi-Level Finances in Canada, 1952-65," *The Canadian Journal of Economics*, II, No. 2 (May 1969), pp. 165-189.

Table 1

NET SHIFT IN POPULATION BY PROVINCE
(as percent of the total net shift)
1946-1966

	1946-51	1951-56	1956-61	1961-66
Newfoundland	—	+ 0.1	— 5.9	+ 2.7
Prince Edward Island	— 3.2	— 5.8	— 3.7	— 2.9
Nova Scotia	—18.3	—18.2	—23.3	—24.8
New Brunswick	— 8.6	—15.8	—14.2	—14.3
Quebec	+14.5	—11.2	+ 4.8	+ 0.1
Ontario	+29.7	+54.7	+48.9	+46.4
Manitoba	—17.2	—17.5	—19.3	—26.8
Saskatchewan	—52.7	—31.4	—33.7	—31.2
Alberta	+26.8	+19.1	+26.7	+ 5.2
British Columbia	+28.9	+26.1	+19.7	+45.7

Note: Population in the Atlantic provinces, Manitoba, and Saskatchewan has not increased as rapidly as in the country as a whole. Ontario, Alberta, and British Columbia accounted for almost all the gains above the national average.

Sources: Dominion Bureau of Statistics, **Canada Year Book**, various years 1946-1961. Reprinted from T. N. Brewis, **Regional Economic Policies in Canada** (Toronto: The Macmillan Co. of Canada Ltd., 1969), p. 258.

chewan have fallen well behind. Table 2 on page 338 shows personal income by province as a percent of the Canadian average over the last forty years. The Atlantic Provinces have the lowest incomes and are followed by Quebec. Reflecting its dependence on wheat production and sales, marked fluctuations have occurred in Saskatchewan. The figure on page 339 shows percentage unemployment by region for 1963-1969, the Atlantic Provinces, then Quebec exhibiting levels of unemployment well above the national average. The heavy concentration of manufacturing employment in Ontario and Quebec is indicated by Table 3 on page 340. (Recently there has been a very sharp drop in capital formation in Quebec in comparison with that in certain other provinces, and the consequences for future economic growth and employment in that province are likely to be significant.) Projected expenditures under FRED plans appear in Table 4 on page 346.

It will be noted from the figure that levels of unemployment show a high degree of correlation across the country, though the swings are very much greater in the Atlantic Provinces. A 6 percent unemployment rate in Ontario in March 1963 was accompanied by an almost 16 percent rate in the Atlantic Provinces, and the same pattern is observable in subsequent years. As discussed more fully in earlier reviews of the subject,[3] past experience indicates that if there is a general slack in economic activity, the Atlantic Provinces suffer much more than the rest of the country. Policies

3. T. N. Brewis, *Growth and the Canadian Economy,* Carleton Library No. 39 (Toronto: McClelland and Stewart Ltd., 1968), pp. 90-111. See also his *Regional Economic Policies in Canada* (Toronto: The Macmillan Co. of Canada Ltd., 1969).

Table 2

PERSONAL INCOME* EXPRESSED AS A PERCENT OF THE CANADIAN AVERAGE
1926 to 1968 (VARIOUS YEARS)

(as percent of national average)

	1926	1929	1933	1939	1946	1950	1955	1959	1961	1963	1965	Revised 1965	Revised 1968[1]
Newfoundland						51	54	55	60	58	59	56	55
Prince Edward Island	57	59	51	53	58	56	55	62	62	63	69	60	63
Nova Scotia	67	71	77	76	86	74	73	75	77	74	75	76	78
New Brunswick	64	65	66	65	75	69	65	66	68	66	69	69	71
Quebec	85	92	94	88	82	85	85	85	88	87	88	90	90
Ontario	114	122	129	124	115	121	120	119	118	117	115	117	115
Manitoba	109	98	93	90	103	100	95	100	97	97	97	95	100
Saskatchewan	102	67	47	77	97	87	93	87	78	107	99	96	90
Alberta	113	92	74	87	108	103	103	104	102	100	99	96	99
British Columbia†	121	128	132	125	114	123	122	118	116	114	115	113	107

*Includes all transfer payments and imputed net income of farmers.
†Includes Yukon and Northwest Territories, 1926 to 1950.
Source: Calculated from Dominion Bureau of Statistics, **National Accounts, Income and Expenditure**, various years. Reprinted from T. N. Brewis, **Regional Economic Policies in Canada** (Toronto: The Macmillan Co. of Canada Ltd., 1969).
1. Not strictly comparable with previous years; national accounts estimates having been revised in 1965.

Figure 1

PERCENTAGE UNEMPLOYED, BY REGION, 1963 to 1969

Source: Dominion Bureau of Statistics, **Canadian Statistical Review,** various months.

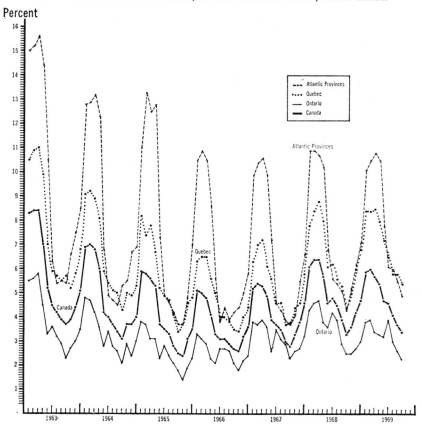

designed to maintain aggregate demand can thus claim a high priority in our measures to reduce the ills which face the Atlantic Provinces specifically. A high level of aggregate demand will not only stimulate growth in the economy as a whole, but it will also do much to reduce the problems of the less-favoured regions.

In Newfoundland, unemployment often runs around two or three times the national average and the seasonal swings are extreme.[4] Had it been possible over the past decade to reduce unemployment in Newfoundland

---

4. The situation in Newfoundland is well portrayed in the *Report of the Royal Commission on the Economic State and Prospects of Newfoundland and Labrador* (St. John's, Newfoundland: Queen's Printer, 1967).

and the Maritime Provinces to between 3 and 4 percent, it is not unlikely that there would have been an increase of close to 40,000 in the employed labour force, contributing a potential $100 million a year to the gross national product from labour income alone. Increased rewards to other factors of production would have raised the figure further.

There is the further consideration that high levels of unemployment are likely to slow down the rate of capital accumulation. The reduction in the upward pressure on wages attendant upon heavy unemployment can be expected to reduce the rate of installation of cost-saving techniques of production.

Given freedom of movement and higher rewards to labour in the Central than in the Atlantic Provinces, one would expect labour to be attracted to the former from the latter and that this would contribute to a more uniform level of income and to a reduction in unemployment. On the face of it, such a movement, conforming with the principles of a simplified equilibrium analysis, would make for a more efficient resource use. In fact, notwithstanding substantial migration from the Atlantic Provinces, marked differences in employment opportunity and incomes continue to persist. At the

Table 3

DISTRIBUTION OF POPULATION, LABOUR FORCE, AND MANUFACTURING EMPLOYMENT
1961

	Percent				
	Atlantic provinces	Quebec	Ontario	Prairies	British Columbia
(a) Population	10.43	28.90	34.26	17.47	8.95
(b) Urban population	7.44	30.79	38.02	14.43	9.32
(c) Labour force	8.70	27.38	37.05	17.93	8.94
(d) Non-primary labour force*	8.40	28.19	38.91	15.13	9.37
(e) Employees in manufacturing	5.54	33.21	45.80	7.41	8.05
(f) Employees in manufacturing (excluding primary and local)†	2.79	37.21	50.39	6.24	3.37

Density measures (concentration of manufacturing jobs relative to other characteristics):

(e) as % of (a)	53.1	114.9	133.7	42.4	89.9
(e) as % of (b)	74.5	107.9	120.5	51.4	86.4
(e) as % of (d)	66.0	117.8	117.7	49.0	85.9
(f) as % of (b)	37.5	120.9	132.5	43.2	36.2

Note: Figures do not add to 100 percent in all cases because of rounding.
*Excluding labour force in agriculture, fishing, forestry, and mining.
†Excluding foods and beverages, wood products, paper products, printing and allied industries, and primary metal.
Source: Dominion Bureau of Statistics, **1961 Census of Canada,** Vol. I and Vol. III. Reprinted from T. N. Brewis, **Regional Economic Policies in Canada** (Toronto: The Macmillan Co. of Canada Ltd., 1969), p. 16.

first Canadian decennial census in 1871, over 20 percent of the Canadian population lived in the three Maritime Provinces of Nova Scotia, New Brunswick, and Prince Edward Island. By 1961, that percentage had dropped to less than 8 percent. Between 1881 and 1931 net out-migration from the Maritime Provinces is estimated to have averaged some 20,000 per decade. If we include Newfoundland, the number increases for the decade 1951-1961 to almost 100,000 out of a total population in the Atlantic Provinces of about two million. In spite of this migration and relative decline in population, per capita income in the Atlantic Provinces remains one-third below that of the rest of the country, and unemployment remains very much higher.

It may be wondered why relative declines in the Maritime population have not improved more substantially the economic situation of those who remain. One possibility is that the migration has not gone far enough. Given that per capita incomes in Newfoundland are 40 percent below those in the rest of the country, it could be argued that if something like one-third of the population were to leave that province, the per capita incomes of the remainder would rise fairly close to the national average. In the absence of what appear to be feasible alternatives, such migration might well seem desirable, but even if it could be induced over, say, the next decade, by various forms of encouragement, a substantial income gap might still remain. For one thing, certain overhead costs would have to be borne by a smaller population and, for another, the decline in population would reduce still further the incentives to produce for a local market. To the extent, moreover, that the migrants consisted largely of young adults, as seems likely, the age distribution of the remaining labour force would be even less favourable than it is at the present time, and this, combined with the decline in local markets, would make the province even less attractive to new industry. Some migration is to be expected and should be facilitated, for market forces alone operate too slowly and painfully; but the net gains from such movement may be disappointing and not such as to make other action to raise output appear less urgent.

The above may appear to be taking a rather pessimistic view of the potential gains from migration, and admittedly there are important offsetting considerations to be taken into account. Thus, in the matter of overhead costs, it should be possible with a declining population to effect economies in educational expenditures by closing down some of the smaller schools, as is currently being done, and such action would have the additional merit of contributing to a rise in educational standards. There is the further consideration that with the passage of time, the number of older people will also diminish. The essential point is to bear the limitations in mind in advocating the merits of a population outflow; otherwise we shall expect too much from it. Internal migration within the province is currently being encouraged. Efforts are being made to close down many of the smaller fishing outports and induce the population to move to larger centres where superior services can be made available and where, hopefully at least, improved job opportunities can be provided.

In general, the larger the region or area under consideration the easier it will be to create employment opportunities. Insofar, for example, as the Atlantic Provinces can regard themselves as a single unit for purposes of development policy, any population movement that takes place within them entails no necessary conflict of objectives. Assistance can be concentrated where it shows greatest promise. If we are faced, however, with provincial loyalties and jealousies and we try to raise employment opportunities within each province individually, the task immediately becomes more complex. Not only do we have to worry about interprovincial migration, but we run the risk of less efficient resource allocation in terms of the country as a whole. If we narrow the boundaries still further—say to a county level or Canada Manpower Service area—then room to manoeuvre decreases sharply. At the township level, room to manoeuvre disappears almost entirely, and we are left with the task of finding employment for workers in localities which show no prospect whatever of developing without continued and heavy subvention. The designation of areas, as well as the criteria for assistance, will depend ultimately on the priorities which are accorded to various objectives. If we are concerned with growth rather than welfare, larger areas will normally appear more appropriate, and those offering greater scope for expansion will be preferred to those which offer less. If it is local welfare in which we are primarily interested, smaller areas will tend to be selected and the measure of their distress rather than their potentiality for growth will assume importance. It is fruitless to seek a concept of designation which will be appropriate for all the objectives which we may have in mind. There may be occasions when a very depressed locality offers the greatest scope for long-run development, and from the standpoint of designating an area this is an ideal combination, but it is not one which is likely to arise frequently. We are faced with the fact that, as a broad generalization, those areas which are most depressed are likely to be precisely those with the poorest growth prospects.

In deciding upon the magnitude and forms of aid that might be made available in the poorer regions, some evaluation of possible costs and benefits needs to be made, crude though these may have to be. Given a sufficient subvention to industry, employment could be found for every potential worker in Newfoundland, but the net rate of return on that outlay would almost certainly be less than that involved from a similar expenditure elsewhere. In estimating whether such is the case or not, it is essential, however, to use social accounting concepts rather than private. If the alternative to government aid is no output at all—where the alternative in other words is not employment elsewhere but unemployment—the "real" cost of spending nothing may be much higher than any subventions which the government might be called upon to make to ensure that work is made available. In short, the encouragement of some redistribution of industry needs to be viewed in the context of larger social and political objectives, and an assessment made of the expected costs and benefits, social as well as private.

As a final observation, it may be noted that there is nothing sacrosanct about present locational patterns of economic activity. Current patterns and trends, which may be regarded as far from ideal for a variety of reasons, could be modified substantially if it appeared that such a task warranted the effort involved. There is implicit recognition of this in government policies of regional development though, as noted below, specific goals and programs have been undergoing continual transformation. It seems highly probable, moreover, that if we fail to take action now to influence spatial patterns of economic activity and population distribution, the task will have to be undertaken in future when it could prove to be immeasurably more difficult. There is no reason why all sorts of other policies to improve the social and economic performance of industry should be regarded as acceptable but that those to influence its location should be taboo. Misgivings over regional economic disparities, problems of pollution and urban agglomeration are all straws in the wind.

It is one thing, however, to have a view on such issues and quite another to introduce and implement effective policies relating thereto. As the following section indicates, Canadian experience has been a chequered one.

THE POLICIES PURSUED

Turning to the policies pursued in Canada to redress spatial inequalities in income and employment opportunity, it may be helpful to glance back at some of the lessons of recent experience. Looking back is usually easier than looking forward, though it is not obvious that such is true in this case. The past decade displays a picture of manifold shifts in emphasis, administration and policy direction. Over the last few years, an observer who took his eye off what was happening for even a short while was apt to find that by the time he looked again the scene and the action had both changed.

The goals themselves are complex. They are not always consistent; they are typically couched in general terms and have rarely remained constant for long. Reduction of unemployment, acceleration of economic growth and structural change, mitigation of poverty and the quest for social justice and national unity have all been woven into the fabric of policy.

The reduction of social injustice may be difficult to reconcile, however, with steps to expand output in the more- rather than the less-promising of the depressed regions, and what seems like justice to one group of people may not seem like justice to another. Measures to encourage migration typically meet with a very mixed reception and efforts to reduce local unemployment in the immediate future may be at the expense of structural changes designed to reduce it in the longer run. With regard to the distribution of industry there is often considerable doubt whether action to assist development in a lagging region will benefit or be at the expense of national output. As for national unity, it might be furthered by actions which favour the poorer parts of the country, though it is worth recalling that in a number of federations the effect has been the other way.

Concern with the plight of impoverished farmers led to the introduction of the Agricultural Rehabilitation and Development Act of 1961, but an earlier emphasis on improving the physical qualities of land and increasing output to improve their lot soon gave way to disenchantment and to new approaches which stressed movement out of agriculture and the broader issues of rural poverty in general.[5] The Atlantic Development Board, established in 1962 to provide special assistance to the Atlantic Provinces and which was originally given only advisory powers, was provided the following year with funds to finance projects likely to contribute to the growth of the economy of the region. The sum was subsequently increased, but now, in a return to the original concept, the Board has been replaced by a Council with advisory powers only. The Area Development Agency, which was created to encourage industrial development in areas of chronic unemployment, began operations in 1963. Ambitions of planning development, however, were stillborn, and the Agency limited its action to providing funds in an automatic way to firms engaged in secondary manufacturing that settled in those areas, without any attempt being made to analyze the needs of the areas in question. Under the wing of the new Department of Regional Economic Expansion, a much more sophisticated role is to be played involving substantial discretion in the granting of aid and the agency as such comes to an end. The emphasis henceforth is to be on the development of "growth centres" and growth potential in large regions, whereas before it was on distress in small ones. In earlier statements of policy the objective of developing the more promising centres had been rejected categorically, the purpose being to steer firms into areas where unemployment was especially severe. As the Department of Regional Economic

---

5. In 1966, reflecting a significant shift in emphasis, the title of the legislation was changed to the "Agricultural and Rural Development Act."

Expansion has said, a fundamental change of policy is involved.[6]

FRED—the Fund for Rural Economic Development—appeared on the scene in 1966. Action thereunder began with tremendous verve. As seen in Table 4 on page 346, several ambitious plans, involving a total outlay of over a billion dollars, were introduced, but within three years the legislation creating the Fund was superseded. During the few years that the government has been active in the regional field, policies have undergone a continual transformation, and agencies have come and gone. As a result, and very understandably, the task of those entrusted with the implementation of action has often been characterized by confusion and frustration. Adjustment to new policies and procedures takes time and the phasing out of earlier programs contributes to difficulties during the transitional period.

Ideally in the implementation of regional policies, one would like to have a fuller understanding of the determinants of growth. With regard to the latter, fashions have changed and confidence has waned. There has been a disposition in some circles to look upon the determinants of economic growth much as one would regard a horse race. Thus a number of years ago stress was being laid on the crucial role of investment expenditures in machinery and equipment and physical assets generally. It is still seen by some as the crucial element in growth. But confidence is not as widespread as it was; that horse has dropped back. "Research" and "technological change" nosed ahead for a while, only to be overtaken by "investment in human capital" and education. Enormous sums have been directed to the latter and some misgivings are beginning to emerge about their magnitude and wisdom. Outsiders such as "development corporations" and "management training" have attracted attention from time to time. Some psychologists appear to favour "achievement motivation." The sociologists talk about "participation," and financiers, as is their wont, indicate a preference for "risk capital and finance." For those who see development in this way, it is a much more open race now, and by the time the pack gets round

---

6. A useful source of information on federal policies is contained in the *Minutes of Proceedings and Evidence of the Standing Committee on Regional Development*, House of Commons, Nos. 1-16 (Ottawa: Queen's Printer, 1968-69). See also T. N. Brewis, *Regional Economic Policies in Canada, op. cit.*; and "Salient Features of Federal-Regional Development Policy in Canada," a paper prepared for the Organization for Economic Cooperation and Development by the Department of Regional Economic Expansion (Ottawa: Queen's Printer, 1969). A more comprehensive study of North American Regional Development is currently being prepared for the United Nations under the auspices of the Resources for the Future, Inc., Washington, D.C. by Professor John H. Cumberland and the author. Excerpts therefrom are included in this paper.

Table 4

FRED PLAN EXPENDITURES AND COMMITMENTS

	Duration of agreement	Federal cost	Provincial cost	Total cost	Population	Cost per capita	Federal cost as percent of total
	(years)	$000	$000	$000	No.	$	%
Hactaquac	10	15,358	5,592	20,900	10,200	2,049	73
North East New Brunswick	10	62,136	27,114	89,250	106,000	842	70
East Quebec	5	212,295	46,495	258,790	322,500	802	82
Interlake Manitoba	10	49,562	35,523	85,085	59,270	1,436	58
Prince Edward Island	15	225,000	500,000	725,000	109,500	6,621	31
Total		564,351	614,724	1,179,025	607,470	1,941	48

Source: Figures provided by the Department of Forestry.

the next bend it is hard to be sure which horse the Economic Council or the Ministry of Regional Economic Expansion will be pinning its hopes on.

The current favourites seem to be urbanization and "growth centres."[7] They are not without merit, but the latter may be a hard horse to ride, and those who attempt it could well end up in the ditch. Experience in other countries shows that aspiring growth centres do not always live up to expectations. Experience also suggests that looking at economic growth in terms of possible winners is not a very fruitful approach. It is becoming widely recognized that a large number of interrelated variables are involved, and concentrating on one or two of them is unlikely to get us very far. Unfortunately, we still know very little about the internal dynamics of development, but there is an increasing disposition to look for "total-systems" approaches to regional development, cutting right across conventional political bailiwicks and administrative boundaries. Inevitably this gives rise to rivalries between departments, jealous of their traditional rights and responsibilities, and there is the added complication in Canada of the allocation of powers under the constitution.

The program of the former Area Development Agency is being completely replaced. Discretion in the granting of aid as now permitted has much to recommend it in principle, but much harm may be done if those exercising that discretion lack the knowledge and competence which is required. It will call for a high degree of professional sophistication. It will be necessary to consider the forward and backward linkages which exist between industries and the extent to which these linkages are likely to be felt in surrounding areas. The local income and employment multiplier effects resulting from the establishment of an industry in an area may be quite nominal, supplies being obtained from other regions and increased earnings being spent largely on goods produced elsewhere. Skilled workers may have to be brought in from outside the region and employment opportunities for the local population may be virtually non-existent.

In the past, ADA policies to assist depressed areas have achieved their greatest impact in those areas which are in the more prosperous parts of the country, those which are typically not far distant from major centres of activity. In contrast, peripheral areas of deep distress have shown little or no improvement. Some of the poorest of these have not attracted any firms at all. The same tendency is seen in the case of industrial estates—those that are relatively far removed from important centres of activity have been less successful than others.

---

7. In a speech delivered at St. John's Newfoundland, September 15, 1969, the Hon. Jean Marchand, Minister of Regional Economic Expansion, stated: "Our concern for the region causes us to look first to the growth of the urban centre and then to the benefits that must spread from it through the region—the growth of the urban community is the key to the program of the people of the region."

It follows that if the most depressed parts of the country are to be assisted to develop, they will have to receive preferential treatment, in some cases probably on a very substantial scale. Such differential incentives may appear warranted on grounds of social justice but not on economic; and if poverty should be considered a prime concern, it might be preferable to look to alternative policies such as guaranteed incomes, negative income tax or other assistance. There is a limit to what the Department of Regional Economic Expansion can be expected to accomplish to reduce poverty, and it might be better to leave the task to others. It is an illusion to believe that industrial expansion will solve the problems of the poorest people, many of whom are not, and are never likely to be, productive members of the labour force.

If the focus is to be on economic growth, as is currently intended, it makes sense to concentrate aid on the more- rather than the less-promising areas of lagging regions, unpopular though that may be. In this regard one of the merits of the new approach to policy is that small designated areas are to be replaced by larger regions. The designation of the latter should permit more effective policies of structural adjustment. Such adjustment must be undertaken if suitable improvements are to be effected. Anything less is likely to prove no more than a palliative.

A strong case can be argued for tailoring aid to the specific needs of individual regions and developing growth strategies on the basis of various assessments as is now being proposed, but it bears repeating that this is no mean task.[8] It is one thing, for example, to recognize the potential merits of growth centres and quite another to realize them. Apart from the political difficulties which are to be expected in their selection, it may be far from clear in individual cases whether growth will benefit or be at the expense of outlying localities, where unemployment and poverty are likely to be more extreme.

In addition to helping the more promising areas, there is a need for policies to facilitate the decline of economic activity in some industries and areas where the prospects are bleak. Remote rural areas with poor natural resources are cases in point. Left to themselves, market forces are too slow and too painful. There is still considerable reluctance in a number of circles to recognize the desirability of encouraging outmigration from some impoverished parts of the country; and unless this attitude changes, public money will be spent to little purpose in trying to restore them. Unless there are reasons for believing that an area can be revived and that it is worth reviving, there is no point in bribing firms to move in. The fact that certain

---

8. As some sceptics have remarked, the government will be hard pressed to achieve as rapid a rate of growth in the depressed areas as in the number of officials concerned with them.

distributions of population and industry happen to exist at the moment is not a sufficient reason to maintain that distribution in the future.

It follows that the pursuit of policies whether for expansion or decline presupposes a view on the prospects of individual areas. There is an urgent need in Canada for more information on which to base an assessment.[9] The nature and magnitude of technological changes involving new products, production, and transport costs profoundly influence the locational patterns of industry. Without a knowledge of new innovations and their expected consequences over the foreseeable future, it is virtually impossible to make sensible decisions on the courses of action that regional development should follow. The implications of these changes are rarely given the attention that they deserve. Admittedly, the future can never be foreseen with certainty, but to the extent that likely trends are discernible, their neglect is almost certain to lead to a waste of effort. We need to have some notion of the forces at work which are influencing the location of industry and population.

Related to the above issue is the practice of closing the stable door after the horse has gone. Canadian policy has been characterized by concentration on the past rather than on a view of the future. Only when unemployment was chronic, for example, was ADA authorized to step in, and ARDA had no mandate to anticipate structural changes in rural areas which were not already depressed. What is needed are policies which will reduce the emergence of distress. This presupposes some understanding of impending changes and the implications of these for future development. If, to mention one illustration, innovations in transport are likely to influence locational patterns to a major extent, then steps to prepare for the consequences need to be taken before the dislocation results. Similarly, if economies of scale are likely to increase (and there are few who doubt it), there is no point in stimulating a multiplicity of small plants across the country by offering substantial incentives. Indeed, the relatively small scale of many secondary manufacturing plants is regarded as one of the factors contributing to higher production costs in Canada than in the United States.

Reviewing the Canadian scene as it has unfolded over the past decade, it is apparent that there have been all sorts of programs but little overriding direction. In the case of the Atlantic Development Board, project engineers and planners went their separate ways, and especially in its early days ARDA allocated funds to all sorts of miscellaneous projects recommended by the provinces without any regard for broader strategies of regional development.

---

9. In this connection, some observers are very uneasy about the analysis which lies behind the FRED plans as well as the capacity and determination of respective governments to carry them out.

The Department of Regional Economic Expansion should improve matters in time; its establishment was a most important advance, but it remains to be seen how far it will succeed in integrating various functions or where it will place its emphasis. Hopefully, it will bring to the fore the regional implications of major policy recommendations proposed by other departments and ensure that they are given due weight before decisions are taken on them. The Department offers the prospect of a more sophisticated approach to regional problems, with its concentration on developing growth potentiality and with a higher degree of administrative coordination than has existed hitherto. Legislative changes, however, are not enough, and governments will be hard pressed to achieve a high degree of expertise. It is one thing to point to the urgent need for a more effective over-all development strategy and quite another to create it. As is well known to those faced with the task of recruitment, there is a severe shortage of people with the skills and judgment required.

Decisions on the various steps considered necessary to create employment opportunities in some of the poorest areas will depend in large measure on agreement with the provinces, and some conflicts of opinion have to be expected. There are times when the provincial governments pursue ends which inhibit the development which others would like to see, and, as has happened in Quebec, the actions of extremist parties can be a factor discouraging investment. In *per capita* terms, investment in the Atlantic Provinces currently exceeds that in Quebec.

Provinces are competing with each other for industry, and this can prove to be an expensive as well as self-defeating practice. There have been notable instances of late where provincial governments have outbid each other for new industry. Industrialists for their part can and do play off one province against another.[10] In a number of cases information on inducements offered is not made public. These are serious matters. National interests will not be served if individual provinces act independently and offer whatever concessions they choose.

A number of provincial governments have been advocating the formation of regional governments, and specific proposals with regard thereto are currently under discussion. It is realized that many of the old administrative boundaries have little relevance in the world as it now exists. The redrafting of such boundaries, though not necessarily undertaken with economic development in mind, can be expected to improve the quality of services. Provincial boundaries are much more difficult to change but, as is currently being recognized in the Atlantic region, some forms of closer economic integration between the provinces appear to be inevitable,

---

10. Not to mention one country against another. The poorest provinces and the poorest countries are the ones most likely to suffer from this type of competition.

for many of their regional economic problems cannot be solved in isolation. It is questionable, indeed, how far it will be possible to proceed with the ambitious policies which are now envisaged without becoming involved in a re-assessment of provincial powers and responsibilities. Certainly there will be a need for joint federal-provincial strategies.

Looking back over Canadian experience, a charitable observer might regard the frequent changes of course and administration as a part of the learning process rather than one of inadequate thought being given at the outset to a highly complex problem. One would hope, however, that with the experience gained in recent years it would be possible to proceed at both the policy and the administrative level with a clearer sense of direction in future.

With regard to past expenditures specifically, evaluation has been skimpy. This is one of the more serious deficiencies of policy. Substantial sums have been and continue to be allocated to various programs, but little analysis of the probable effects has been made public. In some cases little is known, and what is known is not always released. Some bodies and agencies are less ready to make information available than others.[11] It is widely recognized, however, that many outlays, both federal and provincial, show a very poor return and heavy losses have been incurred by some of the poorest provinces. The main beneficiaries of aid in the past have often been large capital-intensive industries rather than the depressed local communities which the subventions were designed to assist. Cost per local worker employed in some cases has been extremely high, amounting in effect to several-years' gross income.

It is strongly urged that a percentage of all expenditures be earmarked for evaluation and analysis and that such evaluation not be left exclusively to those responsible for the implementation of the policies. Even crude estimates of a rate of return on federal outlays may be better than none at all. It is difficult to escape the impression at times that government departments are less disposed to measure the value of their aid by what they accomplish than by what they spend. It may not generally be realized that the federal government alone has already disbursed and committed under its various regional aid programs in recent years a sum far in excess of a billion dollars, and this is additional to federal-provincial transfer payments. Nothing is likely to kill public support for regional development expenditures in future more surely than doubts about the wisdom and efficacy of what is being attempted.

---

11. A number of provincial agencies are especially secretive. Professor Rowat has pointed out that the United States has always had a much more open system of administration than our own. See Donald C. Rowat, "How Much Administrative Secrecy?" *The Canadian Journal of Economics and Political Science* XXXI, No. 4 (November, 1965), pp. 479-498.

some economic aspects of the northland*

Theodore W. Schultz
University of Chicago

ECONOMIC SHADOWS RATHER THAN PRICES

The biological and physical dimensions of the Middle North cast all manner of economic shadows. It is difficult, however, to transform these shadows into prices and economic opportunities for production and consumption. There is much uninhabited room in the area which could become valuable in a world becoming more and more crowded. There is an abundance of unpolluted water and unspoiled land. Settled communities are small, few and far between. Plants and animals, whether natural or domesticated, are not generous in producing a surplus for man. In its support of agriculture, nature is niggardly when capital and human effort are applied to land, especially so when the value of a man's time is as high as it is in Canada and the United States. Yet man does not live for food alone; he also wants untrammeled wilderness, room for privacy and room that will complement his crowded daily routine when vacation and leisure time are his to use. These then are some of the sources of the economic shadows. But shadows are not prices.

   The real prices that link these northern communities to the rest of Canada, the United States and the world abroad are hard to come by. Buying and selling prices are not posted. Private and public rates of return on investment are concealed information. Even the real costs of transportation—over the few roads, railroads, and airlines which reach up from the south and over the rivers, bays and seas northward to the open ocean water during the season when the ice can be broken—cannot be reckoned by

---

* Parts of Canada and Alaska visited as a guest of the Arctic Institute of North America, July 16-30, 1967.

casual observation while travelling and interviewing competent local people. Nor is it possible by this means to determine how much of the economic value of the commodities, goods and services produced or consumed in these northern communities is contributed by the natural endowment (timber, wildlife, minerals, water when it generates hydro energy and locally produced food), or how much is contributed by outside capital (reproducible physical forms) or by people who come from the South to work temporarily in these communities.

OUTSIDE ECONOMIC DEPENDENCE

Yet most of the economic story is in these connecting links to the outside, since none of the communities that we visited is anywhere near self-contained. On the contrary, no country in the world, or region of any country known to me, is as dependent upon outside "markets" for its livelihood as are these northern communities. They are dependent predominantly upon outside prices and wages, upon outside demands for minerals (including that for oil and gas), and upon water and wilderness. They are often sites for government administration, for national research activities and for national defence establishments. Some of them are heavily dependent upon national income transfers to improve the social and economic lot of the Eskimos and Indians. Investment resources for the formation of physical capital and the supply of skilled human beings also come predominantly from the outside.

What this outside economic dependence implies is that the real costs of investment resources are relatively high (concealed in part by the fact that some of these resources are subsidized by the government), that wages and salaries are relatively high, especially so for highly skilled workers, and that the cost of living is also relatively dear (so many consumer items are brought up from the South, and transportation is very expensive). It also implies that the productive services of the natural endowment, where they have an economic value, are relatively cheap. Unpolluted water is abundant and still virtually a free good. The economic value of wilderness is potentially large but is presently small because of inaccessibility. There are unexploited oil and gas reserves which will become economic should the world price rise or the transport costs from these reserves to outside markets be reduced substantially. The picture of other minerals is of many parts. Iron ore obtained by open mining in northeast Canada is undoubtedly a highly successful economic activity even though the price of iron ore has been weakening. The mining of nickle, copper, lead and zinc is booming in response to the strong world demand for these minerals. But the recent high prices of some of these minerals are a consequence of "war"-induced demands and thus are subject to the price instability which such demands imply. The potential amount of hydro-electric power is very large. However, the transmission of this energy over long distances is costly, and when the outside market is 500 miles distant, it is now held that this source of energy becomes more expensive than energy generated from nuclear (atom energy) sources. The cost of producing agricultural products, field crops for food and feed, is presently so high as to make this type of activity, with few exceptions, uneconomic in these northern communities, including Alaska, where technically the potential output is substantial, judging, for example, by the achievements of Finland. However, Finland is producing agricultural products under markedly different economic conditions.

FUTURE ECONOMIC PROSPECTS

But what are the future economic prospects? Will these northern communities come into their own during the next decade or two as a consequence of major changes in the tastes and preferences of people, or as a result of the advance in science and technology, or as a consequence of a growing pressure of population on natural resources, or from other large economic developments and political changes? The substance and scope of many of these changes and how they will alter the economic prospects are matters which are subject to much uncertainty. They are in large part concealed in a fog which our analytical instruments cannot penetrate with much assurance. Nevertheless, thought should be given to these matters in the hope that some limited clarification can be achieved. It is in this spirit that I entered upon the speculations that follow.

The revealed preferences of people for major classes of goods and services, revealed through consumer behaviour, are in general fairly stable in major countries, for example, in Canada and the United States. Building on these revealed preferences, the economist is able to estimate the elasticities of the demand for these goods and services. As personal income rises, the income elasticity of the demand is of major importance. At the level of income that generally prevails in these countries, the income elasticity of the demand for food is low. (In the U.S., a rise in income per family of 10 percent will of itself increase the demand for farm-produced food only about one percent.) But it is high for educational and health services. For the services of parks and wilderness it is very high, in all probability well over unity; that is, a rise in income per family of 10 percent increases the demand for these services well over 10 percent. Thus, looking ahead, as personal incomes continue to rise along with the increase in population, the consumer demand for one important class of services which parts of the Middle North can supply will increase at a high annual rate during the foreseeable future.

Yet I know of no evidence in support of the proposition that people in significant numbers want to leave the urban centres of Canada and the United States because they prefer to live in these northern communities. Temporarily, for the summer and a few of them for a year or two—yes. But as permanent northern residents—no. Thus, what new developments will bring about a substantial net migration from southern Canada and the United States into these parts of the Middle North? Improved (cheaper) transportation is always a two-way street. More and better schooling of the children of Eskimo and Indian families will enhance the opportunities of these children to improve their economic lot by moving south. New economic possibilities within the Middle North would, of course, attract people. The multiplication of mining communities is a real possibility. The agricultural economic opportunities are mostly marginal and small, notwithstanding the world-population food picture to which I shall return. Of the places that we visited, the developing Alberta complex reaching into northern Alberta and beyond has real economic potential; but the core of this viable regional development is largely south of the Middle North.

The social and economic implications of the advance in science and technology, even in the near future, are beset by many imponderables. Thus here we enter the realm of much uncertainty. Will new, cheap substitutes be forthcoming for copper, lead, zinc and nickle? Will energy from atomic sources become even cheaper, and should this occur, what will such development imply with respect to the price (cost) of energy from coal, oil and hydro power? Cheaper electric energy from nuclear installations might set the stage for substantial decentralization of economic activities, which in turn could become a strong factor in the development of some northern communities. The marked technical advance in open-pit mining of iron ore is already an economic reality reducing the real costs of iron ore.

The advance in biology is especially important in the production of agricultural products. The technical possibilities of transforming sunlight, water, and other plant nutrients into food and non-food agricultural products are becoming increasingly more favourable. What will this biological advance imply for the economic development of the Middle North? From the clues now at hand, I would infer that it will increase the comparative advantage of the temperate and near tropical parts of the world in producing agricultural products.

Returning to population and food, will the growth in population throughout the world place so much pressure on the capacity to produce food that an area such as the Middle North, which is now marginal as a producer of food, will become an economic source of a large additional quantity of food? Despite all the uncertainties ahead, there are strong reasons for believing that the answer to this question is in the negative for the next couple of decades and longer.

While it is true that the rapid increase in population during recent decades in many parts of the world has given rise to a population crisis, it is also true that this crisis has reached a turning point for the better. The public and private responses underway support the view that the populations of most major countries will approach an equilibrium by the beginning of the 21st century. The social and economic consequences of the marked decline in death rates are no longer concealed; and the neglect of agricultural production in many of the poor countries has been exposed dramatically, for example, in India by two back-to-back bad-crop years. These bad-crop years may well be viewed by historians as having been a "blessing" in changing public and private thinking and in searching for measures to increase the economic capacity of agriculture and curtail the fecundity of man. In contrast to the vast empty spaces of the Middle North, many rural areas of India have upwards of 1,000 people per square mile. (This paragraph is written as I return from fairly extensive travel over India during late August and early September.) Yet the technical and economic opportunities to produce much more food in the major "rice bowls" of southern India and throughout the Gangetic Plain of northern India are real. Moreover, there is little doubt that the agriculture of India is now moving ahead with substantial momentum. The implications of these observations for the Middle North are as follows: (1) the fecundity of man can and will be curtailed, although much of the necessary effort to achieve this objective is only beginning to be applied; (2) the capacity of agriculture can be vastly increased and measures to increase it are being taken; (3) the advance in scientific knowledge that is useful and economically relevant for increasing the capacity of agriculture is an essential part of modernizing agriculture in poor countries; and (4) this knowledge (mainly biological) has a marked comparative advantage in producing more food and other agricultural products in most of these poor countries in contrast to the possibilities of applying this knowledge to increase the economical agricultural capacity in most parts of the Middle North.

SOME UNSETTLED QUESTIONS

My endeavour has been to clarify the economic dependence of the Middle North upon the national economy of Canada and the United States and upon the rest of the trading world. In view of this dependence, I turn, in closing, to a number of questions pertaining more specifically to the further economic development of the Middle North. These are unsettled questions which in my judgement require competent research.

(1) What are the technical and economic factors that account for the poor performance of agriculture in Alaska despite the large investment

in organized agricultural research, agricultural extension activity and the presence of local markets in which farm-foods are dear?

(2) Although the armed services are contributing substantially in developing the skills of many of the individuals who are drawn into the armed services, they are not, so it would appear, contributing efficiently, for example, to the economic development of Alaska, where the size of the defence establishment is large. A systematic study is warranted to determine the alternative ways by which the armed services can efficiently contribute to the economic development of this area.

(3) The economics of a transitory labour force should be high on this research agenda. It is all too easy to hide this important attribute of much labour in mining, construction, trapping and fishery, in providing services for tourists, and in the employment of teachers, health and administrative personnel. To assume that the main solution to transitory labour in this area is in providing permanent employment (i.e., year-round work) is largely wishful thinking. There is no reason, however, why all economic activity should conform to full-time, year-round employment. On the contrary, there is still considerable economic activity in northern parts of the United States and in southern Canada that is highly seasonal and yet highly productive in economic terms. A 100-percent average annual turnover in the labour force in mining can be taken in stride, thus presumably serving workers' preferences. To find ways of developing economic activities that are efficient in employing transitory labour, is a matter of high priority throughout the Middle North.

(4) The contributions of additional schooling to the economic mobility of the Eskimo and Indian populations can and should be determined. To assume that the higher skills associated with additional schooling should be employed in these communities in the case of Eskimos and Indians is an unwarranted assumption, because it is contrary to the expected and observable behaviour of people as the range of their economic opportunities is enlarged by more schooling.

(5) Some of the communities in this area are predominantly public (governmental) administrative centres. It should be possible in analyzing the experiences of these centres to determine the optimum size and organization needed to provide these governmental services.

(6) The effects of welfare services and payments to families and individuals throughout this area upon the economic incentives to induce them to improve their economic lot and thereby contribute to production are far from clear.

(7) Above all, from an economic point of view, are the *private* and *social* rates of return from the allocation of investment resources to education, health facilities and services, transport, power installations, mining and other extractive activities, wilderness accessibility, forestry, fishery and agriculture, equal?

The art of transforming economic shadows into prices and real opportunities is, above all, a utilitarian art.